Creating Historical Memory

Edited by Beverly Boutilier
and Alison Prentice

Creating Historical Memory: English-Canadian Women and the Work of History

UBCPress / Vancouver

Printed in Canada on acid-free paper ∞

ISBN 0-7748-0640-0 (hardcover)
ISBN 0-7748-0641-9 (paperback)

Canadian Cataloguing in Publication Data

Creating historical memory

Includes bibliographical references and index.
ISBN 0-7748-0640-0 (bound); ISBN 0-7748-0641-9 (pbk.)

1. Women – Canada – Historiography. 2. Women historians – Canada. 3. Women – Historiography. 4. Women – Canada – History. I. Boutilier, Beverly, 1963– II. Prentice, Alison, 1934–

FC149.C73 1997 971′.007′2 C97-910841-1
F1024.C73 1997

This book has been published with a grant from the Social Science Federation of Canada, using funds provided by the Social Sciences and Humanities Research Council of Canada. UBC Press also gratefully acknowledges the ongoing support to its publishing program from the Canada Council for the Arts, the British Columbia Arts Council, and the Department of Canadian Heritage of the Government of Canada.

Set in Stone by Brenda and Neil West, BN Typographics West
Printed and bound in Canada by Friesens
Copy editor: Nancy Pollak
Proofreader: Joanne Richardson
Indexer: Pat Buchanan

UBC Press
University of British Columbia
6344 Memorial Road
Vancouver, BC V6T 1Z2
(604) 822-5959
Fax: 1-800-668-0821
E-mail: orders@ubcpress.ubc.ca
http://www.ubcpress.ubc.ca

For Maxine and Wayne
and for Jim

Contents

Illustrations

Acknowledgments

Many debts are incurred in the creation of a collection of essays such as this one. We would first like to thank Laura Macleod, the Toronto editor for UBC Press whose belief in the project was important from the beginning. When, first, one of us decamped and headed across the continent to Victoria and, a year later, the other crossed the sea to Indonesia, our delightful meetings with Laura had to be replaced by e-mail and phone calls. But her faith never wavered. We are grateful for her continued confidence in our work, as well as her unfailingly fine judgment and good humour.

Second, thanks are due to the many people who assisted with the research for this book. National, provincial, municipal, and university archivists and librarians in Canada, the United States, and Great Britain were enthusiastic and helpful. We thank in particular the librarians and archivists who assisted the editors and authors at Acadia, McGill, and Queen's Universities; at the Universities of Toronto, Saskatchewan, and British Columbia; at the Smith College Archives in Northampton, Massachusetts; and at the National Archives, the Archives of Ontario, the Metropolitan Toronto Library, and the City of Toronto. Their knowledge and dedication were essential to our task. In addition, researchers and support staff at the Ontario Institute for Studies in Education, Carleton University, and the University of Victoria have supported our work in many ways. We want especially to thank Paula Bourne, Elizabeth Fear, and, last but not least, Alyson King, whose skills have added a great deal to the completed volume. Also important to the final product were the interest and insights of the anonymous reviewers appointed by UBC Press and the Aid to Scholarly Publications Programme. Their prompt reports and even-handed criticisms were invaluable.

Finally, we would like to thank our families. Guthrie and Theo, not to mention their wonderful parents, Douglas and Shirley, have sustained and vastly improved the humour of their historian grandmother during many bouts with history over the years. Bob and Margot and Debby and Pat have provided house room when we were on the road, as well as tea and sympathy. Finally, we thank Wayne and Maxine, and Jim, to whom we have dedicated this book. Their belief in our work as historians has been more important than we can possibly ever say, and their support for this book has been unflagging.

Beverly Boutilier, Ujung Pandang, Indonesia

Alison Prentice, Victoria, British Columbia

Creating Historical Memory

1
Introduction: Locating Women in the Work of History

Beverly Boutilier and Alison Prentice

Looking back at the three years she worked as a history lecturer at McMaster University during the Second World War, Margaret Ormsby recalled a time of social and professional isolation. With only one other woman professor as a friend, she looked forward to the twice weekly visits of the classicist, Mary White, who travelled from Toronto to Hamilton to teach at McMaster. Here, the two instructors shared a desk in the only space available to them: the women's washroom. From this inauspicious location, Ormsby conducted her professional life as an academically trained teacher and writer of history before moving to more commodious accommodations at the University of British Columbia, where she taught for the next several decades.

During her brief sojourn in Hamilton, however, Ormsby learned much about women and the work of history. In 1943, McMaster hosted the annual meeting of the Canadian Historical Association (CHA). Ormsby attended as a representative of the university's history department, but found that she also carried an additional burden. As the only university-based woman historian present, she was conscious of an obligation to her sex as well as to her institution and profession. At the meeting, she therefore behaved 'discreetly,' believing, as Hilda Neatby of the University of Saskatchewan did, that it was imperative for women faculty to act with decorum at such functions. But for many years, as she later recalled, it was not likely that she or any other woman could do anything else, 'for some of the provinces where the CHA met were "dry," so the receptions and dinners were held in the men's downtown clubs to which women could not be invited.'[1]

As two of the few women with faculty appointments in university departments of history at mid-century, Ormsby and Neatby were by contemporary definitions 'exceptional' women; however, their passion for the study of history was not. Long regarded as peripheral to the field of historical inquiry, in the past women have nevertheless recorded and written history with varying degrees of energy and success. Historians of European women, for example, have identified a distinct tradition of 'learned ladies' writing history that dates back to medieval times.[2] Similarly, in North America, scholars have shown that in the United States large numbers of women turned to historical writing after the revolution, and later to historic preservation, as a way to legitimate the new republic and women's contributions to it.[3]

Canadian women have likewise been, both individually and collectively, at home and abroad, creators of historical memory. The purpose of this collection is to suggest some of the institutional and intellectual locations from which English-Canadian women have worked as historians and to highlight their surprising variety of reasons for doing so. Although several essays examine the careers of university-trained women, we do not view the work of history as the exclusive purview of academic or 'professional' historians. Indeed, one purpose of the collection is to call into question the legitimacy of the amateur/professional dichotomy as applied to the term 'historian.'

The professionalization of historical practice in the last decades of the nineteenth and early years of the twentieth century formalized a definition of history that privileged male experience and reserved most permanent academic jobs for university-trained men. In Canada, after the turn of the century, even women who pursued advanced academic training in history remained outside the historical profession, unable, for the most part, to find paid work in their chosen field of expertise. There were exceptions to this rule, most notably Ormsby and Neatby, but the hiring of women faculty in more than token numbers by university departments of history in Canada is a comparatively recent phenomenon.[4] Although some Canadian universities demonstrated a willingness to appoint women history graduates to temporary posts and, in a few western institutions by the 1930s and 1940s, to more permanent positions, in general they have not been eager to accommodate women. The University of Toronto, which houses one of English Canada's oldest and largest history programs, did not begin to appoint women to tenured history positions until the 1960s. Today, few of its tenured or tenure-stream history professors are women. Across the country, the proportion of women to men working as historians in Canadian universities remains small, reflecting neither the longstanding numerical parity of male and female undergraduates nor women's increasing representation in graduate history programs.[5]

The problem is not a new one. In the late nineteenth and early twentieth centuries, hundreds of women were actively engaged in the work of history in English Canada. Although some historically minded women earned their livings as writers of history or historical fiction, the great majority did not; their efforts to record and preserve the oral and material heritage of their national and local communities were voluntary. Typically lacking the proper credentials, and often choosing subjects that did not conform to a narrowing definition of historical importance, by the 1930s most of these women had been arbitrarily consigned to the ignominious category of 'amateur' by an increasingly self-conscious historical profession. Although practitioners of the new 'science of history' carried on side by side with their more traditional colleagues into the middle decades of the twentieth century, the view that only graduates of specialized university training in history were now qualified to call themselves historians increasingly prevailed. As before, the object of the professional historian was to render the past intelligible to the present. But, rather than a partisan chronicle of heroic deeds designed to inspire the ideals of loyalty and patriotism in the nation's male and female citizens, academic historians began to view mastery of the 'discipline' of history, and the empirical world view that underwrote it, as necessary precursors to a career in the field.[6]

Women as a group were not seen as fully part of this new historical project. Moreover, because their very gender was thought to embody the sentimental outlook and unrigorous qualities of mind that many male academics attributed to amateur historians generally, the process of professionalization further denigrated 'antiquarianism' by conflating it with femininity on the one hand and by representing it symbolically as the work of 'blue-haired ladies' on the other.[7] This tendency, which was already apparent at the turn of the century, reached its zenith in Canada during the 1930s in the very public battle waged over the place of Laura Secord, and by extension all Canadian women, in history. The academic debunkers of this famous Upper Canadian heroine – and chocolate box icon[8] – argued that her much celebrated walk between Queenston Heights and Beaver Dams had had no discernible impact on the outcome of the War of 1812. This well-publicized assertion infuriated Ontario's local history community, whose female leaders had helped to establish Secord's popularity as a historic figure at the end of the nineteenth century. The debate has never been entirely resolved, but the removal of Laura Secord from the pages of academic history in the 1930s suggests just how closely allied historical professionalization was to the masculinization of history. 'If, after this,' the *Canadian Historical Review* (*CHR*) trumpeted in 1932, 'the public still wants a Laura Secord who "saved the country" in 1813, it must go exclusively to those writers of alluring fiction whose works will not sell unless they drag some woman in.'[9]

As Marlene Shore notes, the *CHR* nevertheless managed in 1940 to publish an intriguing article by Isabel Foulché-Delbosc on women in New France. But its author, who, unfortunately, did not live to see this publication, must have been aware of how out of tune her work was with the general trend. Historians' increasing preoccupation with political records and themes, she explained, meant that 'colonial domestic life was rarely studied.'[10] The general message had been made clear: women might dabble in history, and a few exceptional ones might have something useful to contribute, but they were not – indeed, it was doubtful if they could be – its bona fide intellectual custodians.

The persistent image of the professional historian as a tweed-clad, bewhiskered male continues to emphasize the exceptionality of the female historian. This circumstance has affected the ability of many women, including the small number who have made careers within the academy, to regard themselves as full-fledged historians. Even now, it is all too apparent to many women that their gender sets them apart, leaving some uncertain of their ability or their right, as women, to join the club.[11] Other factors have played a role. For many years, it was assumed that 'career girls' would have to sacrifice the traditionally female roles of marriage and motherhood in order to fulfil themselves intellectually – and unconventionally – as academics. This stark choice delayed some women's identification with a professional path that was defined by the experiences and expectations of men. With few known models of female intellectual achievement before them, and a profession that repeatedly exhibited its reluctance to acknowledge or reward their talents, many intellectual women in English Canada found a career in history a difficult course to chart.

Their dilemma was not unique. In the second volume of her autobiography, the Australian-born scholar Jill Ker Conway, who was one of the first women given tenure in history at the University of Toronto, recollects the moment when she first recognized herself as a historian:

> In the fall of 1968, freed from the albatross of my dissertation, I suddenly realized that I was serious about being a historian. At thirty-three, about to be thirty-four, I saw myself as a scholar. I was not just someone going through the motions of scholarship to please some distant thesis supervisor, or to win some other medal or prize, but the real thing. History was what I did, and would do for the rest of my life.

Conway's belated identification with history as a possible life course mirrors the experience of many women, who, as she notes, often develop a sense of their working selves 'on a different time trajectory' from that of men.[12]

Conway's memoirs also highlight a further problem faced by generations of historically minded women in Canada: an inability to identify their own lived experience with much of the content of history. Although the history of women loomed large in the writings of 'amateur' women historians in the late nineteenth and early twentieth centuries, and even made tentative inroads in the *CHR* during the interwar years, for most of this century academic historians of both genders in English Canada have generally assumed that men alone were makers of history. Focusing largely on Canada's political and economic development as a nation, they initiated a wholesale revision of Canadian historiography that effectively wrote women out of the historical record.[13] Discovering – or perhaps, in light of the work of an earlier generation of women historians, we should say rediscovering – that women, too, have a retrievable and knowable past has been liberating for many women in the latter part of this century. Jill Conway's experience is perhaps, once again, typical. In the early 1960s, when she began her dissertation on American women reformers in the Progressive era, Conway was startled to discover that she had never before looked at *herself* 'through the lens of history,' something that her male colleagues had always done. For the first time she found that she was able 'to engage in an inner conversation' with historical actors of the past with whom she could identify. The experience, she recalled, was 'delightful.'[14]

Since then, the rapidly developing field of women's history has done much to challenge and diminish the androcentric bias of historical writing and teaching.[15] Informed by the political and theoretical perspectives of feminism, historians of women have made gender a historical issue, arguing that the cultural meanings accorded to biological sex, or to 'maleness' and 'femaleness,' are socially constructed and change over time. In the process they have also destabilized the category of 'woman' by working to understand how racial, ethnic, and class differences have shaped and reshaped women's experiences of the past, and our perception of them.[16]

Internationally, historians of women are also starting to focus on their own past, charting the boundaries of the female historical imagination at different times and places. In 1991, for example, the British journal *Gender and History* began featuring a series entitled 'Foremothers,' which sketches the careers of several early twentieth-century women historians.[17] These biographical essays, together with a growing number of collective studies of the scholarly women who worked as historians before the subject was professionalized, or as it was professionalizing, in Europe and North America, are beginning to reveal the full extent of women's long-standing curiosity about the past and women's place in it.[18]

Part of this project is devoted to the rediscovery of historical work by women that was almost totally erased in the interest of enhancing the male historian's image as individual genius. Such was the fate of Athénais Michelet, whose contribution to her famous husband's scholarly output was denigrated and gradually suppressed by some of his influential successors in French history. Bonnie Smith argues that such stories show how the 'authorial presence' of the historian has been 'gendered masculine and how it comes into being through repetitious pairings of a male "original" with a female "copy(ist)" or "falsifier" or "fake."'[19]

Despite such distortions and erasures, we are now discovering that over the centuries Western women have produced an impressive historiography that both parallels the better known canon of male historians and diverges from it in certain significant ways. In the late eighteenth and nineteenth centuries, in particular, a growing number of women in France, England, and the United States entered the field of historical literature as writers of female biography. In much the same way that male historians focused on the lives and deeds of 'great men,' female biographers in this period recalled the lives of 'women worthies,' notable and often noble women whose exercise of social influence or political power had won them a place in history.[20] But this new emphasis on the lives of 'great women' was more than a simple emulation of men's historical preoccupations. For example, women such as Agnes and Elizabeth Strickland, whose multivolume biographies of the queens of England and Scotland went through several editions in the latter half of the nineteenth century, also revealed a new kind of historical sensibility. As well as placing individual women at the centre of history, they suggested that the conventional interests of womanhood, namely domesticity and motherhood, were also areas of legitimate historical concern. In the lives of their female subjects they saw a unity between private and public worlds, as they placed the details of women's everyday experience against the bolder canvas of men's statecraft. But, as Joan Thirsk and Billie Melman note, 'history women' were frequently criticized by 'history men' for these forays into social history because it was thought that their discussions of household cares detracted from the 'real' work of history, which was politics.[21]

There is an emerging consensus among feminist historians not only that women in Europe and North America created a distinct historiography, but also that this tradition of historical writing has its own recognizable periodization and forms. Women have been writing history since at least the medieval period in the West and, viewed as a body of work, their historical writings exhibit certain shared characteristics. The first of these was a common preoccupation with the history of women, whether working in a biographical mode or using the perspectives of scientific history to reconstruct the collective experiences of specific groups of women. Another was a tendency to write histories of their own family members. Indeed, as Natalie Zemon Davis argues, those few women who wrote in the 'great man' tradition of political biography, in the early modern period, were usually related in some fashion to their subjects. Only in this way could these women claim the authority to speak, as women, about matters more typically associated with male expertise.[22]

The impact of historical professionalization on women historians is another area of notable consensus among students of the topic. In Britain especially, the renaissance of women's historical writing that began in the late eighteenth century was over by the late 1930s, as professional history became synonymous with the history of politics and, by extension, the history of men. Most women academics who worked in history during the first three decades of this century aligned themselves with the experimental fields of social and economic history, examining various aspects of the history of women's lives before and after the industrial revolution. When, after the Second World War, political history finally supplanted this area of historical investigation – in part because it was associated with women's history – the status of women historians both within and outside the profession declined. Their work on the history of women and their intellectual inventiveness as social and economic historians were largely rejected by their chosen profession. Only now, more than half a century later, have their contributions to modern historiography and historical practice begun to be recognized.[23]

Our book constitutes a beginning for this kind of work in English Canada. At this stage of the research, we are unable to present a comprehensive survey of all Canadian women who engaged with history or the historical profession. Nor is it yet certain whether the women whose lives are featured in this collection are in any way typical of the women who have taken up the work of history in English Canada. Our limited focus suggests that they are *not*. The essays collected here sketch the relationship of women to the work of history from the particular, although sometimes unspoken, vantage point of English Canada's dominant white, Anglo-Celtic majority. Moreover, all regions of the country are not considered equally: the lens of inquiry is focused predominantly, although not exclusively, on Ontario women. In short, our emphasis is not only on those women who worked in English, but also on the written word and the experiences of white women, the majority from Canada's most populous province. *Creating Historical Memory* nevertheless shows that, within this limited racial and regional grouping, there was considerable diversity.

What, then, do these ten essays suggest about the origin and outlook of women historians in English Canada? One thing they clearly reveal is that class made a difference: most of the historians featured had strong support from their families or their communities, and several came from relatively privileged backgrounds that made their historical studies possible. Yet, as the careers of Sarah Anne Curzon and Constance Lindsay Skinner demonstrate, a woman's class and family status could be tenuous.

Single women and widows, especially, could not necessarily rely on their families for economic support. To the extent that the sources, or space, has permitted, the authors of our essays grapple with these factors.

An examination of the different family, class, and community locations from which women wrote history underscores the extent to which historical consciousness is itself socially constructed. There were many forces that drew women to history; the most powerful, perhaps, was economic. Historical writing has been a means of earning a living from the beginning for many women, not just for 'professional' women historians. Many of the women whose careers are explored in this collection were dependent in whole or in part on the earnings from their historical work. Others engaged in history, either as writers or preservationists, for more overtly ideological reasons. For some, history was a means of expressing their sense of national and racial identity as patriots, while for others historical research was a means of defining or redefining a commitment to their local communities. Similarly, some historical work by women grew out of religious commitment. For professed Roman Catholic women, religion was a catalyst for chronicling the lives of their communities; indeed, Elizabeth Smyth argues that in the world prior to Vatican II, some women religious in Ontario wrote history 'out of obedience.' Faith also frequently informed the writings of Protestant women historians, as the careers of Agnes Maule Machar and Kathleen Wood-Legh show. And faith could be political as well as religious. The women's movements of the late nineteenth and twentieth centuries, for example, generated many new historical preoccupations, including the development of women's history.

Motivation was one thing; the ability to engage in historical work quite another. The biographical studies included here reflect this, as the authors explore the circumstances that informed the daily work of their subjects. Some women historians found space and support for their research and writing relatively easily, but most struggled to integrate their historical work with other demands on their time and energy. From the Maritime historian, Esther Clark Wright, who got into high gear only when her felt obligation to support her husband's career ceased in middle age, to the teaching sisters who sometimes found themselves writing history as very elderly women, fragmented and demanding lives leap from these pages. So, too, does the strength of women who managed to write history in spite of such constraints.

The women featured in these essays wrote in a variety of genres and focused their work on many different topics. Most of the women who wrote from outside the university-based history profession were preoccupied from the late nineteenth century onward with the history of Canada, a subject that not all academic historians considered important until the middle decades of the twentieth century. Several of those who wrote from inside the academy also focused on Canadian themes; some turned to the early practitioners of economic and social history for their inspiration. Indeed, the essays suggest that women historians had a marked tendency to adopt innovative perspectives and methodologies. Their new interests often paralleled, and sometimes derived from, Canadian women's longstanding fascination with the histories of their own local and regional communities. There were also practical considerations influencing the subjects both academic and non-academic women chose. Frequently, women could not afford research far from home, or were constrained by family commitments. Some choices were governed by external demands; others by internalized beliefs, whether spiritual or political. In other cases, the need to make a living and respond to the demands of the marketplace shaped the content of their work.

Two perspectives predominate in this collection. Six of the essays are biographical; the other four approach their subjects as collectivities. Feminist historians have recently reclaimed biography as a tool of women's history, using the analytical vantage point of gender to reconstruct the contours of women's individual lives. Sandra Holton and Barbara Caine, for example, argue that feminist biographies can tell us a great deal about the history of 'the average woman' by providing a wealth of specific information about the life course of differently positioned women, whose lives can then be viewed collectively and comparatively.[24] The authors of our biographical essays work from several different starting points. Beverly Boutilier focuses on the connections between Sarah Curzon's political career as a women's rights activist and her literary work as a writer of historical Canadiana. Similarly, Dianne Hallman dwells, for the most part, on the historical thought of Agnes Maule Machar as expressed in her published writings.

In contrast, the emphasis of Megan Davies, Colin Coates, and Barry Moody is on the personal contexts that shaped their subjects' lives and work. Davies and Coates explore how Kathleen Wood-Legh reconciled her ambition to be a scholar with the challenge of her blindness. In a similar vein, Moody concentrates on the early influences, educational and marital, that shaped Esther Clark Wright's later development as a historian. In his essay on Isabel Skelton, Terry Crowley unites these two perspectives, profiling the private and public dimensions of her work as a writer of history and considering how she managed the constraints and opportunities created by her marriage to O.D. Skelton, Canada's first undersecretary of state for External Affairs. Jean Barman also explores the personal and public aspects of Constance Lindsay Skinner's career, including the challenges she encountered working with her publishers. Each of these approaches was determined, to some degree, by the nature and range of sources available to the authors.

The remaining four essayists examine the historical work of several formal and informal communities of women. Linda Ambrose and Elizabeth Smyth consider two well-established groups. Smyth's study of Roman Catholic women religious is based on records that they themselves created for a number of purposes: to celebrate the achievements of the present and the past; to build a sense of community over time; and to examine the role of providence in history and in the lives of their orders. Linda Ambrose focuses on an altogether different kind of community: a rural women's organization that, from the 1920s onward, actively worked to preserve the heritage of their own townships and districts in an increasingly urban world. The essays by Alison Prentice and Deborah Gorham, in contrast, deal with groups whose sense of identity as communities of women was either somewhat tenuous in the former case, or in the latter grew out of their engagement with the women's movement of the late 1960s and 1970s. Prentice's essay examines the earliest generations of women to study and work in selected Canadian university departments of history. Gorham's essay expands on this theme, tracing the institutional development of women's history as a distinct field of research and teaching in English Canada, a development undertaken at the beginning almost exclusively by women historians. In these two cases, the authors' identification with the communities they study creates a particular problem: how to grapple with the work of women who were either their predecessors or are now their colleagues. Indeed, in each of the four group studies, a degree of negotiation between the authors and their subjects was an essential part of the process of historical creation.[25]

This raises the question of how membership in a given community, real or perceived, affects the historian's work. Or, to pose the question as it relates to the broader theme of this collection: How does gender consciousness influence historical consciousness? Does looking at the past through women's eyes alter the view?

The simple answer is, of course, yes. Especially in the case of those individuals and groups who were preoccupied with the history of women, there is a sense that they looked to the past, in part, to validate their own experience. Moreover, we would argue that consciousness of gender difference helped them to see patterns and problems that most men had previously ignored or dismissed as irrelevant to the real concerns of history. The connection that present-day historians of women have made between the types of history written by women in the past and contemporary attitudes towards their prescribed gender roles is likewise suggestive. Particularly in the nineteenth century, when history was largely regarded as a chronicle of politics, and women's authority as historical interpreters was constrained by the assumption that politics belonged to the world of men, some Canadian women circumvented this constraint by choosing genres and subjects that were more closely identified with their own prescribed 'sphere.' This, in part, accounts for many activist women's interest in the history of women, a subject about which they could assert their expertise.

This was not necessarily true in the twentieth century, when some women's participation in political life and higher education began to narrow the gap between male and female experience, at least in certain quarters. Now it seemed legitimate for women to tackle subjects formerly considered beyond their scope. Gender nevertheless remained an important factor in shaping women's opportunities to work as historians, both within and outside the academy. In a period when an overseas education was still considered the standard of excellence for an academic career, women who would otherwise have chosen a quite different specialization found themselves studying Canadian history by default because they could not afford to do research in foreign archives. These kinds of financial constraints bore more heavily on talented women than on talented men. Women, for example, were ineligible for the Rhodes scholarships that made study at Oxford possible for some Canadian male historians. Moreover, to the extent that advanced historical training was associated with preparation for a life in diplomacy or politics, once again women were disadvantaged.

In the first half of the twentieth century, the nature of historical practice in Canada was in flux as the country's fledgling history departments increasingly adopted the professional norms of 'scientific' history. The general tendency of this process was to reinforce the masculine bias of historical studies. Within this institutional framework, it was nevertheless possible to raise new questions about the past, as many early English-Canadian women historians did. However, not all of these historical innovators were products of the new profession of history as it was being developed within the universities of Canada. Many impressive women of historical sensibility continued to work outside the academy, applying the same empirical standards of research to a very different set of historical preoccupations, including, in the case of Isabel Skelton, the history of women. Nor did all, or indeed most, of the women who pursued academic training in history necessarily aspire to become academic historians. But some women did, and it was this small group who learned from experience that academic excellence was not the only qualification needed to achieve full membership in a self-consciously male professional grouping that was in the process of consolidating its institutional and intellectual boundaries.

Could a 'woman' be a 'historian'? We now recognize, with the help of feminist theory, that both concepts are socially constructed. The essays in *Creating Historical Memory* attempt to problematize, in different ways

University of Saskatchewan Historical Association, 1921

and to varying degrees, the relationship between women and historical practice. If a woman *were* a historian, how and where could she practise her art? If our collection illustrates the many constraints that women faced, it also depicts women who embraced a wide variety of ways of engaging with history. They taught history in schools and, in a few cases, in colleges and universities. They wrote historical novels and history textbooks, articles for historical societies, convent annals, and community histories. Some wrote poetry and plays with historical themes. Several drew deeply on their own experience of time and place in their historical writing, creating a genre that Jean Barman dubs 'experiential' history. A few, more concerned with the orthodoxies of the German scientific school, immersed themselves in archives and documentary evidence as they joined male colleagues in the effort to 'raise standards' and embrace a definition of historical practice that more clearly approached the norms of science.

It is evident from this collection that English-Canadian women historians were intellectually innovative. They were intrigued by regional and local history at a time when national history was fast becoming the norm among professional historians. They researched the lives of ordinary people, not just the famous or politically powerful, and they often demanded that women be the subjects of history as well as men. In this way, in common with their counterparts in Britain and the United States, English-Canadian women helped to pioneer experimental approaches to history and to create topics that had not previously been regarded as part of the historical agenda.

As their work varied, so too did their audiences. Some wrote for small, closed circles, such as those who wrote for their sisters in religion. Many were writing for children and had explicitly educational goals; far from having doubts about the importance of the juvenile market, some made it a priority and devoted a significant amount of their time and energy to this work. There were also those who, like the members of the Women's Canadian Historical Society of Toronto, envisaged their audiences to be chiefly women, who would be empowered through the study of Canadian history to adopt a new image of themselves as patriots and citizens. Many women wrote mainly for local audiences, while the scholarly few targeted learned societies and academic journals, and published in university presses, in order to reach the men whose work and gender defined the historical profession. In the larger, national historical associations, women's role and right to full participation nevertheless remained contested for much of the twentieth century. Although a few women were admitted to the most significant rites of passage – Hilda Neatby and Margaret Ormsby would become presidents of the Canadian Historical Association in the 1960s, and several others would eventually receive honours commensurate with their outstanding achievements – such women tended to be regarded as exceptional even at that late date.

While we hope this collection touches on most of the themes that should inform a work of this kind, we are aware that several remain unexplored or have received only limited treatment. The question of professionalism in history is a topic that deserves extensive exploration, using among other records those of Canada's national and regional historical societies. A related topic is women's involvement in the quest for a 'scientific history' and the rise of the research university in Canada. Both topics suggest the need to examine gender relations in Canada's historical and other scholarly societies and in institutions whose practices defined the boundaries of professional historical work.[26] We need more studies that engage strenuously with the ideas of mid-twentieth-century Canadian women historians, as the Boutilier, Crowley, Hallman, and Barman essays do for earlier women writers of history. It is important also to make more links between the different women who worked in history and to study them collectively, in the context of the institutions they built.

More research is needed as well on the personal contexts in which Canadian women historians constructed their lives, not to mention the contexts of class, ethnicity, and race – topics that only a few of the essays in this book explore extensively. The subjects of mentorship and apprenticeship also receive little attention from our authors and are ripe for further examination. There is very little about women and the teaching of history here, yet we know of women who loved scholarship but ended up, more or less by default, working mainly as teachers; conversely, some women sought careers as teachers and later became deeply involved in historical scholarship. Life course is an obviously related topic. At what point in their lives were women able to write history? Some of our essays begin to answer these and similar questions. But, at this early stage in the research on English-Canadian women and the work of history, perhaps the chief contribution made by these studies is to open up the field to further exploration.

Creating Historical Memory is organized in four sections that reflect the shifting dimensions of English-Canadian women's work as historical writers and activists. We begin with 'Community Building.' Billie Melman argues that one of the prime motives for British women writing history in the nineteenth century was to establish 'woman' as an actor in history alongside the more familiar 'historical man.' Using the genre of individual and group biography, they focused on notable women such as queens and consorts whose impact on their nation as rulers was irrefutable.[27] The three essays in Community Building suggest that English-Canadian women were similarly motivated to prove that women had played a significant role in the development of their national and local communities. Dianne Hallman's study of Agnes Maule Machar's commitment to forging a distinct Canadian identity through history begins this section. Beverly Boutilier's exploration of Sarah Curzon's historical writing and activism reveals a woman shaped by an equally strong commitment to the cause of 'women's rights.' Linda Ambrose considers the connections between rural women's activism and the historical impulse by examining the Ontario Women's Institutes and their formal efforts to record and write the histories of their own communities.

The second section, 'Transitions,' opens with Elizabeth Smyth's analysis of the work of Roman Catholic women religious as historians. Here was another kind of community building, as the appointed record-keepers of these communities created the histories of their own orders and sometimes commented on the world outside. Over time, sisters and nuns sought a wider public for their historical writings, offering their work at academic gatherings and publishing it in historical journals. Jean Barman and Terry Crowley describe women historians whose careers bridged two worlds: that of the so-called amateur, exemplified by women like Machar and Curzon, and that of the professional scholar. Constance Lindsay Skinner engaged with the new scientific history, leaving the biographical mode and substituting a heroic western landscape and its people for the individual subject typical of earlier women's historical work. Isabel Skelton, too, focused on collectivities rather than on individuals, as she sought to introduce the experience of pioneer women into the story of Canada.

The third section, 'The Academy,' documents the careers forged by English-Canadian women as historians in and on the margins of Canadian, American, and British universities. The general context for their experience in Canada is established by Alison Prentice's essay, which shows how women fared in selected history departments across the country, as students and faculty, prior to the 1950s. Barry Moody explores the personal and professional foundations of Esther Clark Wright's career as a Maritime historian. Megan Davies and Colin Coates examine the remarkable career of Kathleen Wood-Legh, a Canadian who made her mark as a scholar in British medieval history while living and working at the periphery of Cambridge University. These essays suggest that women engaged with scientific history in a distinct way. Often focusing on particular religious groups or regions, they emphasized difference rather than the designated centre. As Melman argues for British women historians of the first half of the century, women historians sought to complicate rather than to embroider the existing historical narrative.[28] New work in economic and social history, much of it pioneered by British women scholars, clearly inspired some Canadian women to question contemporary definitions of historical importance well in advance of our own times.

One of the results of this intellectual energy was a renewed interest in the history of women. Between 1940 and 1970, a handful of women scholars had already managed to ignore dominant trends, focusing their research and writing on women and topics in women's history that captured their attention. Their studies ranged from individual biographical studies, through exercises in women's collective biography, to a general account of the Canadian woman suffrage movement.[29] This was the context within which Hilda Neatby encouraged at least one advanced student to consider the history of women as a legitimate field of inquiry in the 1960s; Margaret Ormsby eventually entered the field herself, with the publication of the memoirs of British Columbia pioneer Susan B. Allison in 1974.[30] Deborah Gorham's essay in the last section, 'New Departures,' explores the flowering of a Canadian women's history movement in the early 1970s and its sometimes difficult relationship to feminist thought and activism.

It is with a sense of growing excitement that we present these essays. We are fascinated with the facts about women and the work of history that are coming to light. Like women everywhere, English-Canadian women wrestled with the past in a variety of ways in order to learn from it, to make it meaningful to themselves and others like them, and to derive lessons for the future that suited their own particular ends. They grappled with an established canon of historical literature and thought in which their own experiences as women were often marginalized or entirely absent, and with a profession that sought to formalize a definition of history and historical practice that would perpetuate their absence. The message of this book is that, far from being intimidated or defeated by these struggles, English-Canadian women discovered and developed other paths to historical expression and put forward new and quite different ideas about history for their contemporaries to consider. Their work left a rich and varied legacy for the women who would do the work of history in the generations that followed.

Notes

1 Margaret A. Ormsby, 'A Western Woman Looks at Her Work,' paper delivered at the Canadian Historical Association annual meeting, McMaster University, Hamilton, ON, 7 June 1987, pp. 6-7. Professor Ormsby kindly sent the paper to Alison Prentice in 1991.

2 Natalie Zemon Davis, 'Gender and Genre: Women as Historical Writers, 1400-1920,' in Patricia Labalme, ed., *Beyond Their Sex: Learned Women of the European Past* (New York: New York University Press 1980), 153-82. Gerda Lerner argues that a female tradition of historical writing in Europe can be traced back to the seventh century. See *The Creation of Feminist Consciousness* (New York: Oxford University Press 1993), esp. 247-73.

3 Kathryn Kish Sklar, 'American Female Historians in Context, 1770-1930,' *Feminist Studies* 3, 1-2 (1975-6): 171-84; Nina Baym, *American Women Writers and the Work of History* (New Brunswick, NJ: Rutgers University Press 1995). Explorations of women's historical work now go well beyond the boundaries of North America and Europe. See, for example, Susan Janson, 'Jessie Webb and the Predicament of the Female Historian' and Susan Davies, 'Kathleen Fitzpatrick: Sculptor with Words,' in Stuart Macintyre and Julian Thomas, eds., *The Discovery of Australian History, 1890-1939* (Carleton South: Melbourne University Press 1995); E. Patricia Tsurumi, 'The Accidental Historian, Yamakawa Kikue,' *Gender & History* 8, 2 (August 1996).

4 This pattern of discrimination was general throughout Canadian universities, although there were local variations on the theme. On the experience and status of women as faculty in Canadian universities, see Judith Fingard, 'Gender and Inequality at Dalhousie: Women Faculty before 1950,' *Dalhousie Review* 59, 4 (winter 1984-5): 687-703; Alison Prentice, 'Scholarly Passion: Two Women Who Caught It,' *Historical Studies in Education/Revue d'histoire de l'éducation* 1, 1 (spring 1989): 7-27, reprinted in Alison Prentice and Marjorie R. Theobald, eds., *Women Who Taught: Perspectives on the History of Women and Teaching* (Toronto: University of Toronto Press 1991), 258-84; 'Bluestockings, Feminists or Women Workers? A Preliminary Look at Women's Early Employment at the University of Toronto,' *Journal of Canadian Historical Association* 2 (1991): 231-61; Mary Kinnear, 'Disappointed in Discourse: Women Professors at the University of Manitoba before 1970,' *Historical Studies in Education/Revue d'histoire de l'éducation* 4, 2 (fall 1992): 269-87, reprinted, in a revised form, as chapter 2 of Mary Kinnear, *In Subordination: Women and the Professions, 1870-1970* (Montreal and Kingston: McGill-Queen's University Press 1995).

5 *Women in Canada: A Statistical Report*, 2nd ed. (Ottawa: Statistics Canada 1990), 45-72. See also the papers presented to the 1990 meeting of the Canadian Historical Association in Victoria in the panel entitled 'Three Generations of Women in the Historical Profession': Margaret Prang, 'Personal Reflections on a Career in History'; Linda Kealey, 'Women Historians in Canadian Universities: A Report on the Canadian Historical Association Survey'; Lykke de la Cour, Karen Dubinsky, Nancy Forestall, Mary Ellen Kelm, Lynne Marks, and Cecilia Morgan, '"Here's Where We Separate the Men from the Boys": Comments on Women's Experiences as Students in Graduate History Programmes in Canada.' Kealey's report was published as 'The Status of Women in the Historical Profession in Canada, 1989 Survey,' *Canadian Historical Review* 72, 3 (September 1991): 370-88.

6 Although she does not discuss the question of historians' gender, Marlene Shore explores these trends in '"Remembering the Future": The *Canadian Historical Review* and the Discipline of History, 1920-95,' *Canadian Historical Review* 76, 3 (September 1995): 410-63.

Shore finds that broader interests and traditional, more literary forms shared the pages of this key journal with narrower approaches during the interwar years, only disappearing in the middle decades of the twentieth century. For an account of the development of professionalism that examines some of these issues, see R.D. Gidney and W.J.P. Millar, *Professional Gentlemen: The Professions in Nineteenth-Century Ontario* (Toronto: University of Toronto Press 1994). See, as well, the discussion of Lady Tweedsmuir's 1938 University of Toronto speech, published in the *CHR* as 'The Amateur Historian,' in Linda Ambrose's essay in this collection.

7 Both of us have encountered this kind of gendered characterization of amateur (and local) history as the work of elderly, possibly eccentric, women. In the early 1970s, a male historian presenting a paper to a meeting of professional historians in Toronto referred to the 'little old ladies' of the Kamloops Historical Society, while, in the late 1980s, another long-serving member of the history profession in Ottawa described members of the Ontario Historical Society as 'blue-haired ladies in tennis shoes.'

8 In Canada, Laura Secord's name and image are the trademark of a well-known manufacturer and retailer of chocolates and ice cream.

9 Ruth McKenzie, *Laura Secord: The Legend and the Lady* (Toronto: Macmillan 1971), 120-33, esp. 124. See also the interesting analysis of the Laura Secord story in Cecilia Morgan, '"Of Slender Frame and Delicate Appearance": The Placing of Laura Secord in the Narratives of Canadian Loyalist History,' *Journal of the Canadian Historical Association* 5 (1994): 195-212, reprinted in Joy Parr and Mark Rosenfeld, eds., *Gender and History in Canada* (Toronto: Copp Clark 1996), 103-19. For a discussion of the link between historical professionalization and the masculinization of history, see Bonnie G. Smith, 'The Adolescent Road to Historical Science,' *History of Education Quarterly* 33, 4 (winter 1993): 563-77.

10 Shore, '"Remembering the Future,"' 422. The article was 'Women of New France (Three Rivers: 1651-1663)' and drew, innovatively, on notarial and law court records. It was published posthumously in the *CHR* 21 (June 1940): 132-49. For a brief account of what is known about Isabel Foulché-Delbosc, see Alison Prentice's essay in this collection.

11 The nostalgic image of the bewhiskered professor in a tweed suit, originally put forward by David Bercuson, Robert Bothwell, and J.L. Granatstein, is critiqued in Ruth Roach Pierson's '"Women Have Nothing to Gain from a Harvard of the North": The False Equation of Elitism with Excellence in Education,' in Frieda Forman et al., eds., *Feminism and Education: A Canadian Perspective* (Toronto: Centre for Women's Studies in Education, Ontario Institute for Studies in Education 1990), 277-93. For a recent discussion of the situation of women faculty in Canada, see The Chilly Collective, *Breaking Anonymity: The Chilly Climate for Women Faculty* (Waterloo, ON: Wilfrid Laurier University Press 1995).

12 Jill Ker Conway, *True North* (Toronto: Alfred A. Knopf 1994), 148.

13 On the development of the historical profession in English Canada, see Carl Berger, *The Writing of Canadian History: Aspects of English-Canadian Historical Writing Since 1900*, 2nd ed. (Toronto: University of Toronto Press 1986), and M. Brook Taylor, *Promoters, Patriots, and Partisans: Historiography in Nineteenth-Century English Canada* (Toronto: University of Toronto Press 1989). For a study of the English context of the professionalization of history in English Canada, see Rosemary Jann, 'From Amateur to Professional: The Case of the Oxbridge Historians,' *The Journal of British Studies* 22, 2 (spring 1983): 122-47.

14 Conway, *True North*, 56.

15 For Canada, see the essays in Bettina Bradbury et al., eds., *Teaching Women's History: Challenges and Solutions* (Athabasca: Athabasca University Educational Enterprises 1996); Veronica Strong-Boag, *Work to Be Done: The Canadian Committee on Women's History* (Vancouver: Centre for Research in Women's Studies and Gender Relations, UBC 1995). The rapid expansion of the field is amply documented in Diana Pederson, *Changing Women, Changing History: A Bibliography of the History of Women in Canada*, 2nd ed. (Ottawa: Carleton University Press 1996).

16 For a recent account of the development of women's history internationally that includes Ruth Pierson's perceptive survey of the Canadian scene, see Ruth Roach Pierson, Karen

Offen, and Jane Randall, eds., *Writing Women's History: International Perspectives* (Bloomington: Indiana University Press 1991). See also Joy Parr and Mark Rosenfeld, eds., *Gender and History in Canada* (Toronto: Copp Clark 1996); Gisela Bock, 'Women's History and Gender History,' *Gender and History* 1 (1988): 11-15; Joan Wallach Scott, *Gender and the Politics of History* (New York: Columbia University Press 1988); Ann-Louise Shapiro, ed., *Feminists Revision History* (New Brunswick, NJ: Rutgers University Press 1994); Cheryl Johnson-Odim and Margaret Strobel, eds., *Expanding the Boundaries of Women's History: Essays on Women in the Third World* (Bloomington: Indiana University Press 1992).

17 See, for example, Ellen C. Dubois, 'Foremothers I: Eleanor Flexner and the History of American Feminism,' *Gender and History* 3, 1 (spring 1991): 81-90, and Maxine Berg, 'Foremothers III: Eileen Power and Women's History,' *Gender and History* 6, 2 (August 1994): 265-74.

18 For example, Maxine Berg, 'The First Women Economic Historians,' *Economic History Review* 45, 2 (1992): 308-29, and Bonnie G. Smith, 'The Contribution of Women to Modern Historiography in Great Britain, France and the United States, 1750-1940,' *American Historical Review* 89, 3 (June 1984): 709-32.

19 Bonnie G. Smith, 'Historiography, Objectivity, and the Case of the Abusive Widow,' in Ann-Louise Shapiro, ed., *Feminists Revision History*, 24-46, esp. 43. See also, Natalie Zemon Davis, 'Women and the World of the *Annales*,' *History Workshop Journal* 33 (spring 1992): 121-37.

20 The phrase 'women worthies' was coined by Natalie Zemon Davis in '"Women's History" in Transition: The European Case,' *Feminist Studies* 3, 3-4 (1975-6): 83-103.

21 Joan Thirsk, 'The History Women,' in Mary O'Dowd and Sabine Wichert, eds., *Chattel, Servant or Citizen: Women's Status in Church, State and Society* (Belfast: The Institute of Irish Studies, Queen's University of Belfast 1993), 1-11; Billie Melman, 'Gender, History and Memory: The Invention of Women's Past in the Nineteenth and Early Twentieth Centuries,' *History and Memory: Studies in Representation of the Past* 5, 1 (spring/summer 1993): 5-41.

22 Davis, 'Gender and Genre.'

23 Maxine Berg, 'The First Women Economic Historians,' and *A Woman in History: Eileen Power, 1889-1940* (Cambridge: Cambridge University Press 1996); Miranda Chayter and Jane Lewis, 'Introduction,' to Alice Clark, *Working Life of Women in the Seventeenth Century* [1919] (London: Routledge and Kegan Paul 1992), ix-xli.

24 Sandra Holton, 'The Suffragist and the "Average Woman,"' *Women's History Review* 1, 1 (March 1992): 9-24; Barbara Caine, 'Feminist Biography and Feminist History,' *Women's History Review* 3, 2 (June 1994): 247-61.

25 Linda Ambrose has written an official history of the Ontario Women's Institutes: Linda M. Ambrose, *For Home and Country: The Centennial History of the Women's Institutes of Ontario* (Erin, ON: Boston Mills 1996).

26 See Jacqueline Goggin, 'Challenging Sexual Discrimination in the Historical Profession: Women Historians and the American Historical Association, 1890-1940,' *American Historical Review* 47, 3 (June 1992): 769-802, for an interesting look at one such organization in the United States. Laura Macleod explored Canadian women's participation in scholarly publishing in 'Proper Care and Work Well Done: The University of Toronto Press, 1929-1960' (unpublished paper, University of Toronto 1995).

27 Melman, 'Gender, History and Memory.'

28 Ibid.

29 For example, Elsie Pomeroy, 'Mary Electa Adams,' *Ontario History* 41, 3 (1949): 106-17; Mary Quayle Innis, ed., *The Clear Spirit: Twenty Canadian Women and Their Times* (Toronto: University of Toronto Press 1966); Catherine Cleverdon, *The Woman Suffrage Movement in Canada* (Toronto: University of Toronto Press 1950). At the time of writing, Pomeroy had access to Adams's diaries, most of which were subsequently lost. Innis's edited volume was commissioned by the Canadian Federation of University Women, probably to celebrate Canada's centennial. Ramsay Cook's introduction to the second edition of Cleverdon's book provides an account Cleverdon's choice of topic. She was an American doctoral student who was prevented by the Second World War from travelling to England to do research for a thesis in British history and was persuaded to

choose a Canadian subject instead. Cleverdon was at Columbia at the time and was supervised by 'expatriate Canadian' J.B. Brebner. She had initially intended to write her doctoral thesis on the political influence of Queen Victoria. Cook, 'An Introduction,' *The Woman Suffrage Movement in Canada,* 2nd ed. (Toronto: University of Toronto Press 1974), vii.

30 Margaret A. Ormsby, ed., *A Pioneer Gentlewoman in British Columbia: The Recollections of Susan B. Allison* (Vancouver: UBC Press 1976).

Part 1:
Community Building

2
Cultivating a Love of Canada through History: Agnes Maule Machar, 1837-1927

Dianne M. Hallman

A brief biographical portrait of Agnes Maule Machar (1837-1927) written by A.E. Prince in 1934 indelibly imprinted a picture of her as an old spinster who lived alone with several cats – 'a fragrant memory to those privileged to know her. Her quaint little figure, her mid-Victorian dress and manners, her eccentricities.'[1] Prince was not alone in evoking an impression of the writer from Kingston, Ontario, as belonging to an age gone by. Upon Machar's death in 1927, R.W. Cumberland, a regular visitor to both her house on Sydenham Street and her island retreat Ferncliff, described her as 'a little bit of yesterday,' and as belonging 'so completely to the nineteenth century that the twentieth cannot accept her with enthusiasm.'[2] The image of Agnes Machar as a picturesque literary figure from the distant past has persisted in late twentieth-century assessments

Agnes Maule Machar

of her.[3] Yet Machar's own contributions to the recording and interpretation of the past have received less critical attention than other aspects of her work.[4] History was, nevertheless, either the focus or a substantial theme in much of her writing, and her considerable contributions to the historical record reveal much about Victorian Canada's dominant paradigm of historical writing and how one woman stood in relation to it.

The private dimensions of Machar's life seem doomed to die with the 'fragrant memories' of those who knew her. There are no personal papers conveniently housed in an archive where one can go to assimilate and distil the many dimensions of her life and work, to re-create her consciousness of history, or even to reconstruct the basic chronology of her life. The few personal letters that have been retrieved from the papers of correspondents give tantalizing glimpses into the person she was, but this essay on Machar as a historian must rely mainly on description and analysis of her published work. Here the corpus is substantial, spanning sixty years from 1859 to 1919.

As was the case for many of her contemporaries, both men and women, Machar's historical interests found expression in a number of genres: memorials, local history, historical fiction, and poetry. Her other significant contributions to the field were history books for children, such as *Stories of New France*, *Stories from Canadian History*, and *Stories of the British Empire*.[5] Several of her essays published in the *Canadian Monthly and National Review*, its successor *Rose Belford's Canadian Monthly and National Review*, and *The Week* (often under her pen-name Fidelis) had historical themes; her novels and poetry also instructed her audience in the morals to be drawn from history as well as the virtues of patriotism.

In an age when English-Canadian writers unabashedly promoted a particular Canadian national identity and many Canadian historians were occupied with illuminating the importance of the St. Lawrence River and its connections to Britain, it is appropriate to consider Machar's written legacy with respect to the sense of national identity that she promoted.[6] In her study of Machar's nationalism, Ruth Compton Brouwer focused on two components: Machar's concern to demonstrate the historic contributions of French Canada to the nation and to assure 'the recognition of a place for French Canadians in the country's future as well as its past'; and 'the formulation of an imperialism tempered and complemented by positive attitudes toward the American republic.' Brouwer concentrated on the remarkable capacity of Machar to reconcile the competing interests of Britain, English and French Canada, and the United States in her sustained efforts to promote national unity and a broad concept of patriotism. The underlying idea that fired and sustained Machar's sense of patriotism was the Anglo-Saxon providential sense of its mission to cast Christian light into all the 'dark' corners of the globe.[7] Thus Machar's conciliatory methods were subordinated to an Anglo-Saxon and Christian triumphalism that promoted a decidedly Whiggish view of history. She was, in fact, both an avid reader and producer of historical texts that reflected a conception of history as the unfolding of God's eternal purpose and reinforced the notion that a social order premised on Anglo-Saxon ascendancy and asymmetrical gender relations was God's will. At the same time, her essays reveal an interest in and knowledge of what today would be called women's history. Here, a tradition of female excellence was recalled and pressed into service to substantiate claims for the extension of women's sphere and to validate a view of human perfectibility and progress.

A belief that God's hand guided history and provided for His people is hardly surprising, given the strength of her Presbyterian heritage. A.B. McKillop refers to Agnes Machar as 'one of the most articulate and intelligent lay defenders of Christian orthodoxy' who was 'deeply committed to her Presbyterian heritage, [and] never doubted the fundamental truths of her religion.'[8] For Machar, the paradox of Divine Predestination and human free will was one that she was willing to acknowledge and let lie: 'Both are facts, contrary, but not contradictory.'[9]

Her father, Rev. Dr. John Machar (1796-1863), had grown up in Forfarshire, Scotland. Shortly after completing university studies at Aberdeen and Edinburgh, he was ordained as the minister of St. Andrew's Church, Kingston, Upper Canada. Reverend Machar arrived in Canada in the fall of 1827 to take the position left vacant by the premature death of the recently founded church's first minister. To this ministry he devoted the rest of his life. He was one of the founders of Queen's College in 1841 and served as its Principal from 1846-53.[10] As was the case for many ministers, particularly in colonial circumstances, his home became a centre of intellectual and cultural life. His large and excellent library expanded the minds and widened the horizons of young men like John A. Macdonald and Oliver Mowat, who later became prominent statesmen.[11] It was presumably here in the 'shadowy manse library' that the young Agnes 'spent long hours ... devouring rows of metaphysical Scottish divines or translating Bossuet's sermons for fun.'[12]

The primary account of Reverend Machar's life remains the book edited 'by members of his family' and published ten years after his death.[13] This account was obviously prepared for the consumption of the parish and left unsaid anything that might arouse controversy. However, chronic fatigue, delicate health, solitary travel, and worry about his sinful state were recurring threads. Reverend Machar's attention was absorbed by a busy pastorate, the fledgling and faltering Queen's College, and political controversies within the church and the colony. He deplored the schism imported from Scotland in 1844 that resulted in the formation of the

Free Church. His own parish remained 'in connexion with the Church of Scotland,' the Auld Kirk, and establishment tradition.[14]

Belief in God's providential care permeates Reverend Machar's *Memorials*. In 1848, John Machar was on his way to Scotland to attend Church Assembly and to enjoy a much needed rest. He went ashore in the port city of Halifax and was apparently misinformed regarding the time of the ship's departure, for he returned in time to see 'the vessel steaming out of the harbour.' Left alone in a strange city with no luggage, little money, and no immediate means to continue his voyage, John Machar nevertheless took a sanguine view of his predicament, later writing to his family, 'This thing was evidently in the Providence of Him who ruleth over all; for wise and gracious reasons I can have no doubt, I was not permitted to go in the Acadia [name of vessel].' On another occasion during that same eventful journey, John Machar had reason to rejoice in the providence of God, for he and fellow passengers were spared in a train wreck.[15]

All reference to domestic life was very circumspect in this text; readers were assured that Reverend Machar 'was a devotedly affectionate husband and father.'[16] His wife, Margaret Machar (1798-1883), had left the Scottish manse of her father to come to a remote colony to marry him in 1832. They married in Montreal and made their way to Kingston. Their first son David was born the following year and died a few weeks later. Agnes was born in 1837, and a son John followed in 1841.

Although she was accorded a privileged position among the elite of Kingston by virtue of her husband's vocation, it is clear that Margaret Machar, already in her mid-thirties, had to forge a new life and raise a family amid considerable stress and turmoil, with a husband who was always tired. These were unsettling times for both the church and the embryonic state: the fractious question of the clergy reserves, the political rebellions (1837), the struggle for survival of the newly founded Queen's College (1841), the 'Great Disruption' within the church (1843-4), and the ongoing threat of cholera were among the things that tried the body and vexed the spirit within the Machar household. During the 1830s and 1840s, Kingston was struck by recurring cholera epidemics that heightened anxiety about the heavy influx of immigrants and left in their wake many widows and orphans with no means of support. A person attending church on Sunday might well have died and been buried by Monday.[17] While her husband worked ceaselessly to bury the dead and comfort the bereaved, Margaret Machar directed her philanthropic concerns through the church and the Female Benevolent Society, helping those whose lives had been shattered.[18]

It is difficult to penetrate the politeness and the piety that pervade what little is known of her parents in order to discover any revealing sense of Agnes Machar's relationship with them. Certainly her father's position and active encouragement of her intellectual scholarship exposed her to a world of books and ideas, and instilled a love of learning that continued throughout her long life. Indeed, every Sunday sermon would have been a lesson in biblical and church history as well as morality. Examples of Reverend Machar's sermons, attached as appendixes to *Memorials*, reveal careful attention to scriptural exegesis and historical context. Moreover, his letters to his children show attempts to make their history lessons personal and immediate. For example, while in Scotland, he wrote of dining at the Palace of Holyrood in a room where Mary Queen of Scots once sat.[19]

It was through disciplined self study under her father's supervision that Agnes Machar formed her knowledge of the philosophy, theology, science, literature, and history that ultimately gained her admission to the circle of knowers who debated the intellectual and social issues of the day in national newspapers, journals, and books. It was an education that enabled her to match wits with intellectuals like Goldwin Smith, W.D. LeSueur, and J.A. Allen in the pages of the *Canadian Monthly*;[20] to lobby George Monro Grant, fellow Presbyterian and Principal of Queen's College, on church and university issues;[21] to become a mentor to and collaborator with T.G. Marquis in writing Canadian history; and, finally, to become a respected writer in her own right.

As an adult, Agnes Machar maintained the family tradition of making her home and her island retreat in the Thousand Islands centres of intellectual life. Her contemporary Helena Coleman confirmed this when she wrote, 'In her [Machar's] garden, at her parties, island neighbours met

Pinehurst Island, 1911. From left to right (back), Agnes Maule Machar, Ethelyn Wetherald; (front) Marjorie Pickthall, G.B. Lancaster

men and women of eminence in the world of letters overseas, artists, scientists, writers.'[22] Guests of prominence at Ferncliff included evolutionist Alfred Russell Wallace, social gospeller Lyman Abbott, author Grant Allen, politician Richard Cartwright, and biologist George Romanes.[23] Nor was her intellectual life nourished solely by men; Louisa Murray, Annie Rothwell, Helena Coleman, and A. Ethelwyn Wetherald were some of the community of women writers who sustained and enriched Machar's thinking.[24]

The gender ideal that Margaret Machar promulgated by example cannot be underestimated. A eulogy of Mrs. Machar written at the time of her death by Rev. D.J. MacDonnell, who boarded at the St. Andrew's manse as a young student at Queen's, leaves a lasting impression of the living exemplar she was. MacDonnell emphasized her unremitting work with Kingston charities and missionary organizations, work that was portrayed as the outward expression of her rich spiritual life. Her 'personal intercourse with the needy, the sick, the sorrowful, and the erring' was remembered as well as her wise counsel to family and church colleagues. In short, 'she proved herself to be both to the congregation and to the community all that "the minister's wife" is expected to be.'[25]

But what was the minister's daughter expected to be? We know that her younger brother studied at Queen's and in Europe,[26] and that Agnes did not undertake formal studies at any institution beyond a year of study at a Montreal boarding school under the direction of Miss Hannah Lyman.[27] In the 1850s, there were in fact no institutions in the Canadas where she would have been able to undertake university studies, and the ladies' colleges and seminaries that were available may not have matched the advantages of her private education.[28] However, we do not know if the lack of formal training was a matter of resentment or regret on her part. We know that Margaret Machar initially did not encourage her daughter's literary aspirations 'from a belief that a literary vocation was not likely to promote a woman's happiness, and also from a distaste of anything like notoriety.'[29] We do not know to what degree Agnes found her mother's attitude to have been an impediment.

Certainly Agnes Machar seems to have taken her mother's ideal of active service in the Lord's name to heart. The text 'to whom much is given, of him shall be much required,' was her personal credo, and one that she stamped on her fictional characters, both male and female, for the purposes of instructing her readers in their social obligations.[30] A strong consciousness that class privilege created a debt to be repaid in Christian service pervades her work. It followed that Machar was no mere commentator on social conditions; she always tried to connect thought with action. The scope and intensity of her organizational and reform work were breathtaking. As well as her mission and church work, she was a founding and very active member of the National Council of Women of Canada, the Kingston Local Council of Women, the Young Women's Christian Association, the Children's Aid Association, and the Kingston Humane Society. She served on various art and historical societies including the Women's Art Association, the Canadian Society of Authors, the Ontario Historical Society, and the Canadian Women's Historical Society.[31]

Her unwavering faith, uncompromising principles, and rigid self discipline unquestionably earned her contemporaries' respect, although some, like the younger Elizabeth Shortt, one of Queen's first female graduates in medicine, saw her as somewhat of a fossil even when Machar was still actively publishing. In a letter to her family in 1895, Shortt commented, 'Miss Machar of course is all right as a literary light & a woman who really lives up to her preaching as far as I know & although she is a most ridiculous woman in appearance & in some of her ideas she is in earnest.'[32] Helena Coleman noted Machar's strict discipline in a charming reminiscence of her daily 'dip' in the river: 'even when her years were almost as many as the ninety wobbly steps that she must descend, she would rise at six to immerse her delicate frame in the cold waters of the St. Lawrence.'[33] Whatever good or ill effects this swim had on her constitution, it exemplifies the strength of her convictions. The 'noble ideals' that Machar demanded of Canadian writers were imprinted on all her work.[34]

In her recent study of Canadian women writers of non-fiction, Anne Innis Dagg noted that biography was a genre that was attractive to women because they could become experts on subjects close at hand without necessarily having access to libraries or archives. Of the titles Dagg surveyed, Machar's 1859 memorial of John Anderson, a Queen's College janitor, is the earliest biographical work.[35] Machar would have been personally acquainted with John Anderson before his death, as her family was closely associated with Queen's.

F.L. MacCallum, an early twentieth-century reporter, referred patronizingly to Machar's first and anonymous publication as stories of Anderson's 'unexampled devotion' that 'the child' (she would have been twenty-two) pieced together with his letters.[36] Nonetheless, Machar's portrayal of Anderson's life appeared self-consciously constructed to show that 'true Christian greatness may lie in the humblest path and most commonplace routine.' Despite his 'lowliness of station,' Anderson's life exemplified for Machar true Christian piety. She concluded on a didactic note: 'May each reader of this little book find this love awakened in his heart, and having come as a repentant sinner to Him who will in no wise cast out, – go on, by prayer, by watchfulness, by constant working for Him – to *live* the *life* of "the righteous."'[37]

Machar's valorization of Anderson's fulfilment of Christian duty precluded any analysis of the harsh working conditions under which he laboured at the college. His letters to his family in Scotland, however, revealed a less-than-joyous acquiescence to his lot:

> This winter I have just wrought as hard as ever I was able, – from six in the morning till ten at night, – so many stoves and so much shovelling of snow. There is no end of it, for it is sometimes to be cleared away three times a day. It is a very confining berth too, – you must be there every hour, as you have to ring the bell every hour. I was not farther than the market this twelve month.[38]

On this aspect of Anderson's Christian service Machar had no comment, although later in her career she did take up the cause of factory workers, lobbying strenuously for legislation to protect them against abuse.[39]

Machar's second major writing endeavour was also biographical, and also on a subject close at hand. This was the volume on her father's life and ministry, mentioned previously, that Agnes undoubtedly had the greatest hand in. As with Anderson, this work was based on letters and recollections, although the range and scope of her father's correspondence were considerably wider than Anderson's. Machar was primarily concerned with portraying her father as a model of Christian piety, fulfilling God's eternal purpose as it was revealed to him; or, as it was put in the preface, 'to present a true, unvarnished history of his faithful and incessantly laborious life among his people.'[40] Nevertheless, *Memorials* supplies some fascinating personal glimpses into the social, political, and institutional changes wrought in early Anglo-Ontario, including the founding of Queen's and the growth of Kingston's charitable societies.

In the 1870s, Machar came into her own as a writer, publishing four novels, her father's biography, at least twenty-four essays, and twenty poems in this decade alone. Her writing was abetted by the national literary fervour inspired by Confederation and the creation of the *Canadian Monthly and National Review*, a journal initiated and sustained by Graeme Mercer Adam and Goldwin Smith. While maintaining a non-partisan editorial policy, this magazine for all intents and purposes represented the views of the Canada First movement founded in 1868 and was devoted to developing a sense of national consciousness and patriotism. From 1871 to 1882, the *Canadian Monthly* and its successor *Rose Belford's Canadian Monthly and National Review* served as a forum where English-speaking Canadians elaborated their vision of the new country. Machar was a regular and respected contributor to the journal, most often writing under her pen-name Fidelis.[41]

The War of 1812 still kindled imaginations some sixty years after the fact and was a popular topic of historical romance, the favoured genre of English-Canadian writers. Machar's third novel, *For King and Country: A*

Story of 1812, first published in serial form in 1874 in the *Canadian Monthly* and later brought out as a book, was centred on the events of this war. Carole Gerson has pointed out that the war 'was always interpreted as the vindication of monarchism and British values,' and Machar's effort, as the title suggests, was no exception in this regard.[42] However, Machar's central character, Ernest Heathcote, embodied the pain of divided loyalties in this 'terrible unnatural evil,' as he was American by birth, the orphaned son of a Quaker mother and a Republican soldier killed in the Revolution.[43] After his parents died, Heathcote was raised in Canada by an aunt and uncle who were United Empire Loyalists. With the declaration of war, aspersions were cast on his character, and he was suspected of being disloyal to the British Crown. His young love Lilias was forbidden to see him by her father, a major, but Heathcote redeemed himself by exemplary service and by preventing the elopement of his cousin (and Lilias's friend) with a low-life soldier. In the end, Heathcote's rival for Lilias's affections, the very English Captain Percival, was conveniently killed in battle, leaving Ernest and Lilias ruminating on the war, united in an 'open and acknowledged bond.'[44]

Ruth Compton Brouwer cites this as an example of Machar's promotion of Canadian nationalism and amity towards the United States.[45] But it is also a story of men fighting and dying for the imperial cause, and discussing it after dinner over tobacco while 'Lilias, with a bit of delicate muslin embroidery in her hand took a low seat at a little distance from the gentlemen, listening to their talk.'[46] While Machar's concept of patriotism was relatively inclusive of competing and even conflicting interests, it was also very gendered. Men were expected to risk their lives for their country; women, if visible at all, watched from the sidelines. The notable exception to women's retirement from war matters was Laura Secord. Her legendary and timely warning to the British soldiers was celebrated by Machar in a later poem proclaiming that 'British gallantry and skill' might well have failed had it not been for her 'dauntless heart.'[47]

Apart from the memorials of her father, Machar's non-fiction work in the 1870s appeared as essays in the *Canadian Monthly*. One of these sketched the events of the War of 1812.[48] Other essays revealed her nascent social Christianity as she began to reconcile the 'eternal truths' of her religion with empiricism and to compare them, to the advantage of Christianity, with Buddhism.[49] It was during this time that she also took up social issues, arguing forcefully for the restriction of the liquor trade and advocating higher education for women.[50] The latter pieces in particular formed the basis of her reputation as a moderate feminist and are of interest here for their use of history.

In 1878, just as Queen's College was grudgingly opening to women, Machar published her second article on the higher education of women and women's work.[51] In this article she moved beyond the debates about the dangers to women of an education identical to that of men to consider women's work in its broadest context, both productive and reproductive. She argued that men's work in the public sphere and women's work in the domestic sphere were interdependent; that to separate them would be like separating 'the sap which courses through the budding trees from the tissue that holds and is fed by it.' However, over the course of time, women's traditional work had been devalued. In a manner that anticipates modern-day feminist historians, Machar hypothesized that in early patriarchal societies 'the strong and superstitious desire for male children gradually lowered the idea of the wife and mother to that of a mere link in the generations, and encroaching polygamy lowered it still further.'[52] She described a growing gulf between 'man's word and woman's work' as societies became increasingly complex; yet she was concerned to show that women had always had a formative influence on society and that exceptional women had always risen above patriarchal constraints: 'scattered all along the dim centuries we call the Dark Ages, we find exceptional cases, as distinct as those of Sappho and Aspasia, to show that genius knows no bounds of sex, and that the gulf conventionally interposed [between men and women] did not exist in the nature of things.'[53]

Machar's acquaintance with India, no doubt fostered through her wide reading and active work in her church's Juvenile Mission to India,[54] was revealed in her allusions to female heroines of Hindu literature. She also made reference to several learned ladies of medieval Europe: Queen Edgitha, Betisia Gozzadini (Doctor of Laws), and Lady Jane Grey to name a few. Furthermore, an 1880 trip to Heidelberg inspired Machar to write a biographical portrait of Olympia Morata. Machar described her as a learned lady of the Renaissance, so esteemed that she had been invited to lecture at the University in Ferrara: 'The life of Olympia Morata is worth a dozen treatises on the "higher education" of woman,' Machar concluded.[55]

A significant proportion of the 1878 article was taken up in discussion of the suitability of the medical profession for women. Machar reminded her readers that the prejudice against women practising medicine was a relatively recent phenomenon, and that, in fact, women had a long history of practising the healing arts. She sketched this history from ancient Greece, with reference to Olympias Thebes, Aspasia, and Oenone, to eighteenth-century women such as Anna Moranda Maggiolini and Maria Petraccini: 'Why this sacred office, belonging to her of old, should have been considered by intelligent men and even by intelligent women, as unbecoming her womanhood, while the kindred office of *nurse* is universally admitted to be eminently befitting it – seems inexplicable ... In this case however, it is the prejudice which is the real *innovation.*' Machar devoted considerable attention to promoting the restoration of medical practice to women on the grounds that it was 'work for which woman is peculiarly fitted and peculiarly needed.' Integral to this 'peculiar need' was a preference for women physicians to attend women 'in what are called civilized countries,' and the demand for female medical missionaries in countries where men were not permitted to attend women. Machar concluded the article with a message that she repeated in several others: that both men and women 'should be left entirely free to choose that life work to which they are led by the natural gifts with which God has endowed them, combined with that providential guidance which all who seek it shall surely find.'[56]

With her allusions to a historical heritage of learned women and women's need for freedom to choose their own paths, Machar was still careful to assuage the age-old concern that a methodical education might unsex a woman and make her less likely to marry and have children. In all her writing on this subject, Machar maintained that marriage and child-rearing were woman's happiest destiny and that the responsibility of moulding character entrusted to women as wives and mothers was in fact the best argument for a rigorous, liberal education to prepare them for this 'noble' task. Machar magnified the benefits that a superior education for women would accrue to the nation in terms of decreased infant deaths, the assiduous preparation of future citizens and statesmen, and the regeneration of the Christian faith. As wives and mothers, women were seen to have a peculiar role to play in saving the nation through their promotion of the faith and their work of forming Christian character.[57] At the same time, she argued that women should 'develop as God would have them to do.' Any contradiction that this posed was slipped over by the assumption that 'what is truly best for the *individual* is truly the best for the race.'[58]

What is of interest here is that history became almost a heuristic device to illustrate the unity of providentialism, progress, and a particular construction of national character – one that assumed a Eurocentric basis, Christian values, and differentiation by gender. But also significant was Machar's effort to make women visible in history, to make their long-standing contributions to culture more widely known. In this Machar participated in a process that is ongoing, for it seems that every generation of women scholars must rediscover its legacy. Women's historical achievements and contributions have yet to be made part of the canon that is passed on to succeeding generations.

With the demise of *Rose Belford's Canadian Monthly* in 1882, the main forum for Machar's writing became *The Week*, a weekly literary magazine published in Toronto under the forceful guidance of Goldwin Smith. It would seem that Machar was not overly impressed with this new literary venture: she complained to Louisa Murray about Smith's editorial control, which allowed only 'the appearance of papers which ... echo his own opinions or else have no opinions at all.'[59] It is difficult to imagine that she would have counted her own among the latter, but her published work in *The Week* did veer towards laudatory poetry more than political commentary, literary criticism more than social critique, especially in the 1880s.

The format of *The Week* did not allow for the long expository essays or lengthy debates between authors that had been the style of the *Canadian Monthly* and *Rose Belford's Canadian Monthly*. Machar's brief essays on social issues covered pretty much the same ground as her earlier articles, although in the 1890s she did comment extensively on current debates such as reciprocal trade with the United States and protective labour legislation for women.[60] However, generally speaking, *The Week* was not the forum where Machar expounded her historical interests. The most notable exceptions were a five-part series entitled 'Roamings in Classical Massachusetts' and a two-part 'Ramblings on the Sources of Canadian History.'[61]

These pieces were written reflections on various trips taken to the United States and the Maritime provinces. In the former, Machar focused on what united rather than what divided America and Canada: 'two civilized nations, lying side by side, whose origin, interests, and general characteristics are identical.'[62] The pieces read like a modern-day Michelin guide. The tour focused on mainly literary sites – a visit to the poet John Greenleaf Whittier, whom Machar greatly admired, and Nathaniel Hawthorne's former home at Concord, among others – but Machar also self-consciously used the occasion to review the sites of the American Revolution, 'the spots where were fired the first shots of the combat that lost to England a colony and gave to the world a new Anglo-Saxon nation.' Here she somewhat patronizingly reminded her Canadian readers of significant events in early American history while smoothing over any remnant of ill feeling in Canadian-American relations:

> Much as we may regret the unhappy breach, and the strife and bitter feeling which it awoke, – much as we may sympathize with the unquenchable loyalty of those whose unswerving devotion to the 'Old Flag' was the foundation of British Canada, – still if fair-minded, we cannot help admitting that the spirit which conquered old England then was the very spirit that her traditions had nourished in New England.[63]

In her enthusiasm to show that Canadians and Americans were 'brothers in tongue, tradition and literature,'[64] Machar momentarily overlooked

Canada's French heritage and the other distinct cultures, particularly aboriginal cultures, that constituted its polity. However, Machar typically was sensitive to at least the French component of Canada's plural society.

French-English relations in the post-Confederation period were rocky to say the least. The Métis uprising of the 1870s, the rebellion of 1885, and the Jesuits' Estates Act of the late 1880s provided opportunities for English Canada to assert its dominance and/or to vent hostility against French Canada and Roman Catholicism. While Machar wrote little about the Northwest, she did, as Brouwer has shown, consistently call upon her fellow English Canadians to show tolerance, respect, and a conciliatory attitude towards French Canada.[65] Her views may have been influenced by her brother's first-hand experience as commissioner sent to settle Métis claims after the first rebellion.[66] Still, her congenial stance would have placed her in direct opposition to her close friend, Rev. D.J. MacDonnell, who actively supported the Equal Rights Association, a Toronto-based group that mobilized public opposition to the Jesuits' Estates Act.[67] Machar promoted harmonious relations primarily by romanticizing early French exploration, settlement, and missionary work. Her approach was biographical; her audience young people.

From her earliest published and prize-winning novels written for Sunday school to the end of her career, Machar directed much of her writing towards the edification of a juvenile audience.[68] In the 1890s, her subjects for these pieces were the French pioneers. Her first efforts in this regard were undertaken in collaboration with T.G. Marquis, to whom, she confessed to the reporter MacCullum in 1924, 'she left "the battles and other horrible things."'[69] (Little is known of her relationship with Marquis. The fact that she left her island retreat to him and another colleague, Lawson Chambers, upon her death would seem to indicate a close and enduring friendship.[70] Marquis was instrumental in bringing out a posthumous booklet of her poems exalting her beloved Thousand Islands, the place he referred to as her 'poetic domain.')[71]

Machar's *Stories of New France* appeared soon after the tense relations between the English and French in Canada had been exacerbated by the Jesuits' Estates Act issue. Styled by Brouwer as an exercise in 'literary crisis management,' the book romanticized early French explorers and colonists, as did her later contributions to Marquis's *Builders of Canada*.[72] Anglo-Saxon ascendancy was nevertheless a foregone conclusion. The conquest of the French colony by the British was foreshadowed in her stories of Cartier's moral lapse in taking, by force, the Indian chief Donnacona and some of his men back to France. While honouring Cartier as the 'discoverer of Canada [*sic*],' Machar went on to say: 'Both name and fame would have been brighter but for the cruel act of treachery to his Indian friends, which so seriously interfered with the success of the attempted colony, and which was wiped out in after years ... So true is it that "The evil that men do lives after them."'[73]

Despite Machar's knowledge and interest in the activities of women in history, female settlers were most conspicuous by their absence in these largely biographical narratives. The single chapter about a woman was a sentimental account of Marguerite de Roberval's heroic efforts to survive a long and arduous exile to the Isle of Demons with her ill-fated lover. A 'female Robinson Crusoe,' Marguerite survived to bury her lover, child, and 'an old nurse,' and, 'utterly alone,' continued to hunt and skin animals for food and clothing, hoping for the rescue that eventually came. Once delivered from her prison isle, this Amazon-like woman retreated into the background, and the narrative returned to the unsuccessful expeditions of her cruel uncle.[74] While this rendering of Marguerite's life may have evoked some sense of admiration in its readers, it would have hardly persuaded young girls and boys that their foremothers contributed significantly to the so-called 'founding' of the nation. The important contribution by religious women to the development of the colony of Montreal was outlined in another chapter, but again, the ultimate fate and welfare of the colony was attributed to the actions of men, especially to their self-sacrifice and spilt blood in warfare.[75] For, despite her disclaimer that she left the battles to Marquis, it was military activities that most engaged Machar in her historical writing, something that profoundly distinguishes her work from that of her younger contemporary, Isabel Skelton, whose book *The Backwoodswoman* is discussed by Terry Crowley in this collection. Given her earnest interest in women's past achievements, Machar's very brief attention to women's historical contributions to the making of the nation is somewhat surprising. Perhaps to Machar's mind, Canada had yet to produce the 'women worthies' who warranted historical treatment.[76]

Three years later, Copp Clark brought out *Stories from Canadian History*, based on *Stories of New France;* ten years later, Machar contributed chapters on Jacques Cartier, Samuel de Champlain, and Robert de la Salle to a volume edited by Marquis entitled *Builders of Canada from Cartier to Laurier*. These covered much the same ground as her earlier work and reveal her indebtedness to the American historian, Francis Parkman, whose fascination with the struggle between France and England for dominance in North America generated a seven-part series.[77]

Machar's novel *Marjorie's Canadian Winter*, published in 1892 and brought out again in 1906, also gave voice to her particular brand of historical determinism, Christian triumphalism, and Canadian nationalism.[78] History lessons were taught in a fictional format. The plot centred on Marjorie, a young American girl, who spent a winter with relatives in Montreal while her father recovered his health. Here she was regaled with stories of the early Jesuits' attempts to convert 'the Indians,' recounted by the indomitable Professor Duncan, a friend of the family. Professor Duncan was the vehicle for the retelling of Parkman's popular tales of the seventeenth-century Isaac Jogues and other French 'heroes.' These stories of martyred Jesuits and doomed colonists seem to have served a number of explicit purposes: they recognized and affirmed the early evangelizing zeal of French Catholics that Protestants had only recently carried into effect; they demonstrated that the United States and Canada had a shared history and therefore much in common and, moreover, that Canada owed a debt to the American Parkman for recording that history; and they served as a backdrop and were made analogous to a contemporary story of 'heroism,' the fall of General Gordon in Khartoum.[79]

However, the stories also implicitly expressed the common view that the demise or assimilation of native peoples was inevitable and desirable, while reinforcing the crudest stereotypes of native peoples as heathen savages and barbarians. The commemoration of the work of missionaries was tied to the vilification of native peoples whose 'conversion,' both on a personal and cultural level, was the object of missionary work. One passage from the novel will serve as an example. Professor Duncan used the occasion of a moonlight trek in search of a Christmas tree to hold forth on the French pioneers. Alan, one of Marjorie's cousins, responded to Duncan's lengthy oration on the cruelty suffered by colonists and missionaries at the hands of the Iroquois:

> 'Well, it beats me,' said Alan, 'to understand how those people [Jesuits] could give up everything, and go on suffering all they did, for such a set of stupid miserable savages as those Indians were.'
>
> 'Ah my boy!' the professor replied, 'that's one of the lessons we can learn from only one Master! We can't understand it until we get some of the spirit of him who came to "seek and save the lost."'

Professor Duncan went on to list heroic Christians from St. Paul to General Gordon whose mission was to 'follow Him who thought none too low to care for.'[80] At that very moment he interrupted his lecture to point out the scintillating northern lights whose symbolic associations with Christianity had already been drawn for readers by Marjorie's father, who had retold the legend of Aurora Borealis.[81] The recurring metaphor of light and the special brilliance of northern lights – made more so by the depth of the darkness surrounding them – were perhaps intended to convey the uniquely enlightening influence and generally salubrious effects of Christianity. Heroes were lights shining in the darkness. But the achievement of this effect depended on constructing Native American Indians as part of 'the darkness,' and thus robbing them of humanity and dignity.

The dominant belief in the inevitable colonization of native peoples was also expressed in Machar's poetry. 'The New World,' published in her single major volume of poetry *Lays of the True North*, was initially empathetic:

One hemisphere lay hid in misty night;
  God said, 'Let there be light!'
And straight a bark from Palos steered its way
O'er trackless ocean towards the setting day –
...
The red men, standing by in feathered pride,
  Gazed wondering – open-eyed –
To see upon their strand remote and lone
These pale-faced strangers from a world unknown.
Little *they* dreamed, who paddled close to shore,
  Afraid to fare forth on the trackless sea –
Little they dreamed of what those white wings bore
  For them, what omens dark of misery;
Little they knew of what the coming years
Must bring to them of strife and blood and tears –
  The ancient empire of their fathers spurned;
Fled the wild subjects of their bows and spears;
  Their hunting-grounds to yellow cornfields turned;
  Their lodges levelled and their forests burned!

Yet Machar's apparent sympathy towards the indigenous peoples of the so-called 'new world' soon gave way to the repetition of the notion of the historic and moral inevitability of their demise or assimilation:

So must the tide of human progress go
Past every barrier, till it overflow
  All wastes where the dull savage lived and died
Amid the common round of instincts low –
The chase, the strife, the skill of spear and bow –
  Till quickened life o'erspread those regions wide
  With higher impulse in its swelling tide,
And nobler men to nobler stature grow
  In a new world which God hath purified![82]

Her 'Ramblings about the Sources of Canadian History' was a historic pilgrimage that began 'where the hardy Norman pioneers made their first historic foothold on the edge of the great unbroken wilderness [*sic*] of North America.'[83] Like the former series on Massachusetts and two of her novels written in the 1890s, these ramblings followed a travelogue format thick with descriptions of picturesque villages, wooded isles, and multi-hued sunsets that, as Patricia Jasen points out, were increasingly in vogue as the tourist trade developed.[84] Interwoven with the scenery was historical information, some apparently drawn from the writings of Marc Lescarbot, who accompanied de Monts to Acadia in 1604. As well as tracing the routes of early French explorers such as Champlain, de Monts, and Poutrincourt, Machar chided Canadians for their ignorance of their history, urging readers to learn the historical associations of their own communities and those they visited:

> The apathy shown by the great mass of Canadians toward the sacred places of their own history is both an indication and a cause of the low tide of patriotic feeling among us as a people ... Let us hope that a better and more enlightened era is approaching, when every Canadian who visits Annapolis will have the eventful story of such a place as Port Royal stored up in his heart, to add its thrilling interest to the natural charm of the scene.[85]

Two novels written in the 1890s assumed the style of travelogues. In *Down the River to the Sea* (1894) and *Heir of Fairmount Grange* (1895), Machar celebrated the St. Lawrence waterway extending from the Niagara to the Saguenay as imbued with historical, spiritual, and political significance.[86] A voyage by boat down the St. Lawrence in the first novel (and upriver in the second) provided the vehicle for Machar, following a popular convention among writers of the time, to insert 'chunks of historical or geographical information' into her fiction.[87] At the same time, geography and history were correlated to promote nationalistic feeling as the 'sights' and artefacts visited along the way enshrined, in Jasen's words, 'myths of historical significance.'[88] The introduction of American characters, inevitably ignorant of Canadian history, served as a convenient device for Machar to expound on her two special historical interests: the War of 1812 and early French settlement. The trips on the river provided the scenes of historical denouement.

Her next major historical project also closely correlated geography with history. In a period that has been called the 'golden age of local history in Canada,'[89] Machar made her contribution to this category in 1908 with a detailed study of her home city. She dedicated the work to the 'Memory of the Good Men and True Who Built Up Old Kingston, and to all citizens of today who follow their traditions and example.'[90] Here, Machar built upon her historical sketch of Kingston, published in the *Canadian Monthly* in the early 1870s, in which she paid tribute to its European beginnings as a French fur-trading post and, later, as a Loyalist town.[91] In her larger work, Machar expanded her narrative of the

War of 1812, the rebellions of 1837, Kingston's brief service as the capital of the Canadas, and the development of its educational, church, and charitable institutions – institutions with which her own family had been intimately connected. Machar also drew on the records of the Ontario Historical Society, founded in 1888, to which she belonged.

She acknowledged her debt to several historians including Margry, Mahan, Parkman, McMullen, Dent, and Canniff. As in all her work, this history revealed Machar's ability to synthesize a number of authors and integrate them with her own views. Her interest in Kingston's past was limited to its European past; her vision for its future had European associations as well: 'May we not predict for our old Canadian town the enviable destiny of becoming, perchance, in the future, a Canadian Weimar, the home of philosophers and sages, where the Arts and Muses may find a congenial abode?'[92]

With the demise of *The Week* in 1896, Machar's periodical publishing had declined as well. She published a couple of pieces in *Canadian Magazine,* but her attention to writing was now primarily devoted to projects of a larger scale. Perhaps it was only at this relatively late stage in her career that, as an established writer, she had the time, connections, and financial security to tackle large pieces. *Lays,* a collection of her poetry, was brought out in 1899, and an enlarged edition in 1902; her history of Kingston was published in 1908; and her last major historical work, *Stories of the British Empire,* came out in two series in 1913 when Machar was well into her seventies. Here again, her work was directed towards young people, or 'young folks and busy folks' as the full title indicated. Her approach was biographical, a fact that commended it to the Dean of Manchester, Right Rev. J.E.C. Welldon, who wrote the preface. Machar reminded her young readers that this was not '*a complete history,*' and gave instructions on how they should read it – one chapter a week, with the intervening time spent in reflection on the persons and events described and in supplemental reading. Interwoven in many of the stories were lines from the poems of Tennyson, Cowper, and several minor poets so that literary lessons were fused with historical ones.

The first series consisted of thirty chapters focused on early England, beginning with a description of cavemen drawn from the work of Grant Allen, a writer well known to the Machar family,[93] and ending with the death at the scaffold of 'beautiful and ill-fated' Mary Queen of Scots.[94] The second series began with 'Good Queen Bess' and focused on the expansion of the Empire and military exploits ending with the Boer War of 1899-1902. In the chapter on the conquest of Canada, Machar again stressed the unity of English Canada and the New England states, where the news of Wolfe's victory was greeted with joy, prompting one young minister to predict that 'British America would grow into a mighty empire – to which he added that he did not mean an independent one.'[95] The imperial tenor of all the stories was best described in the Foreword: 'no one, surely, with any adequate belief in the Divine Ruler of the Universe, can study the wonderful Story of our British Empire without being impressed with a sense of its Divine purpose, its final mission to humanity, as the end for which the shoot of Saxon freedom, planted in British soil, has grown into the greatest Empire this world has ever seen.'[96]

Machar's storytelling voice was intimate and pastoral, evocative of a genteel grandmother, a horsehair sofa, and an interminable Sunday tea. Pictures of military exploits were vividly drawn and a moralizing tone was never far away. Whether children were captivated by these richly detailed stories or found them as boring as a dry sermon in church is impossible to ascertain. However, the fact that a second edition was brought out the following year would seem to indicate that sales were brisk.

While certain elements in the style of writing popular history changed in the early decades of the twentieth century, basic premises remained the same, if comparison with Stephen Leacock's 1940 *The British Empire* is any measure. Machar began her *Stories of the British Empire* with a sensual and biblical river trope: 'the story of our great British Empire may be compared to the course of a mighty river, taking its rise from springs hid among the misty hills, and fed by stream after stream, as it winds on its way, till it swells at length into a great and bountiful tide, spreading its waters throughout the world, and bringing larger life and fruitfulness to many a barren soil.'[97] Leacock's opening prose is less purple but conveyed the same message:

> The rise and development of the British Empire is one of the great features of the world's history. Its vast extent, its accumulated wealth and latent resources, its close association in language and culture with the United States of America render it a chief factor in the situation of mankind today. In it and in its external associations lie the chief hopes for mankind tomorrow. As seen by many of us, it offers ... a basis for an orderly and stable world of justice, peace and plenty.[98]

While Leacock's history is focused more on the places of British colonization than on the people who carried it out, many of his premises – the historical inevitability and rightness of British domination, the sense of Canadian fraternity with the United States, and the romanticization and/or dismissal of colonized peoples – were the same as Machar's. This had nothing to do with direct borrowing (Leacock does not cite Machar), but with an intellectual hegemony that took many years to change.

So what, if anything, did Agnes Machar contribute to the writing of history in Canada? If her work is assessed solely on the grounds of breaking new intellectual terrain or even of offering a conventional history of a new area, then there is reason for disappointment. However, if her work is assessed from within the context of a single woman successfully forging a literary career in mid-nineteenth-century Canada and extending it into the twentieth, then there is much of interest. The first question of immediate interest is how it was that she was able to write history at all.

Natalie Zemon Davis suggests three things are needed for a learned woman to write history: physical access to materials about her subject, 'access to the genres of historical writing, to the rules for expressing historical material,' and a 'sense of connection ... with the areas of public life considered suitable for historical writing.'[99] Davis assumes that the woman writing history is a learned woman, but becoming a learned woman in mid-nineteenth-century Canada was no mean feat. Although she was born too soon to have the advantages of university studies, Machar was privileged to have a superior private education that included wide reading in history, and close proximity to and stimulating exchange with the province's leading intellectuals. Little is known of her particular financial circumstances, yet she was a woman of considerable property who travelled fairly widely in the United States and Europe, visiting monuments and sites of historical interest. At the same time, the subjects she wrote most fully about were relatively close at hand: family, acquaintances, her community, and later the nation – in a sense what Davis calls, borrowing a phrase from Margaret Lucas, 'particular histories' with perhaps a marginally 'widening circumference of truth.'[100]

Her education did give her access to the genres of historical writing: Sir Walter Scott the model for historical romance; Francis Parkman her most acknowledged mentor for popular history. Indeed, Machar was not alone in her admiration of Scott and Parkman. Carole Gerson argues that English-Canadian fiction developed in the 'long shadow' of Scott, so widely were his romances idealized and imitated.[101] Kenneth Windsor details the pervasive influence on Canadian historical writing of Parkman, whose popularity and credibility extended into the twentieth century despite his extreme ethnocentricity.[102]

If it is indeed 'the historian's business ... "to digest voluminous collections,"' then Machar lacked nothing.[103] Her work on both contemporary and historical topics synthesized an enormously wide range of reading and made it accessible to her intended audience. What, in fact, is most intriguing about Machar's work is how closely it conformed to convention not only in form, but also in substance – history (read: British empire-building), like a predictable plot in one of her novels, was unfolding as it should. Her legacy of historical writing is interesting exactly because it typified the styles, conventions, and thought of the times.

The third need of a historian is, according to Davis, a sense of connection to areas of public life that were deemed worthy of historical inquiry.[104] In a newly federated nation, what could be more worthy of historical inquiry (or conducive to patriotism) than the elaboration of a shared past: '"The one thing I have tried to do ... is to cultivate a spirit of Canadianism and a deeper love of Canada in the hearts of her own people,"' Machar once told a journalist.[105] She was connected to the making of the nation in a number of ways: her family was closely associated with the politicians who brought it into being and who ran it; she was actively involved in cultural institutions and reform organizations with distinctively nationalistic and patriotic agendas; and she was one of, and closely acquainted with, the writers who were defining what the new nation was and, implicitly, what it was not. History, then, became one means (and only one) of articulating her vision and love of Canada.

Acknowledgments
I acknowledge the partial financial support of a Social Sciences and Humanities Doctoral Scholarship in the early stages of this research. I thank Alison Prentice for her ongoing encouragement of my work on Machar, and Thomas E. Ritchie for his invaluable assistance and for providing such an attractive space in which to write.

Notes

1 In Charles G.D. Roberts and A.L. Tunnell, eds., *A Standard Dictionary of Canadian Biography: The Canadian Who Was Who*, vol. 1 (Toronto: Trans-Canada Press 1934), 314-15.

2 R.W. Cumberland, 'Agnes Maule Machar,' *Queen's Quarterly* 34 (January 1927): 331, 333; see also by the same author, 'Agnes Maule Machar,' *Willison's Monthly* 3 (June 1927): 34-7; 'Remembering Agnes Maule Machar,' *Historic Kingston* 21 (April 1973): 22-7.

3 See, for example, Mary Vipond, 'Blessed Are the Peacemakers: The Labour Question in Canadian Social Gospel Fiction,' *Journal of Canadian Studies* 10, 3 (1975): 32-43; Nancy Miller Chenier, 'Agnes Maule Machar: Her Life, Her Social Concerns, and a Preliminary Bibliography of Her Work' (M.A. thesis, Carleton University 1977); Carole Gerson, 'Three Writers of Victorian Canada,' in Robert Lecker, Jack David, and Ellen Quigsley, eds., *Canadian Writers and Their Works* (Downsview, ON: ECW Press 1983).

4 For discussion of her religious thought, see Ramsay Cook, *The Regenerators: Social Criticism in Late Victorian English Canada* (Toronto: University of Toronto 1985), 186-92; Ruth Compton Brouwer, 'The "Between-Age" Christianity of Agnes Machar,' *Canadian Historical Review* 65, 3 (1984): 347-70; Dianne M. Hallman, 'Religion and Gender in the Writing and Work of Agnes Maule Machar' (Ph.D. diss., University of Toronto 1994). For her advocacy of protective labour legislation, see Constance Backhouse, *Petticoats and Prejudice: Women and Law in Nineteenth-Century Canada* (Toronto: Osgoode Society/Women's Press 1991), 276-88. For her literary work, see Vipond, 'Blessed are the Peacemakers'; Gerson, 'Three Writers'; Ruth Compton Brouwer, 'Moral Nationalism in Victorian Canada: The Case of Agnes Machar,' *Journal of Canadian Studies* 20, 1 (1985): 90-109.

5 *Stories of New France, Being Tales of Adventure and Heroism From the Early History of Canada* was published in two series: first series by A.M. Machar, the second by T.G. Marquis (Boston: D. Lothrop 1890); T.G. Marquis, ed. *Stories from Canadian History* (Toronto: Copp Clark 1893); *Stories of the British Empire for Young Folks and Busy Folks* (Toronto: Briggs 1913; 2nd ed. 1914). *Stories from Canadian History* was based on *Stories of New France*. I have determined that Machar did not write the biography *Mere Marie-Rose,*

Foundatrice de la Congregation des S.S. Noms de Jesus et de Marie au Canada, although it has been attributed to her. It was written by Rev. Jules-Henri Pretot, Oblate of Mary Immaculate.

6 For an explication of Laurentianism and its enduring influence, see Michael Cross, 'Canadian History,' in Carl Klinck, ed., *Literary History of Canada,* 2nd ed., vol. 3 (Toronto: University of Toronto Press 1976), 63-83.

7 Brouwer, 'Moral Nationalism,' 91.

8 A.B. McKillop, *A Disciplined Intelligence: Critical Inquiry and Canadian Thought in the Victorian Era* (Montreal and Kingston: McGill-Queen's University Press 1979), 137.

9 Fidelis, 'Prayer and Modern Doubt,' *Canadian Monthly and National Review* 8 (September 1875): 230.

10 Biographical file, 'Rev. Dr. John Machar' in United Church Archives (hereafter UCA), Toronto, ON. For Rev. John Machar's work at Queen's, see Hilda Neatby, in Frederick W. Gibson and Roger Graham, eds., *Queen's University, Vol. 1, 1841-1917* (Montreal and Kingston: McGill-Queen's University Press 1978), esp. chapters 1-3 and chapter 5.

11 Donald Creighton, *John A. MacDonald: The Young Politician* (Toronto: Macmillan 1952), 39, 83-4. See also Cumberland, 'Agnes Maule Machar,' *Willison's Monthly* 34. For a brief biographical sketch of Oliver Mowat, see A. Margaret Evans, 'Oliver Mowat: Christian Statesman of Ontario,' in W. Stanford Reid, ed., *Called to Witness: Profiles of Canadian Presbyterians,* vol. 2 (Committee on History: Presbyterian Church in Canada 1980), 47-55. Oliver Mowat's father was an elder at St. Andrew's Presbyterian Church in Kingston; his brother John Mowat taught at Queen's from 1857-1900.

12 F.L. MacCallum, 'Agnes Maule Machar,' *Canadian Magazine of Politics, Science, Art, and Literature* 62 (November-April 1924): 354.

13 *Memorials of the Rev. John Machar, D.D., Late Minister of St. Andrew's Church, Kingston,* ed. by members of his family (Toronto: James Campbell & Son 1873).

14 One of the clearest explications of the Disruption and of distinctions between Kirk and Free is found in Richard W. Vaudry, *The Free Church in Victorian Canada, 1844-1861* (Waterloo: Wilfred Laurier University 1989), esp. chapters 1 and 2. See also John Webster Grant, *A Profusion of Spires: Religion in Nineteenth-Century Ontario* (Toronto: University of Toronto Press 1988), 123-7; John S. Moir, *Enduring Witness: A History of the Presbyterian Church in Canada* (Bryant Press, ca. 1975), chapter 6. In brief, there were three main Presbyterian bodies in Upper Canada at the beginning of the nineteenth century. Two of these united in 1840 to form the Synod of the Presbyterian Church in Canada in connection with the Church of Scotland. This body split into Kirk and Free in 1844. In 1875, the Kirk and Free Churches of Canada and the Maritimes united. For a discussion of how the Disruption affected Queen's, see Neatby, *Queen's University,* 45-50.

15 *Memorials,* 97-8.

16 Ibid., 115.

17 Ibid., 56. On disease and the poor, see Patricia E. Malcomson, 'The Poor in Kingston, 1815-1850,' in Gerald Tulchinsky, ed., *To Preserve and Defend: Essays on Kingston in the Nineteenth Century* (Montreal and Kingston: McGill-Queen's University Press 1976), 281-97.

18 See Agnes Maule Machar, *The Story of Old Kingston* (Toronto: Musson Book 1908), 229-30 and 255-62. As well, see Katherine M.J. McKenna, '"The Union Between Faith and Good Works": The Life of Harriet Dobbs Cartwright, 1808-1887,' in Elizabeth Muir and Marilyn Färdig Whiteley, eds., *Changing Roles of Women within the Christian Church in Canada* (Toronto: University of Toronto Press 1995). While little information in McKenna's essay bears directly on Margaret Machar, it details the life of an Anglican clergyman's wife in Kingston with whom she was well acquainted. Dobbs Cartwright, the wife of Rev. Robert Cartwright, shared Margaret Machar's social concerns and charitable work. Despite their different positions on the question of the clergy reserves, the Reverends Cartwright and Machar were close friends (see *Memorials,* 63-4). Malcomson, 'The Poor in Kingston,' 291-5, outlines some of the work of the Female Benevolent Society and its successors.

19 *Memorials,* 99.

20 For these articles, see Marilyn Flitton, *An Index to the Canadian Monthly and National*

Review and to Rose Belford's Canadian Monthly and National Review 1872-1882 (Toronto: Bibliography Society of Canada/University of Toronto 1976).

21 See William Lawson Grant and Frederick Hamilton, *Principal Grant* (Toronto: Morang 1904), 151-64; Agnes Machar to George Monro Grant, 13 July 1888, microfilm C-1872, 2290-2304, George Monro Grant Papers, National Archives of Canada, Ottawa.

22 Helena Coleman, 'Chipmunk Hollow,' 3, undated typescript, box 1, file 11, Helena Coleman Papers (hereafter HCP), Victoria University Library Special Collections, Toronto. I am grateful to Johanna Selles-Roney for making me aware of this collection. See also A. Ethelwyn Wetherald, 'Some Canadian Literary Women – II – Fidelis,' *The Week* 5 (5 April 1888): 300-1.

23 Cumberland, 'Agnes Maule Machar,' *Willison's Monthly* 36, and 'Remembering,' *Historic Kingston* 23. Grant Allen's sister was married to Agnes Machar's brother.

24 For a glimpse into the informal networks among women writers, see the article from an unnamed magazine in the 'Elsie Pomeroy Material,' box 6, file 148, HCP; see also the correspondence between Louisa Murray and Agnes Machar in file 15, and between Louisa Murray and Susie Harrison (*Seranus*) in file 10 of the Louisa Murray Papers (hereafter LMP), York University Archives, North York, ON.

25 D.J. MacDonnell, 'In Memoriam: Mrs. Machar,' *Canada Presbyterian* 11, 46 (November 1883): 732, clipping in the biographical file 'Rev. Dr. John Machar,' UCA. Agnes Machar wrote a poem for MacDonnell upon his death entitled 'Tenos: Thou Good One, – A Tender Farewell!' *The Week* 13 (8 May 1896): 571.

26 Fidelis, 'Queen's University and What It Has Done for Canada in the Past,' *Canada Educational Monthly* 11 (March 1889): 95.

27 Wetherald, 'Fidelis,' 300-1. Hannah Lyman became first Lady Principal of Vassar College. On her strict regimentation of students' lives at Vassar, see Lynn D. Gordon, *Gender and Higher Education in the Progressive Era* (New Haven and London: Yale University Press 1990), 122.

28 For an overview of education facilities available to girls and young women in nineteenth-century Canada, see Charles E. Phillips, *The Development of Education in Canada* (Toronto: W.J. Gage 1957), chapter 20.

29 Wetherald, 'Fidelis,' 300-1.

30 See, for example, Agnes Maule Machar, *Lucy Raymond; or, The Children's Watchword* (Toronto: James Campbell and Son 1871), 3. This novel exemplified the demands of Christian duty for a Sunday school audience.

31 Henry Morgan, *Men and Women of the Time: A Handbook of Canadian Biography* (Toronto: Briggs 1898), 693-4; John William Leonard, ed., *Women's Who's Who of America (1914-1915)* (New York: American Commonwealth 1914), 521; *A Standard Dictionary of Canadian Biography: The Canadian Who Was Who,* vol. 1, 315; Cumberland, 'Remembering,' 27; and Leman A. Guild, 'Canadian Celebrities: Agnes Maule Machar (Fidelis),' *Canadian Magazine of Politics, Science, Arts, and Literature* (May-October 1906): 499-501.

32 Elizabeth [Smith] Shortt to Mother and Sister, 14 April 1895, in the Elizabeth Smith Shortt Papers, University of Waterloo Library. Also cited in Veronica Strong-Boag, *Parliament of Women: The National Council of Women of Canada*, National Museum of Man Mercury Series History Division, no. 18 (Ottawa: 1976), 150. Elizabeth Smith was one of the class of women who attempted to study medicine at Queen's and who suffered the coeducation fiasco of 1882-3. As Elizabeth Shortt, she was active in the Kingston Local Council of Women. See also Strong-Boag, ed., *A Woman with a Purpose: The Diaries of Elizabeth Smith, 1872-1884* (Toronto: University of Toronto Press 1980), xxvi-xxxiv and 235.

33 Coleman, 'Chipmunk Hollow.'

34 Agnes Maule Machar, 'Views of Canadian Literature,' *The Week* 11, 17 (23 March 1894): 391-2.

35 Anne Innis Dagg, 'Non-Fiction and Early Women Writers,' *Journal of Canadian Studies* 27/2 (1992): 116.

36 MacCallum, 'Agnes Maule Machar,' 355.

37 Agnes Maule Machar, *Faithful Unto Death: A Memorial of John Anderson, Late Janitor of Queen's College* (Kingston: James M. Creighton 1859), 2-3 and 66.

38 Ibid., 29. Janitors at the Toronto Normal School laboured under similarly difficult conditions; see Susan E. Houston and Alison Prentice, *Schooling and Scholars in Nineteenth-Century Ontario* (Toronto: University of Toronto Press 1988), 93-4.

39 See, for example, Machar's novel *Roland Graeme: Knight, A Novel of Our Time* (New York: Fords, Howard and Hulbert 1892); her articles on female factory workers, 'Healthy and Unhealthy Conditions of Woman's Work,' *The Week* 13 (27 March 1896): 421-3; 'Unhealthy Conditions of Woman's Work in Factories,' *The Week* 13 (8 May 1896): 566-9; National Council of Women of Canada, *Report* (1895), 173-8, and (1896), 358-60. For a sustained discussion of Machar's views on poverty, see Brouwer, '"Between-Age,"' 364-9; Backhouse, *Petticoats and Prejudice*, 277-88; Hallman, 'Religion and Gender,' chapter 5.

40 *Memorials*, viii.

41 On the Canada First movement, see Alvin Finkel, Margaret Conrad, with Veronica Strong-Boag, *History of the Canadian Peoples: 1867 to the Present*, vol. 2 (Toronto: Copp Clark Pitman 1993), 143-4; Flitton, *An Index*, introduction.

42 Carole Gerson, *A Purer Taste: The Writing and Reading of Fiction in English in Nineteenth-Century Canada* (Toronto, University of Toronto Press 1989), 92.

43 Agnes Maule Machar, 'For King and Country,' *Canadian Monthly* 5 (1874): 102-3.

44 Ibid., 500.

45 Brouwer, 'Moral Nationalism,' 100-1.

46 Agnes Maule Machar, 'For King and Country,' 199.

47 Agnes Maule Machar, 'Laura Secord,' in *Lays of the 'True North' and Other Canadian Poems*, 2nd ed. (London: E. Stock 1902), 32-5.

48 Agnes Maule Machar, 'Historical Sketch of the War of 1812,' *Canadian Monthly* 6 (July 1874): 1-24; see Brouwer, 'Moral Nationalism,' 101

49 See Brouwer, '"Between-Age."'

50 See Machar's three essays entitled 'The Temperance Problem,' published in April, August, and October 1877 in *Canadian Monthly*; 'Higher Education for Women,' *Canadian Monthly* 7 (February 1875): 144-57; 'Woman's Work,' *Rose Belford's Canadian Monthly* 1 (September 1878): 295-311; 'The New Ideal of Womanhood,' ibid., 2 (June 1879): 659-76.

51 Although 1878 has long been held to be the year Queen's formally admitted women, recent scholarship suggests it was later. See Jo LaPierre, 'The Academic Life of Canadian Coeds, 1880-1900,' in Ruby Heap and Alison Prentice, eds., *Gender and Education in Ontario* (Toronto: Canadian Scholar's Press 1991). For a brief overview of women's entry into Canadian universities, see Alison Prentice et al., *Canadian Women: A History* (Toronto: Harcourt Brace and Jovanovich 1988), 155-62.

52 Machar, 'Woman's Work,' 296, 299. For twentieth-century feminist theory of the origins of patriarchy, see, for example, Gerda Lerner, *The Creation of Patriarchy* (New York: Oxford University Press 1986).

53 Machar, 'Woman's Work,' 300.

54 For her involvement in the Indian Orphanage and Juvenile Mission scheme, see *Presbyterian Record* 1, 2 (January 1876-December 1877): 190. Her report to the Assembly had to be read by a clergyman because it was 'wholly unwarranted by Scripture and the practice of the Church' that a lady's name should appear in the official records.

55 Fidelis, 'Olympia Morata,' *Rose Belford's Canadian Monthly* 5 (September 1880): 252.

56 Agnes Maule Machar, 'Woman's Work,' 304, 308, 311.

57 Fidelis, 'Higher Education for Women,' 144-57.

58 Machar, 'The Higher Education of Women,' *The Week* 7 (27 December 1889): 55-6.

59 Agnes Machar to Louisa Murray, 11 April 1884, file 15, LMP.

60 Brouwer, 'Moral Nationalism.'

61 Agnes Maule Machar 'Roamings in Classical Massachusetts,' part I, *The Week* 8 (2 October 1891): 702-3; 'At Amesbury,' part II, 8 (30 October 1891): 767-8; 'At Concord,' part III, 9 (11 December 1891) 22-3; 'At Wellesley and Andover,' part IV, 9 (25 December 1891) 54; 'Farewell Visits,' part V, 9 (19 February 1892): 181-2; 'Ramblings about the Sources of Canadian History – In the Footsteps of the First Explorers,' part I, *The Week* 11 (26 October 1894): 1,112-5; part II, 11 (26 October 1894): 1,136-9.

62 Machar, 'Roamings,' part I, 702.
63 Machar, 'At Concord,' 23. See her poem, 'The Sons of the United Empire Loyalists and the Old Flag,' *The Week* 13 (31 January 1896): 233.
64 Machar, 'Farewell Visits,' 183.
65 Brouwer, 'Moral Nationalism,' 93-7.
66 Chenier, 'Her Life,' 8.
67 Opposition coalesced around the issues of papal intervention in Canadian political life and compensation to the Jesuits for property confiscated by the Crown after the British conquest of 1763. For a full discussion of the act and MacDonnell's views on it, see J.F. McCurdy, ed., *Life and Work of D.J. MacDonnell* (Toronto: William Briggs 1897), chapter 28.
68 Her earliest Sunday school novels were *Katie Johnstone's Cross: A Canadian Tale* (Toronto: James Campbell and Son 1870; Edinburgh: William Oliphant 1870); *Lucy Raymond.*
69 MacCullum, 'Agnes Maule Machar,' 355. Machar, *Stories of New France.*
70 Cumberland, 'Remembering,' 27.
71 Agnes Maule Machar, *The Thousand Islands,* The Ryerson Poetry Chapbooks (Toronto: Ryerson 1935). See Thomas Marquis, 'English-Canadian Literature,' in A. Shortt and A.G. Doughty, eds., *Canada and Its Provinces, a History of the Canadian People and Their Institutions* (Glasgow, Brook: Toronto 1913), 588.
72 Brouwer, 'Moral Nationalism,' 95.
73 From her portrait of Jacques Cartier in T.G. Marquis, ed. *Builders of Canada: From Cartier to Laurier* (Detroit and Brantford, ON: Bradley-Garretson 1903), 17; for a similar treatment, see Machar, *Stories of New France,* 27-31.
74 Machar, *Stories of New France,* 36, 39-41. The story first appeared in sixteenth-century writings: Marguerite de Navarre, *L'Heptameron,* Paris: 1559, and André Thevet, *Cosmographie Universelle,* 1575.
75 Machar, *Stories of New France,* chapter 10.
76 For a discussion of the 'women worthies' tradition of historical writing, see Natalie Zemon Davis in '"Women's History" in Transition: The European Case,' *Feminist Studies* 3, 3-4 (1976): 83-103.
77 For a discussion of Francis Parkman's work and his subscription to Anglo-American superiority and the 'Great Man school of history,' see W.J. Eccles' biographical portrait in Francess G. Halpenny, ed., *Dictionary of Canadian Biography* XII (Toronto: University of Toronto Press 1990), 823-7.
78 Agnes Maule Machar, *Marjorie's Canadian Winter, A Story of Northern Lights* (Boston: Lothrop 1892; Toronto: William Briggs 1906).
79 See *Marjorie's Canadian Winter,* 291 and passim. On General Gordon, see her poem, 'Wednesday, January 28, 1885,' *The Week* 2 (5 March 1885): 217, and her essay 'Ten Years Captivity in the Soudan,' *The Week* 11 (26 January 1894): 202-5. In the novel and the poem, the fall of Khartoum was made to coincide with the symbolic seige of the ice castle during Carnival week.
80 Machar, *Marjorie's Canadian Winter,* 162-3.
81 Ibid., 23-8.
82 Machar, *Lays,* 9-10.
83 Machar, 'Ramblings,' part I, 1112.
84 Patricia Jasen, 'Romanticism, Modernity, and the Evolution of Tourism on the Niagara Frontier, 1790-1850,' *Canadian Historical Review* 72, 3 (1991): 283-317.
85 Machar, 'Ramblings,' part II, 1,137.
86 Agnes Maule Machar, *Down the River to the Sea* (New York: Home Book Company 1894); *The Heir of Fairmount Grange* (London: Digby Long 1895; Toronto: Copp Clark 1895).
87 Gerson, 'Three Writers of Victorian Canada,' 226ff.
88 Jasen, 'Evolution of Tourism,' 291.
89 Kenneth N. Windsor, 'Historical Writing in Canada to 1920,' in Carl Klinck, ed., *Literary History of Canada* (Toronto: University of Toronto Press 1965), 238.
90 See Machar, *Old Kingston.*
91 Agnes Maule Machar, 'An Old Canadian Town,' *Canadian Monthly* 4 (July 1873): 1-18; Brouwer, 'Moral Nationalism,' 93.

92 Machar, *Old Kingston*, 286.
93 Machar wrote a biographical sketch of him for the prominent Canadian series, although Grant Allen never lived in Canada as an adult. See 'Prominent Canadians XXXVII – Grant Allen,' *The Week* 8 (10 July 1891): 510. Like his father before him, Grant Allen was a follower of Herbert Spencer.
94 Machar, *Stories of the British Empire*, 314.
95 Ibid., 198.
96 Ibid., x; Brouwer, 'Moral Nationalism,' 97-8.
97 Machar, *Stories of the British Empire*, 1.
98 Stephen Leacock, *The British Empire: Its Structure, Unity and Strength* (New York: Dodd Mead 1940), 1.
99 Natalie Zemon Davis, 'Gender and Genre: Women as Historical Writers, 1400-1820,' in Patricia H. Labalme, ed., *Beyond Their Sex: Learned Women of the European Past* (New York and London: New York University Press, 1980), 154-5.
100 Ibid., 174-5.
101 Gerson, *A Purer Taste*, chapter 5.
102 Windsor, 'Historical Writing.'
103 Davis, 'Gender and Genre,' 169.
104 Ibid., 155.
105 Guild, 'Canadian Celebrities,' 500.

3
Women's Rights and Duties: Sarah Anne Curzon and the Politics of Canadian History

Beverly Boutilier

In December 1898, members of the Women's Canadian Historical Society of Toronto gathered to remember their founding president, Sarah Anne Curzon, who had died the previous month. 'For more than thirty-five years she has lived among us in Toronto,' the group's new leader recalled, 'and by her pen and personal influence has done much for our intellectual and national life. Beneath a frail and gentle bearing dwelt a brave spirit, and with many disadvantages of health and fortune she accomplished much ... Those who knew her kind and retiring nature would hardly have suspected the strength that lay beneath.' To some extent, this hagiographic portrait of Curzon as a woman whose life embodied spiritual rather than physical strength can be viewed as a typical product of late Victorian culture. But, in this case, the language used to sketch this portrait suggests that the Women's Canadian Historical Society had a very specific comparison in mind. Drawing on the same feminine lexicon of service and sacrifice, in the 1880s and 1890s Curzon herself had claimed a place in Canadian history for Laura Secord of Queenston, Upper Canada, as 'the heroine of the War of 1812.' Viewed in this light, the society's message was clear: As a woman who had surmounted great personal challenges to write and preserve the history of her country, Sarah Curzon had demonstrated the same selfless qualities and devotion to duty that had sustained Laura Secord in 1813. As such, she, too, was indisputably a true heroine of Canadian history.[1]

Cecilia Morgan argues persuasively that the heroic image of Laura Secord popularized by Sarah Curzon and other women authors in late-nineteenth-century English Canada functioned as a gendered commentary on the Loyalist 'tradition' of Canadian history.[2] But there is another, equally compelling context for assessing the historical writing and activism of Sarah Curzon and for reading her interpretation of the Laura Secord saga. Although her work on Laura Secord helped to disseminate the history of loyalism, it was in order to further the cause of

Sarah Anne Curzon

women's rights, and thus to redefine the parameters of female citizenship, that Sarah Curzon initially turned to the writing and preservation of Canadian history. Through a steady literary output of historical prose and poetry during the 1880s and 1890s, and most notably through her pointed resurrection of Secord as a national and imperial heroine, Curzon attempted to move the cause of women's rights to the centre of Canadian political discourse by asserting a historic relationship between the sacrifices of Canadian women in wartime and the preservation of Canada as a British nation – a national identity with specific social, religious, and racial meanings.[3] Viewed from this perspective, Laura Secord served as an intellectual bridge between the two political worlds that Sarah Curzon occupied as an activist: the Ontario local history movement on the one hand and the Toronto women's rights community on the other.

As a women's rights activist, from the mid-1870s onward Sarah Curzon worked through a variety of mixed-gender and single-sex organizations to extinguish women's political disabilities and to provide elite young women of her daughter's generation with the kind of higher education and professional opportunities denied to herself. Already enjoying a degree of public notoriety in Toronto for her women's rights politics, in the late 1880s Curzon used her newfound authority as the champion of Laura Secord's claim on history to negotiate a position of some distinction within Ontario's newly invigorated local historical movement. This male-dominated movement was aligned through a common membership and a shared ideology with the imperial federation movement, whose elite male leadership sought the creation of an imperial parliament in

London and, through it, direct constitutional authority over imperial policy-making for Britain's so-called 'white dominions.'[4] Curzon shared this imperial outlook and worked assiduously, as both a writer of Canadian history and an activist within the local historical movement, to identify the cause of imperial federation not only with Canadian national development, but with the cause of 'woman' as well.

That history was used in late Victorian Canada to promote a partisan political cause is not in itself remarkable. As M. Brook Taylor argues, throughout the nineteenth century a succession of 'promoters, patriots and partisans' used history as a tool of Canadian nation-building, with each moulding the history of Canada to support its own particular ends.[5] But what is remarkable, as the example of Sarah Anne Curzon attests, is the extent to which the politics of gender also became entangled with the politics of Canadian history in the last two decades of the century. Untangling the political meaning that Sarah Curzon accorded to history in her campaign for 'woman's rights' is the subject of this paper.

Women's Rights

Too little is yet known about the personal and political histories of the individual women who comprised the early Toronto women's rights community to declare Sarah Curzon either a typical or atypical representative of the group.[6] Born in or near Birmingham, England, in 1833, Sarah Anne Vincent was a daughter of the provincial English middle class described by Leonore Davidoff and Catherine Hall.[7] Her father, George Philips Vincent, owned a Birmingham glass manufactory, but the enterprise does not appear to have been either very large or particularly noteworthy. As an adult, her extended family of cousins included a prominent Birmingham physician, an Anglican clergyman, and Edward White Benson, the archbishop of Canterbury from 1882 to 1896, whose ascent from Birmingham's lower middle class by way of Cambridge University and the Church of England was engineered by a series of wealthy patrons. Although she briefly attended a ladies' school in Birmingham, Sarah Curzon's own education was conducted mostly at home by tutors and by her parents, who enjoyed a reputation as learned and intellectual individuals. After a short career as one of Britain's legion of anonymous 'lady scribblers,' she married Robert Curzon of Norwich, England, in 1858.[8] This decision reoriented her life dramatically, for within a decade she found herself riding the crest of the last great wave of nineteenth-century British emigration to Toronto, where the Curzon family first appears in the city directory of 1866.[9]

In Toronto, whose population in 1871 was not yet 60,000, the family's fortunes appear to have vacillated for several years between financial risk and financial security. Robert and Sarah Curzon initially settled in the lakefront commercial district next door to the import-export firm where he worked as a bookkeeper. In 1872, the family moved to a midtown Toronto neighbourhood, and Robert established himself as an independent coffee and pickle merchant. The venture did not succeed, and the Curzon family briefly disappears from view. Indeed, the family's residential pattern between 1866 and 1877, when Sarah Curzon's public career as a women's rights activist began, suggests that its hold on middle-class status was somewhat precarious. Despite these apparent economic setbacks, however, as Britons, Anglicans, and Tories, Robert and Sarah Curzon nevertheless shared the predominant racial, religious, and partisan demeanour of the city's well-to-do, propertied, Protestant elite.[10]

In 1877, Sarah Curzon joined the Toronto Women's Literary Club. Inspired by the examples of Sorosis in New York City and the recently founded American Association for the Advancement of Women, the group's ostensible aim was to educate, edify, and entertain its female membership. But, in practice, its purpose was more political than cultural. Its principle founder was Dr. Emily Stowe, a Toronto physician and women's suffragist. From the beginning, she envisaged the Toronto Women's Literary Club as an educational forum for introducing the women of Toronto to the cause of 'woman's rights,' a cause that her own experience as the first female school principal in Ontario and the first female doctor in Canada had taught her to embrace. Given the hostility accorded to 'public' women in this decade, and to Stowe in particular, one should not wonder that she and her followers chose to dissemble about the true nature of their new 'club.'[11]

By the mid-1870s, alterations in Sarah Curzon's personal circumstances made membership in an organization such as the Toronto Women's Literary Club a very attractive proposition. After eighteen years of marriage, Robert Curzon had finally abandoned his various commercial ventures and joined the Treasurer's Department of the City of Toronto full-time as a clerk.[12] The unprecedented degree of financial stability that resulted from this change of occupation coincided with the easing of Sarah Curzon's child- rearing responsibilities and the resumption of her literary career as a poet, dramatist, and essayist at mid-decade. For a woman like Curzon, who sought artistic recognition from the country's so-called 'national' literary community, actual membership in a women's literary club must have been a welcome outlet for her creative talents. There is evidence to suggest, too, that the wider political objectives of this group were amenable to Curzon, who soon emerged as one of its leading advocates of women's admission to the University of Toronto. Similarly, after the club reconstituted itself as the Canadian Women's Suffrage Association in 1883, she publicly endorsed its now undisguised and expanded program of women's rights reform.[13]

In the early 1880s, Sarah Curzon took a leading role in the campaign mounted by the Toronto Women's Literary Club and the Canadian Women's Suffrage Association to institute co-education at the University of Toronto. A confluence of personal and public politics seems to have inspired Curzon's support for this issue. Although none of her three sons attended university before commencing paid work in the early 1880s – as a travelling sales agent, engraver, and clerk, respectively[14] – in 1885, Curzon's daughter Edith became a living symbol of her mother's repeated assertion that women had an equal capacity for higher learning. In that year, she entered University College with a small class of women students and four years later became the first woman to graduate from the University of Toronto with a B.A. in Natural Science.[15] The evident alacrity with which Edith Curzon greeted the opening of University College degrees to women by the Ontario legislature in 1884 points persuasively to a strong connection between the intellectual aspirations of one generation and the political activism of the other – a connection shared by more than one advocate of women's higher education in Toronto during this decade.[16]

Curzon entered the battle over women's higher education most forcefully in 1882, when she wrote a short blank-verse comedy entitled 'Sweet Girl Graduate' for the Toronto *Grip-Sack*. In it, she challenged the frequently laid charge that higher education alongside of men would 'unsex' women. Using the well-worn literary device of female cross-dressing, Curzon engineered a plot that asked readers to reconsider the 'impropriety' of women seeking 'the teaching that is chained – / Like ancient scripture to the reading desk – / Within [the] College walls.' In the play, Miss Kate Bloggs, whom Curzon described as the daughter of a wealthy merchant, masquerades as Mr. Tom Christopher in order to complete her university education. When she finally reveals her true gender identity, after graduating as a Master of Arts and winning class prizes in each subject of the university's reputedly 'masculine' curriculum, her startled but suitably chastened classmates accept the evidence before them and concede women's intellectual equality.[17]

But was it proper, Curzon asked, that a woman of such evident ability was unable to test the full spectrum of her individual talents without first disguising herself as a man? Kate's inner struggle to reconcile her ambition to attend university with her misgivings about the moral dangers of male impersonation were dwelt on at length by Curzon. When her cousin, Orphea, asks what Kate will do to realize her goal, she responds:

> A deed without a name!
> A deed will waken me at dead of night!
> A deed whose stony face will stare at me

With vile grimace, and freeze my curdling blood!
Will make me quake before the eye of day;
Shrink from the sun, and welcome fearsome night!
A deed will chase my trembling steps by ways
Unknown, through lonely streets, into dark haunts! –
Will make me tremble if a child observes
Me close; and quake, if, in a public crowd,
One glances at me twice!
A deed I'll blush for, yet I'll do't; and charge
Its ugliness on those who force me to't –
In short, I'll wear the breaks.

Curzon was careful to stress the selfless character of Kate's actions. As well as exchanging her fashionable silks for masculine trousers, Kate characterizes the cutting of her 'abundant brown hair' as 'an offering to my sex; a protest strong / 'Gainst man's oppression.' This sacrifice of her 'woman's simple pride' was made doubly painful by the knowledge that elsewhere in the British Empire other young women already enjoyed the academic privileges she now sought through subterfuge:

Not let me in! We'll see. I'll beat 'em yet.
To think that down in Canterbury, girls,
Like my poor self, have had the badge bestowed
That I so fondly covet. To think that they
Enjoy the rights I ask, and have received
The Cambridge University degree, B.A.
Not only wear the gown and cap
As college students, but the hood. The hood!
And shall Macaulay's proud New Zealanders
Thus sit on me? Not if I know it. No!
I'll don the dreadful clothes, and cheat the Dons.[18]

Curzon used the tears shed by Kate over her degraded femininity to make the play's central point: that 'womanliness' was not incompatible with an ambition to learn. Rather than unsexing women, Curzon argued that co-education would unsex academic knowledge and thereby free talented young women like Kate Bloggs, and Edith Curzon, to realize the full potential of the humanity they shared with men.

The complete scope of Curzon's commitment to women's rights reform became apparent in 1883 when she agreed to represent the Canadian Women's Suffrage Association as an editor at the *Canada Citizen and Temperance Herald*, a Toronto weekly that promoted the 'woman's vote' as an electoral antidote to the spiritual affliction of intemperance. Under her direction, the paper's Ladies' Department became a political forum for local and international news about the progress of women's suffrage reform and the work of university-educated women professionals in Britain and North America. This dual focus, combined with her periodic reportage of local efforts to found a separate women's medical college in the summer and autumn of 1883, suggests that, contrary to her male colleagues at the *Canada Citizen*, Curzon distinguished between the rights of women as individuals and the political power that women might wield as a group once enfranchised. Although she could speak the millenary language of temperance reform, and later joined the Toronto Woman's Christian Temperance Union,[19] Curzon did not invoke 'the political power of enfranchised womanhood' to justify the extension of electoral privileges to women. Instead, she declared that it was a woman's 'right as a human being to the freedom inherent in humanity' to vote, attend university, and enter any occupation for which her education and God-given personality fitted her. As such, the full extent of women's political power would not be fully realized in her estimation until 'the general question of Woman's Rights' was first addressed and resolved.[20]

The emphasis Curzon placed on women's individual rights did not mean that she believed the civic responsibilities of women and men were identical, or that she equated female individuality with the self-interestedness that contemporaries associated with masculine professionalism.[21] To refute such insinuations of 'mannishness,' Curzon argued that, if allowed to cultivate themselves as scholars, as professionals, and as electors, women would use the power of their newfound individuality to fulfil their gendered duties as citizens.[22] For Curzon, the primary political obligation of women citizens would be to consider 'the bearing of civil and national politics upon the home, the *real practical life* of the nation'[23] (emphasis in the original). Reconstituted as a gendered political mandate, their prescriptive responsibility for the home was transformed in Curzon's philosophy into a civic obligation to make the 'health, welfare, education, and comfort' of the people a priority of local and national government. Canada's ongoing development as a 'centre of civilisation' within the British Empire was thus irrevocably linked to its leaders' recognition of women's collective and individual right to self-representation. 'I trust,' she told the editor of the *Dominion Illustrated* of Montreal in 1890, 'that the time is not far distant when our men, laying aside their selfishness, jealousy and prejudice, may say to woman, "come over and help us," not only in making pure and righteous homes, but in making our nation.'[24]

Women in History

Proving that women had already played a vital role in bringing Canada to its present state of national development was a central objective of

Sarah Curzon as a writer of history. On the whole, Curzon agreed with the prevailing nineteenth-century view that the principal subject of 'history' was politics. The work of history was to chronicle the lives of civil and military heroes and to document the fortunes of nations. As a writer of historical Canadiana, Curzon explored those themes best suited to illustrate the preservation of Canada's racial heritage as a British nation and its political identity as a monarchy. Her inclusion of women in the historical record thus did not by itself constitute a new way of looking at history. But what it did represent was a new way of thinking about politics and about the political impact of women's work in the home on the nation-state over time.

Curzon viewed a knowledge of history as an essential ingredient of national identity. Looking back to her own girlhood reading, she recalled that 'as soon as she had conquered the rudiments of reading and grammar at school, she was set to learn English History, and so become acquainted with the past of her country.' She was therefore astonished to hear educated Canadians assert that '"Canada had no history."'[25] Stories about the nation's pioneer settlers, and the sacrifices made by the United Empire Loyalists on behalf of the British Crown, convinced Curzon that a rich vein of historical material was yet to be mined by the nation's budding literary community. As a writer of historical prose and poetry in the 1880s and 1890s, Curzon sought to awaken the dormant spirit of patriotism that she associated with citizenship and national development. Her initial choice of subject, however, suggests that she also viewed history as a tool of women's rights politics.

In common with most other women historians in nineteenth-century Britain and North America, Curzon viewed the past through the lens of women's history.[26] In choosing Laura Secord as her subject, she also conformed to the 'great woman' tradition of female biography, the genre through which most women in this period expressed their historical sensibilities. As a group, women historians emphasized the achievements of exceptional women: queens, heroines, and noblewomen whose lives had intersected in some definite way with the male-dominated political realm. Their work nevertheless had a broader import, for not only did it present women and their domestic experiences as worthy subjects of study, it also suggested, as Billie Melman argues, that 'world historical man' was not the only actor in the human drama.[27] As the century wore on, and Darwinian social science relegated white women and non-white peoples of both genders to the margins of evolution, this contention assumed added political significance. In this context, writing even a few women into the existing historical narrative became a political act because it challenged the persistent notion that history, and therefore politics, was an innately 'masculine' preserve.[28]

By historicizing white women's experience of loyalism and warfare in late eighteenth- and early nineteenth-century Upper Canada, Sarah Curzon joined this broader pattern of dissent.[29] But for her, the introduction of these women into the historical narrative of Canadian nation-building had a deeper political meaning. In 'Betty's Choice,' for example, a short story published in *The Week* in 1889, Curzon's heroine is faced with an unwelcome dilemma. Living in Massachusetts at the time of the revolutionary war, she must choose between political loyalty to Great Britain and personal loyalty to her republican fiancé. Betty ultimately leaves Massachusetts for a new life under the Union Jack in Upper Canada, deciding that she must put duty to country before all other considerations, no matter how painful the results.[30] By placing the fictional Betty at the centre of one of North America's greatest political upheavals, Curzon implied that, in common with their male counterparts, white Loyalist women had actively chosen their fate. Canadian history thus not only demonstrated the capacity of 'woman' to share power with 'man,' but also proved her moral right – and fitness – to do so.

How, then, did Sarah Curzon structure her narrative of Canadian history? Starting with the assumption that Canadian history was synonymous with European history, Curzon represented late Victorian Canada as the culmination of three centuries of British beneficence in North America. The divine inspiration of British rule in this region was unquestioned in her estimation. Writing in 1896 about the British conquest of New France in 1760, she declared: 'Nothing remained to France but Britain's grace. / But what more shall we ask save grace of God?' The principal characters in this divinely inspired history were the United Empire Loyalists and their patriotic descendants, who, with a little help from their friends in the British regulars, had also defeated the American army in the War of 1812. Women as well as men featured as protagonists in Curzon's historical accounting of Canadian history; however, her repeated characterization of the American Revolution as a family squabble between mother Britannia and 'some wayward sons' underscored the limited racial scope of her own definition of historical agency. Although native peoples might qualify as Britons in time of war, for example, when their military prowess and loyalty to the Crown could be applauded and even celebrated, in general Curzon, like Agnes Maule Machar, used the stock image of the 'noble savage' to underwrite the importance of Canada's political, cultural, and racial 'evolution' as a *white* British nation.[31]

The exodus of the United Empire Loyalists from the United States to British North America, and to Upper Canada in particular, was for Curzon *the* defining moment in Canadian history, which at this point in her narrative she increasingly equated with the history of Ontario. In contrast to her representation of Americans as unfrocked Britons, Curzon portrayed the United Empire Loyalists of Upper Canada as noble gentlemen and gentlewomen who had sacrificed all they owned to remain true to the social, political, and religious ideal of British monarchy. As the selfless progenitors of Greater Britain in Canada, their memory had to be preserved. It was Curzon's fervent hope that Canadians of her own time would recognize their indebtedness to these early patriots by working to promote the political destiny of Canadians as 'Britons':

O Britain! Mother-land! to thee we turn
With proud high hearts and eyes alight with love
Knowing thee ever true and ever great.
Our kindling souls to-day find in thy name
Our richest boast. Canadians! Britons!
We ask no more; the rest is in our hands.[32]

Sarah Curzon's most ambitious historical work was a blank-verse drama entitled *Laura Secord: The Heroine of 1812*, published along with a selection of shorter works at her own expense by C. Blackett Robinson of Toronto in 1887. Although the production of this work nearly bankrupted the Curzon family,[33] its publication enhanced Curzon's fame as a Canadian woman of letters and, because it included an appendix of historical documents designed to substantiate Secord's wartime heroism, established her reputation as a historical authority of some reknown.[34]

The play, which was actually written eleven years earlier in 1876, describes how one brave Canadian woman thwarted the United States army during the War of 1812, thus saving Upper Canada from certain military defeat and proving the patriotism of yet another generation of 'loyalist' women. By her account, Curzon first encountered the story of Laura Secord in 1873, when the question of pensions for veterans of the War of 1812 was before the House of Commons. The failure of Canadians at this time to recognize Secord's wartime exploits as a form of national service equal to that rendered by men-in-arms dismayed her. She attributed this oversight in part to the historical myopia that prevented late Victorian Canadians from clearly seeing their country's past. But, since there was no corresponding reluctance to celebrate the wartime experiences of men, she concluded that Secord's exclusion from 'the roll of Canadian heroes' must be due to her gender. '[I]t could not pass without observation,' Curzon recalled in 1887, 'that, while the heroism of the men of that date was dwelt upon with warm appreciation and much urgency as to their deserts, Mrs. Secord, as being a woman, shared in nothing more tangible than an approving record.' It was first and foremost to set Laura Secord on 'a pedestal of equality' with the male heroes of the war, and thus to inspire the current generation of Canadian women to similar acts of 'loyal bravery,' that Curzon wrote and eventually published *Laura Secord*.[35]

Using the formal language of blank-verse poetry, Curzon chronicled the ordeal of a woman beset by circumstances not of her own making. Although ensconced in the supposed safety of her home, which is now in enemy-held territory, Laura Secord overhears four American soldiers, who have claimed victor's rights to dine at her table, discuss American plans to attack a small British garrison on the other side of the Niagara Peninsula. With her husband James already disabled by battle wounds, Secord decides that she herself must undertake the perilous journey from Queenston to Beaver Dams in order to warn its British guard of the approaching Americans. But it is as a wife and mother, not as a soldier, that Secord undertakes her unsought and arduous task. Over and over again, Curzon forced Secord to defend her actions, and to explain her apparent readiness to deprive her children of their mother's care. Believing that her children would distinguish between the selfless aim of her actions and the sacrifice her death would impose on them, Secord argues that the primary duty of women and men in wartime is to preserve their country and soldiers from harm.[36] More than anything else, Secord's decision to risk her life to safeguard a group of men who were unrelated to her by family ties revealed the high price that Curzon believed women had already paid, and were yet willing to pay, for full participation in national life.

Like any good hero, once decided to action, Secord is beset by a series of trials designed to test her courage and resolve. Setting out at first light on her twenty-mile hike, Secord must pass through three American sentry posts to reach the home of her sister-in-law Elizabeth at St. David's Mill. Here, she is given one last chance to abandon her extraordinary scheme and assume her rightful place in the domestic fold, symbolized by Elizabeth and her kitchen. Undeterred, Laura Secord continues along her chosen path, but as the day progresses the terrain she must cover becomes less and less familiar – and more and more dangerous. At nightfall, Secord finds herself in dense woods that, under normal circumstances, she would never have entered alone. Tired and afraid, her worst fears are suddenly realized when, within a short distance of the British camp, her path is blocked by a group of Mohawk warriors. Marshalling all her remaining courage, Secord speaks to them and discovers that they are British scouts. With their help, she reaches her destination in time to warn Lieutenant James Fitzgibbon of the impending American attack. Her duty done, Secord faints with fatigue as the soldiers prepare for a battle they are now destined to win.

Although Curzon clearly intended the play as a contribution to the history of Canadian loyalism, her principal objective was to illustrate the heroic capacity of Canadian women to serve their country in wartime, not as soldier-citizens like men, but as wives and mothers in the home. On this level, the play reads as a justification of Curzon's basic political contention that women and men shared a common humanity that was at once equal and complementary. Curzon made this point most effectively in Act I, when Laura and James Secord debate the scope of their respective duties to each other and to the nation. When Laura reveals her plan to James, he objects, stating 'I cannot let thee go, my darling. / Did I not promise in our marriage vow, / And to thy mother, to guard thee as myself?' To which Laura Secord responds:

> And so you will if now you let me go.
> For you would go yourself, without a word
> Of parley, were you able; leaving me
> The while in His good hands; not doubting once
> But I was willing. Leave me there now, James,
> And let me go; it is our country calls.

In the exchange that follows, Curzon used Secord to challenge the scriptural foundations of women's inequality, arguing that for a man to love his wife as himself, he must also love her as his neighbour, and therefore as his equal. 'Why now, fond ingrate!' Laura says to her husband,

> What saith the Book?
> 'THE GOOD, with all thy soul and mind and strength;
> Thy neighbour as thyself.' Thou must not love
> Thyself, nor me, as thou *must* love the Good.
> Therefore, I am thy neighbour; loved as thyself:
> And as thyself wouldst go to warn Fitzgibbon
> If thou wert able, so I, being able,
> Thou must let me go – thy other self.
> Pray let me go![37]

Since women, as Curzon argued, were the equals of men in the eyes of God, any reading of the Christian marriage contract that consigned them solely to the protection of their husbands, or reserved to men exclusively the duties and privileges of citizenship, was spiritually and legally invalid.

It is the mutual obligation of James and Laura Secord as Canadians, as Britons, and as Loyalists to warn Fitzgibbon and his men of the impending American offensive. Since James is disabled by battle wounds, the duty, which would normally be his, devolves on Laura as his 'other self.' But Laura Secord was not merely playing the role of a surrogate male. As a woman whose home and family were now at the centre of an armed international conflict, Curzon contended that Secord had her own peculiar interests to protect *as a woman*. Nor did she represent Secord as an exceptional woman. Each of the several minor female characters in the play also contribute, either by word or by deed, to Curzon's general argument that women shared an equal capacity and desire to serve their nation in wartime, when the obligations of citizenship were most onerous. Indeed, the entire play can be read as an extended discussion of the nature and scope of female citizenship, which Curzon defined as the performance of one's appointed duty, including the conventional prescriptive duties of womanhood. In this way, Curzon accorded a political significance to the work of domesticity and to the home itself. In the last resolve, Secord was a heroine not because she transcended the bounds of woman's 'sphere,' but because she claimed the nation as a part of it.

As a woman who had exerted a tangible and documented impact on the course of national and international politics, Secord was indisputably a heroine in Curzon's eyes and, as such, a maker of history. But Secord was also a slave owner, a fact that Curzon presented without comment or apparent concern. In total there are two episodes of inter-racial contact in the play: between Laura Secord and her two black slaves, one male and one female; and between Secord and the Mohawk scouts in the forest near Beaver Dams. In the racialized culture of late Victorian Canada, these encounters between non-white men and a white woman would be interpreted in relation to a whole series of stock images and ideas about the relative importance of 'race' and 'sex' as demarcations of power and authority.[38] In the play, their currency became an additional, almost unspoken, means for Curzon to advocate the 'natural' right of white women not only to represent their own political interests, but to protect those of the British 'race' as well.[39]

In Act I, Secord scolds Pete, her adult male slave, when he tries to evade the American soldiers who have entered the Secord house in search of dinner: 'You'll stay / And wait upon these men. I'll not have Flos / Left single-handed by your cowardice,' she says. When one of the soldiers criticizes Secord for the 'saucy' behaviour of her slave, she rebukes him for his own bad manners as an uninvited guest in her home.[40] Although this encounter does nothing to advance the plot, it is not entirely gratuitous. The broken language and simple-minded speeches that Curzon gave to Pete, for instance, place him outside of 'civilization' and establish the authority of Laura Secord not only as the mistress of her home, but as the 'master' of some men as well. Despite the temporary enmity of their two nations, and the poor manners of the Americans, the scene between Secord, Pete, and the soldiers serves as a none-too-subtle reminder of the racial bond of whiteness – and ultimately of Britishness – that Curzon clearly believed set Secord and her American adversaries above the world's 'black races.'

Curzon conveyed a similarly racialized message when she made Secord face her fear of Britain's 'red allies' in Act II.[41] The distinction between 'savage and civil' was an important element in Curzon's representation of Secord as a heroine. According to the stage directions, the Mohawk men who confront Secord in the forest 'seem to spring from the ground,' a description that reflected the popular nineteenth-century image of the 'noble savage' as an unchanging product of nature rather than of culture. Although Curzon represented these men as valued allies of the Crown, she also undermined their status as 'Britons' by contrasting their child-like loyalty to King George – which was purchased, she implied, with a few plugs of tobacco – to the selfless and complex patriotism that motivated 'true' Britons like Secord and Fitzgibbon. Moreover, by juxtaposing one white woman's imperilled femininity with the stereotypically 'savage' masculinity of aboriginal men, Curzon further exploited the late Victorian concept of racial hierarchy to argue that the political authority of white women must accord with the racial authority they already wielded as 'civilizers' within the empire.[42] Thus, rather than incidental additions of dramatic colour, black and indigenous men function in the play as two-dimensional foils for whiteness and for a racially privileged citizenship that, for Curzon at least, had both a male and a female face.

Historical Activism

Contemporary reviewers praised Sarah Curzon's book as a noteworthy contribution to Canadian literature and annals but largely ignored her portrayal of Secord as an everywoman fulfilling her appointed duties as a citizen. Instead, they constructed both Secord *and* Curzon as exceptional women: the former because of her bravery and the latter because of her evident political sensibilities.[43] Curzon's representation of Secord as a national and imperial heroine nevertheless struck a chord with the well-to-do men who led Ontario's expanding local and provincial history movement in the late 1880s and 1890s. As a group, these historical activists embraced Laura Secord as an icon of Canada's past, present, and future loyalty to the British Empire and to the social and political principles of British monarchy. Their response to Sarah Curzon as her biographer was more equivocal, however. Although they could commend Secord as a maker of history *in the past*, Sarah Curzon's reputation as a politically self-conscious woman *in the present* was, for them, a less digestible concept.

For Sarah Curzon, on the other hand, the Ontario local historical movement was a point of access to the dominant male political culture. First as an invited speaker and pamphleteer, and later as the founder of the Women's Canadian Historical Society of Toronto, she used the authority accorded to her as the champion of Laura Secord's claim on history to articulate an explicit link between the two political causes that animated her adult life: women's rights and imperial federation. Curzon's support for imperial federation stemmed from a passionate belief in the necessity of expanding and formalizing Canada's leadership role within the British Empire. This would secure its future prosperity and help guarantee the continued predominance of British 'civilization' throughout the world. In common with supporters of the Canadian imperial federation movement generally, Curzon's endorsement of this cause was precipitated in part by a corresponding growth in the popularity of annexationist sentiment in the late 1880s and early 1890s, both in Canada and the United States. But, for Curzon, support for imperial federation entailed more than advocating a new constitutional or fiscal arrangement between Canada and Great Britain. It was also a means of asserting, she declared in 1891, that 'England is Canada, and Canada is England,' and that their interests were one and the same. As she confided to the noted historian William Kirby, her historical writing was conceived as a vehicle for promoting this idea: 'To me Canada is an integral part of England and if any book of mine fosters a healthy national spirit I shall be well rewarded.'[44]

The male and female imperial federationists whose patriotic ardour fuelled the local historical movement in Ontario perceived their activism as a means of collecting the necessary proofs not only of Canada's British destiny, but of their own ancestors' role in preserving the racial and political heritage of Canadians as Britons. Many historical activists were the descendants of United Empire Loyalists or early Upper Canadian pioneers. In such cases, personal as well as political considerations informed their individual and collective efforts to portray the United Empire Loyalists as the founders of the Canadian nation and the defenders of Greater Britain in North America. By advancing this imperialistic nation-building narrative, they claimed not only pride of place for their own forefathers in Canadian history, but also attempted to legitimate an enhanced leadership role for themselves in the present as the rightful stewards of the new Canadian nation.[45]

Although a few pioneer societies had been established in Ontario before the 1880s, it was not until the latter half of this decade that an identifiable historical movement took shape in the province with the foundation of the Pioneer and Historical Association of Ontario (PHAO) in 1888. The object of the PHAO was to unite in concerted action the several existing local historical societies and thereby foster the expansion of patriotic sentiment in the province through the preservation and dissemination of historical records and relics that celebrated Canada's Loyalist past. Because the men who founded and led the PHAO in the 1880s and early 1890s viewed the past as a moral guide for the future of the nation, and therefore as an inherently political occupation, they initially perceived the work of history as the natural preserve of men like themselves. The executive roster of the PHAO and its local affiliates reflected this assumption. In 1895, the year that Sarah Curzon and Mary Agnes FitzGibbon applied to the PHAO for permission to found a separate women's historical society, none of its executive positions was held by a woman, no affiliated society sent a woman as its delegate to the annual meeting, and only one of its seven member societies had elected a female officer.[46]

Many women were nevertheless anxious to participate in the historical movement, sharing as they did many of the same political and cultural preoccupation's as their male counterparts. A few notable women such as Janet Carnochan, who presided over the Niagara Historical Society for many years, occupied positions of leadership within mixed-gender societies, but most women assumed auxiliary or supportive roles within these organizations.[47] The experience of women in the Wentworth Historical Society (WHS) of Hamilton is perhaps typical. Although the WHS was one of the few local historical societies in Ontario to open its membership rolls to both women and men, its female members by no means took an equal share in the governance or work of the society. Within a few years of its foundation in 1889, the WHS's male leaders had channelled the society's large female membership into a separate Ladies' Committee, complete with its own roster of female officers. Initially this committee functioned as a female auxiliary to the WHS, raising funds for the men's museum-building program. But in 1900, this arrangement ceased when the Ladies' Committee changed its name to the Women's Wentworth Historical Society, purchased a historic house, and began raising funds for its own restoration program.[48]

The historical movement as a whole acknowledged and used Sarah Curzon's intellectual authority as an eminent and well-known woman author for its own political and patriotic ends, but before 1895 she was never welcomed as a full member of any one society. Instead, her activism within this movement was limited to honorary memberships in men-only groups such as the Lundy's Lane Historical Society and to auxiliary memberships in groups such as the York Pioneers of Toronto. Several societies, including the Niagara Historical Society, the Wentworth Historical Society, and the Lundy's Lane Historical Society, also invited Curzon to speak or read selections of her poetry before their meetings. The Lundy's Lane Historical Society, in whose historical jurisdiction Laura and James Secord were buried, was especially attentive to Curzon. In the early 1890s, its male leadership commissioned Curzon to write a prose sketch of the heroine. It was hoped that the funds raised by the sale of this pamphlet, which went through two editions between 1891 and 1898, could be used to erect a modest stone memorial to Secord at her grave site.[49] Despite these indications of support for Curzon as a historian, the men who founded and led the Ontario historical movement were still unwilling to accord Curzon full access to the work of history as they defined it. It is clear that Curzon nevertheless interpreted their endorsement of her expertise as confirmation of their support for an imperial politics that recognized the historical claims of Canadian women, and Canadian men, to an equal share in the governance of the Empire.

At the same time, there is considerable evidence to suggest that Curzon was aware of the peripheral position that she and most other historically minded women occupied within the historical movement as a whole. In an 1891 address to a meeting of the Wentworth Historical Society, for example, Curzon prefaced her remarks with an extended tongue-in-cheek aside about the propriety of a woman making a speech before a historical society:

> When your president ... conveyed to me your kind invitation to read a paper before you, the honor came to me with all the force of novelty. I did not hope that anything I could say would be of sufficient value to arrest the attention of your honorable society, seeing that I am but a dabbler as it were in historical records, nor did I think that you had sufficiently understood that I was one of a sex that had never been recognized as in its place when upon a platform, even the very modest platform of an essayist. So that at first I felt compelled to decline your courteous invitation lest I might offend some whom I would be sorry to displease, or place my sex at a disadvantage to the eyes of others whose good word we shall always desire to deserve.

Curzon had finally decided to risk censure and accept the WHS's invitation to speak for two reasons. Because the society had invited someone who had for twenty years been 'upholding the doctrine of the equal rights of woman as a human being,' Curzon contended that its leaders had 'tacitly admitted' the veracity of this doctrine and thereby acknowledged her right *as a woman* to speak. Moreover, by opening its membership rolls to women as well as to men, Curzon believed that the WHS had signalled its endorsement of a historical and political world view that acknowledged the central role that women had played, and continued to play, as builders of the Canadian nation.[50]

Curzon's remarks to the WHS can be read as a form of advocacy not only on behalf of her own authority as a public woman, but also on behalf of the many other women who aspired to take up the work of history and call it their own. By claiming a place for herself as a leader within the historical movement, Curzon also worked to imbue women as a group with a collective political identity as nation builders. For Curzon, women's responsibility for homemaking was 'the incentive, the anchor, the object of nation-building.' It was therefore only fitting that women should join with men to preserve the memories of their mutual forebearers. 'Together,' she told the WHS, 'men and women built up this noble country by whose name we call ourselves; together they must preserve and develop it; and together they will stand or fall by it.'[51] Curzon nevertheless worried that women – the group best equipped to teach the lessons of history to the young – were not adequately represented within this movement or perceived as a legitimate audience for its patriotic message. In order to ensure that women received and understood the importance of preserving Canada's Loyalist past, it was first necessary to draw more of them into the historical movement. To do this, Curzon eventually concluded that a new institution tailored to fit the precise contours of women's lives would have to be created.

From 1895 to her death in 1898, Curzon attempted to forge an explicit intellectual and institutional link between women, nation-building, and the work of history as the co-founder and first president of the Women's Canadian Historical Society of Toronto (WCHST). In February 1895, at the request of Sarah Curzon and Mary Agnes FitzGibbon, another well-known woman historian,[52] the PHAO passed a motion at its annual meeting that 'authorized' these women to form a separate women's historical society. Curzon and FitzGibbon wanted a separate history organization specifically for women for two reasons. As Curzon explained to the WCHST's inaugural meeting in November 1895, they wanted to form 'a more distinctly woman's society' that would emulate the proven ability of the newly launched National Council of Women movement to spread 'a knowledge of any subject brought before it.' Their second reason was more general: 'to establish in the minds and understandings of incoming settlers' the history of the country before 'the opportunity [was] lost beyond recovery.'[53]

Both Curzon and FitzGibbon were inspired by the ideal of female unity embodied by the National Council of Women of Canada (NCWC), an experimental federation of local and national women's societies founded two years earlier in 1893. As a leader of the Dominion Women's Enfranchisement Association – as the Canadian Women's Suffrage Association was now known – Curzon was already an active participant in this new organization. Although the NCWC did its best to avoid the whole question of 'woman's rights' in the 1890s, Curzon viewed the existence of this organization as a symbol of women's concerted power for social and political reform. She hoped the spirit of unity that had inspired the Council movement would not only help them achieve the vote, but also help them realize 'a higher ideal' in their collective work for the nation – an ambition shared by the vast majority of Council leaders in this decade.[54]

In much the same spirit, Curzon worked through the WCHST to harness the concerted energies of its members in the service of the nation. Curzon envisaged the WCHST as a vehicle for uniting the historically minded women of Toronto in a common purpose. As such, its general aim would be to provide the women of Toronto with a forum for united action *as women* on behalf of Canadian history. Its specific aims were to promote and preserve the history of Canada and, through these means, to encourage the growth of loyalty and patriotism among the populace, especially Canadian women and children. In this respect, the WCHST institutionalized the goals of the late nineteenth-century historical movement in Ontario, functioning as both a heritage organization and an advocacy group. But its exclusive female membership and its contention that history was an especially fitting form of women's work also set it apart from the male-dominated movement as a whole. As did the assumption of its founders that historical activism was a means by which women could assert a collective civic identity as citizens.

Despite its separatist form, and the influential leadership of Sarah Curzon, the WCHST was never a women's rights organization. Instead, its elite roster of leaders drew selectively on Curzon's historical message, rejecting her rights-based reading of female individuality on the one hand, but accepting her less controversial, but still politicized, contention that women and men had different spheres of influence, each of which was essential to national development, on the other.[55] FitzGibbon, for example, did not share Curzon's analysis of women's rights. However, she was in complete accordance with her friend's understanding of homemaking as a peculiarly feminine form of nation-building. As an immigration activist, FitzGibbon strove to acquire for Canada hardy British women whose labour in the homes of Canada would help build up the nation and perpetuate its ties to Greater Britain. To this extent, both Curzon and FitzGibbon envisaged the WCHST as a politicized institution because each supposed that their new organization would provide women of their time with additional opportunities to prove that they, too, were nation builders in the service of Canadian history.

Although Curzon did not use the WCHST as a platform for her women's rights politics, she clearly viewed it as a vehicle for teaching women to see themselves as historical agents and to understand the full scope of their duties as female citizens. Through an annual program of lectures and meetings, the WCHST disseminated an interpretation of Canadian history that celebrated Canada's past and future as a British nation and highlighted the role of women like Laura Secord in preserving this imperial tie. In this way, during the three short years of her presidency, Curzon introduced several hundred women to her basic political contention that homemaking and nation-building were synonymous concepts. For Curzon, then, this group functioned as a symbol, rather than as an advocate, of her wider argument that women had a right to fulfil their gendered duties as citizens and needed the vote to do so.

Conclusion

What does the example of Sarah Curzon tell us about the role of history in late nineteenth-century women's rights politics? Or, to pose the question in a slightly different way, why did Sarah Curzon use Canadian history to press the cause of women's rights? From 1877 until her death in 1898, Sarah Curzon promoted an ideal of female citizenship in which women's political rights and duties were at once general and specific. As an activist within Toronto's women's rights community, Curzon elaborated a definition of female individuality that claimed political, economic, and intellectual freedom for women as a basic human right. Curzon tempered this focus on female individuality by distinguishing between the political duties of women and men on the basis of gender. Enfranchised women, she argued, would use their newfound civic power not to advance narrow, selfish ends, but rather to secure greater representation for the home and family in Canadian national life.

In the 1880s and 1890s, Curzon embraced Canadian history as an essential tool in her campaign for bringing this vision of women's rights and duties to fruition. In particular, she used the image of Laura Secord to represent the full spectrum of women's potentiality as equal citizens. In characterizing Secord as a heroine of Canadian history, Curzon represented her as an exceptional woman and an ideal standard for her sex to emulate. But Curzon also portrayed Secord as the archetypal Loyalist woman through whom all women who resembled her could be historicized. As an activist in Ontario's historical movement, and more particularly as the founder of the Women's Canadian Historical Society of Toronto, Curzon attempted to institutionalize this vision of women as makers of history. Although ultimately a limited vision that privileged the experience of white Loyalist women and their descendants, Curzon's efforts to claim a place for some women in Canadian history nevertheless had a profound political significance. In a period when 'history' was synonymous with politics, her contention that women, as well as men, had been nation builders – and thus makers of history – politicized women as a group and recast their work in the home as a form of national service. In this context, the heroic efforts of Laura Secord to preserve Canada as a British nation served as historical proof not only of women's moral fitness to exercise power alongside men, but also of the political necessity, both for themselves and for the nation, of their recognition as full citizens.

Acknowledgments

The financial support of a Postdoctoral Fellowship from the Social Sciences and Humanities Research Council of Canada made this research possible. Thanks also to Alison Prentice, Deborah Gorham, Marilyn Barber, and Sara Burke for commenting on various versions of the essay.

Notes

1 Lady Matilda Edgar, 'Mrs Curzon,' Women's Canadian Historical Society of Toronto (hereafter WCHST), *Transaction No. 2*, 1899, 3-4. Sarah Anne Curzon, *Laura Secord, The Heroine of 1812: A Drama and Other Poems* (Toronto: C. Blackett Robinson 1887), 11-68; 'A Ballad of 1812,' ibid., 69-83; *The Story of Laura Secord, 1813* (Welland, ON: Lundy's Lane Historical Society 1891). A second edition of this pamphlet was issued in 1898 and was still available for purchase from the Society as late as 1919; see *The Centenary Celebrations of the Battle of Lundy's Lane, July 25th, 1914* (Niagara Falls, ON: Lundy's Lane Historical Society 1919), 152.

2 Cecilia Morgan, '"Of Slender Frame and Delicate Appearance": The Placing of Laura Secord in the Narratives of Canadian Loyalist History,' *Journal of Canadian Historical Society/Revue de la societé historique du Canada* (1994): 195-212. See also 'Fidelis' (Agnes Maule Machar), 'Mary Secord [*sic*]: a Canadian Ballad of 1813,' *Rose Belford's Canadian Monthly and National Review* (June 1880): 575-7; Ruth McKenzie, *Laura Secord: The Legend and the Lady* (Toronto: McClelland and Stewart 1971).

3 Linda Colley, *Britons: Forging the Nation 1707-1837* (London: Pimlico 1992).

4 On the local history movement in Ontario, see Gerald Killam, *Preserving Ontario's Heritage: A History of the Ontario Historical Society* (Ottawa: Love Printing Service 1976). On the imperial federation movement, see Carl Berger, *The Sense of Power: Studies in the Ideas of Canadian Imperialism 1867-1914* (Toronto: University of Toronto Press 1970).

5 M. Brook Taylor, *Promoters, Patriots and Partisans: Historiography in Nineteenth-Century English Canada* (Toronto: University of Toronto Press 1989).

6 On the Toronto women's suffrage movement, and the Canadian women's suffrage movement generally, see Carol Lee Bacchi, *Liberation Deferred?: The Ideas of English-Canadian Suffragists, 1877-1918* (Toronto: University of Toronto Press 1983); Ernest Forbes, 'The Ideas of Carol Bacchi and the Suffragists of Halifax,' *Atlantis: A Women's Studies Journal* 10, 2 (spring 1985): 199-26; Catherine Cleverdon, *The Woman Suffrage Movement in Canada* (Toronto: University of Toronto Press 1950), 19-45. On the importance of making the connection between 'formal' and 'informal' politics in activist women's lives, see Sandra Holton, 'The Suffragist and the "Average Woman,"' *Women's History Review* 1, 1 (1992): 9-24; and Philippa Levine, *Feminist Lives in Victorian England: Private Roles and Public Commitments* (Oxford: Basil Blackwell 1990).

7 *Family Fortunes: Men and Women of the English Middle Class 1780-1850* (Chicago: University of Chicago Press 1987).

8 Edgar, 'Mrs Curzon,' in *Transaction No. 2*; Henry Morgan, *Canadian Men and Women of the Time: A Hand-book of Canadian Biography* (Toronto: William Briggs 1898), 235-6; 'Mrs S.A. Curzon,' in Archibald MacMurchy, *Canadian Literature* (Toronto: William Briggs 1906), 89-91; Lorraine McMullen, 'Vincent, Sarah Anne (Curzon),' in *Dictionary of Canadian Biography*, vol. 12 (Toronto: University of Toronto Press 1990), 1,075-6. It does not appear that George Vincent's manufactory was either very large or very distinguished, for he is not mentioned in the available histories of the Birmingham glass trade: 'The Birmingham Glass Trade 1740-1930,' *Transactions*, Society of Glass Technology, 1927, 374-86; D.N. Sandilands, 'The Birth of Birmingham's Glass Industry,' *Journal of the Society of Glass Technology* 5, 20 (1931): 227-31; Charles R. Hajdamuch, *British Glass 1800-1914* (Woodbridge, Suff.: Antique Collecters' Club 1991). My thanks to the reference librarians at the Royal Ontario Museum Library for bringing these materials to my attention. On Benson, see *Dictionary of National Biography From the Earliest Times to 1900*, vol. 22, supplement (Oxford: Oxford University Press 1921-22), 171-9.

9 *City of Toronto Directory*, 1858-66, Metropolitan Toronto Reference Library, Department of Special Collections.

10 J.M.S. Careless, *Toronto to 1918: An Illustrated History* (Toronto: James Lorimer 1984), 201, table 5.

11 On Sorosis and the American Association for the Advancement of Women, see Karen Blair's *The Club Woman as Feminist*. On the gender- and class-based meanings of the term 'public woman', see Mary Ryan, *Women in Public: Between Banners and Ballots, 1825-1880* (Baltimore: Johns Hopkins University Press 1990), and Glenna Matthews, *The Rise*

of Public Woman: Woman's Power and Woman's Place in the United States 1630-1970 (New York: Oxford University Press 1992).

12 *City of Toronto Directory*, 1866-76; City of Toronto, *Annual Statement of Receipts and Expenditures*, 1877 (p. 77), 1878 (p. 85), 1879 (p. 85), 1888 (p. 175), and 1894 (p. 92), City of Toronto Archives. My thanks to Elizabeth Cuthbertson, Archivist, for tracing Robert Curzon through city records on my behalf.

13 Emily Stowe, 'Report of the Dominion Women's Enfranchisement Association,' in *Women Workers of Canada: Being a Report of the Proceedings of the First Annual Meeting of the National Council of Women of Canada* (Ottawa: Thoburn & Co. 1894), 48-9, and Dr. Emily Stowe, 'The Enfranchisement of Women,' ibid., 229-33.

14 *City of Toronto Directory*, 1883-1898.

15 University of Toronto, *Register of Graduates, &c., for 1886* (Toronto: Henry Rowsell 1886), 74; *Register of the University of Toronto for 1914* (Toronto: University of Toronto Press 1914), 16. For biographical information about Edith Curzon, who worked as one of Ontario's first university-trained teachers of 'domestic science' before her early death by drowning in August 1903, see newspaper clipping: 'Miss Curzon is honored,' Toronto *Globe* (9-6-1905) Graduate Records, accession no. A73-0026, box 076, file 57, University of Toronto Archives; 'Funeral of Miss Curzon,' newspaper clipping, n.d., n.p., Augusta Stowe Gullen Collection, box 1, scrapbook, Victoria University Library, University of Toronto.

16 Anne Rochon Ford argues that the editorial support given to co-education at the University of Toronto by George Brown at the Toronto *Globe* is at least partially attributable to the aspirations of his own daughters, who were among the earliest graduates of University College: *A Path Not Strewn with Roses: One Hundred Years of Women at the University of Toronto 1884-1984* (Toronto: Governing Council, University of Toronto 1985), 11-12.

17 Sarah Anne Curzon, 'Sweet Girl Graduate: A Comedy in Four Acts,' *Grip-Sack* (Toronto), 1882, reprinted in Curzon, *Laura Secord, The Heroine of 1812: A Drama and Other Poems* (Toronto: C. Blackett Robinson 1887), 122-37, esp. 135.

18 Ibid., 126-7. See also Nancy Ramsay Thompson, 'The Controversy Over the Admission of Women to University College, University of Toronto' (M.A. thesis, University of Toronto 1974).

19 Edgar, 'Mrs Curzon,' *Transaction No. 2*, 4. On the attitude of the Ontario Woman's Christian Temperance Union towards women's suffrage, see Sharon Anne Cook, *'Through Sunshine and Shadow': The Woman's Christian Temperance Union, Evangelicalism, and Reform in Ontario, 1874-1930* (Montreal and Kingston: McGill-Queen's University Press 1995), 99-102.

20 *Canada Citizen and Temperance Herald* (6 July 1883): 5. See also 'The Opening of Toronto Women's Medical College,' ibid. (26 October 1883): 202-3; S.A. Curzon, Letter to the Editor, *Dominion Illustrated* (21 June 1890): 398; S.A.C. [Sarah Anne Curzon], 'The Women's Medical College of Toronto,' *Dominion Illustrated* (23 May 1891): 501.

21 R.D. Gidney and W.P.J. Millar, *Professional Gentlemen: The Professions in Nineteenth-Century Ontario* (Toronto: University of Toronto Press 1994).

22 For a discussion of the relationship between the politics of female individuality and female citizenship in a British context, see Jane Rendall, 'Citizenship, Culture and Civilisation: The Languages of British Suffragists, 1866-1874,' in Caroline Daley and Melanie Nolan, eds., *Suffrage and Beyond: International Feminist Perspectives* (New York: New York University Press 1994), 127-50.

23 *Dominion Illustrated* (21 June 1890): 398.

24 Ibid.; S.A. Curzon, 'A Diamond in the Rough,' *The Week* (26 April 1889): 325.

25 Curzon, *Laura Secord*, preface.

26 Joan Thirsk, 'The History Women,' in Mary O'Dowd and Sabine Wichert, eds., *Chattel, Servant or Citizen: Women's Status in Church, State and Society* (Belfast: The Institute of Irish Studies, The Queen's University of Belfast 1993), 1-11; Billie Melman, 'Gender, History and Memory: The Invention of Women's Past in the Nineteenth and Early Twentieth Centuries,' *History and Memory: Studies in Representation of the Past* 5, 1 (spring/summer 1993): 5-41; Bonnie G. Smith, 'The Contribution of Women to

Modern Historiography in Great Britain, France and the United States, 1750-1940,' *American Historical Review* 89, 3 (June 1984): 709-32; Nina Baym, *American Women Writers and the Work of History* (New Brunswick, NJ: Rutgers University Press 1995).

27 Melman, 'Gender, History and Memory,' 8.

28 Christina Crosby, *The Ends of History: Victorians and the 'Woman Question'* (London: Routledge 1991), 1-11; Johanna de Groot, '"Sex" and "Race": The Construction of Language and Image in the Nineteenth Century,' in Susan Mendus and Jane Rendall, eds., *Sex and Subordination: Interdisciplinary Studies of Gender in the Nineteenth Century* (London: Routledge 1989), 89-130.

29 Not all the women who resettled in Upper Canada from the Thirteen Colonies in 1784 were free women; see Adrienne Shadd, 'The Lord seemed to say "Go": Women and the Underground Railroad Movement,' in Peggy Bristow et al., *'We're Rooted Here and They Can't Pull Us Up': Essays in African Canadian Women's History* (Toronto: University of Toronto 1994). See also Janice Potter-MacKinnon, *While Women Only Wept: Loyalist Refugee Women in Eastern Ontario* (Montreal and Kingston: McGill-Queen's University Press 1993); Mary Beth Norton, 'Eighteenth-Century American Women in War and Peace: The Case of the Loyalists,' *William and Mary Quarterly,* 3rd series, 33 (1976): 386-409.

30 Sarah Anne Curzon, 'Betty's Choice,' *The Week* (28 June 1889): 471-2.

31 Sarah Anne Curzon, 'Centennial Poem,' read to the Niagara Historical Society on 17 September 1896, and later published in *Niagara Historical Papers* no. 2 (1897): 1-2. The poem was also published as 'Lines,' *The Week* (16 October 1896): 1,123.

32 Ibid. See also the following poems: 'The 74th Anniversary of the Battle of Lundy's Lane,' *The Week* (2 August 1889): 558; 'A Centenary Ode,' ibid. (29 July 1892): 550; 'Imperial Federation,' ibid. (9 December 1892): 30; 'The York Pioneers Log Cabin (1794-1894),' ibid. (12 October 1894): 1,093.

33 'An Appeal to Patriotic Canadians,' Louisa May to the Editor, *The Week* (10 May 1889): 362. Evidence of Curzon's precarious financial state can also be found in her correspondence with the historian, William Kirby, to whom she appealed for a loan in 1888: see S.A. Curzon to William Kirby (21 November 1888), reel 542, correspondence A-5, William Kirby Papers, Archives of Ontario.

34 Review of *Laura Secord* (1887), *The Week* (20 October 1887): 759; Archibald MacMurchy, *Handbook of Canadian Literature (English)* (Toronto: William Briggs 1906), 89-91.

35 Curzon, *Laura Secord* (1887), preface.

36 Ibid., 34.

37 Ibid., 18-22, esp. 21-2.

38 Joanna de Groot, '"Sex" and "Race": The Construction of Language and Image in the Nineteenth Century,' in Susan Mendus and Jane Rendall, eds., *Sex and Subordination: Interdisciplinary Studies of Gender in the Nineteenth Century* (London and New York: Routledge 1989), 89-130; Mariana Valverde, '"When the Mother of the Race is Free": Race, Reproduction and Sexuality in First-Wave Feminism,' in Franca Iacovetta and Mariana Valverde, eds., *Gender Conflicts: New Essays in Women's History* (Toronto: University of Toronto Press 1992), 3-26.

39 Antoinette Burton, *The Burdens of History: British Feminists, Indian Women, and Imperial Culture, 1865-1915* (Chapel Hill and London: University of North Carolina Press 1994). See also Vron Ware, *Beyond the Pale: White Women, Racism and History* (London: Verso 1992), and 'Moments of Danger: Race, Gender and Memories of Empire,' in Anne-Louise Shapiro, ed., *Feminists Revision History* (New Brunswick, NJ: Rutgers University Press 1994), 217-45.

40 Curzon, *Laura Secord* (1887), 16-18.

41 Ibid., 44.

42 Rendall, 'Citizenship, Culture and Civilisation.'

43 *The Week* (20 October 1887): 759.

44 Sarah Anne Curzon, 'Historical Societies,' Wentworth Historical Society *Journal and Transactions,* 1 (1892): 112; S.A. Curzon to William Kirby (8 October 1887), reel 542, A-5, William Kirby Collection, Archives of Ontario. See also *Canada in Memoriam, 1812-14. Her Duty in the Erection of Monuments in Memory of her Distinguished Sons and Daughters. A paper read July 25, 1890, by Mrs Curzon, of Toronto, at the Annual Commemoration of the*

Battle of Lundy's Lane, of 1814, before the L.L. Historical Society (Welland: Telegram Stream Publishing House 1891), 4.

45 Killam, *Preserving Ontario's Heritage.*

46 In 1895, two of the five officers of the Thorold and Beaverdams Historical Society were women. See Pioneer and Historical Association of the Province of Ontario, *Report of the Annual Meeting* (1895): 28.

47 John L. Field, *Janet Carnochan* (Markham, ON: Fitzhenry and Whiteside 1985).

48 Minnie J. Nisbet, ed., *Souvenir Book and Program for Military Encampment Given by the Ladies Committee of the Wentworth Historical Society* (November 1895), 3-6, and *Souvenir Book and Program for Ye Pioneers of One Hundred Years Ago. An Entertainment Given Under the Auspicies of the Women's Wentworth Historical Society* (April 1900), 3-4; National Council of Women of Canada, *Women of Canada: Their Life and Work* (Ottawa: Department of Agriculture 1900), 395.

49 Sarah Anne Curzon, *The Story of Laura Secord, 1813* (Welland, ON: Lundy's Lane Historical Society 1891). A second edition was published in 1898.

50 Curzon, 'Historical Societies,' 106.

51 Ibid.

52 In Toronto, Mary Agnes FitzGibbon was as well known for her illustrious family heritage as she was for her published writings and activism on behalf of female immigration. Her paternal grandfather was Col. James FitzGibbon, whose name Sarah Curzon had so thoroughly linked with that of Laura Secord as the hero of Beaver Dams. Her maternal grandmother was Susanna Moodie, one of the famous Strickland clan of writers whose number also included Agnes Strickland, the famous 'biographer of the queens of England.'

53 Women's Canadian Historical Society of Toronto Records, MU 7840, series B-2: General Minutes, book 1 (19 November 1895), F1180, Archives of Ontario.

54 Sarah Anne Curzon, 'Report of the Dominion Women's Enfranchisement Association,' in National Council of Women of Canada, *Women Workers of Canada* (1895), 65-7. See also Sarah Anne Curzon, 'Development of National Literature in Canada,' ibid., 235-41.

55 For a discussion of the various definitions of female citizenship within the English-speaking women's movement in Canada during the 1890s, see Beverly Boutilier, 'Gender, Organized Women and the Politics of Institution Building: Founding the Victorian Order of Nurses for Canada, 1893-1900' (Ph.D. diss., Carleton University 1994), chapter 2.

4
Ontario Women's Institutes and the Work of Local History

Linda M. Ambrose

Although the Women's Institutes of Ontario are best known as promoters of domestic science education,[1] these rural women's groups are also widely recognized as keepers of local history. Gerald Killan notes in his history of the Ontario Historical Society that the Women's Institutes 'often chose to include history within their terms of reference and became in effect, the rural counterparts of the urban women's historical societies.'[2] For more than seventy years, women across the province have been busy compiling their volumes of local history. Commonly known as 'Tweedsmuir History Books,' their works range in size and quality from a few scrapbooks housed in members' private homes, to large leather-bound volumes stored in museums or public libraries, to published works financed with the support of municipal governments and local historical societies. Writing about the practice of local history as a form of popular culture in Ontario, Royce MacGillivray describes the historical offerings of the Women's Institutes as 'impressive and bulky works, half written history and half scrapbooks,' and comments that they 'are mines of information on the everyday aspects of rural life.'[3] Because the books were authored solely by members of the Women's Institutes, they provide an opportunity to explore the work of women who practised history outside of academic circles and who wrote for a very specific audience – the members of their own communities.

For one hundred years, the Women's Institutes of Ontario have been a vital organization in rural communities and small towns throughout Ontario. Recent research shows that more than 2,000 of these groups have existed since the founding of the first local branch in Stoney Creek in 1897.[4] At the height of their popularity in the 1950s, the Women's Institutes in Ontario could boast a membership of almost 50,000 and more than 1,500 active branches across the province.[5] Most of those groups compiled books of local history. Although it is impossible to make an accurate count, by 1964 one source had estimated that 'well over 1,100'

Tweedsmuir History Books existed, and that 1,209 women were currently involved in compiling those local history books.[6]

The large quantity of these books is a clear testament to their popularity. Thousands of women devoted countless hours to the exercise of compiling them, and the books enjoyed large audiences as community members eagerly read the compiled tales of their own local histories. Although Tweedsmuir History Books are highly valued at the local level, there is an ongoing debate among professional historians about their relative merit as works of history. This paper illustrates that women who practised history as a hobby attached various meanings to their work throughout the century. Striving to validate their work, WI historians sought the endorsement of public figures and the adjudication of academic historians. While they welcomed the recognition that came through these contacts, Women's Institutes historians were not willing to have outsiders dictate the content they should include nor the approach they should take. They were determined to maintain control over their history, despite the criticisms levelled by professional historians.

Origins of the Tweedsmuir History Books

The Tweedsmuir History Books were named in 1940 to honour the memory of a former Governor General of Canada, John Buchan, who had died earlier that year in Montreal. His wife, Lady Susan Tweedsmuir, was an active member of the Women's Institutes in Great Britain, and during their time in Canada from 1936 to 1940, she served as honorary president of the Women's Institutes of Canada. Prior to their arrival in Canada, she had served as president of a local institute at Elsfield, and for many years she was president of the Oxfordshire Federation.[7] By the mid-1930s, the British Institutes were actively compiling local histories – what they called 'village histories' – and some sources suggest that the idea of compiling local histories in Ontario came from Lady Tweedsmuir herself. That notion is based on records from the 1940s, including correspondence between Susan Tweedsmuir and the Federated Women's Institutes of Ontario (FWIO) in which the official name of Ontario's local WI histories was settled and Lady Tweedsmuir agreed to sponsor a competition to award prizes to the best-kept history books. However, when the first 'Tweedsmuir Competition' was held in 1947, the work of compiling history by local Ontario Institutes had already been under way for twenty years, long before the name 'Tweedsmuir' was associated with it.

The first mention of the FWIO's historical research appeared in the 1926 *Annual Report* of the Institutes Branch of the Ontario Department of Agriculture. According to that account, this task had been added to the agenda of the provincial organization a year before. 'Historical Research' was only one of several standing committees under FWIO sponsorship. The full roster of committees, which included Health and Child Welfare, Agriculture, Immigration, Relief, Community Activities, and Legislation, reflected the wide range of interests that engaged the Women's Institutes. The authors of the report contended that the history committee had

> already undertaken work of real interest and national value ... In some counties, they have already begun to compile the history of the whole county and in many Institutes a beginning has been made on local history, including individual farms, industries, public buildings, etc. A record is being made of the first settlers, their methods of living and their accomplishments, the history of the first schools and the first church in the district is being recorded.[8]

It is significant to note that the women who did this history work were referred to as 'curators' not 'historians.' The task that women in the branch organizations took up when they agreed to collect materials of historical interest was to compile and organize information and to act as caretakers and guardians of the local heritage. The title 'curator' evokes images of an antiquarian, one who indiscriminately strives to collect as much material as she can possibly find. Yet to suggest that the members of the Women's Institutes were driven by a collector's instinct is not to say that they amassed their information without a sense of purpose.

Evidently, the history that the women were striving to record was in keeping with the historiographic trends of the period, which promoted the notion of progress.[9] The curators were encouraged to record the stories of their communities' first settlers and, in so doing, to illustrate the hardships that had been overcome and the accomplishments that made those early citizens successful and prosperous. It was a history characterized by a preoccupation with 'the most powerful myth in Ontario – the myth of the pioneers.'[10] The FWIO committee responsible for overseeing this work suggested to members that it was worthwhile 'that a little more time be given to the study of local history,' and they rationalized that approach by emphasizing that the curators would 'gain a greater insight into the lives and thoughts of our ancestors in this country.'[11]

These books were obviously intended to go beyond the exercise of collating farm techniques or plotting out the maps of early settlement patterns. The early curators were hoping to uncover the very 'thoughts' of their forebears. There was consensus around the notion that those thoughts and feelings were undoubtedly ones of local pride of place. After all, as the first report explained, compilation of the local history books was 'proceeding on the belief that every community has a history which should be preserved.'[12]

Why did the preservation of local history seem so urgent to FWIO members? There are several explanations. The year 1927 would mark the sixtieth anniversary of Confederation, and with feelings of nationalism running high, Women's Institute members were eager to contribute to the celebrations. That same year was also an important milestone for the WI movement itself, for it marked the thirtieth anniversary of the famous founding meeting of the Women's Institutes in Stoney Creek in February 1897.[13] Commemorating significant historic anniversaries continued to preoccupy WI members. Early in 1934, for example, the members were reminded that there was plenty to celebrate since it was the year of 'the fourth hundredth [*sic*] anniversary of the discovery of Canada, and in Ontario the one hundred and fiftieth anniversary of the coming of the Loyalists to this province, and the one hundredth of Toronto's cityhood.'[14]

There was also a certain urgency about doing local community history at this time: the rural population of Ontario was steadily declining and had been for several decades. By 1931, only 39 per cent of Ontario's population was still living in rural areas, a sharp decrease from 1901 when rural residents could still pride themselves on being the majority, with 57 per cent of the population.[15] Given this trend, concerns about rural depopulation were close to the surface, and the psychological need to preserve and record the rural past was understandably strong. Members of the WI were convinced that there was a great deal of work to be done in collecting the rural past and, particularly, that it was important to do so in a systematic way.

The First Historical Research Convenor

To provide a primer on how to do local history research, the first convenor of the FWIO Committee on Historical Research regularly wrote a column in the Women's Institutes' own periodical, *Home and Country*. 'Someone is always asking How shall we begin?' Miss E. Appelbe wrote in 1934. 'That depends on how your county records have been kept, and whether there has already been anything of historic value published.' Appelbe provided concrete advice based on her own experience researching Halton County settlers, and sought to guide novice researchers through a variety of local and provincial government records and archives.[16] She offered a systematic plan for approaching the research, and with her encouragement, dozens of other women followed in her footsteps. In a relatively short period, the Women's Institutes could boast of real success in their attempts to collect history, boldly estimating in 1934 that 'the knowledge of local and Provincial history has increased by 50% since the committee has been carrying on this work through the Institutes over less than [a] ten year period.'[17]

To popularize the work of local history among the WI membership, the provincial convenor urged them to think of it as a hobby. 'People are talking of the necessity of learning how to use our leisure,' Miss Appelbe noted. 'Let me recommend to you this subject of Historical Research and Current Events. You may make of it either a quiet indoor occupation or an active outdoor recreation. You may pore over records, maps, family or state documents, or you may search out natural beauty spots or places of historic interest and photograph them or seek out almost forgotten tales of by-gone industries, stories of schools, churches, roadmaking, and water traffic, from the oldest inhabitants.'[18]

Women's Institutes researchers employed a wide variety of methods to collect their information, including the use of oral history – 'house to house visitation' as Appelbe called it.[19] In communities where written reminiscences were scarce, members were taught to respect the oral tradition of local pioneer stories and urged to incorporate them into the written record. For example, in 1935 the Parry Sound Women's Institute was applauded 'in its choice of a [branch history] curator who realizes that there is no time to be lost in securing firsthand information from those pioneers who are still living.'[20] Reporting on the activities of various branches across Ontario, *Home and Country* revealed that one elderly member, who was particularly keen about history, had organized a guided tour of her historic home for members of the community.[21]

Appelbe urged local curators to be vigilant in their ongoing research. 'Historical Research does not mean having just one meeting in the year devoted to that subject,' she reminded them. 'It means keeping constantly on the alert for any historical news that may be heard or read, digging up other bits that may form strong links in the chain of facts, and recording, in some permanent form, the current events of your township, town or county.'[22] Her column became a forum for exchanging information on particularly interesting historical cases and for sharing the delightful intrigue of solving the puzzles and mysteries that inevitably arise during historical research. 'Somewhere in the northern section of Victoria and Ontario counties and probably on through Simcoe County to Orillia there appears to have been a stage road, and there was a little book written about it called Nancy McFay of the Monk Road. Nancy kept a tavern and appears to have been quite a character. (Has anyone ever heard of it?),' Appelbe wondered. This female innkeeper sparked the curator's curiosity, as did other stories of outstanding women.

However, WI historians did not limit themselves to the exploits of unusual or outstanding women; the typical or 'average' woman was also of great interest. In 1935, for example, the Fisherville WI in Haldimand County reported that one of their meetings was a 'grandmothers' programme' where they 'had each grandmother describe her wedding garments' so that information about changing bridal fashions could be included in the record of the community's social history. The question of what to include in a history book went beyond the accepted canon of historical importance established by academic historians, most of whom were more interested in the 'official' history of politics, economics, and industry – and the local dignitaries who brought that history to life. Members of the Women's Institutes had different ideas about what was historically significant. For them, recording 'everyday life' for posterity was of paramount importance. As a result, the compilers of WI history books were equally anxious to document their current experiences for future generations.[23] Appelbe counselled:

> If some one in each branch, or even two or three in each district, would write the story of an ordinary day's doings on the farm, or a day of village life, and another of a threshing day, or somebody's wedding, a fall fair or a day in the kitchen, and describe in connection with these the food that was prepared and served, the clothing worn, and various other details, we would have a wonderful picture of every day life in rural Ontario in 1933.[24]

The result of this advice was an eclectic mixture of family folklore, extended community genealogies, pioneer profiles, and histories of local institutions, providing a wealth of information for students of social and women's history.

To preserve and present that history, the Women's Institutes did not limit their involvement to creating written records. In several counties across the province, WI branches made their research findings even more accessible to the public by supporting the establishment of local museums. Two typical examples from the 1930s serve to illustrate the energy the Institutes put into historical preservation. A 1935 report from the Hamilton area celebrated the establishment of a museum at Cayuga. The local Institutes had successfully lobbied for financial assistance from Haldimand County as well as the use of a room in the municipal offices.[25] A similar report came from Simcoe County the same year, where the local Women's Institutes had begun a collection of artefacts that they housed in the Barrie Library. They were happy to report that their growing collection had recently been transferred to 'a fire-proof building donated by their county officials.'[26]

Members took up the work of history enthusiastically and, during the height of the Depression, Appelbe boasted that 'there is no depression in the work of Historical Research. If there is anyone out of a job it is from lack of interest and not from scarcity of work. History is always in the making.'[27] Of course, it was not paid work, and real devotion to the task meant that women had to have the personal resources – time and money – to travel for research. As provincial convenor, Appelbe evidently had both. In addition to research trips, she frequently observed and participated in the activities of other organizations that shared her love of history. In the winter of 1933, she travelled from Georgetown to Toronto to attend an exhibition sponsored by the 'Women's Historical Society of Toronto' at which 'all sorts of family treasures, carefully guarded, were displayed and every afternoon and evening it was crowded with visitors.' Excited by what she had seen, Appelbe suggested that local branches of the Women's Institutes should mimic the idea: 'similar exhibition[s] might prove very profitable in the smaller cities and in the towns.'[28] In the same season, the provincial convenor reported that she had also attended the forty-seventh annual meeting of the American Historical Association 'held in Canada for the first time, by invitation of the University of Toronto during Christmas week, 1932.'[29]

In 1936, the international WI organization, the Associated Country Women of the World, held its second triennial convention in Washington, DC. At that event, Appelbe introduced delegates from around the world to the history work done by Ontario Institutes, proudly noting that they 'were informed that Ontario was well in the lead in its work in historical research.' Despite the accolades, there was still a lot of work to be done. 'Are we, as it were, sitting with a self satisfied air, secure in the knowledge that we have accomplished great things,' she wondered, 'or are we accepting it as a challenge to carry on with undiminished effort until every county of our province can truthfully say, Oh yes, we have the early history of our settlement gathered in and we are keeping track of current events as the years go by?'[30]

The War Years

Appelbe continued in her role as provincial convenor until Mrs. Florence Reesor of Scarboro Junction took on the job in 1939. Reesor acknowledged her predecessor's long service record and promised that she would continue the work along the same lines. She stressed that WI members should take the initiative to compile reference materials and to foster research contacts. Reesor observed:

> Your Institute convenor of Historical Research is in reality a community archivist. In her possession should be a copy of every address relating to this topic and a record of all current events of historical importance. These should be carefully preserved and passed on to each succeeding convenor. Soon a collection of valuable material will be available to form the nucleus of an interesting and authentic history of your township or county.[31]

Reesor clearly intended to continue the tradition of systematically compiling reference materials, but she also introduced important new initiatives to further enhance the reputation of Women's Institutes historians.

It was Florence Reesor who came up with the idea to seek Lady Tweedsmuir's endorsement for the history books. 'When I first thought of this idea, I was afraid to venture any further with it,' she confided to the secretary of the FWIO board, Mrs. W.B. Leatherdale. '[I was] thinking it might be regarded as a somewhat far-fetched and vague plan, and so am rather amazed to see [it] in actual print.'[32] The convenor's proposal was in fact a straightforward request to Lady Susan Tweedsmuir well in keeping with her expressed interest in the compilation of local histories in Canada and Britain. The British Women's Institutes were engaged in the same kind of historical research, and, during her husband's tenure as Governor General in the later 1930s, Lady Tweedsmuir had suggested that WI members in Ontario make a concerted, province-wide effort to expand their projects. Reesor therefore asked the FWIO secretary to correspond with Lady Tweedsmuir and seek her formal endorsement for the planned series of community histories.

In April 1940, the request went out. The FWIO secretary explained that the 'Village Books would be a simple, effective and worth-while project, with the objective of collecting, preserving and retaining in the community, the histories of the pioneers.' She asked Lady Tweedsmuir to 'entertain the idea' that local histories 'be known as the Tweedsmuir Books or some name relating to the Tweedsmuir tradition.' The object, she explained, was to pay 'tribute to the memory of Lord Tweedsmuir's life and interest in the Women's Institute and to the inspiration which your presence here had provided us.'[33] Lady Tweedsmuir's answer arrived promptly, indicating that she was fully in support of the idea. 'Thank you very much for your very nice letter,' she wrote. 'Yes, indeed my husband was always interested in Women's Institutes and thought so highly of the work you are all doing. I think it would be very nice if you call the books you are compiling Tweedsmuir Village Histories.'[34]

It is significant that the Institutes sought this formal link with the Tweedsmuir name as a form of validation for the historical work they were performing. Although the women themselves valued their historical research and the resources they were compiling, they were still self-conscious about it. Reesor wondered if seeking recognition was not a rather 'far-fetched' idea, but, at the same time, she recognized that it was important for the Institutes to raise the profile of what their members were doing. Tweedsmuir had been a popular figure, and his recent death was a matter of much public attention. Women's Institutes members hoped that the use of his name would enhance the reputation of their books, raising them from being mere 'scrapbooks' to works deemed to be 'of outstanding worth,' even meriting the name of Tweedsmuir.[35]

Although the popularity of documenting local history grew within the WI throughout the 1930s and 1940s, interest levels had also fluctuated.

To promote the work, the provincial headquarters offered helpful instruction for WI members in a pamphlet produced by the provincial convenor and circulated by the WI's 'Loan Library.' Through the library's mailing service, members could learn about a variety of topics; the service was most commonly used by women who were responsible for preparing monthly programs for their local branch meetings.[36] In 1937, for example, a total of 4,144 members used materials from the library, with home economics and education topics being the most popular at 727 and 693 requests, respectively. That same year, 75 members asked for help with their historical research. The following year, 106 local history curators turned to the library for instruction.[37] However, in 1940 – the year Reesor's request was forwarded to Lady Tweedsmuir – only 66 women used the library for help with their histories. Evidently the war was responsible for that declining interest: WI members were preoccupied with their volunteer work for the war effort.

WI members made enormous contributions to the war effort both in fundraising and in the physical work of knitting, canning, and farm labour. Although the record of the provincial organization (FWIO) alone was impressive, the bulk of the work was performed at the local level,[38] and women had no spare time to devote to the 'hobby' of history. In 1943, the new provincial history convenor, Mrs. Gordon Maynard, expressed her concern about this trend. 'I regret to say that since the war commenced there has been a definite lag in the interest in Historical Research in our Institutes. Women have said to me We haven't time for Historical Research now. The needs of the present are all-engrossing. It is true that the winning of the war is our first objective, but it is also true that to understand the present we must know the past.'[39]

Maynard was concerned that in their zeal to contribute to the war effort, women might be guilty not only of neglecting their historical research, but of actively contributing to the destruction of valuable archival materials in the name of patriotic duty. 'Every day old documents, letters, newspapers and photographs are being destroyed in the interest of salvage and to accommodate more people in the home due to the housing shortage,' she warned. With a growing sense of urgency she pleaded with WI members to think carefully about the value they placed on those old documents. 'The only method we have of rescuing these priceless treasures from the salvage piles and bonfires,' Maynard continued, 'is to arouse the interest of all inhabitants of our communities in the local history; so that they will look twice at any article before discarding it.'[40] Her priority was to preserve materials that should be stored in an archival facility, whether private or public. Again, the Institutes members' interest in history went beyond recording the written record to protecting and safeguarding the physical objects and material culture that revealed that history.

Maynard continued to urge members to participate more fully in recording their local histories despite the fact that the war had not yet ended. She justified historical research to WI members as 'a national duty for us to perform.'[41] By invoking the rhetoric of patriotism, she hoped that busy WI women would see the work in a different light. Maynard recognized that there were competing demands on women's time during the hectic war years, and so she emphasized that this was not merely a hobby for women of leisure, but a form of service to the country. Although Maynard attempted to redefine the WI's historical work as a 'national duty,' she did not equate 'history' itself with politics. On the contrary, the emphasis remained squarely on local history and, even more specifically, on the social history of everyday experiences.

As early as 1944, Maynard was thinking beyond the immediate demands of the war to the valuable role that history work could play in the postwar period. A concern about integrating 'new Canadians' in the postwar years helped to shape her thinking about the importance of the WI's historical research. She reminded members that their history books had an important role to play in helping newly arrived immigrants learn about the traditions of Ontario's past. She represented the Tweedsmuir History Books as one tool that could help 'Canadianize' these newest citizens. Maynard was convinced that the Women's Institutes' history books would inspire the new arrivals, 'awakening in them the love of Home and Country, our history, our culture and our pursuits.'[42] According to the WI strategy then, the best means of instilling loyalty into the hearts and minds of new Canadians was through a greater appreciation of history. With an undeniable emphasis on pride of place, the women argued that it was to be local history, not national political history, that would best achieve that goal.

The Postwar Years

The lag in historical work within the WI was short-lived and, in the immediate postwar years, interest in research surged again. Requests to the Loan Library increased dramatically, with more than a five-fold increase from the 1943 numbers. In 1946, 292 members requested help with their history books, while one year later 305 requests came in; in 1948, there were 428.[43] With the war over, women could once again turn to history as the kind of leisure activity that Appelbe had originally envisioned ten years earlier.

There were also new chapters to be written for almost every community in Ontario, as the records of local military personnel were added to the Tweedsmuir History Books. Rural participation in the First World War was already included in most of the Institutes' local history books, and additions were now necessary. Photographs and biographies of the young soldiers, sailors, and airmen predominated, and the young women who served overseas were not overlooked. Local curators also included accounts of their organizations' own volunteer efforts. Receipts for the branch donations to the Red Cross, stories of knitting competitions, and letters from grateful service personnel who had received their 'comfort boxes' containing socks, cigarettes, and other treats were all added to the Tweedsmuir books.

The growth of the organization itself likewise accounts for the increased interest in the work of doing local history. After the war, the Ontario Women's Institutes movement entered the period of its highest popularity ever. By 1953, 1,503 local branches were meeting, and the membership had risen to 47,000 women. Not surprisingly then, there was a corresponding expansion in historical research activities as new branches began their own Tweedsmuir books.

This increased attention to history was due in part to the fact that the Women's Institutes of Ontario celebrated their own fiftieth anniversary in 1947. Plans for the gala event began early, and when the day of celebration arrived in June 1947, 12,000 women crowded on to the campus of the Ontario Agricultural College at Guelph. They came from all across the province to mark the special occasion. The highlight of the day's festivities was the presentation of a historical pageant that depicted the roots and activities of the WI movement. The pageant conveyed a romanticized version of its history, emphasizing in particular the role of Adelaide Hoodless, whom the playwright elevated to the status of saint. The idealization of homemaking and family life depicted through Hoodless's emphasis on domestic science found a very receptive audience among the postwar homemakers of the WI, and the pageant had a profound impact on the WI members in attendance. For some, it motivated them to seek out historical parallels in their own communities. When the members returned home, they were determined to honour and elevate the women who had founded their local branches, thus creating a local version of the founders' story that emphasized the greatness of the Institutes' first leaders.

A romanticized version of the past was in keeping with the WI women's sense of nostalgia about a world that was fast disappearing within their local communities. Members were acutely aware that they were living in the midst of rapid social change and, to preserve the memory of their own small communities, felt compelled to record those changes. When Lady Susan Tweedsmuir agreed to allow her husband's name to be associated with the books, she wrote about why she thought they were so important, highlighting the process of change that she observed. Remarks from her correspondence with the FWIO in 1940 were widely circulated and adopted as the standard foreword that introduced each local book.

She wrote, 'I am so glad to hear that the Women's Institutes of Ontario are going to compile village history books. Events move very fast nowadays; houses are pulled down, new roads are made, and the aspect of the countryside changes completely sometimes in a short time.' In light of that rapid rate of change, she continued,

> it is a most useful and satisfying task for Women's Institute members to see that nothing valuable is lost or forgotten and women should be on the alert always to guard the traditions of their homes, and to see that water colour sketches and prints, poems and prose legends should find their way into these books. The oldest people in the village will tell fascinating stories of what they remember, which the younger members can write down, thus making a bridge between them and events which happened before they were born. After all, it is the history of humanity which is continually interesting to us, and your village histories will be the basis of accurate facts much valued by historians of the future. I am proud to think that you have called them The Tweedsmuir Village Histories.[44]

As a further indicator of the importance she attached to the documentation of community histories, Susan Tweedsmuir initiated a process for recognizing those women who excelled in their research efforts. The national Tweedsmuir Cup competition was first administered as part of the ongoing festivities throughout the WI's fiftieth anniversary year. There were three silver cups to be awarded, one for the best handicraft, one as a prize for an essay competition, and one for the best Tweedsmuir history. In the 1947 provincial competition for history books, the Berwick WI in York County won first prize. Second place was awarded to a branch named Carry-On WI in Wellington County, and honourable mention was given to Classic WI in Perth County.[45] The winner of this competition went forward to compete at the national level for the silver cup provided by Lady Tweedsmuir. In that first year, the prize for the best Tweedsmuir History Book in Canada went to the Hampton Women's Institute from New Brunswick: 'work of Mrs. Guy Humphrey and her sister.' The national competition was to be held every second year, with the results announced at the biennial meeting of the Federated Women's Institutes of Canada. As the competitions became more firmly established, the rules continued to develop. It was decided that the individual curator of the book would be 'custodian' of the cup until the next competition was held, and the name of her Women's Institute branch would be engraved upon it. Once a branch had won the prize, they became ineligible to enter future competitions.[46]

Worthy recipients were judged according to strict criteria, and the first guidelines for the Tweedsmuir History Books competition were published in the fall of 1945. Maynard outlined the standard layout for the preliminary pages of the books, which were to include Susan Tweedsmuir's foreword, a photograph of Lord and Lady Tweedsmuir, and one of Adelaide Hoodless. A suggested table of contents was laid out, and in the first part of the book members were instructed to include one section each on: 'History of Local Women's Institutes; Geography and Topography; Natural Resources; Indians; Pioneer Settlements; Institutions including Churches, Schools, Libraries, Industries; Newspapers and Fraternal Organizations; and the History of Achievement of the local Women's Institutes in marking historical spots by Cairns, etc.' The second part of the book was to be devoted to current events. For example Maynard wrote, compilers should include war service records and the local peace celebrations to mark the return of local service personnel. She justified why a 'history' book should also include what some deemed to be recent news saying, 'the desire to perpetuate the memory of noble sacrifices and heroic deeds is both natural and useful. [That] the future generation may know the spirit of the generations who served their country so nobly in World Wars Nos. 1 and 2 it is our duty to perpetuate these things.'[47]

The Tweedsmuir History Books' emphasis on local heroism and noble sacrifices was overt and unapologetic. The women were instructed that their mandate was to build local pride and foster a sense of admiration for community builders. As Maynard told them, 'the purpose of the Tweedsmuir Village Histories is to stimulate and maintain interest in local history and to build up a permanent historical record of the pioneer days and subsequent progress of our country.'[48] Such a bold declaration of intent is rare among historians – either amateur or professional. At the same time, Maynard urged local curators to maintain their credibility through a commitment to careful research. 'All data recorded should be absolutely authentic,' she reiterated. She was convinced that the Tweedsmuir books would 'form a permanent record and will be regarded as authoritative historical documents.'[49] In her mind, the exercise of glorifying local heroes in a celebration of progress was not incompatible with her call to write 'absolutely authentic' history and to create 'authoritative historical documents.' Others were not so sure. Striking a balance between accolades and accuracy would be no easy task.

Professional Connection

As the reputation of the Tweedsmuir histories grew and the competitions continued, professional historians were drawn into the circle. In the late 1940s, two historians from Toronto, George Glazebrook and George Spragge, were closely associated with the work of the Women's Institutes histories, acting as judges for the history book competitions. G.P. de T. Glazebrook, professor of history at the University of Toronto, judged the submissions for the first Tweedsmuir Cup competition in 1947. At the time of the second competition two years later, Professor Glazebrook's career path had taken him out of the classroom and into the Department of External Affairs, where he spent the next fourteen years.[50] There are some indications that he would not miss the task of adjudication. One wonders whether he was completely comfortable with the work of the WI histories; his experience with the 1947 competition led to the creation of a committee 'named to draft rules for the next competition.'[51] In one of his later publications, Glazebrook remarked that 'there are a great many local histories – of townships, counties, towns, cities and other areas – but few of them have more than marginal value.'[52] He did not elaborate on that judgment, but in the list of resources that he considered valuable for studying local history, he made no mention of the Women's Institutes' Tweedsmuir books. In another context he advised aspiring writers, 'work regular hours and don't get emotional.'[53] The emotion attached to chronicling local heroes and celebrating community life may have lowered the value of the Tweedsmuir histories in his eyes.

Glazebrook shared his disdain for most works of local history with many other academic historians. In 1952, the Canadian Historical Association (CHA) held a symposium on local history at its annual meeting. Discussing strategies for forging links between the CHA and local history societies, Hilda Neatby of the University of Saskatchewan made some harsh judgements in pointing out the problems inherent in that field. 'As all historians know,' she began,

> the pursuit of history is not without its dangers. It may, by overemphasis on the trivial, the picturesque, and the pseudo-dramatic, produce the painful type of pedant who has so often been caricatured. Or, by way of reaction it may go to the other extreme and lead to endless and aimless counting and listing, sociological pedantry at its worst. Local history also nourishes the reminiscer. The editors ... know how much tact is required to maintain friendly relations with correspondents who have a natural desire to tell their stories and have them printed, but who lack discrimination in the selection of material and experience in the verification of facts.[54]

Neatby went on to assert that while the enthusiasm of local historians was admirable, they were mostly 'people with little academic knowledge of history.' What they needed, she argued, was to develop the skills of critical analysis. The exercise of criticism was hardly in keeping with the declared purposes of the FWIO's Historical Research Committee. It was difficult, therefore, for academics like Glazebrook or Neatby to unconditionally endorse the Tweedsmuir histories.

A definite division existed between the professional and the amateur historian, and this had been openly discussed in the pages of the *Canadian Historical Review* (*CHR*) several years earlier. In 1938, when Lady Tweedsmuir received an honorary degree from the University of Toronto, her remarks about the differences between the two kinds of historians were reprinted in the *CHR*. Noting the irony in the fact that while she was considered an 'amateur,' she was being honoured by academics, she spoke in defence of the work of local historians. 'After all even amateurs have their uses. They cannot bring the search-light of a trained mind and the battery of skilled application to their subject,' she admitted, yet their work 'sometimes help[s] to reveal something ... of the past which has been left out and forgotten in the march of time.' While amateurs might not possess strong analytical skills, she argued that they should be recognized for the important roles they had played in preserving local historical records. Fully aware of the differences between the two kinds of historians, Susan Tweedsmuir concluded her remarks by saying that she wanted to 'salute' the professional historians and make 'a plea for the amateur.' With thanks to the University of Toronto for giving her the degree, she remarked that 'I and my fellow amateurs will go on our way happy in this generous acknowledgement of our services.'[55]

But the professional historians were never unanimous in their ideas about the amateurs. At the same symposium in which Neatby raised serious concerns about the weaknesses of local historians and cautioned the CHA about getting too closely involved with their work, her colleague Lewis H. Thomas, of the Saskatchewan Provincial Archives, came to their defence. As he urged the CHA:

> Let us not consider local history solely from this highly important but austere point of view. What other branch of historical study gives us more vivid impressions of the hopes, the trials, the prejudices, the pleasures, the frustrations and the achievements of people than does the history of a community if it is written with sympathy, perceptions and literary grace? What, except for biography, brings us closer to human beings as they really are than local history?[56]

Thomas was not alone in his call for a sympathetic reconsideration of the value of local history. The man who had replaced Glazebrook as the judge for the Tweedsmuir History Book competitions was in full agreement with Thomas's position.

George Warburton Spragge, who served as the Archivist of Ontario from 1946 to 1963, agreed to act as the judge for the second Tweedsmuir Cup competition in 1949. Spragge's commitment to local history was demonstrated through his important contributions to the Ontario Historical

Society. He served as its secretary-treasurer from 1948 to 1952, and according to the society's official history, Spragge 'did a great deal to strengthen the society's image in academic circles.'[57] He had the rare ability to act as a liaison between the academics and the amateurs. Spragge was fully convinced of the value of local history and defended it at the CHA's 1952 symposium, arguing that the CHA should look to the American Association for State and Local History for a model of how to encourage local history societies in their preservation efforts and publication work.[58]

When he turned his attention to the Tweedsmuir History Books, Spragge did not revisit the old debates about celebration and subjectivity, but concentrated instead on urging WI curators to raise their standards by paying careful attention to their citation techniques. His four specific pieces of advice were:

1. That it would add very much to the value of these histories were the sources of information given, wherever possible.
2. The source and date of each newspaper clipping should be given.
3. Pictures should have titles giving the place, date and as far as possible, the names.
4. That it would be advantageous to have the books made up in the order given in the instructions.[59]

Spragge's ability to combine demanding professional standards with a 'profound empathy with those for whom history is an avocation'[60] meant that he could gently nudge the WI historians towards writing better history. In his first year as judge, the two best submissions from Ontario were the St. George WI Tweedsmuir History from Brant County and the Russell Village WI Tweedsmuir History from Russell County. Spragge awarded the national cup that year to the Ascot WI Tweedsmuir History from Quebec.[61]

The silver cups of the national competition were coveted prizes, and winning one quickly came to be recognized as a very prestigious honour in Institute circles. But internal awards were only one part of the growing recognition accorded to Women's Institutes historians and their books. As their reputation for keeping local history grew, the Women's Institutes were honoured by other historical organizations, and George Spragge was instrumental in supporting that recognition. At the annual meeting of the FWIO board in November 1949, board members were pleased to learn that their work had earned an Award of Merit from the American Association for State and Local History, the organization that Spragge held up to the CHA as a model. The award, an engraved certificate, was presented to Mrs. E.E. Morden, the president of the Federated Women's Institutes of Canada.[62] Thirteen years later, similar recognition came from the Canadian Historical Association, when the CHA's 1962 annual meeting announced that the Women's Institutes were being presented with an Award of Merit for their contribution to local history.

Although the prizes and awards were a welcome form of recognition for some local curators, they left others feeling uneasy. The idea that their work was being assessed by outside adjudicators caused some controversy. The WI women wanted to be very clear about the fact that they themselves were not professional historians, nor did they aspire to be judged by the standards of academic history. In November 1956, the issue came to the floor of the provincial board meeting at the Royal York Hotel in Toronto. Just as professional historians had discussed the amateurs at their CHA symposium, now it was the academics who came under the scrutiny of the Women's Institutes. The feelings of distrust, it would appear, were mutual. After some discussion, a resolution was passed about the Tweedsmuir competitions, stating:

> That the judges [should] realize that these Books are not being compiled by Historians, history teachers, etc., but by women of ordinary calibre and by family members of the communities concerned, with the object of preserving the history of said community, and with human interest stories, to show the historical growth, advancement and achievement of said community, and therefore be judged in that light. The content of the books should not be compared to texts of history books.[63]

Evidently some women thought that having the books assessed by outside authorities meant that the work of history was becoming too competitive, and that the rigour associated with academic works or reference books was not appropriate for WI local histories. Although they enjoyed the work of preserving their local community history, not all the members welcomed the intrusive introduction of standards that dictated how their history should be written.

It was a familiar dilemma. The tension centred on whether the Tweedsmuir histories should concentrate on collecting anecdotal information that reflected the personality of the curator as she practised her hobby, or whether they should attempt to compile a definitive and official historical record. Not every WI historian aspired to fulfil the role of county archivist or to be regarded as an expert reference for the school curriculum. No one in WI had overtly stated that academic standards of excellence were incompatible with local works of history, but in the minds of some Tweedsmuir curators, too much emphasis on standards set by professional historians would diminish the leisure function of doing history. In other words, the professionals were taking the enjoyment out of history by taking control over its form and even its content. Above all, the WI historians who complained were determined that the process of doing history should remain accessible to their own community members and not be judged by outsiders according to some rigid set of criteria.

The 1960s and Beyond

The WI members were not unanimous in their attitudes to the professional historians. Some women welcomed the instruction offered by academic historians and concurred with the judges on the need for standardization and attention to research excellence. Mrs. R.G. Walker from St. George, Ontario, was among those women. When she took on the job of curator of the Provincial Tweedsmuir History Books in 1957, she was convinced that there was much room for improvement among the compilers of WI local histories. Walker was part of a community that was actively involved in local history work. Her home in Brant County was very close to the birthplace of Adelaide Hoodless, and the two nearest Women's Institute branches, St. George WI and Blue Lake and Auburn WI, had impressive records of preserving and promoting the importance of the movement's founder. In 1937, a memorial cairn honouring Hoodless was erected at the intersection of the two highways just outside the village of St. George, and the Ontario Department of Highways was persuaded to set aside a two-acre park where a flag was erected to mark the site. The St. George Tweedsmuir History Book was a serious contender in provincial competitions, and Walker was partly responsible for the high calibre of that book.

Mrs. R.C. Walker (second from right) urged women to balance their creativity with careful citation techniques when compiling their Tweedsmuir History Books

It came as no surprise, then, that Walker would be very keen to raise the standards held by local WI history curators. One of her main contributions was the publication in 1962 of a thirty-nine-page handbook entitled *Manual for Compiling Tweedsmuir Histories*. The suggested content outlined in the manual was virtually unchanged from the 1940s. Walker stressed the importance of accuracy and listed the resources that should be consulted to verify factual information in a section called 'References for Authenticity.'[64] While she called for careful attention to citation, Walker balanced it with a call for creativity. After outlining the suggested table of contents, she remarked that 'these are [the] fundamental sections or chapters of your book, any others that you wish to include make your book more interesting and enlightening to your readers. Stretch your imagination and see how far you can go.'[65] The emphasis was squarely on history as entertainment, and Walker's manual included a section on how to host a 'Tweedsmuir Tea' to show off the books for the enjoyment of community members.[66]

The invitation to be creative and eclectic gave a contradictory message to curators. Walker urged the women to be as thorough as possible. 'As you toy with the ideas passed along here in this Manual, I am sure you will realize there are many other fields which you may include as definite Sections for your historical records. Do not be afraid of straying but do not let anything of value escape the pages of your book.'[67] At the same time, she warned the curators that they had to be systematic and selective in their collecting. 'So often it has been said, let's get everything in the book and sort it out after. This is never done! Never attempt anything that is going to make extra work for someone, because there just isn't that extra time. Make a definite plan first, and then work to that end.'[68] Such a liberal policy of inclusiveness, no matter how systematic, would surely tend towards the uncritical collector instinct that led Professor Neatby to characterize some local history works as 'sociological pedantry.'

Walker's contradictory instructions led to mixed results. Some Tweedsmuir curators regarded their books as 'a scrapbook of odds and ends of community life as they happen,' while others took pride in putting together 'an authentic story of the community' designed 'to aid students in thesis [*sic*]' and 'to aid statisticians searching for authentic data.' Walker did not see the two purposes as mutually exclusive. She was thoroughly convinced that by following her manual, every curator could competently create both an entertaining volume and an exacting account of community history. In reality, only the most capable historian, whether amateur or professional, manages to achieve both goals simultaneously.

When Canada celebrated its centennial five years after Walker's manual was circulated, Women's Institutes were given a chance to demonstrate

Keeping local history scrapbooks was a hobby for members of the Women's Institutes, which sometimes allowed them to display other talents such as leathercraft in creating the covers of the books

their creativity in presenting history. Regarded as the resident experts in the field of local history, WI members were reminded that 'the Women's Institutes for many years have been conscious of the importance of preserving the history of their communities. This year they are the leaders, in many cases, in planning Centennial programs.'[69] At open houses, parades, tea parties, drama presentations, and fashion shows, WI members welcomed local community members whom they entertained. As *Home and Country* boasted:

> Celebrations of many kinds are being planned or already have taken place. Attics are being ransacked for the articles that grandmother tossed out as junk and that are now known to be irreplaceable. Clothes are being taken out of old trunks. Stories are being recalled and there is a growing appreciation of the deeds and hardships of the pioneers ... The ingenuity that our women are showing in some of their plans is worth recording.[70]

In the festivity of those celebrations, deliberations about academic standards for judging history books were set aside.

Conclusion

When the celebrations were over, this close association with celebratory history left the WI with a legacy that was not entirely positive. The

Centennial parades were a favourite venue for Women's Institute members to promote local history by dressing up in pioneer costumes

expertise of the WI in historical pageantry and costuming worked to the detriment of WI historians, as they came to be seen as the very characters they had been impersonating. Images of WI members dressed in costume to celebrate the past lingered, and many people connected the WI and history so closely that they assumed the WI itself was now a relic of the past. 'I personally worry about the future of the WI, and so do others that I have talked to from time to time,' wrote Mary E. James, a member of Union Hall WI in Lanark North District. 'So far, in *Home and Country*, I see all kinds of anniversaries being celebrated, but I also want to see the NOW celebrated. Adelaide Hoodless lived NOW, and her NOW was 1897; ours is 1979. In *Home and Country* please.'[71] Coming to the organization's defence, editor Margaret Zoeller stressed that there was much more to the WI than the celebration of the past. She pointed out the voluntarism, the social stimulus, the resolutions, the international projects, and the WI's role as 'mouthpiece in government and industry' to emphasize that the WI was very much a part of the present. However, not all readers were convinced. Throughout the 1970s, membership in the Women's Institutes declined as many younger rural women dropped their affiliation in favour of newer farm women's organizations, which they deemed more relevant to current rural issues.[72]

Ironically, the work of local history, which had once served to elevate the reputation of WI members, was now regarded as a cause for disdain and criticism, not only in the academic community, but among some of the WI's own members.[73] Those who were committed to writing history did so for their own pleasure, in order to chronicle and entertain the members of their own communities. Therefore, they cared little about the academic criticisms or the disregard of younger members who were less interested in history than in current issues.

In assessing the merits of local histories written by WI members, it is difficult to generalize. The Tweedsmuir History Books vary in quality, and some are more successful than others in contributing to an understanding of local history. Just as academic opinion was divided over the relative value of these works, the women themselves were never unanimous about what they were hoping to achieve or how they should best go about the task. Curators clearly recognized that they were working outside academic circles, and most of them revelled in that position. Although they might entertain advice from professionals, they made it clear that they had no desire to join their ranks or write in the same genre.

Typically, a Tweedsmuir curator saw her work of history as a hobby, her way of contributing to the chronicle of the community. At certain times, she elevated that work to the status of a patriotic duty or redefined it as a tool for integrating new immigrants. But despite those changing purposes, she maintained a focus on celebrating local experiences and documenting the theme of progress. Although she might welcome the recognition attached to winning an award from an external judge, she was not willing to relinquish control over the content of her book or the way in which she presented the material. She was eager to chronicle change, but not to change the way she wrote her chronicle.

Notes

1 Terry Crowley, 'The Origins of Continuing Education for Women: The Ontario Women's Institutes,' *Canadian Women Studies* 7, 3 (fall 1986): 78-81.

2 Gerald Killan, *Preserving Ontario's Heritage: A History of the Ontario Historical Society* (Ottawa: Love Printing Service 1976), 29.

3 Royce MacGillivray, 'Local History as a Form of Popular Culture in Ontario,' *New York History* (October 1984): 368.

4 For a complete list of those branches and a fuller understanding of the organization's many different roles over the years, see Linda M. Ambrose, *For Home and Country: The Centennial History of the Women's Institutes in Ontario* (Erin, ON: Boston Mills Press 1996).

5 Although it is relatively easy to trace the membership statistics, it is much more difficult to measure the class composition, race, or ethnicity of WI members. It seems that the WI membership was mostly made up of white, Anglo-Saxon Protestant women, although the organization prided itself on being 'inclusive' of all women. This is probably a reference to the fact that the groups successfully drew together women from various churches and helped them to foster relationships among women of different

Protestant denominations. On the question of class, Margaret Kechnie argues, in her study of the movement up to 1919, that the activists and leaders in the organization were town and village elites, and that despite the claim that 'there is no class distinction in our ranks,' nevertheless the leaders were most often quite wealthy. See her 'Keeping Things Clean for "Home and Country": The Federated Women's Institutes of Ontario 1897-1919,' (Ph.D. diss., OISE at University of Toronto 1996), especially chapter 5. More work needs to be done to determine class and ethnic composition of the membership-at-large, particularly in the period after 1919.

6 Minutes of provincial board meeting (24-7 November 1964): 17, Federated Women's Institutes of Ontario Collection (hereafter FWIOC), University of Guelph Archives and Special Collections.

7 'Her Excellency Has Graciously Accepted the Office of Honourary President,' *Home and Country* (hereafter *H&C*) (January 1936): 1.

8 Ontario, Department of Agriculture, Institutes Branch *Annual Report* (1927): 31.

9 For more on the use of history as a celebration of progress, see the essays by Boutilier and Hallman in this book.

10 MacGillivray, 'Local History,' 371.

11 Institutes Branch *Annual Report* (1927): 31

12 Ibid.

13 An account of the meeting is recorded in the Tweedsmuir History Book of the Stoney Creek Women's Institute, Archives of Ontario. The tale of the stormy winter evening when Adelaide Hoodless addressed a meeting of 101 women in Squire's Hall in Stoney Creek, Ontario, has been retold countless times by WI members, including the commemorative histories published to date: Viola M. Powell, *Forty Years Agrowing: A History of Ontario Women's Institutes* (Port Perry: The Port Perry Star 1941); Walker et al., *Fifty Years of Achievement* (Toronto: Federated Women's Institutes of Ontario 1947); *The Women's Institute Story: In Commemoration of the 75th Anniversary of the Founding of the Ontario Women's Institutes of Ontario* (n.p.: Federated Women's Institutes of Ontario 1972). For a version of the tale that contextualizes the meeting, see Ambrose, *For Home and Country*, especially chapter 1.

14 *H&C* (February 1934): 4.

15 Statistics Canada. Cited by Randall White, *Ontario 1610-1985: A Political and Economic History* (Hamilton: Dundurn Press 1985), 340.

16 E. Appelbe, 'Historical Research,' *H&C* (September 1934): 7.

17 Ibid., 6.

18 Ibid.

19 Ibid.

20 *H&C* (January 1935): 4.

21 Ibid., 7.

22 *H&C* (May 1937): 1.

23 Ronald D. Lambert, 'The Family Historian and Temporal Orientations Toward the Ancestral Past,' *Time & Society* 5, 2 (June 1996): 115-43; Lambert, "Looking for Genealogical Motivation," *Families* 34, 3 (August 1995): 149-60.

24 E. Appelbe, "Historical Research," H&C (September 1933): 5.

25 *H&C* (January 1935): 4.

26 Ibid.

27 *H&C* (September 1933): 5.

28 Ibid.

29 Ibid.

30 *H&C* (May 1937): 1

31 *H&C* (summer 1939): 3.

32 Florence Reesor to Mrs. W.B. Leatherdale, 29 May 1940, Tweedsmuir Competition and Files Ontario – FWIC. XR1MSA555, FWIOC.

33 Mrs. W.B. Leatherdale to Lady Tweedsmuir, 24 April 1940, FWIOC.

34 *H&C* (summer 1940): 2.

35 Ibid.

36 For a discussion of members' dependence on the library's resources, see Linda M.

Ambrose, 'What Are the Good of Those Meetings Anyway? Early Popularity of the Ontario Women's Institutes,' *Ontario History* 87, 1 (March 1995): 1-20.

37 Institutes Branch *Annual Report* (1937, 1938).

38 Ambrose, *For Home and Country*, chapter 6.

39 *H&C* (fall 1943): 2.

40 Ibid.

41 *H&C* (fall 1944): 2

42 Ibid.

43 Institutes Branch *Annual Report* (1946, 1947, 1948).

44 Susan Tweedsmuir to Mrs. Leatherdale, Tweedsmuir file, FWIOC. Also quoted in *H&C* (summer 1940): 2.

45 *H&C* (spring 1947): 4.

46 *H&C* (spring 1947): 1.

47 *H&C* (fall 1945): 4.

48 Ibid.

49 Ibid.

50 'Glazebrook, G(eorge) P(arker) de T(wenebrokes)' in Frances C. Locher, ed., *Contemporary Authors*, vol. 102 (Detroit: Gale Research 1981), 218; John Robert Colombo, *Colombo's Canadian References* (Toronto: Oxford University Press 1976), 205.

51 *H&C* (spring 1947): 1.

52 G.P. de T. Glazebrook, *Life in Ontario: A Social History* (Toronto: University of Toronto Press 1968), 300.

53 Glazebrook cited in Locher, 218.

54 Hilda Neatby, 'The Canadian Historical Association, the *Canadian Historical Review*, and Local History: A Symposium,' Canadian Historical Association *Annual Report* (1952): 49.

55 Lady Tweedsmuir, 'The Amateur Historian,' *Canadian Historical Review* 20, 1 (March 1939): 1-3.

56 CHA *Annual Report* (1952): 60.

57 Killan, *Preserving Ontario's Heritage*, 231.

58 CHA *Annual Report* (1952): 64.

59 *H&C* (fall and winter 1949-50): 15.

60 Killan, *Preserving Ontario's Heritage*, 231. Killan points out that under Spragge's direction and in consultation with Professor J.M.S. Careless of the University of Toronto, the OHS raised its own publication standards with the creation of the journal *Ontario History*, another of Spragge's initiatives.

61 *H&C* (fall and winter 1949-50): 11.

62 Albert B. Corey, Chairman, Committee on Awards, American Association for State and Local History, to Mrs. E.E. Morden, FWIC President. Cited in *H&C* (fall and winter 1949-50).

63 Board meeting minutes (5-8 November 1956), FWIOC.

64 The Women's Institutes of Ontario, *Manual for Compiling Tweedsmuir Histories* (Federated Women's Institutes of Ontario 1962), 5-6.

65 Ibid., 20.

66 Ibid., 6.

67 Ibid., 38.

68 Ibid., 24.

69 *H&C* (summer 1967): 24.

70 Ibid.

71 *H&C* (winter 1979): 3.

72 For a discussion of these new organizations for farm women, see E.A. (Nora) Cebotarev, 'From Domesticity to the Public Sphere: Farm Women, 1945-86,' in Joy Parr, ed., *A Diversity of Women: Ontario 1945-1980* (University of Toronto Press 1995), 214.

73 For a further discussion of the changing directions of the WI movement in the 1970s and 1980s, see Ambrose, *For Home and Country*, chapter 8.

Part 2: Transitions

5

'Writing Teaches Us Our Mysteries': Women Religious Recording and Writing History

Elizabeth Smyth

It is a well known fact that the experience of women religious in Canada is a record of female firsts: the first teachers, nurses, hospital administrators, and college presidents. Less well known is the fact that women religious were also among the first women to record women's experiences for future readers. Marie Guyart, in religion the Ursuline Mère Marie de l'Incarnation, was one of the first chroniclers of everyday life in New France. She was acutely aware of the power of recording history. In a 1670 letter to her son, she responded to his questions regarding how the aboriginal peoples preserve 'the tradition of their history and of what happened in times past,' describing their lack of a written language as 'the cause of their traditions being mixed with a great many fables and irrevelances, which increase continually with time.' For Mère Marie, there was power in the written word. As she explained to her son, 'writing teaches us our mysteries.'[1] Nor was she alone in this belief. For the many hundreds of thousands of Canadian women who, like Marie de l'Incarnation, entered religious life, historical writing was a powerful instrument. It had both spiritual and practical value. Community mysteries were revealed through historical writing.

The community-oriented historical work undertaken by women religious took various forms. As Gerda Lerner notes, 'women's efforts at History-writing followed the same pattern men had much earlier created: the making of lists of notables and heroines; the documenting of individual lives and exploits; the documentation of the histories of communities; the interpretation of past documentation from a particular point of view, and, finally, in the 19th and 20th centuries, "scientific History."'[2] Initially, women religious documented their communities' past, in both written and oral tradition, by celebrating the lives of the women and often, when describing the formative stages of the community's establishment, the male clerics who served as their institutional and local founders. Interpretation of the past focused on the relationship between their temporal and spiritual existence. The purpose of their lives on earth was preparation for life with their God in the hereafter. This spiritual journey was often the framework in which community history and the histories of individuals was cast. Only within the past few decades have women religious begun to examine their history from what Lerner describes as 'scientific' principles, using feminist theology and historiography as analytical tools.

Lerner views female religious as self-supporting and economically independent women whose community lifestyle created a context for cultural affirmation. She cites the 'Sister books,' a collection of nine works by fourteenth-century German Dominican nuns, as an early example of history 'written by women about women'[3] and for women, concluding that, although these works 'may have been initially inspired by the desire to spread a religious message ... [they] should also be seen as efforts of historical documentation.'[4] Gertrund Jaron Lewis further argues that the Sister books 'add yet another example to our growing awareness that there has always been, parallel to the dominant male Tradition, a feminine tradition [of historical writing] waiting to be explored.'[5]

In this essay, I seek to broaden Lewis's observation by exploring the historical work of women religious in English Canada. I explore how, prior to the 1960s, when the reforms of the Second Vatican Council[6] and the almost simultaneous impact of feminist historiography and theology dramatically altered the historical mindset and daily living of many women religious, a culture of women writing and recording history, supported by the structures of the Catholic church, existed among communities of sisters and nuns.[7] Further, I argue for the substance and significance of the body of historical work created by this subset of Canadian women – a subset that, by the mid-twentieth century, contained members of some 229 canonically recognized institutes and societies working in health care, social service, and education.[8]

The sources analyzed in this essay are drawn from the archives of three communities of Ontario women religious: the Religious of the Precious Blood, Mount Olivet, Toronto; the Ursulines of the Chatham Union; and the Congregation of the Sisters of St. Joseph of Toronto. The communities were selected to document both the diversity and the commonality of the historical work of women religious. The Religious of the Precious Blood, established in Toronto in 1869 as the first branch of this Quebec-based institute, were cloistered nuns whose orientation was to a life of continuous prayer. This community demonstrates that historical writing played a part in the temporal and spiritual lives of women living entirely within the cloister walls. The Ursulines of the Chatham Union, established at Chatham, Ontario, in 1860 by Mother Mary Xavier Le Bihan, a member of the Ursuline Convent at La Rouet, France, were a community of sisters dedicated to education, with particular emphasis on education of girls and women. The Congregation of the Sisters of St. Joseph, established in Toronto in 1851 by Mother Delphine Fontbonne, a pioneering founder sent to North America from St. Joseph's Convent at LePuy, France, worked in education, social service, and health care. The Ursulines and the Sisters of St. Joseph show women religious engaged in the work of history not only within their own community setting, but also in the more public domains of schools, colleges, and professional historical societies.

Purposeful History for Particular Communities

Communities of women religious are characterized by intergenerationality. Institutional memory is maintained by the presence of women who represent a continuum of age and experience, from postulants – generally younger women exploring their suitability for religious life – to elderly women who have spent their lives in religion. Second, institutional memory also has a physical manifestation: the motherhouse residences, which dotted the Canadian landscape by the mid-twentieth century. These large buildings attested to the stability of their communities. Although the religious themselves frequently moved from mission to mission, they came and went from a central home. Thus, unlike other groups of women whose lives were continually fragmented, women religious had a structure of community stability to support them and preserve their records and stories. Third, the Code of Canon Law identifies women religious as historical beings, instructing that community records were to be maintained in a 'properly equipped and carefully arranged' archive.[9] Among the community records that the code prescribed were the annals.[10]

The annals, also known as chronicles, were kept by each local house in which religious lived. They were the permanent records of community events. The keeping of annals was usually one item in a long list of other duties typically executed by a woman with no historical training. In the motherhouses, it fell to the community secretary; in local houses, it was an additional chore assigned to a sister engaged full-time in other activities. Annalists were directed to record 'any remarkable or edifying occurrence,'[11] which often provided the opportunity for including vivid accounts of community life and its evolution. Annals supplied a running commentary on daily life and work and were often complemented by scrapbooks of printed reports from both the religious and secular press documenting community events. Typically, notices of public ceremonies in the life of the community and its enterprises were found in the scrapbooks. The annals often cross-referenced events and named the community member who wrote the copy or provided the background information. The title 'annalist' was frequently used in community records referring to the woman who currently performed these tasks. Yet, in spite of the dictates of canon law, there were often gaps, sometimes of several years in length, when no one was appointed to keep the annals. Explaining the sporadic nature of some of the entries, one annalist noted as a postscript to her work, 'in the early days of the Community, no one had the time to keep records.'[12]

The self-published three-volume *Community Annals of the Sisters of St. Joseph of Toronto* are fine examples of this genre of historical writing. It is from these sources that the examples cited from throughout the following pages are drawn. In the preface to Volume 1, The Sisters of St. Joseph wrote:

> The Annals of our Community have been printed in book form in order to preserve, in all its richness, the information of our past, whether it be strictly historical or of community and personal interest ... The original records of our early history have not in any way been changed. The literary style of each writer and the characteristics peculiar to each period have been maintained.[13]

Although the community annalists were to conduct all official writing and correspondence in a manner that was 'clear, precise and full of sweetness, and spirit of piety which is the distinctive mark of the Congregation,'[14] their personalities shone through.

The annals revealed much about the women who lived in the community. The entries ranged from the mundane ('extra dainties and good things for meals')[15] to the profound ('today the 19 th. Century comes to a close; its joys and its sorrows shall soon be recollections of the past').[16] They contained records of community business transactions, elections, and decisions concerning where to deploy personnel. Sometimes they contained snatches of oral history, with reminiscences about the achievements of a member of the community, former pupil, favourite priest, or relative and statements related to the evolution of community customs. Frequently, the annals provided the insights of the community, filtered through the eyes of the annalist, regarding political events both at home and abroad. For the annalist bidding farewell to the nineteenth century, events overseas were clearly the cause of considerable distress: 'Alas! That its closing days should have been marred by scenes of violence and bloodshed – the South African War with its harrowing scenes of slaughter and the terrible "Boxer" movement in China.'[17]

The debate on the qualifications of teaching sisters that raged throughout Ontario in 1905 provoked some strong reactions. The *Globe* reported that the Sisters of St. Joseph were henceforth requiring that all women seeking admission to their religious community must have teaching certificates. The annalist wrote (and the reader can almost hear her intoning):

> Well, Well! That is news indeed. Where did the *Globe* get its information ... no such instructions have been given. Of course, such a publication is no discredit to us professionally, rather to the contrary ... Reverend Mother wishes me to write to the Editor of the *Globe* to contradict the erroneous statements mentioned above ... She desires me to point out how misleading the article would be to eligible candidates.[18]

What emerges from these comments is the fact that the sisters viewed the public discussion of what was ostensibly a community policy as a double-edged sword. If they were portrayed in the press as having higher expectations of potential members, a theme that often emerged (especially in the reporting of examination results), the sisters feared that women who were unable to meet these qualifications, yet who could teach such skill-based subjects as music and art, or who possessed business and commercial skills, or who could serve the community as 'house sisters' performing primarily domestic chores, might not apply for membership. From a public relations and recruitment perspective, action needed to be taken. The community was fully prepared to engage in debate in the public press.

The annalist was equally engaged when it came to the progress of the First World War. Dual themes of patriotic commitment and the mounting cost of victory, viewed through a providential lens, were echoed through the war years. In writing about Vimy Ridge, the annalist observed: 'No praise of Canadian achievement could be excessive ... Canada has poured out her thousands ... She has sent across the ocean an army greater than Napoleon ever commanded ... A Day of Glory, April 9, 1917 will be in our beloved Canada's history.'[19] At the same time, the suffering associated with war had a divine purpose.

> The world is suffering from this dreadful and deadly war; but the world needs suffering. The insolent materialism of European civilization which waxed proud and rebellious before the Lord, its God, needed the dreadful calamity of War to chasten and rebuke it ... All over the world prayer is offered for our dear ones in peril. Our chapel reverberates with the sound of voices – pleading, pleading with our Divine Spouse for aid with our dear Blessed Mother and St. Joseph to intercede for us.[20]

War was thus viewed as a means of bringing people back to God. This was not to say that the Toronto sisters were not active and enthusiastic supporters of the Canadian war effort; there was more than one reference to 'a grand patriotic concert in our Auditorium for the benefit of invalided soldiers.'[21] Similarly, there were frequent references to drives for humanitarian relief such as sending 'eight hundred garments to the Secours National' for suffering French children.[22]

The annals recorded community perceptions of the roles of women religious within the secular world and vice versa. When the Sisters of St. Joseph journeyed to Prince Rupert, the annalist noted that 'The Mayor of the town ... told the Sisters they had been highly complimented by the Contractors for their business ability. The contractors were evidently not accustomed to meeting women who could undertake the erection of buildings.'[23] An annalist expressed her opinion on the suffrage movement: 'the writer ... whilst deprecating the unwomanly and lawless conduct of the Suffragists thinks that if women had a voice in certain public matters, there would be less corruption in the world than there is.'[24] Similar reflections can be found in the annals of virtually all communities of women religious.

The annals also documented the cycle and rituals of community life, often using the metaphor of women religious as the brides of Christ. Women were described as being received into the community, dressed as brides with 'magnificent satin and silken robes borne by "Angels."'[25] Silver and golden jubilees of taking the veil were celebrated as wedding anniversaries with 'the Brides being Mother M. Teresa, Mother St. John and Mother M. Philomena ... the centre of the table was ornamented with a delicious looking three-story bridal cake.'[26] The sisters' deaths were often described as answering the call of their 'Divine Bridegroom.'[27] While the death of a member was listed and briefly commented upon in the annals, a separate volume, a necrology, was also kept by the annalist. Typically, a necrology contained 'a short account of each deceased Sister, the year, day and place of her death and burial, with an abridgement of the principle which characterized her during life and the offices she held in the Community.'[28] Since, with a few exceptions, women religious rarely left personal diaries or other pieces of personal writing, necrologies are often the only accounts historians have of individual lives. Necrologies were a temporal and spiritual memorial. They were also a personal history of the community and its evolution.

The words of Mother St. Joseph Caouette (1842-1913), co-foundress and first Toronto superior, are recorded in the prologue of the first volume of the necrologies of her community, the Religious of the Precious Blood:[29] 'Let us not forget those who sowed the seed, whose tears moistened it. Whose love warmed it, whose prayers and whose sacrifices fructified it.'[30] Remembering would help build a sense of community over time and across distance. The writings were deliberately inspirational and instructive, describing the characteristics of the sister or nun in her daily domestic and spiritual duties.

Like many other necrologies, the necrologies of the Religious of the Precious Blood began with the lives of the first superior and four founders of the Toronto community. Biographies such as these have been traditionally dismissed as hagiographic,[31] yet, as Natalie Zemon Davis suggests, women's writings can reveal much concerning 'centers and hierarchies' and how women carved out a life for themselves as they lived 'on the margins.'[32] One might expect that the lives led by women in cloister would be far removed from engagements with the outside world. Yet what emerges from the necrologies is a community with deeply embedded traditions and ties to life outside the convent walls.

The unpublished individual necrologies were comparatively lengthy documents, generally about fifteen double-spaced typewritten pages. Their narratives followed a similar pattern. They contained considerable demographic, personal, and spiritual detail, indicating the links with the secular world that the particular religious gave to the community. Each necrology began by contextualizing the life of the religious in God's providential plans for humanity: 'The life and especially the last days of the dear Sister whose life we are about to sketch would seem to have been an exemplification of her own words ... God prevails in the end, showing us once more how wonderful are the designs of Providence when dealing with souls God wishes to be His in a particular manner.'[33] Background on the late nun's family was given before the details of her life were shared; the background sometimes included a description of the family's socioeconomic status, the religious and educational background of her parents, and the number and names of her siblings, with details of those who entered religious life.

Details concerning the early life of the religious and those forces that influenced her decision to enter a religious community (and especially a cloistered community) were given. Often poetic and mystical terms were employed: 'The gradual growth of a religious vocation in a soul is always interesting, but it is not possible to depict this in words as the workings of the Holy Spirit are gentle and hidden, but when the flower unfolds we may judge of the tree and look for the fruit.'[34] This is not to say that the ordinary aspects of community life were neglected. Portions of letters circulated within the communities describing pets found their way into necrologies, 'our budgie, Pat, keeps us amused. He pulls the pins out of the Sisters' veils and even their clothes and then sits and cocks his head.'[35]

The characteristics of a 'good nun' were highlighted. Women were described as 'a shining example of all that a good religious should be.'[36] 'Fidelity to the rule ... Charity, love of Holy Poverty and a Careful use of every moment'[37] were celebrated. Obedience was praised as a cardinal virtue: '[She] was working diligently in the Altar Bread Rooms without any complaints about her failing health and strength.'[38] Another religious, a necrology noted, 'towards her Superiors, was always most deferential and submissive – she who was naturally independent could be almost childlike in this respect.'[39]

Necrologies also recorded the business side of religious life. Financing a contemplative community required entrepreneurial skills as, unlike active communities, the religious did not garner income from outside employment. The necrology of one nun recorded that, in order to finance the building of a new monastery in 1965, 'a decision was made to produce a record "Sisters Sing Favourites for You," with selections from Rogers and Hammerstein 2nd. and a negro spiritual ... [S]he went around the monastery practicing the word "church" with an English accent during the days immediately preceding the recording.'[40]

Not surprisingly, much focus was given in the necrologies to the rituals surrounding illness and death. Spiritual preparation for death was a hallmark of the life of a good religious: 'the sunshine and sweetness of [her] character had its foundation in a deep and solid piety, a great spirit of prayer.'[41] What one takes away from these readings is a sense of a supportive, loving community that rallied around its members especially in times of crisis, illness, and death. As the community gathered, 'praying at the bedside' of a dying nun, her death was described as 'the precious life flickered like the flame of a blessed candle, but now it was the flame of a death candle, not the golden flame that had shed its rays of love and cheer over our daily life.'[42]

The annals and necrologies are but two of the various forms of community-based historical writings in the archival holdings of religious communities. Nuns and sisters wrote historical fiction: poetry and short stories that were contributed to community newsletters and other circulated materials. Sometimes these pieces found their way into more public venues such as the annuals of the convent schools frequently attached to the motherhouses of teaching orders.

The flagship convent academies of the two teaching orders discussed in this essay both had long-running annuals. *Echoes from the Pines* was the publication of the Ursuline's Chatham Academy; *The Lilies* was the publication of the Sisters of St. Joseph's Toronto Academy. Both publications were combinations of literary journals, yearbooks, and alumnae magazines. As well, both served as chronicles of the activities of the religious communities. Obituaries of sisters were published in them, as were descriptions of celebrations of community life. They were truly collaborative efforts among the religious communities and past and present members of the schools.

The annuals produced by convent academies served as venues for the writings of sisters and their past pupils. They were also sites where works by authors deemed significant by the editors could be reproduced. Sections of these publications were targeted at specific audiences: current pupils (including the mimms – the little girls), recent graduates, and senior alumnae. In the prose and poetry, opinion pieces, and works of nonfiction and fiction they contained, the publications of convent academies served to reinforce the values and further the links created by schools. While well beyond the scope of this essay, there is need for a systematic study of this body of literary work. It represents a subset in the genre of women's writing that can shed insight into the construction of gender.

Historical drama was a popular form of writing. Plays were written and performed by the women religious themselves for members of their community. These plays commemorated significant events in community history. *In the Footsteps of the Martyrs*, a three-act play penned by a 'Sister of St. Joseph, Toronto, Canada' in 1921, depicted the experiences during the French Revolution of Mother St. John Fontbonne, the 'second founder' of the order. In the play, Mother St. John Fontbonne confronts a regiment of soldiers that had come to force her to sign the Civil Constitution of the Clergy. Her defiance causes one of them to observe: 'This woman's lost her reason. She is mad. / Call the other nuns and we shall see / If we can find some sense among them all.' Mother St. John replies: 'Nay, just a moment please. 'Tis clear you know / Nothing at all about our Convent ways. / Else you would know that every Sister here / Is of one mind with me.'[43] Courageous, unyielding, placing complete faith in God, trusting her community – these were the characteristics of Mother St. John revealed through the dramatic dialogue.

Plays of this type are found in the archives of many communities of women religious. Like the necrologies and annals, they were written largely for the women religious themselves and were structured to reveal characteristics and behaviours to which the audience should aspire. Frequently, they drew their dialogue from primary archival sources, supplemented by fictional characters who aided in the interpretation of writings and events. In almost every instance, the author of the play was an 'anonymous sister.' Sometimes the identity of the woman can be uncovered through cross-referencing within the annals or necrologies, where the authorship is attributed.

Such are some of the historical and historically based writings produced within communities of women religious for internal consumption. Among the themes found within this community-based writing are images of admirable women with behaviours and characteristics all should emulate, tales of the mysteries of divine intervention, and heroic accounts of women overcoming almost insurmountable odds. Rather than summarily dismissing them as hagiographic, these tales need to be examined for what they were: venues for community development and instruction intended for an exclusive audience of nuns or sisters.

History for Schools and Colleges

In the many Roman Catholic communities of sisters that focused on education, women religious often served as teachers of history at the elementary, secondary, and university levels. They were creators and producers of historical drama for public consumption and commissioners of historical monuments. Their historical works were published by mainstream publishers and were reviewed in the secular and scholarly press. Members of the Ursulines of the Chatham Union were among those sisters who did this public historical work.

The Ursulines were dedicated to teaching, which they held as 'the assured means of fulfilling their holy vocation.' Their constitutions directed them to 'apply thereto all their strength and attention'[44] and lead 'so holy a life as to serve as an example to the children confided to them ... They shall be equally zealous and devoted whether teaching children of the poor and lower classes or those of the upper classes.'[45] Further, they were instructed to 'prepare themselves for the worthy exercise of their ministry towards youth by striving to acquire, under the control of obedience, such knowledge and ability as will enable them efficiently and fruitfully to accomplish this holy task.'[46]

As with many teaching communities, the Ursulines of the Chatham Union generated a variety of instructional resources to support their teaching sisters. Teaching manuals detailed, in both theory and practice, how subjects were to be taught. History was among these subjects:

> History should be made a particularly interesting subject to the pupils and should be presented in as vivid and entertaining a manner as possible. The teachers should make a thorough study of the subject beforehand and read many authorities on it, particularly Catholic ones, so that they may be perfectly familiar with the topics they are to teach, through which they should constantly endeavour to train the hearts and judgements of their pupils, to lead them to God and to point out to them the workings of Divine Providence in all the events that have happened in the history of the world.[47]

Just as God was to be the centre of the curriculum taught within the Ursuline schools, history was 'providential.' All historical events bore God's imprint.

The Ursulines of the Chatham Union followed these constitutional directions in their primary, secondary, and tertiary schools. Their two best-known educational enterprises were their convent academy, The Pines, established in Chatham in 1860, and Brescia College. Religious who staffed these institutions played significant roles in the Ursulines' historical work.

The foundations of Brescia College were laid in London, Ontario, in 1913 when, with the departure of the Religious of the Sacred Heart, diocesan Bishop Michael Fallon requested that the Ursulines take over the work of higher education for girls and young women in that city. In September that year, the Ursulines opened St. Angela's College. Six years later, this Ursuline college, renamed Brescia Hall, successfully affiliated itself with the University of Western Ontario. In the words of the affiliation agreement, 'The Ursuline College shall constitute a college of Arts, and as such shall enter into and form a part of the Faculty of Arts of the Western University; it shall enjoy the rights and assume the obligations common to all such affiliated colleges ... its staff of teachers shall have equal standing and rights with the officers of instruction of the University College of Arts.' Further, the university agreed to accept the history courses taught at Brescia College as 'substitutions and requirements for its degrees.'[48]

Between 1919 and 1956, the history courses taught at Brescia were delivered exclusively by Ursuline sisters, who lived highly regulated lives.[49] Early rising, prayers said in community, meals taken in community and in silence or accompanied by spiritual readings, a year structured around the liturgical seasons and punctuated by retreats and general chapters – all these were features of daily life. Little time was available for the pursuit of personal scholarly interests. More significantly, in their choice to lead a life as an Ursuline sister, these women had vowed obedience. Thus, they agreed to abide by the decisions made on their behalf by the general council of the community. This included decisions concerning educational and professional paths: who should be sent to study, what they should study, and where they should be assigned to teach. Under obedience, the sisters agreed to 'keep the order prescribed by the Superior for the distribution of their time and occupations, faithfully acquitting themselves of the various duties confided to them.'[50] These duties were to be carried out with humility. The sisters were to 'avoid singularity and all that can draw attention to themselves ... Should God work anything extraordinary in them they shall be careful to hide it and speak of it only to those who have the direction of their souls.' If the Superior 'find anyone inclined to pride, she shall exercise her in lowly occupations in order to help her acquire humility.'[51]

The women religious who engaged in the study, writing, and teaching of history thus did so within narrow parameters. Their vocation, responding to the call to serve God through service to neighbours, integrated their lives as religious with their historical work. Obedience and humility were to be the characteristics of their professional demeanour. Yet this did not prevent outstanding individuals from emerging, and indeed flourishing, within the Ursuline community.

Mother St. Michael Major was Brescia's first instructor of history. Her experience illustrated the costs exacted by the vow of obedience. Mother Major had been educated by the Ursulines in England and had received

Summer School, Brescia College, 1953. The sisters pictured are members of the Ursulines of the Chatham Union, Sisters of St. Joseph, and Holy Name Sisters

her B.A. in literature and history from the University of Liverpool. Dr. I.N. Mackay, Professor of History at Liverpool, described her as 'an admirable student, in my opinion, one of the best in her year ... She has the scholarly qualities which go to make a true teacher.'[52] Following further education in languages, she received her teacher certification from the Liverpool Mount Pleasant Training College, where she was observed by the principal as 'an exceptionally intelligent student ... [as] a teacher, Miss Major is intelligent, clear, precise, capable of handling any subject well and of dealing with the difficulties of the scholars.'[53] She began her teaching career in England. In 1913, she emigrated to join her family in Leamington, Ontario. The following year, she entered the Chatham Ursulines.

Brilliance and ill health characterized Mother Major's career. The *Annals of Brescia College* recorded that, after the college was established, it needed faculty and 'the telephone carried a message and [Mother] St. Michael, then in Dublin [Ontario] on sick leave, was told to be prepared to start for London at a moment's notice to attend lectures leading to the M.A. degree at Western University ... on Tuesday October 25 [1919], [Mother] St. Michael was duly registered and till the following May ... regularly attended lectures at Western University when the degree of M.A. was conferred upon her.' The *Annals* further recorded that following 'an interview with Rev. R.R. Rankin SJ, Dean of the Graduate School, Fordham University [a]rrangements were made with him for the recognition of ... [Mother] St. Michael for the Ph.D. degree. The latter was allowed to take part of the work extramurally, part in attendance at the summer sessions held at Fordham.'[54] Mother St. Michael began her studies towards her doctorate in the summer of 1920 and commenced her duties as lecturer in English and history and registrar of Brescia College in the fall.

The onerous combination of teaching, college administration, and pursuing her own studies, all squeezed into the heavily regulated day of a religious, seem to have made her already frail health worsen, for she was sent to the Grey Nuns Sanatorium at St. Agathe to recuperate. In a poignant letter dated 28 February 1926 to Reverend Mother Clare Gaulker, she asked permission to come home to the Chatham motherhouse to die. She described herself as 'a rather frightened little soul in St. Agathe' who makes 'a humble petition that you will help me prepare to meet my God if He should soon call for me.'[55] True to her premonition, Mother St. Michael died at the Chatham motherhouse on 14 April 1926. Writing to convey his sympathy to the community, Western's W. Tamblyn described the personal sense of loss that the university community felt at the death of this woman. He recalled 'how delightful, how able and how perfect Mother St. Michael was' and expressed his sorrow at the 'valuable' life 'lost to all of us.'[56]

Although Mother St. Michael Major's short academic career and life did not yield surviving contributions to the writing of history, they demonstrate the complexities inherent in examining this cohort of women historians. Her necrology was telling: 'Naturally endowed with a brilliancy of intellect given to few, a student of rare ability, a teacher of exceptional talents, yet modest and retiring, she was loved by all with whom she came in contact as an ideal religious teacher, whose salutary influence will long remain a happy memory to those who were so fortunate as to have been placed under her guidance.'[57]

The death of Mother St. Michael was a staggering blow both to the community and the fledgling Brescia College, necessitating a reassessment of personnel and skills to complete the academic staff. To fill the void, Mother Mercedes Toohey was taken from the staff of the diocesan elementary schools and prepared for a place on the faculty. She was assigned to Brescia in 1928, completed her B.A. in 1930, and subsequently enrolled in the M.A. program, where she wrote a thesis entitled 'The History of the Ursulines of Ontario' as the first graduate student of Dr. Hartley Thomas at the University of Western Ontario. Upon completion of this degree, Mother Mercedes became head of Brescia's history department. She retired in 1960 and was named Alumna of the Year by the student body. She was well respected by her Western colleagues. Dr. Thomas, her

M.A. supervisor, remarked that 'he had considered it a privilege to work with a student as keen and scholarly as Mother Mercedes.'[58] Up to her death, she continued to work on her manuscript dealing with the history of the Ursulines of the Chatham Union.[59] Mother Mercedes Toohey's career was typical of many women religious. She began in the elementary school system, received her undergraduate and graduate degrees as a mature student, simultaneously holding teaching positions and community administrative posts, serving, for example, as general treasurer of the Ursuline Chatham Union, in addition to carrying on her work as head of the history department.[60]

At the same time as Mothers St. Michael Major and Mercedes Toohey were undertaking their work at Brescia College in London, Mother St. Paul Coveny was engaging in the writing of community history at the convent academy in Chatham. *From Desenzano to 'The Pines': A sketch of the Ursulines of Ontario, with a brief history of the Order compiled from various sources* was commissioned by the Alumnae Association of The Pines. The dust jacket to the 1941 Macmillian edition described Mother St. Paul as

> a teacher and educator of rare attainment and success. History, languages and religion are her specialities and she is a Latin scholar of the finest type. She has resided at The Pines for over half a century, shared in the varied experiences and hardships of early days and was intimately associated with the foundress for many years. She is, therefore, highly qualified to record with accuracy and vivid interest the story of the foundation and development of that institution.[61]

Unlike her two contemporaries, Mother St. Paul received no formal post-secondary education. She was a graduate of The Pines and, except for three brief mission assignments, spent her entire career there. For the majority of those years, she also served as community treasurer.

The evolution of *From Desenzano to 'The Pines,'* as told through the correspondence in the Ursuline Archives, is an instructive tale about the challenges of writing community history. Bringing the book from manuscript to publication was a lengthy process, spanning well over a decade. Significantly, it was the community, not the publisher's outside reader, that requested that the author make major changes to the historical content of the manuscript. Macmillan Press was to publish the work. Its reader assessed the work as 'precisely what its sub-title indicates ... a good book and one which we think would be more than acceptable to any girl or woman who has ever had the good fortune to be under the instruction of the Ursuline Sisters. It is a book, too, which would grace any publisher's list, and the reader has no hesitation whatever in saying that it would be acceptable to the house of Macmillan.'[62]

The community viewed the manuscript in a different light, and Mother St. Paul's superior directed her to change it. In a letter addressed to Reverend Mother dated 17 February 1935, the author responded to suggestions that she should eliminate sections on the history of the order from 1535 to 1835. Mother St. Paul focused first on the many demands on her time. 'I was forced to await the weekend before acknowledging your letter. Three hours in class daily and all that goes with them seem to be sufficient to keep a *seventy seventh* [*sic*] year old busy for five days in the week and even Saturday and Sunday have their share of claims on my time' (emphasis in original). She then went on to explain why the early history of the Ursulines was important to relate.

> The Nuns of the Sacred Heart, the Carmelites, Jesuits, those of St. Mary of the Woods, etc. have the account of the beginning and progress of their Order written. Why not the Ursulines? As a Councillor and speaking from a self-disinterested point of view, I assure you, I say 'Leave the matter of the book as near as possible to what it is now.' Of course, the part regarding the work in the London Diocese could be enlarged a little. But Mother Vicar no doubt remembers that ... in our [1912] endeavours to trace the planting of the Cross in America ... we naturally, it would seem, brought in the works of Venerable Mother Mary of the Incarnation. The verdict seems to have been 'The Ursulines praise themselves.' Since then the thought of it gives me nausea. I notice that it is a priest or some one else outside the community that writes these particulars of other Orders.[63]

This obviously heartfelt statement revealed much. Writing a community history was an activity that was interspersed with other duties – in this case, teaching at the convent academy, The Pines. Writing was also a community event. Additional correspondence revealed the work of other women from the community in the significant revision of the text that took place. Also revealed was a competitive spirit among religious communities: what was good for male religious (the Jesuits and Carmelites) was also good for women religious (the Religious of the Sacred Heart and the American-based Sisters of Providence of Saint Mary of the Woods). Finally, Mother St. Paul firmly believed and graphically stated her belief that the Ursulines were the appropriate authors of their own history.

Although revisions to the manuscript were made by other members of the community, its author was identified when the book was published in 1941. No longer just a 'member of the Ursuline Community of The Pines, Chatham, Ontario, Canada,' as she was named on the original Macmillan reader's report, Mother St. Paul, now in her eighties, was given credit for her work. The book was reviewed in over a dozen periodicals.

The reviewer for the *Globe and Mail* praised it as contributing to 'our knowledge of what the Church is doing and has done' by relating 'an integral part of the story of Catholicism in North America.'[64] The review in the *Canadian Historical Review* was balanced and reflected the debate described above. The reviewer described the work as 'a careful, competent piece of work ... [that] should appeal to an audience far wider than the preface would indicate' and concluded: 'If the story of the Ursulines at Quebec had been given fuller treatment, or if more space had been devoted to changes in Ursuline organization and the entry of the order into new fields of educational activity, the book would have been of more general interest.' There were some criticisms of the style, which the reviewer found 'naive and rather unctuous ... Many readers will dislike the pious obituaries and occasional moralizing.' Yet, despite this criticism, the review was essentially a positive one. '[T]the book is interesting and accurate and should be useful as an introduction to a more profound study of the influence of the Ursulines upon Canadian educational and social development.'[65]

Another reviewer compared *From Desenzano to 'The Pines'* to the history of the Sisters of St. Ann, *Herald of Christ the King,* highlighting the fact that both authors were octogenarians. This produced a letter from Sister Mary Theodore, author of *Herald,* to Mother St. Paul, citing the comment about the 'two eighty-year-old authors, you dear Mother St. Paul and myself.' Sister Mary Theodore confessed that she had not seen herself as a historian. 'I really wrote under obedience – not prompt, cheerful obedience either – but once I had begun I found the work most absorbing.'[66] Pursuing a task undertaken under obedience through the years generally reserved in the secular world for leisure and rest was not an uncommon experience among women religious who wrote history.

Today, the Ursulines of the Chatham Union describe themselves as 'Listening Women, Treasuring Women ... who walk in mutuality with other women ... Dangerous Women ... who challenge the status quo ... question the unchangeable ... dream of new possibilities.'[67] Brescia College at the University of Western Ontario remains a symbol of the community's continuing focus on education and especially the education of women. From its Halls of Women, which are corridors lined with the representations of historically significant women, to the circular sculpture of women dancing that graces one of Brescia's entrance as a memorial to the women engineering students who were victims of the 6 December 1989 massacre at Montreal's Ecole Polytechnique, the Ursulines ensure that they, their students, and their visitors are reminded of Marie de l'Incarnation's concern for the communication of historical events.

Countless examples of visual history are repeated throughout the enterprises of the women religious of English Canada. Stained glass windows in their hospital, school, and college chapels capture vignettes from the lives of women in ecclesiastical and secular history. In addition to the ubiquitous image of the Blessed Virgin Mary, depictions of women who were doctors of the Catholic church (Teresa of Avila), religious founders (Angela Merici), and saints are also common. Murals portraying the arrival of the women religious and their works are found in both the public and private spaces of many buildings. Virtually all motherhouses have Heritage Rooms. These rooms are dedicated to visually displaying the history of the community and are fine examples of historical representation through material culture. Heritage Rooms contain samples of religious habits, convent furnishings, and artefacts from enterprises of the community such as school desks and hospital furnishings. They also contain many examples of fine arts – including painting, drawing, china painting, and sculpture – that were done by members of the community or their pupils. Many historical subjects are found in such displays: portraits of founders and patrons, pupils and property, events and anniversaries. It was not exclusively through the written word that women religious communicated their historical knowledge and experience, yet it was through the written word that women religious began relating their history to the larger historical community.

History for the Scholarly Community

As women religious began to teach history at the post-secondary level and systematically to write their own history, they became involved in professional organizations such as the Canadian Catholic Historical Association (CCHA). The CCHA was established in 1933 under the driving influence of James Kenney,[68] a career civil servant with the Public Archives of Canada. Modelled on the American Catholic Historical Association established some seventeen years earlier, the CCHA had two prime mandates: the promotion of research on and interest in the history of the Catholic church, and the preservation of its historical sites and documents. It also sought 'to unite Canadian workers in Catholic history and to assist them in presenting the results of their investigations to the public, to assist historical study and teaching with bibliographies and catalogues of archival sources ... and to assist Catholic educational institutions in raising the standards of history teaching.'[69] An organization with such goals appealed to historically conscious communities of women religious as well as to individual sisters. Through its newsletters and journal, the CCHA gave them vehicles for continuous communications. Through its annual meeting, the association offered them a forum to discuss, with like-minded professional colleagues, their research and their teaching interests, and an opportunity to share their communities' concerns for the preservation of their documents and historical places.

The first CCHA annual meeting was a bilingual program with papers given alternatively in English and French. The following year, the English and French sections met in tandem, with papers presented in different parts of the same building and the membership assembling as a whole for dinner and other events. In 1961, the English section decided to meet in conjunction with the Learned Societies; this resulted in a split of the organization along linguistic lines. Subsequently the CCHA has occasionally met as a unit but has always published the proceedings of both sections – English and French – in one volume, currently entitled *Historical Studies / Etudes d'histoire religieuses*.[70]

An analysis of the first forty-five years of the CCHA's published proceedings reveals the extent to which women generally, and women religious in particular, participated in the scholarly work of the organization. The overwhelming number of papers, some 89 per cent, were presented by men, 53 per cent of whom were members of the clergy. Of the 11 per cent of the papers delivered by women, over half (6 per cent) were presented by women religious. Among the latter, the first was a paper by Rev. Mother M. St. James Hickey, an Ursuline of the Chatham Union, Professor of English and Dean of Brescia College.[71] For its content, style, and setting of precedent, the paper 'Three Hundred Years in Quebec: 1639-1941' warrants commentary.

Mother St. James's paper, a personal reflection upon the contributions and significance of the Ursuline experience to Canadian history, focused on Marie de l'Incarnation. While it had overtones of the providential

Mother St. James Hickey when she was Dean of Brescia College

history somewhat typical of its decade, it clearly foreshadowed a contemporary feminist critique – albeit a maternal feminist one. The paper began and ended on a highly religious note. Mother St. James opened with a series of statements on the role of the divine: 'Human history is all of a piece. Its pattern lies before God, Who sees our past, our present and our future.'[72] She concluded with a prayer for the canonization of Marie de l'Incarnation: 'O GOD GLORIFY THY SERVANT MOTHER MARY OF THE INCARNATION WE BEG OF THEE THROUGH THE MOST SACRED HEART OF JESUS'[73] (emphasis in original). Yet, within the core of the paper, some surprisingly contemporary elements were present. Mother St. James challenged the traditional view that the history of New France can be written as the achievement of Laval, Talon, and Frontenac. She argued for the inclusion of Marie de l'Incarnation in their midst, as she 'left a woman's mighty impress on the young colony, an impress of perpetuity which comes to a nation only through the quality of its homes.'[74] She situated Marie de l'Incarnation within the Ursuline tradition and described its founder, Angela Merici, as

> a modern feminist in many ways, a shock to her times by her fearless Christianity, a social service worker at Brescia [Italy] who did her work according to careful formulas. THE OLD WAY she called it and THE NEW LIFE ... Here in Canada a hundred years later is her spiritual daughter, the first woman missionary in the entire world bringing her teaching project to America ... Angela would have understood. THE OLD WAY and THE NEW LIFE.[75]

Mother St. James called for an alternative approach to the viewing of Canadian history, one that included and celebrated the achievement of women. She commented, 'As I stood on the rock of Cape Diamond ... I understood more about Canada than I have ever been taught from textbooks. Here, I found, was a woman's will projected across three hundred Canadian years right before my wondering eyes.'[76] She observed that when buried, the bones of Marie de l'Incarnation were mingled with those of the initial group of Ursulines, 'very fitting in the eyes of historians ... [since one] woman could not have done it alone.'[77]

Mother St. James's passionate and personal reflections about Marie de l'Incarnation remind us about the power of the institutional memory within religious communities. Historical writing, oral tradition, and the sense of being surrounded by history were the key means of its preservation. With this paper, Mother St. James began the tradition of women religious presenting their work before the CCHA, work that was sometimes candidly, and other times not so candidly, critical of the institutional church, especially for its treatment of the leadership of religious communities and for its lack of focus on the historically significant role of women.

Mother St. James and her paper were representative of a significant portion of papers delivered by women religious to the CCHA. Between 1933 and 1978, 82 per cent of the papers presented by women religious were about women religious. The presenters were, for the most part, archivists or academics who were faculty at the colleges administered by their communities; however, it should be noted that they were not necessarily those who taught history who were charged by their community, or invited by the CCHA to prepare research on topics that honoured community anniversaries. Members of the Congrégation de Notre Dame, Sisters of St. Joseph, the Ursulines, the Sisters of Service, the Sisters of Charity of Halifax, the Grey Sisters, and the Institute of the Blessed Virgin Mary presented papers on aspects of their congregational history.

The importance of this community-based research cannot be overestimated. Given the overwhelming number of historical sources such as annals, necrologies, personnel records, and correspondence files stored in community archives, and given that these archives were, and remain, private sources, women religious were among the few individuals admitted by the community archivists to undertake research. As with any private archives, be they corporate or that of associations, permission for admission was not freely given – even to communities' members.

There are few examples found within the CCHA programs of historians from outside of religious communities investigating the history of women religious. There is one example of a lay woman researcher working in this area. There are six examples of papers written by men: four papers by male religious and two by lay males. The male historians tended to examine the spirituality of women's communities and the influence of male clergy thereon or to describe aspects of interaction among male and females religious communities in their missionary enterprises. With the notable exception of the work of the Sisters of Charity of Halifax, the papers by women religious generally focused on community histories, highlighting the works of specific women and documenting the evolution of the communities' endeavours.

A sampling of some of the papers presented by women religious before the English section of the CCHA gives an indication of this type of historical writing. In 1945, Mother Margarita O'Connor, a member of the Institute of the Blessed Virgin Mary (IBVM, specifically the Loretto Sisters) became the second woman religious to present before the CCHA. Like Mother St. James, Mother Margarita was a college dean, serving in this capacity at Loretto College, University of Toronto, where she taught a number of subjects, including English and German. Mother Margarita's paper, 'The Institute of the Blessed Virgin,' traced the history of the

Canadian foundation from 1847 to 1945. It concluded with a commentary on the reinstatement of Mary Ward as the founder of the community, describing her as a 'valiant woman [who] had survived the machinations of the powers of darkness.'[78] This is a fitting analysis of the experiences of Ward, a seventeenth-century English woman whose attempt to establish a community of learned women religious, 'female Jesuits,' caused charges of heresy to be brought against her. Further, for centuries, all references to Ward as the founder of the IBVM were obliterated. This paper was one of the first public references to a subject who would remain one of Mother Margarita's passions throughout her life. It culminated in the 1962 publication of her biography of Mary Ward, *That Incomparable Woman.*

Sister St. Mariam of the Temple Scott Congregation of Notre Dame (CND), the author of the 1953 paper 'The Congregation of Notre Dame in Early Nova Scotia,' was the first woman religious listed in the CCHA program with the title Ph.D., awarded in English from Fordham University in 1947. In her paper, Dr. St. Mariam identified the challenges that were inherent in writing the history of pioneering women religious: 'At no period, however, was documentation held so cheap as at this time of reorganization after apparent chaos. Numbers and names mattered little to these pioneer women; records were difficult to keep. Souls were the great concern; all energies were directed toward reaching them.' The absence of records generated by women religious was all the more problematic when those surviving sources were suspect. The writings of male clerics were not to be completely trusted. She used an example to prove her point: 'The question also arises as to the reliability of Monseigneur de Saint-Vallier as a chronicler ... Objectivity, moreover does not seem to have been his outstanding characteristic.'[79] Dr. St. Mariam's analysis illustrated that women religious were employing the tools of historical analysis to test the validity of documentary sources.

Like Mother Margarita O'Connor, Dr. St. Mariam Scott was an educator and continued her work on the origins of the community and its founder, Marguerite Bourgeoys, throughout her life. Among her other contributions to her community's history were a three-act play about Bourgeoys (*The Constant Heart)* and an analysis of the writings of Bourgeoys (*A Spirituality of Compassion).*

The contributions of members of the Sisters of Charity of Halifax to the CCHA represent a unique and significant collection of work. This community, established by members of the Sisters of Charity of New York in 1849, became an independent foundation in 1856. Among its educational enterprises was Mount St. Vincent Academy, which has played a key role in higher education in the Maritime provinces since 1873. The Mount was chartered as a university in 1925 and given the power to grant degrees in arts, science, and music.[80] An analysis of the academic careers of the Sisters of Charity of Halifax would make a fascinating study and is one that cries out to be done, yet is much beyond the scope of this essay. Suffice it to say that this community was actively interested in promoting historical scholarship among both its members and its students. Five papers presented before the CCHA by members of the community between 1953 and 1976 focused on an array of topics related to the history of the Maritimes, and one dealt with social service among Irish immigrants in Quebec. Unlike papers presented by members of other religious communities, the role of the Sisters of Charity of Halifax is not the focus of any of them. The titles of the papers reveal much: Sister M. Liguori Wilson's 'Haliburton and the Uniakes: Protestant Champions of Catholic Liberty'; Sr. Francis Xavier Walsh's 'Educational Legislation in Nova Scotia and the Catholics'; Sr. Rita Mary Twohig's 'Failure of a Mission'; Sr. Mary Olga McKenna's 'The History of Higher Education in Prince Edward Island'; and Sr. Marianna O'Gallagher's 'Care of the Orphan and the Aged by the Irish Community of Quebec City, 1847 and Years Following.' These contributions are a reminder that not all the historical work undertaken and presented by women religious was self-reflective community history.

Papers presented by women religious before the CCHA covered a range of topics related to the history of women religious in Canada and to the broader area of the history of Catholicism in Canada. Themes that emerge from the papers include the challenges faced by women attempting to create innovation in religious life; struggles of women against social and ecclesiastical authority; a questioning of sources; and the lack of documentation of the historical experience of women. It should be noted that members of communities also reported before other professional historical bodies that were more appropriate venues for historians working in fields other than those defined by the CCHA.

In addition to offering papers to the CCHA, women religious always formed a large portion of the association's membership. Reviewing the CCHA's membership and mailing lists, one quickly sees that schools, motherhouses, archives, and individual women religious themselves have long been among its major supporters. Yet within the time period scanned, it is also noteworthy that women, lay or religious, did not play a prominent public role in the organization. As was the case with other professional organizations of historians that are documented elsewhere in this book, women were significantly under-represented at the executive table, both as subjects and generators of historical research. When women did appear on the program, either as researchers or subjects of scholarly investigation, the majority of them were women religious.

A Gendered Profession

The women religious of English Canada who recorded and wrote history represent a unique subset among the women analyzed in the essays of this book. To situate them in the history of the historical profession raises many interesting questions about both women religious and the idea of professionalism. As R.D. Gidney and W.P.J. Millar's seminal work on the professions in nineteenth-century Ontario suggests, the professions are 'gendered through and through.'[81] They argue that the professions excluded 'gentlewomen ... and women, genteel or not, who ministered to the care of bodies and souls,' even though life as a professional was a vocation: 'a sacred calling, a sacred duty, a commitment not only to service of others but to the larger social good.'[82] Women religious defined themselves and their work as service to God and neighbour through education, health care, and social service – and their work in history, as writers and recorders of their communities' past, as academic researchers, and as teachers in schools and colleges was, to them, a part of this larger vocation or profession.

In the period under study in this essay, the history generated by women religious can be seen as broadening its purpose and becoming more integrated with the world outside the convent walls. The initial types of historical writing analyzed – the annals and necrologies – were targeted exclusively for internal use within the community. While both these types of writing continued to exist (and indeed do exist to the present day), other kinds of historical writing emerged. This second stage also reached specialized audiences: the graduates of convent schools and interested Catholics. These types of history writing were done mostly 'under obedience' and appeared in many cases anonymously as written by 'a member of the community.' Even when communities engaged in a more public forum, it was not, for the most part, in the wider secular world. Their work was shaped by their vows and the structures of a pre-Vatican II Roman Catholic Church. They wrote too at a time in Canadian historiography when the discipline was generally not concerned with the history of women, especially women engaged in education, social service, and health care.

The thirty years since Vatican II brought great changes to the lives of women religious who wrote history as well as to the historical context within which they lived and worked. Although the impact of Vatican II on women religious has been the subject of much debate and analysis,[83] for academic women religious, the emphasis seems to be on the changes in their lives made possible by the implementation of 'Perfectae Caritatis: Decree on the Up-to-Date Renewal of Religious Life' (1965). This document, issued by the Second Vatican Council on 28 October 1965, accelerated a change process that had begun under the pontificate of Pius XII.

While religious life was transformed in many ways, including governance, daily routines, and dress, two changes were most significant for the historical work of women religious. First, more personal input into careers and professions was allowed, enabling women who wished to pursue further study in history and its related fields to do so. Second, religious were urged to 'return to the sources of the whole of Christian life and to the primitive inspiration of the institute,'[84] thus stimulating a wave of projects focusing on community histories. This was undertaken within a very different conceptualization of history than the one held by the women described in this essay. History as a field had changed. The tools of scientific analysis were being brought to bear on historical events at a time when women religious were encouraged to seek their roots. Feminist scholarship provided exciting new frameworks useful for communities exploring their past. The use of gender as a category of analysis as well as the interplay of gender with ethnicity, race, and class began to inform their writings.[85]

The writing and research of women religious reflected these changes. Stimulated by Vatican II, the program committee of the CCHA annually extended an invitation to one community of women religious to present a paper on some aspect of their historical experience. The history of women religious thus gained a higher profile among their own communities and within the membership of the CCHA. Unfortunately, this interest did not extend very far into the larger scholarly community. With notable exceptions among the historians of French Canada, the history of women religious has not yet captured the interest of wider secular scholars, and especially in English Canada, the 'profound study' called for by the reviewer of Mother St. Paul's book in the December 1941 issue of the *Canadian Historical Review* has yet to be undertaken.[86]

The history of women religious in English Canada remains a largely neglected topic. One explanation may be found in the challenge of researching sources within private convent archives. In a 1983 paper, J.S. Moir reminds the CCHA membership of the need to provide access to such sources:

> Without historical records there will be no historical research ... The churches [and communities] fear that the researcher may be unsympathetic to their particular positions (and in a minority of cases they are probably right) but in fact they are doing no more than denying their own creatureliness. Mistakes will be made by historians, but the road to truth is surely paved with mistakes and with their rectifications.[87]

Without the collaboration and support of the religious communities, much-needed research into the historical experience of women religious cannot be undertaken. Unless religious and lay researchers are allowed access to the relevant materials, what will emerge will be an incomplete picture of the historical record, with documents drawn from other public and private repositories. At the same time, as women religious journey further down the path of the writing and recording of their history, collaboration with secular scholars is increasingly evident; as each year passes, more scholars are allowed access to community records. At present, there are examples of collaboration, with both religious and secular scholars preparing work for both the larger academic community and the public.[88] Working together with secular historians, women religious can undoubtedly play a significant role in 'the coming of age' of Canadian Catholic historiography called for by J.S. Moir. Together, they can explore the historical work of past generations of women religious. Together, they can explore comparisons between the communities of English and French Canada, between diocesan and international communities, and within the same community over generations.

This essay merely begins the study of the writing and recording of history by women religious. It barely touches the surface of the historical experience of an extremely small percentage of the communities of women religious who have made foundations in Canada. The treatment of those few communities analyzed in this paper is neither exhaustive nor complete. There is much work needed here. Yet this essay gives a glimpse of the potential of these sources. Through their writing, the women religious indeed revealed to us many mysteries. In the words of the contemporary Ursulines of the Chatham Union, their work reveals how they listened to women who, through oral tradition, built a sense of historical community across time. They treasured women, who preserved the records of their past, often amidst trying conditions. And they were – and are – dangerous women whose analysis of their own past and of the experiences of their founders and pioneering women challenged existing norms. Women religious are indeed women with a sense of the past.

Acknowledgments

The author acknowledges the support of the Social Sciences and Humanities Research Council of Canada for its assistance in the preparation of this essay. The author thanks the leadership teams and archivists of the Sisters of St. Joseph of Toronto, the Ursulines of the Chatham Union, and the Religious of the Precious Blood for their support of the research reported here.

Notes

1 Marie de l'Incarnation to Claude Martin, Quebec, 1670. In J. Marshall, trans. and ed., *Word from New France* (Toronto: Oxford 1967), 371.

2 Gerda Lerner, *The Creation of Feminist Consciousness* (New York: Oxford 1993), 249.

3 Ibid., 255.

4 Ibid., 268.
5 Gertrund J. Lewis, *By Women, For Women, About Women: The Sister-Books of Fourteenth-Century Germany* (Toronto: Pontifical Institute of Medieval Studies 1996), 285.
6 The Second Vatican Council (1962-5) will hereafter be referred to as Vatican II.
7 Although the terms sisters and nuns are commonly used as synonyms, they have quite distinct meanings. Sisters live under simple vows, and their work is described as that of active apostolates. They serve God through serving their neighbours in education, health care, and social service. Nuns live under solemn vows, serving God in a cloistered life of prayer and contemplation. For further details, see M.A. Neal, *Nuns to Sisters* (Mystic, CT: John XXIII 1990), 30-1.
8 M. Theriault, *The Institutes of the Consecrated Life in Canada* (Ottawa: Supply and Services 1980).
9 J. Creusen, *Religious Men and Women in the Code*, 5th English ed. (Milwaukee: Bruce 1951), 286.
10 Before the 1917 codification of the Code of Canon Law, the requirements were somewhat more flexible than they became subsequently. Canon 282 of the 1917 Codification required bishops to ensure that 'two copies of documents' related to diocesan enterprises and residing 'confraternities' be made and that 'one copy shall be kept in the respective archives and the other in the episcopal archives.' In S. Woywood, *A Practical Commentary on the Code of Canon Law*, vol. 1 (New York: J.F. Wagner 1926), 138. Canon 88 requires Pontifical Institutes to generate quinquennial reports and submit them to Rome. Among the questions that institutes are required to answer is: 'Are the Archives of the Institute and of the individual houses properly equipped and carefully arranged?' In Creusen, *Religious Men and Women*, 286.
11 Sisters of St. Joseph of Hamilton, *Usual Customs and Observances* (Hamilton: Park Street 1885), 41. The constitutions of religious communities were often accompanied by a companion volume entitled *Customs and Observances*, which contained commentary and elaboration of clauses in the constitutions. Frequently, detailed role descriptions were included. Having such details in a separate volume facilitated revision, as amendment of customs and practices did not require the same complex and canonically bound protocols as amendment of the constitutions would have required.
12 Postscript, Congregation of the Sisters of St. Joseph of Toronto, *Annals*, vol. 1 (1851-1914): 486.
13 Ibid., Preface.
14 Sisters of St. Joseph, *Usual Customs*, 41.
15 *Annals*, vol. 1 (20 February 1898): 226.
16 *Annals*, vol. 1 (31 December 1900): 258.
17 Ibid.
18 *Annals*, vol. 1 (4 March 1905): 383-4.
19 *Annals*, vol. 2 (11 April 1917): 515.
20 Ibid.
21 *Annals*, vol. 2 (1 January 1916): 500.
22 *Annals*, vol. 2 (27 April 1917): 495.
23 *Annals*, vol. 2 (9 November 1917): 533.
24 *Annals*, vol. 1 (17 June 1909): 444.
25 *Annals*, vol. 1 (21 November 1876): 59.
26 *Annals*, vol. 1 (15 October 1879): 90.
27 *Annals*, vol. 1 (23 September 1901): 281.
28 Sisters of St. Joseph, *Usual Customs*, 41.
29 This cloistered community dedicated to perpetual adoration and prayer was founded in St. Hyacinthe, PQ, in 1861. As a revenue generator, the nuns produced altar breads.
30 Mother St. Joseph Caouette, as cited in 'Introduction,' *Necrology of Our Dear Departed Sisters of Mount Olivet (Toronto)*, typewritten ms., September 1992, n.p. Archives of the Religious of the Precious Blood (hereafter *Necrology*).
31 J.S. Moir, 'Coming of Age, but Slowly: Aspects of Canadian Religious Historiography since Confederation.' *CCHA Study Sessions*, 50 (1983): 91.
32 Natalie Zemon Davis, *Women on the Margins: Three Seventeenth Century Lives* (Cambridge,

MA: Harvard University Press 1995). Davis selects the Ursuline Marie de l'Incarnation as one of her three subjects.

33 *Necrology,* Series C (1913-45), 169.

34 *Necrology,* Series D (1947-91), 100.

35 *Necrology,* Series C (1913-45), 200.

36 Ibid., 283.

37 , 254.

38 *Necrology,* Series D (1947-91), 140.

39 *Necrology,* Series C (1913-45), 282.

40 *Necrology,* Series D (1947-91), 123.

41 *Necrology,* Series C (1913-45), 250.

42 Ibid., 252.

43 A Sister of St. Joseph, *In the Footsteps of Martyrs,* 1921. Archives of the Sisters of St. Joseph of Toronto.

44 *Rule of St. Augustine and Constitutions of the Ursuline Religious of the Diocese of London and their foundations* (n.p: 1929): 13. Ursulines Archives (The Pines), Chatham, ON (hereafter UA).

45 *The Rule and Constitutions of the Institute of the Religious of St. Ursula, of the Diocese of London, Ontario, Canada* (n.p.: 1915), 63-4. UA.

46 *Rule of St. Augustine and Constitutions,* 11-2, UA.

47 Education of Youth. Part III of Regulations for the Ursuline Religious (n.p. 1933-4), 58, UA.

48 Reprinted in Mother M. Toohey, 'The History of the Ursulines of Ontario' (M.A. thesis, University of Western Ontario 1937), 214-5.

49 P.G. Skidmore, *Brescia College 1919-1979* (London: Brescia College 1980), 92-98.

50 *Constitutions of 1915,* 34, UA.

51 Ibid., UA.

52 I.N. Mackay, LL.D., University of Liverpool, 22 July 1907, Mother St. Michael Major file, UA.

53 E.M. Bellord, Principal, Training College, Mount Pleasant, Liverpool, 10 June 1907. Mother St. Michael Major file, UA.

54 *Annals of Brescia College 1919-79.* London ON, 2-3, UA.

55 Mother St. Michael Major to Mother Clare Gaulker, 28 February 1926, Mother St. Michael Major file, UA.

56 W. Tamblyn to the Ursuline Sisters, 19 April 1926, Mother St. Michael Major file, UA.

57 'Necrology,' Mother St. Michael Major file, UA.

58 Mother Mercedes file (Catherine Christine Toohey), UA.

59 The incomplete manuscript is in the UA.

60 As American educational historians point out, this pattern was repeated among secular teachers as well, as they moved from careers in secondary education to careers at the college level. See, for example, D.F. Labaree, 'Career Ladders and the Warly Public High-School Teachers: A Study of Inequality and Opportunity,' in D. Warren, ed., *American Teachers: Histories of a Profession at Work* (New York: Macmillan 1989), 157-89.

61 Mother St. Paul [Coveny], *From Desenzano to 'The Pines': A sketch of the Ursulines of Ontario, with a brief history of the Order compiled from various sources* (Toronto: Macmillan 1941).

62 Reader's report on *From Desenzano to 'The Pines,'* UA.

63 Mother St. Paul Coveny to Reverend Mother, 17 February 1935, Mother St. Paul Coveny file, UA.

64 Review of *From Desenzano to 'The Pines,' Globe and Mail* (28 June 1941), UA.

65 V. Jensen, review of *From Desenzano to 'The Pines,' Canadian Historical Review* 22, 4 (December 1941): 444.

66 Sister M. Theodore, SSA to Mother St. Paul, 26 September 1941, Mother St. Paul Coveny file, UA.

67 *Who Are These Women?* Membership brochure, Ursulines of the Chatham Union, 1995.

68 Kenney was a star pupil of George Wrong, the head of history at the University of Toronto. He was a graduate of University College, University of Toronto (B.A. 1907), the University of Wisconsin (M.A. history 1908), and Columbia University (enrolled 1909, reinstated and Ph.D. 1927).

69 G.T. Wright, 'James Francis Kenney, 1884-1946: Founder of the Canadian Catholic Historical Association,' *CCHA Study Sessions* 50 (1983): 13-45.
70 Since its foundation, the journal appeared under the following names: *CCHA Report/Rapport* (1933/4-65); *CCHA Study Sessions/Sessions d'étude* (1966-83); *CCHA Historical Studies/Etudes d'histoire religieuses* (1984 to present).
71 Mother St. James Hickey taught at Brescia College from 1924 to 1955, with the years 1945 to 1947 being spent on Ph.D. work. Skidmore, *Brescia College*, 44.
72 Mother St. James, O.S.U., 'Three Hundred Years in Quebec 1639-1941,' *CCHA Report* 8 (1940-1): 11.
73 Ibid., 20.
74 Ibid., 11.
75 Ibid., 16.
76 Ibid., 11.
77 Ibid., 14.
78 Rev. M. Margarita, IBVM, 'The Institute of the Blessed Virgin,' *CCHA Report* 12 (1945): 81.
79 Sister St. Mariam of the Cross, CND, Ph.D. 'The Congregation of Notre Dame in Early Nova Scotia.' *CCHA Report* 20 (1953): 68.
80 Sr. Martha Westwater, 'The Sisters of Charity and Mount Saint Vincent University.' Paper prepared for the Blueprint Planning Committee (2 March 1993), Archives of the Sisters of Charity of Halifax. In 1925, the Mount had four sisters on faculty with Ph.D.s, in the fields of English, mathematics, Greek and Latin, Latin, and Greek. The first Ph.D. in history held by a member of the community was granted to Sister Francis D'Assisi McCarthy in 1932 by Fordham University. Sr. Liguori Wilson received a Ph.D. in history from the University of Ottawa in 1961.
81 R.D. Gidney and W.P.J. Millar, *Professional Gentlemen: The Professions in Nineteenth-Century Ontario* (Toronto: University of Toronto Press 1994), 8.
82 Ibid., 10.
83 For a recent example, see P. Wittberg, *The Rise and Decline of Catholic Religious Orders* (Albany, NY: SUNY Press 1994).
84 'Perfectae Caritatis,' in A. Flannery, ed., *Vatican II: The Conciliar and Post Conciliar Documents* (Northport: Costello 1975), 612.
85 Communities of religious, such as the Sisters Servants of the Immaculate Heart of Mary of Monroe Michigan (IHM), labelled their historical project as 'Claiming Our Roots: IHM Interdisciplinary Feminist History Project.' Their seventeen working assumptions include 'in practice, a range of feminist ideologies exist, but feminist approaches to history accept as a starting point that patriarchy exists in society and in its institutions, including churches.' The influence that this project will have, especially through international organizations such as the History of Women Religious Conference (HWR) and its Internet discussion group Sister-L, remains to be seen.
86 V. Jensen, review of *From Desenzano to 'The Pines.'*
87 J.S. Moir, 'Coming of Age,' 97.
88 In the aftermath of Vatican II, many communities of religious adapted a 'comic book' format for their history. V. O'Reilly, *Frontier Women: Sisters of St. Joseph of Canada: The Canadian Adventure* (Turin: Sadifa Media 1986), which appeared in the *Great Moments in Canadian Church* series, is one such example. The Sisters of St. Joseph of Hamilton commissioned Peggy Savage to prepare a centenary history of health care in Hamilton: Peggy Savage, *To Serve with Honour* (Hamilton: Dundurn Press 1990).

6

'I walk my own track in life & no mere male can bump me off it': Constance Lindsay Skinner and the Work of History

Jean Barman

Constance Lindsay Skinner was a transitional figure in the work of history.[1] It was during her lifetime, 1877-1939, that history writing was transformed from craft into scholarly discipline. No longer could the drama of human experience be acceptably interpreted by its most perceptive participants or observers; graduate study and academic employment became the effective prerequisites. The shift was almost entirely a male enterprise, the first female doctorates in history being only awarded, somewhat grudgingly, at the end of the nineteenth century.[2] Ironically, because so few women were permitted within the new paradigm, a few individuals like Skinner who were particularly talented and had some claim to legitimacy through life experience were sometimes given the opportunity to write alongside their professionalizing male counterparts. Examination of the public and private dimensions of Skinner's encounter with history demonstrates both the sacrifices some women made in order to participate in the work of history and the great extent to which the boundaries that the male hierarchy was drawing around itself were as much grounded in self-protection as in their superior talents.

Constance Lindsay Skinner wrote as an experiential historian. Born in 1877 in the Cariboo region of British Columbia, she lived as a child on the frontier that she then evoked, imagined, and generalized in adulthood. Her father was a Hudson's Bay Company fur trader, and her paternal grandparents one of three gentry families brought out from England prior to the gold rush to colonize southern Vancouver Island. About the turn of the century, young Skinner left British Columbia for the United States, and the longer she remained away, the more usable became the frontier of her childhood. Skinner worked as a journalist in Los Angeles and Chicago, and in 1912 made the big leap to New York City, the literary and publishing centre of North America.[3] As she explained in a letter of 1920, 'Alas! Canada has, as yet, failed to provide a market for her writers; and writers must live – at least we *think* we must!'[4] Skinner became

The public Constance Lindsay Skinner in 1926

what she later termed 'a free lance,'[5] supporting herself until her death in 1939 by writing in a variety of genres from newspaper features and book reviews to juvenile and adult fiction to poetry, plays, film, and history.

The public Skinner survives through her extensive publications comprising four historical monographs, four adult and nine juvenile novels, a book of poetry, and innumerable poems, short stories, plays, and newspaper and magazine features.[6] The private woman is less easily retrieved, and then only in snatches. As the young historian Henry Steele Commager wrote in her obituary, 'all of her life she was something of a lone wolf, independent and even remote.'[7] The passage of time served to cull Skinner's private papers, held by the New York Public Library. Letters located in the papers of various correspondents, including the Arctic explorer Vilhjalmur Stefansson, give other glimpses of the private Skinner.[8] This essay draws on these sources to explore the public and private dimensions of a Canadian woman writing history in the early twentieth century.

Skinner's photograph of Vilhjalmur Stefansson

The Public Dimension

The public dimension of Constance Lindsay Skinner's encounter with history affirms her multifaceted talent. In about 1918, Skinner became one of 'The New Historians,' a group of thirty-six scholars who wrote for Yale University Press's fifty-volume *Chronicles of America* series edited by Allen Johnson, Professor of American History at Yale. Conceived in 1916, the series' goal was to present all of American history 'in living form, through a continuity of short narratives ... so to make the traditions of the nation more real and vivid to those of our citizens who are not in the habit of reading history.'[9] Each volume promised 'a live, vivid, gripping story' emphasizing 'the biographical rather than the institutional.'[10] Intended for the general reader and for students, *Chronicles of America* was perceived to have 'from the outset vast educational possibilities and opportunity for distinct service to the country.'[11] The series was inspired by the success of the very similar thirty-two-volume *Chronicles of Canada* series. Its Toronto publisher, who had also instigated the earlier twenty-three-volume *Canada and Its Provinces* series, in 1915 talked Yale University Press into the new venture and then opened a New York office to oversee it.[12] One of just three women in the series and one of eleven individuals authoring more than a single volume, Skinner wrote *Pioneers of the Old Southwest: A Chronicle of the Dark and Bloody Ground* published in 1919 and *Adventurers of Oregon: A Chronicle of the Fur Trade* appearing a year later.[13]

Series editor Allen Johnson was responsible for securing the cooperation of the major historians of the day, no easy task as he confided to Skinner: 'You must know that my professional brethren feel that I have fallen from grace in attempting to "popularize" history.'[14] His strategy was designed to flatter egos, invitations to prospective contributors suggesting that they had been carefully selected as expert in their field. As indicated by the lengthy biographical profiles in a promotional brochure, Johnson was remarkably successful in his quest. For two-thirds of the contributors, all men, their credentials lay, as it would do increasingly over the twentieth century, in a graduate degree and academic position.[15] Contributors included William Munro of Harvard, Frederick Ogg of Wisconsin, Herbert Eugene Bolton of California, Samuel Orth of Cornell, and George Wrong of Toronto, all department heads, and their colleagues at Charleston, Chicago, Clark, College of New York City, Columbia, Cornell, Grinnell, Harvard, Louisiana State, Minnesota, Princeton, Queen's, Wisconsin, Wyoming, and Yale. However difficult it might have been, the series editor had snared many of the leading professional historians of the day from across North America.

The remaining third of the contributors, including the three women, belonged to the older, experiential, literary tradition popularized by

Francis Parkman and others. Often lacking graduate degrees or, in the case of the three women and two of the men, any university training at all, they were by occupation lawyers, journalists, editors, or simply writers. Their legitimacy as historians rested, at least in part, on their facility at generalizing their own life experiences. The man who wrote about seafaring was lauded as having sailed on a steamer running arms to Cuban rebels; his counterpart who portrayed the California gold rush had as a young man 'set out for the Black Hills in search of gold.'[16]

According to the series' promotional brochure, Skinner's legitimacy as an experiential historian predated even her own birth: 'Constance Lindsay Skinner is a blend of hereditary culture and pioneer environment. Through successive generations there have been writers on both sides of her family ... Born at a fur-trading post, Miss Skinner's childhood was spent in the wilderness in touch with the life of the fur traders, which she has pictured so vividly in *Adventurers of Oregon*.' The biographical sketch went on to evoke her career as a journalist, poet, and playwright, including such lines as: 'These poems, breathing the same spirit of the wilderness which is so masterfully expressed in Miss Skinner's two books in the *Chronicles*, established her reputation as an artist.'[17]

Three other contributors were also Canadian, all of them male academics: Munro of Harvard who wrote about New France; Wrong of Toronto whose two volumes examined New France and the American Revolution; and Oscar Skelton of Queen's who traced the history of Canada from 1760 to the First World War.[18] Unlike Skinner, who transcended national boundaries, they essentially wrote as Canadians.

The publisher of the series, Robert Glasgow, who first encountered Skinner in Vancouver in 1899 when she asked him for advice on her writing, invited her into the series to replace dismissed fellow Canadian writer Agnes Laut, author of three volumes on the fur trade and British Columbia in the earlier *Chronicles of Canada* series.[19] Series editor Johnson later mused, 'I heave a sigh when I think of the worries which that woman cost me,'[20] and by comparison he must have found Skinner a pleasure to work with. Volumes were to some extent written to formula in order to ensure consistency. A concept and then a detailed outline had to be approved by the series editor before a potential contributor received a contract; on its signing, the projected volume was given a provisional title.[21] By December 1918, Skinner had submitted her first manuscript, with Johnson responding that, although he was going to tone down 'a few sentences of hero worship,' not to worry: 'it's a good book – a beautiful book.'[22] Over the next couple of years, Skinner clearly held her own. 'May I say with perfect sincerity that your two *Chronicles* are among the very best in the series,' Johnson wrote. Indeed, 'the ease with which you have adapted yourself to historical writing has made me doubt more than once whether all this erudition which students are supposed to amass in a graduate school is not a positive burden.'[23] 'You have great gifts as a writer of history.'[24]

For her part, Skinner became so taken up that she began using note paper headed 'Yale University Press – Chronicles of America Agency – 522 Fifth Avenue – New York' even for her private correspondence.[25] In 1921, Skinner explained the appeal of the work of history: 'I have been absorbed for 3 years & expect to be so for 2 years more on the greatest poem ever writ on earth's pages by men & women – the pioneer history of these states; have had 2 vols pubd under my name & written a third for another author, have some 50000 words on my present book still to do, i.e., 1/2 of the book.'[26]

Skinner depicted the frontier as lived experience. Not unexpectedly, given Skinner's childhood, her frontiers were distinguished by Indians as real people with names and attributes; well-crafted portraits of men, women, and children; and ongoing reference to family and intellectual life. In the case of women, even those about whom Skinner could find out little were acknowledged, viz.: 'There are no portraits of her. We can see her only as a shadowy figure moving along the wilderness trails beside' her husband with whom she had ten children.[27] *Pioneers of the Old Southwest* used Daniel Boone's family as central characters to tell the story of early European settlement in Kentucky and Tennessee; *Adventurers of Oregon* traced the early fur trade in the Pacific Northwest from the time of Captain James Cook to the mid-nineteenth century. As to Skinner's goal as author, 'what interested me most in doing the book was the opportunity to tell the unified story of the N.A. fur trade and to show that the fur traders dictated the development of America as an English-speaking country.'[28] Both books were solidly based in primary sources, as Skinner stressed at the beginning of *Pioneers of the Old Southwest*: 'This narrative is founded largely on original sources – on the writings and journals of pioneers and contemporary observers.'[29]

As well as writing two *Chronicles of America* volumes, Skinner 'revised and contributed chapters to several' others.[30] The principal volume that she edited, to some extent rewrote, was *The Spanish Borderlands: A Chronicle of Old Florida and the Southwest* by Herbert Eugene Bolton, head of the Department of History at the University of California at Berkeley and curator of its Bancroft Library.[31] Bolton had proposed a volume on Spain in America in the literary style of Francis Parkman almost as soon as the series was announced in 1916, but other writing projects and the demands of his positions postponed a rough manuscript's completion to the end of the next year. Despite his desire to 'Parkmanize' Spanish exploits in North America and despite having been told early on that 'the volumes are not to contain discussions or expositions, but the story element,' and that 'they should deal with character, incident, personality, and life in its entertaining and dramatic aspects as far as possible,' Bolton's manuscript proved unacceptable.[32] The text was too learned and too detailed: 'just throw to the winds your scholarly instinct to be exhaustive and give me a graphic picture of types.' Series editor Johnson queried Bolton as to 'what you propose to do or just what you expect me to do with the manuscript – shall I return it to you for rewriting?'[33] For the next year Bolton equivocated, unable to cope with a draft 'to be revised in the direction of levity.'[34]

In March 1919, Bolton submitted a shorter, 'completely rewritten' manuscript,[35] but one that Glasgow considered little improved. He queried Johnson: 'What is to be done? It appears as though Professor Bolton has not the artistic faculty sufficiently developed to write one of our books. And yet he is a scholar of distinction and it is apparent that he has a theme well adapted to a living narrative full of color and movement ... But we cannot print the book as he has written it, nor does it seem likely that we should be willing to print any revision of it that he would be capable of making.' Even judicious editing would not rescue the manuscript; the only hope lay in 'another kind of revision, meaning a new projection by an author of imagination, based upon the materials which the first author has collected.'[36]

So Johnson wrote a very circumspect letter to Bolton, praising him for having 'labored long and hard to give literary form to your material,' then reminding him how he had 'expressed the laudable desire to do for Spanish America what Parkman did for New France.' Johnson reiterated Glasgow's suggestion: 'We can find a writer of literary distinction who will re-write and re-shape your book, using your material, and we could publish the book under your name, with a preface in which you acknowledge the services of so-and-so as your assistant or revisor.' Johnson admitted that the proposal might be 'repellent to you at first,'[37] and indeed, Bolton was crushed, even though he agreed to the plan. 'Your spirit is kindly, but I get little comfort on being told that I did my best and failed ... I am humiliated beyond expression.'[38]

Enter Skinner, who worked anonymously, principally from Bolton's initial, longer manuscript. Johnson refereed, telling Skinner, 'I hope that you can make something out of Bolton's manuscript, but it is an awful mess.'[39] Skinner wanted to extend the manuscript's time period, and Johnson gave her his 'blessing' to 'go to it and give us the borderlands of Spain in all their retrospective and prospective significance,' with the proviso: 'Only beware! They are doing an immense amount of research on early California history at the University of California and at Leland Stanford, and the pedants will be on your trail with war-clubs if you show any lack of familiarity with their scientific monographs.'[40] Johnson soothed Bolton: 'I may not reveal the name of your revisor, but I can assure you that you may trust his literary as well as his sense of historical values.'[41] But Skinner's comments were not designed to mollify: 'The difficulty is that Dr. Bolton's point of view is that of the antiquarian rather than the historian.'[42] Repeatedly, Bolton became 'hopping mad' at what he termed 'X's' willingness to go beyond 'matters of style and selection of incidents' into 'matters of general historical interpretations.'[43] Although 'some parts written by the revisor appear to me to be very good,' 'some of his work is rotten.'[44]

Amidst all of the fury, Johnson sent off yet another comforting letter to Skinner, which also laid bare the highly gendered nature of the profession and the academy:

> What a job you had! My fear is that he wont know the difference between your work and his own. You see, you haven't the proper amount of reverence for The Fact – as Carlyle would say. Now to the professorial mind a fact is a sacred thing, whether it means anything or not; and the more of these sacred things you can mass together the bigger man you are. I believe that Bolton would turn a handspring which would land him across the continent, if he had any inkling that a mere woman had revised his manuscript.[45]

Johnson's characterization of Bolton's attitude towards women is defensively confirmed by his very sympathetic biographer, a Bolton student and longtime academic:

> Bolton's feeling was that a woman's place is primarily in the home, but he was also realistic, for in his day the profession was anti-feminist, being not particularly favorable to woman historians. He was perfectly willing to see endowed girls go on to the master's degree, which could be valuable to them as teachers, both personally and financially, but he encouraged few to go beyond to the doctorate. In his day history was a field almost universally considered to be a man's profession with the positions in women's colleges somewhat limited. More than once Bolton told aspiring young women that he was dead set against accepting a graduate student in a doctoral program unless he felt he had a reasonable chance of placing the student in a position properly commensurate with his/her training.[46]

Only in October 1920, when the manuscript's organization, interpretation, and wording had been agreed on, did Bolton learn Skinner's gender and identity. Bolton, whom Glasgow once called to his face 'the most thorny and perverse man with whom I have done business,'[47] reduced his acknowledgment of Skinner to two concluding sentences of *The Spanish*

Borderlands' preface: 'My original manuscript for this book was written on a much larger scale than the Editor desired. In the work of reduction and rewriting, to fit it for the Series, I have had the able assistance of Miss Constance Lindsay Skinner.'[48] According to Bolton's biographer, the extent to which Skinner rewrote *The Spanish Borderlands* is unclear: 'The drafts of the volume are not complete in the Bolton Papers but there is enough to show that the final book is Bolton's; he did accept occasional paragraphs from Miss Skinner's rewrite and did, in many instances, follow the episodes which she winnowed out of the earlier edition. In any event, between them they produced a notable book.'[49] A more recent Bolton scholar has termed Skinner *The Spanish Borderlands'* 'unacknowledged coauthor' and concluded that it was 'Bolton, Johnson, and Skinner who together produced the book' that would become Bolton's signature publication.[50] As for Skinner, she was buoyed by the experience, quipping in its aftermath: 'I am, as my "Boss" would tell you, a particularly capable "intellectual" type of person, better able to grasp essential facts & correlate them than some of the author-Professors who haven't the handicap of being poets.'[51]

Skinner's final project with Yale University Press was her co-authored *Adventures in the Wilderness,* which appeared in 1925 as the first volume of a new pictorial history of the United States, *Pageant of America.*[52] Skinner was 'the only woman contributor' to a series a reviewer described as 'frankly pictorial.'[53] 'There is text, but only to give running comment on the pictures.'[54] Skinner become increasingly dissatisfied with the *Pageant* concept, and on seeing some proofs in mid-1925 fired back: 'I refuse positively to allow such shoddy scholarship to be accredited to me. I would not be guilty of writing a newspaper article in this trivial fashion, much less a chapter which is to be dignified by the name of history.'[55] After demanding changes, she agreed to 'appear as the author.'[56]

As Skinner engaged in the work of history, so she increasingly considered herself a historian. Glasgow was likely only half kidding when he wrote her in May 1918 that she had so 'got yourself into the good books of the Editor' that 'if you keep on he will be wanting you to lecture in his department at Yale University after the big job of the Chronicles is done.'[57] Skinner increasingly identified with the work of history, as in a letter to a friend two years later:

> I researched for 6 months for each of my short volumes in the Chronicles of America; and have corrected some minor errors accepted till my day in the history of the sections & periods I treat of. And have contributed one new fact. All this might have been done by others, but they balked at the various Colonial Records, 15 to 30 vols for different States, most of 'em unindexed. Needles in haystacks, hard to find, are facts under those conditions. But I happen to love to dig.

For Skinner writing good history went further: 'historical truth is much more than facts, names, & dates. It is interpretation and, as such, touches us today as well as remembers yesterday – else it were useless.'[58]

Skinner felt sufficiently comfortable to publish an essay in 1919 entitled 'History as Literature: And the Individual Definition.' In this hard-hitting defence of experiential history, Skinner blamed Americans' lack of knowledge about their country on 'writers of American history' who present a narrative 'shrouded in dullness, befogged by blind prejudice and willfully perverted through partisanship and propaganda.' 'All he has learned is that he should cross his fingers, blow hard, and curse England on every fourth of July, and, on the other three hundred and sixty-four days of the year, prepare for the chance to go and take Canada away from her.' Skinner asserted that 'American written history ... has no vitality in it because it is not literature. It is dead stuff because the drama of human souls has been left out of it.' 'The writers [of history] have not perceived that the drama of human feelings, motives, and inspirations is essential to true historical narrative, they have told us practically nothing about the character, the habits and customs, domestic and social, of the common people during significant periods.'[59]

Skinner's self-confidence was bolstered by her contact with noted frontier historian Frederick Jackson Turner of Harvard University. He praised *Pioneers of the Old Southwest* at the annual convention of the American Historical Association in December 1920, so series editor Allen Johnson excitedly reported back to Skinner: 'You will be pleased to know that Professor Turner of Harvard inquired with the utmost enthusiasm, "Who is Miss Skinner?"' and '"What is her record?"' 'I hope you will appreciate the subtle compliment that lies beneath this inquiry from one of the foremost historians of the United States.'[60] Shortly thereafter Skinner reviewed Turner's *The Frontier in American History* for the predecessor to the *Saturday Review of Literature*, and sent him a copy of the review that asserted that he had not given enough credit to her ancestors, the Scots. A vigorous correspondence ensued in which, according to Skinner, he made 'merry over my Scotch ardor and clannishness, and accused me of bringing "Scotch Metaphysics" in to bolster my theory.' Turner asked 'about myself, my ancestry and youth,' and became 'interested that I, like himself, was frontier-born.'[61]

In correspondence extending into 1923, a meeting of minds developed. Turner observed that he and Skinner had 'a common outlook upon the problem of history.'[62] Not only did they share the frontier but, in Skinner's view, Turner 'was a great scholar without being scholastic.' 'He could never forget that history is the story of human beings, of individuals composing a mass called society. He distrusted the modern glibness about "forces," "causes" and "main courses."' Skinner saw in Turner's writing 'a sound of beauty and sometimes a look of brightness, a shining,' which she was convinced, based on her own experience, originated 'in his frontier childhood.'

> Certainly, he was not unconscious that his look at the historical frontier was that of a frontiersman looking upon his own; nor that in his interpretation of the life of the frontier, and its significance, he drew upon his experience as a man who had first become aware of a human society, and of himself as an individual and integral part of it, in any environment of rhythmic freedom and beauty.[63]

The basis for Skinner's judgment that she and Turner were fellow experiential historians lay in an autobiographic letter in which Turner wrote to her at length about his own background 'because he knew I could understand and feel it all – it was like my own life in childhood at a northern fur-trading post.' Indeed, some of Turner's recollections of his Wisconsin childhood were extraordinarily similar to Skinner's own:

> There were still Indian (Winnebago) tepees where I hunted and fished, and Indians came in to the stores to buy paints and trinkets and sell furs. Their Indian ponies and dogs were familiar street scenes. The town was a mixture ... My school fellows were from all these varied classes and nationalities, and we all 'got on together' in this forming society ... Is it strange that I saw the frontier as a real thing and experienced its changes?[64]

Frederick Jackson Turner was not the only professional historian to become aware of Skinner. The *American Historical Review*, whose outlook was essentially that of the academy, gave considerable critical attention to the *Chronicles of America* series. It was not quite sure what to make of Skinner:

> Miss Skinner is a newspaper and magazine writer, dramatic and musical critic, and playwright, not particularly associated with the development of historical scholarship. However ... she has succeeded much better than would have been expected ... The rhetoric may be occasionally a bit exuberant, but none can deny that she has presented [in *Pioneers of the Old Southwest*] a reasonably truthful and worthy story of the eventful days and stalwart people whom she describes.[65]

The *American Historical Review*'s assessment of *Adventurers of Oregon* was positively glowing:

> This book is a delight. The author treats the dramatic scenes and incidents in the background of Oregon's history, achieving therein a wholly

> unusual degree of literary perfection. Thus she has produced a narrative which, for adult readers, deserves to take very high rank in its special field ... In her treatment the author exhibits a good knowledge of the facts, a comprehension of relations, critical insight, and a mastery of artistic arrangement rarely excelled. Her critical acumen is manifested not merely in the correct analysis of documents, a common enough accomplishment, but in that higher intellectual gift which enables its possessor to interpret complex human situations.[66]

The series' editor was very pleased, informing Skinner that 'it is not often, I would assure you, that a writer fares so well in the pages of this orthodox review.'[67]

As a female experiential historian, Skinner probably achieved as much as any woman could have, given gender assumptions of the day, and has been so recognized in the United States. The highly respected scholarly biographical dictionary *Notable American Women 1607-1950* contains some 1,300 women who achieved 'distinction in their own right of more than local significance,' and includes Skinner among just twenty-six 'Historians.'[68] Had Skinner been within the academy, she might have revelled in her newfound status. But she was not, and the private dimension of writing history for a living was very different for Skinner, and likely for most women historians, than it was for their professional counterparts.

The Private Dimension

The private dimension of Constance Lindsay Skinner's encounter with history was far more complex than its public face suggested. She did not, like most of the male historians with whom she interacted, have the luxury of an academic post from which to write or the benefit of spousal support. Bolton, during the time Skinner was working on his manuscript, held to an equally rigorous daily schedule but at the end of each day phoned home to be 'picked up' at Berkeley's North Gate by a devoted family member in time for dinner.[69] One of his sons recalled that 'Dad's domesticity was limited to dressing himself ... and to getting his dirty clothes down the laundry chute ... I doubt if he could boil water, let alone an egg.'[70]

In sharp contrast Skinner was a woman alone, dependent on her own resources. The bottom line had to be, and always was, that private borderland between money and ambition. She had to write and then write some more in order to survive financially and to pursue her unflinching goal of writing as she would. The breakneck pace at which she worked then, and throughout her career, likely accounted for Commager's somewhat tongue-in-cheek suggestion that she write a biography of the African explorer G.M. Stanley: 'That would be something to do during these long winter evenings when you have nothing else on hand but a few children's books, novels, histories, reviews, articles, speeches, and editorial work on two or three series.'[71] Instead of the more usual royalty arrangement, contributors to the *Chronicles of America* received a lump sum, in the case of *Pioneers of the Old Southwest* $1,100 plus $50 for undertaking any necessary revisions.[72] For the *Pageant of America* volume, Skinner received sixteen cents a word.[73] It is unclear how she was paid for her other editing and writing for Yale University Press, but it was likely also on a piecework basis.

The importance of the income that came from writing history was magnified by three dynamics entangling Skinner during these same years: a dependent mother, unrequited love, and illness. Each presented a fundamental human dilemma threatening to engulf her career as a writer. Skinner's encounter with the work of history must be contextualized to be understood and appreciated.

Skinner's ambivalent relationship with her mother long preceded her debut as a historian. Born into an impoverished Victoria family with pretensions to gentility, Skinner's mother existed within a traditional frame grounded in female fragility and 'delicate health.'[74] Physically she was 'a small woman,' which likely encouraged the image that she sought to project.[75] Skinner's father willingly participated, referring to her as 'My own darling little Girlie'[76] and taking pleasure in being congratulated 'on my possessions and I do feel rich when I think that I own you too.'[77] When Constance was ten, the Skinners left the Cariboo for a more comfortable Vancouver, where her mother took up social reform but, after her daughter's departure, increasingly found life a difficult proposition. Following Skinner's visit home from California in 1905, her father urged, virtually begged, her to write as often as possible, if only a postcard, since her mother sees 'all gloom' and needs some brightness.[78]

Skinner was an only child, tugged by her parents in two different directions. Her mother endlessly worried, crying at night if a letter did not arrive. According to her father, 'I know that if she could have her way you would be here by her side always.'[79] But she must remember that her mother 'hardly exists outside of sentiment – it colors more or less most women's view of things – with her it is *the* view.' 'I am proud of you my darling and I don't misunderstand your wanting to be independent. I think if you'll remember I always encouraged you to exercise independence of thought.'[80] Repeatedly, Skinner's father buoyed her up and gave practical advice: 'Industry – Economy – Integrity – are the way – and there is none other that is not full of pitfalls and miseries – life is like business – and life is a business.'[81] She should have fun and pleasure, but 'don't get hurt.' 'You are a wise young woman of discretion – therefore be discreet, be wise – take care of yourself – because if you don't no one else will – men are selfish animals at the best – and pain to them is a little thing compared to the pain that is sometimes wrought by them – some without wishing it – to others – keep those two French words in your mind – "Guardez vous."'[82] He responded to her comment that she was 'not going to fall in love with any of those most agreeable and fascinating impossibles' by advising her that she should not monopolize anyone or let them monopolize her.[83] Skinner must take care of herself since no one else would.

The remnants that survive of Skinner's years in Los Angeles and Chicago suggest an enthusiastic social life as well as a burgeoning career. She was in her twenties, attractive, intelligent, and ambitious. One of the most tantalizing clues is a California photograph album that Skinner kept through her lifetime with some pictures removed, others with their names scratched out.[84] Photos of good-looking young men include several of writer Jack London, whom she interviewed as a reporter, in one looking somewhat insolently into the camera, in another with a note at the bottom removed. In 1908, when Skinner had just turned thirty, she assured her mother: 'Because I amuse myself with a man or with men don't be alarmed about me. Had I been going to shipwreck myself I'd have done it long ago. I had chances enough.' Her parents had to trust her:

> Dad knows & he can tell you that underneath all my temperament there is a bedrock of granite. I walk my own track in life & no mere male can bump me off it. I know too much to put myself into a hole that hasn't another exit. You, dearest wee Mother, don't know one half so much about the wicked world as I know. You have not had my opportunities and you have not wanted to know. I've had opportunities and I've wanted to know. So I know, and it hasn't soured me a bit. And it is the knowledge that is Power.[85]

On her father's death in 1909, Skinner inherited responsibility for her mother. At first she sought to maintain the established relationship, reiterating to her how different their lives had become:

> I wish you could see my life and see it & know how good it has all been for me. It has broadened my outlook and made a real woman of me. It has been the best life possible for me. It has made me know & understand – and that was always what I wanted ... You & I can't think alike on all points because we are two persons and our experiences have been different ... I would not give up the past ten years & what they have taught me – not for a kingdom. I wish you could see that you have no cause to worry about me; and that I am not weaned away from you just because my life has not been what you wish. It is the life God chose for

me and it has been good for me. I can say that honestly though it has had none of the great happiness that every true woman longs for, it has given what I needed more than happiness – knowledge & work.[86]

Over time Skinner's mother became more dependent, and Skinner was forced to assist her financially as well as struggle to support herself: 'I am so glad my money has helped you with the taxes too. How I wish I could make it more.'[87] The only solution seemed to be to bring her mother to live with her in New York, which she likely did sometime in 1914.[88] 'We shall have a nice happy time together with ease of mind and enough to live on without distress or the old scrimp.'[89] The reverse quickly became the case. Skinner was stifled, recalling how: 'I was in a prison of "duty" to the will of another person – the iron will of a narrow little person, as pathetic as cruel in her hatred of my work, my religion, my views of life and, in short, of all that gave life any meaning to me.'[90]

I was on my own, in a hard job, desperately lonely, in a city where I had no friends (and no time to make friends) – and with an ailing dependent – my mother ... Many times, I did not know how I would manage the rent and, sometimes, where even our next meal was coming from. My family were nearly all dead, dispersed, or busy with their own troubles. I had no one to help me or to give me advice.[91]

For Skinner, the best hope of emotional survival lay in the second dynamic of these years. Now in middle age, she became enamoured with the exploits of the Arctic explorer Vilhjalmur Stefansson, two years her junior but ostensibly the same age since by this time Skinner was fudging by a couple of years.[92] Like Skinner a Canadian, being the son of Icelandic immigrants to Manitoba, Stefansson had been a graduate student in anthropology at Harvard when he began the Arctic adventures that would bring him widespread popular recognition as an explorer, writer, and lecturer.[93] During the time that Skinner's mother lived with her, it was Stefansson's published 'brief messages from the Ice Realm' that keyed her up so she could 'better work with my pen.'[94] 'In the nights after she slept I sat at the window – it is the moon & skies I remember & the stars — and prayed for a peace, a courage, a steadfastness, a freedom in my soul, like that of the skies, and always I thought of the man I did not know & never expected to see, and I prayed for him ... For my soul's sake as well as for his own, he must not fail.' The contrast between Stefansson's and Skinner's circumstances could not have been greater: 'I felt that I could bear my own lot & be thankful if I could see the man win – i.e., the ideal realized. And I began to think that I knew him & divined his qualities – as true, sincere, chaste, generous, good, large. And I loved him for these things.' The press reported that Stefansson was lost in the Arctic: 'My mother read it aloud at breakfast. She said, "It is too bad but why will men do such crazy things." Without thinking I answered, "it isn't true. While they are saying he's dead Stefansson has succeeded & he will be heard from later." And I was promptly snubbed for another of my ridiculous notions.'[95] And so the gulf widened between mother and daughter, leading to the former's return to Vancouver after an absence of 'several years.'[96]

By late 1918, about the same time that Skinner was completing her first manuscript for Yale University Press, she was again on her own and sought to realize her passion. It is testimony to Skinner's tenacity and strength of character that, not only did she manage to meet Stefansson, but she established ongoing communication with him. The returned hero was slated to lecture at Carnegie Hall. She wrote to him on the morn, using all her literary wiles to capture his attention. Flattering Stefansson as 'the Canadian Viking,' she suggested that 'one Far Western Canadian may write to another without apologies' and then proceeded to tantalize with snippets of her career, from having been 'rather a good interviewer of celebrated persons' to now being 'one of the very ancient and self-lawed Tribe of Bards who should not be judged & condemned by conventional standards of etiquette even when they err so wildly as to write letters to distinguished Canadians whom they have never met.' To underline the point, Skinner enclosed a 'little magazine containing a group of my Indian poems' which 'need not be *read*.'[97]

Skinner warned Stefansson that she was going to introduce herself to him after his lecture, and she did. She wrote again shortly thereafter in even more provocative fashion, making reference to 'the perfect combination of virile masculinity and wishful tenderness, & superb artistic restraint – a force never brutish, a tenderness never mushy, a wistfulness colored by faith & hope & thus never despondent or maudlin.' And at the end: 'Of course I shall like to see you on your return [to New York City] if you care to find time for a meeting. I'll even append my 'phone no. "Schuyler 2950."' Stefansson noted to himself at the top of the letter, 'Saw her.'[98] Two months later, having 'read most of your book last night and enjoyed it,' Skinner rephrased her first approach in a manner to 'accord with those of your friends the non-Christian Eskimos.' 'I am Constance Skinner. My intentions are friendly. I have no knife. May I come in?!' The letter ended with an invitation: 'If you would care to call on me on Sunday afternoon which [is] my deserved leisure time from the arduous toil of history concoction I should be very pleased to see you ... The latch string is out – my door opens inwards.'[99]

Thereafter came frequent long letters from Skinner and Stefansson's less frequent shorter notes, sometimes dictated to a secretary, or return phone calls or visits, as noted on the top of her letters kept by him. The relationship, such as it was, puttered along, likely assisted by Skinner's offers of editorial assistance. Skinner pointed out that, although she had supported herself for over two decades, it had not made her unattractive as a woman: 'Since 18 yrs of age I've had no other protector than my Reason & no discipline but my own, & you perceive that I am not a wreck & that my face is not that of a woman who has lived an ill-ordered & fantastic life.' Thanking 'Stef' for 'that wonderful picture & your inscription which makes me very proud,' she cautioned: 'Don't be frightened at my use of the word "love."'[100] Yet Skinner was ever the realist: 'To be able to revere manhood in a concrete form is the essential thing for me. With that image in my mind I can live alone more than content ... It proves the ideal to be the real: and shows that the lower concept (which seems so much in evidence throughout the younger years of an attractive woman's life) is the false one.'[101] If she could not possess the Stefansson of her dreams, the platonic version was better than nothing at all.

But even this receded as time passed. Responding in early 1922 to one of Skinner's frequent entreaties to meet, Stefansson dictated a far less intimate response: 'I am so much behind with my work that I am afraid I shall not have the time to come down and see you. If it is necessary to talk something over just call me on the phone here at the office in the daytime or in the early morning at my apartment, as shown in the telephone directory.'[102] Skinner continued to put the best possible interpretation on their spasmodic relationship, writing just over a week later: 'When you have the will to give me again some of this spirit, or moral urge, which I always get from you, come to bestow it. I've done work of a better thought-quality since our friendship became a practical, no longer only an ethereal thing. Cooking chops is a stabilizing & solidifying experience -- and the candy dish is again full.'[103] And two weeks later in reference to Wrangell Island about which Stefansson had just written: 'I wish some of the $ of Isabella or Elizabeth were mine, to gamble on this isle with you. Those queens had opportunities I lack but no more sporting blood than I. I can of course wait on the ice boy & the candy dish bulges: and my spirit needs a sweep of the north wind.'[104]

Over time a certain honesty grew up. Skinner wondered, with a touch of cynicism: 'How long can our friendship endure, thus? We have really but *one* thing in common & that is our great love for Stefansson.'[105] At the beginning of 1923, as Stefansson was about to leave town, she quipped, 'Wish you were as virtuous as you are dear.' All the same, her letter ended, 'Would like to equal – if not beat you – at something – (at something besides loving; I put it all over you at that – *alas*!!).'[106] A month later she lamented: 'That Icelandic suspiciousness of yours – (my research books inform me that that is a Norse trait) – shuts the door on so much simple & genuine affection – gift that is being offered you. Poor brilliant blind Great One – you have thrown away some good gold for dross. But maybe just the glitter without the substance (substance creates responsibilities) was what you wanted ... Finis.'[107]

But it was not over, and never could be for Skinner. Money entered the relationship. Skinner's ties with Yale University Press were ending, and she had not only to support herself but assist her mother in Vancouver. Allen Johnson had resigned as series editor in 1921, Robert Glasgow died suddenly the next spring, and thereafter the tone of her correspondence with the press became more perfunctory.[108] By the beginning of 1923, matters were serious: 'I am coming in a week or two to the end of my Yale U.P. work unless I will continue at a figure ruinous to me (not that [Arthur H.] Brook [now in charge] doesn't know the worth of my work, but he does know my financial situation & my responsibilities re mother, which he learned from Mrs. Glasgow – & he is for putting the screws on – & I can't stand any more of it).'[109]

As well as working for Yale University Press and writing fiction and poetry for anticipated sale, Skinner was also doing outside editing, 'working every Sunday all day – 11 am to 1 am; Sat afternoons & pms & all other evenings from about 7 to after midnight.'[110] All this fell short as illness, the third dynamic threatening to engulf Skinner's life, intruded. Like her mother, Skinner had always been prone to periods of poor health. In her late teens she was so ill that she had to lie 'as still as death – almost in an unconscious state for hours.'[111] Indeed, it was this bout that introduced her to the United States when she was, as she later told a reporter, 'sent to an aunt in California to recuperate.'[112] At one point, while her mother was living with her, she had lain 'on my couch with a cough tearing my chest and two deaf ears ringing, (the result of abscesses) and burning with fever.'[113] In mid-1923 Skinner began her letter to Stefansson: 'I've been hoping never to write this particular letter but the ugly facts of my everyday life drive me to do it. Financially I am at a low ebb and attacks of illness have handicapped me so that I haven't finished the stuff I started to work on in the Spring; & now comes August when the editors & publishers leave town, & authors can't sell to them. I couldn't renew my lease on my "house" this month — am hoping I can later before some other tenant takes it.' Skinner appraised her financial prospects:

> If I can get through the next 6 months, things will be o.k. with me. I have still 4 chapters, long ones, of my novel to do & the final revision of the whole. It is a story with magazine serial & motion picture possibilities. I have some short stories also under way to finish & revise carefully with a view to the bigger paying periodicals. I have a publisher much interested in my projected history – the synopsis has been favorably

> considered by their editorial board; but as their chief is off to Europe for 2 months they won't take it up with me finally till September. I can't talk 'advance' to them yet – &, such is the nature of good businessmen, if they knew the straits I'm in they'd give me a poor contract & I'd get next to nothing out of the sales.

Skinner was much more candid than usual: 'And oh Stef dear I am weary of being "*done*" like that – confess it, I have *not* deserved it, cuz I never "did" anyone in my life & never expect to – unless it's you!'[114]

Skinner needed help, and she was willing to beg for it. 'At present I have enough to pay July's food & rent for me & Nip [her cat], and the rent but no food for August & no $ to send home where I am responsible for my mother's expenses, including the maid she has to have, & 300.00 taxes on the house.'[115] Receiving no response, Skinner was forced, a month later, to mortify herself. 'You are the only person except my father of whom I have, in all my life, asked help of that kind. I felt so sure I could ask it of you; but it wasn't easy, at that, &, but for mother's claims on me, I wouldn't have asked even you.'[116] Only two weeks later did Skinner receive a cable from the travelling Stefansson: 'Two letters just arrived regret unable help now hope may have money November.'[117] A fuller explanation soon followed: 'Your financial difficulties came at a hopeless time for me. I am having considerable trouble borrowing enough money to live myself.' His 'lecturing season' began in the fall, so 'by the end of November I shall be able to help you a little.'[118] How Skinner actually survived is uncertain, although a month later Stefansson reported from London that an intermediary, possibly a literary agent, 'had some luck in selling your second-hand stories –- the ones you have already published in America.'[119]

Stefansson likely lent Skinner some money late in 1923, but her plight worsened, as she wrote early the next year: 'Stef dear I hope this is the last time I'll impose on you.' 'The 1st of the month, rent date, begins to loom up before me with its scarifying shadow: & as yet no kudos has come in to reward my pen-labors.' She had been writing as fast as she could and then attempting to sell what she wrote. 'The editor of Ainslees [magazine] said she wanted my story but no price was named before the "grippe" took her out of the office indefinitely. I phoned today but she is still away.'[120] Stefansson again assisted: 'Thank you for the check which came a few days ago.'[121] However desperate the situation might be, Skinner was insistent that her penury not become known: 'But please Stef dear whatever you do or don't do, please don't mention my "hard times" or ill health to *any one*. Those things get about and hurt the writer in his market. As long as I can stand up, I've got to bluff.'[122]

Increasingly Skinner accepted that her emotional well-being would have to depend not on Stefansson but on her own passion to write: 'To see you conquer seems to make the defeat of my own drama easier to bear. I've never wanted anything in my life with a single-hearted desire, but writing – i.e., writing developed into art – and it seems I can't have that. The thirst for perfection is a dread thing. It gets in the way of practical living and the facile sensuous joys – the pleasing glint of easy money and the touch of superficial kisses.'[123] Skinner finally acknowledged the platonic nature of their relationship on paper, in reference to a mutual acquaintance: 'he knows that no such intimacy has been between you & me; but he also knows that, because you exist, there is no other man for me.'[124] She was even more brutally honest in a hasty pencilled note two days later by daring to refer to Stefansson's ongoing relationships with other women:

> Dear Stef
>
> I'm pretty much 'down' (& lost as to pride) or I wouldn't write this note, which is a hard one to write. It is so obvious that if you wanted to come here you would. Yet couldn't you do it merely out of kindness? I am oppressed with anxieties -- feel pretty much the cornered rat. I would appreciate kindness. I am not so selfish that I want you to deprive yourself of hours with someone else much dearer to you -- or to interfere with your work. I only mean that if you would think about it you might find there was a little time for me too. C.[125]

Such stocktaking only magnified Skinner's two other dilemmas. In the middle of 1924, her mother took to her bed in Vancouver, and her family expected her to return home to assume the traditional female role of caretaker. Skinner agonized, writing to Stefansson, who was then in Australia: 'if I leave N.Y., I will either store my belongings in your name ... or sell them myself & deposit the amount in your name in repayment of your generous loan to me.'[126] But Skinner stayed in New York, as a consequence becoming 'the target for every arrow of defeat with the bitter condemnation of one's family heaped also on one in weekly budgets.' Her health again deteriorated: 'The air is so thick with depression sometimes it is hard to see my way. I don't know that this matters – that I am *afraid,* and don't believe I *can* go through another siege of privation of several months – my vitality is not much now -- I give out on these stairs.'[127]

This was not all. Skinner was being beseeched to marry. Now in her mid-forties, even by the age of her imagination, she faced a fundamental life choice: Should she continue to walk her own track in life alone? Having recognized that her love for Stef would remain unrequited, should she settle for some emotional second best? Writing to Stefansson in October 1924, Skinner described her decision:

> I went through a pretty tough time mentally trying to make myself agree to marriage but could not do it ... I know you hoped I would say yes to him & indeed I did try to do it. I am not able. You must forgive me for it and help me get onto my own feet with my work – which I love & which is all I have or can hope to have in my life & give me some happiness ... As to my situation, I do hope you will think it worth while to stand by me and really help me to do what my talents can do if given a chance to go beyond pot-boiling stuff. I know you wanted me to do the other thing & would think me more intelligent if I had done it – & more dignified than to remain in debt & ask for more. I have no excuse except that it was not possible for me.[128]

Stefansson had offered to continue to assist Skinner financially if that was the only reason she felt compelled to marry, and a month later she made clear that she might have to take up his offer: 'With that promise to nerve me I did close the door finally ... I knew I'd have suffered intolerable irritations for about 6 months & then shot myself as the only decent way out. I felt that your friendship and promise were by me to save me from that.' Skinner closed the letter: 'If you no longer feel the same urge to send me my rent monthly, I don't like to ask you to do it. One wants these things done in the same spirit as they were offered: the spirit, the warmth, the interested encouragement are almost life itself ... If you feel too differently now about my home & the rent, will you tell me so at once?'[129]

It seemed for a time that Skinner would crumple. The decision to put her writing ahead of the financial security that marriage, even a loveless marriage, offered was not taken easily. Neither was her decision to stay in New York against her family's expectations for her. Skinner suffered a new bout of illness, which then interfered with her writing and hence her ability to support herself and her ailing mother: 'I seem to have less bodily strength than formerly; for long hours of work, distress of mind and privations have an effect now they did not have years ago.'[130]

The next year, 1925, was decisive. About the same time as her final history volume with Yale University Press approached publication, it seemed as if the private woman that was also Constance Lindsay Skinner might not survive. Even as she was slowly detaching herself from emotional subservience to Stefansson, referring to him by the end of the year as 'old dear,' her mother's condition deteriorated.[131] By the time Skinner received her aunt's angry letter of early 1925, her mother had been confined to her bedroom for about eight months.

> Your mother needs you with her, not for a visit but permanently. She needs a daughter's love and daily attention and the attention in things

> a servant cannot undertake. It is your privilege to leave New York entirely until such time as your mother does not need you ... on receipt of a letter or wire from you I will send you money for your fare to Vancouver ... P.S. It is absolutely essential for your mother's welfare that she should have with her always from now on her daughter and with patience and kindness – you should be there now – Delay in coming is most unwise I think. Your mother suffers great pain & all worries should be kept from her. You should handle the funds of the house & ease her this worry.[132]

Skinner remained in New York, but at the cost of her health. As the months wore on, she became less and less able to cope: 'I am worked thin, & tired to the point of hysteria; and my B.C. relatives (B.C. not only geographically) choose this time to be particularly nasty to me. I shiver at the sight of a Canuck stamp on a letter.'[133] Still Skinner stayed, determined to write but able to do so only through mortgaging her future as well as abandoning her mother: 'I haven't paid any of my June 1st bills because I can't – rent, phone, light etc. My scrubwoman and her daughter who is my seamstress look after my needs and wait for their money because they have worked for me for 4 years & know that I pay generously when I am able.'[134]

Skinner did not return to Vancouver, not then, not several months later on receiving notice that her mother was dying, not for the funeral, and not subsequently. In a letter to the family solicitor, a friend referred to Skinner's 'nervous overwrought condition, due to general physical collapse hastened by overwork and protracted anxiety.'[135] Yet Skinner's illnesses largely disappeared thereafter, which she attributed to Christian Science, her new 'religion.'[136] As with unrequited love, the two fundamental human dilemmas of her health and a dependent mother had resolved themselves, leaving intact her public image as a historian and writer. Once again, she walked her own track in life.

Maturity

From the mid-1920s, the public and private dimensions of Skinner's life coalesced. Her concern that her reputation as a historian and writer remain untarnished never lessened. 'The real job seems to be to keep from getting "down" & heartsick & unproductive mentally & showing the callous $ world that I'm poor – in which case it would want even less to do with me than it does now.'[137] Even during Skinner's low point in mid-1925, she considered it essential to keep up appearances: 'I have to put up a "front" or quit; because N.Y. editors are not interested in the poor.'[138] What changed over time was that Skinner had less to hide.

At the beginning of 1926, Skinner's debt to Stefansson stood, according to her calculations, at $1,221[139] and in early 1927 at an even $1,000 when 'I wish I could make a bigger dent in it but I can't just yet.'[140] Another $222 was repaid in April 1927,[141] and $50 in February 1928 when 'I wish it were more,' but '*think* it will be settled in full this year.'[142] Not until the end of 1934 was the debt again mentioned on paper:

> Here is 200.00 of the debt of fore – very late, but nonetheless as soon as possible! ... Money has been so elusive & demands on it so urgent, & too many, that – to use an original phrase – much time has elapsed; but I have a warm & vital type of memory as well as a tidy account book – I hope the remainder will follow soon. As always – CLS I *can* send this *now*: so don't try to start an argument![143]

It is perhaps the strongest indication of Skinner's growing independence from Stefansson that she repaid so little money, even as she became more financially secure.[144]

Skinner's relationship with Stefansson grew more reciprocal. If writing less frequently, they continued to see each other from time to time, as indicated by a short note of September 1929 – 'When are you coming in for another dose of chops? Nip is eager to see you again.' – and Stefansson's pencilling on its top, 'Shall phone some time.'[145] Increasingly they very skilfully promoted each other's work through writing favourable reviews and making contacts. So far as Skinner was concerned, Stefansson became 'one of my "best publicity agents" (!!).'[146] Writing in 1931 to a third party, he described her in glowing terms:

> Constance Lindsay Skinner, of 12 East 11th Street, telephone Stuyvesant 9-0082, is a historian of national and really international reputation as author of volumes in the 'Chronicles of America' series of the Yale University Press – history of the frontier. She came to this field logically, for she is the daughter of a factor of the Hudson's Bay company and was born in the Indian country of northern British Columbia. She is a poet of distinction and in that field a foremost interpreter of the Indians. She is also a novelist and the author of successful juveniles – her publishers are the Macmillan Company, Coward McCann, and others. Recently, Miss Skinner has made a success as a broadcaster and afternoon lecturer at Women's Clubs.[147]

For Skinner the most important consequence of her encounter with the work of history was precisely as described by Stefansson and, increasingly also by others. By the mid-1920s, so Skinner claimed, *Pioneers of the Southwest* had become 'the standard work on its period in the history of the settlement of Tennessee and Kentucky,' and *Adventurers of Oregon* had 'taken first rank in university circles because it is the only complete history of the North American fur trade.' 'Over 400,000 persons (students and general public) have read these books.'[148] And 'motion pictures made by the Chronicles of America Picture Corporation from my *Pioneers of the Old Southwest* and *Adventurers of Oregon* are being used in the teaching of history in 4500 schools already.'[149] Skinner took pride in *Chronicles of America*'s widespread use as texts in American history, commenting in the early 1930s that 'more than a million' school children had read them despite their being originally written for general readers and for students in colleges and universities.[150]

Skinner's writing career increasingly built on her reputation as an experiential historian uniquely able to interpret the frontier. In 1917, she had published her first novel *'Good-Morning, Rosamond!'* a romance embodying some of the attributes of her genteel maternal heritage, but thereafter it was to her frontier background that she turned.[151] Her second novel, published in London in 1925 and in New York a year later, was *The Search Relentless,* a contemporary romantic adventure set in the Peace River district and incorporating British Columbia frontier history.[152] While *The Search Relentless* did not make a lot of money, Skinner nonetheless considered it a gem: 'a northern story which presents the background of country accurately and sincerely; and which uses the common externals of the life there, such as an R.N.W.M. Policeman, Indians, bad-men, gambling dens, etc. to produce not a thriller but a work of art.'[153] Even as Skinner struggled against filial obligation, she had delighted in receiving 'some English reviews of my book'[154] and 'an article re my novel printed in the New York Times last Sunday.'[155]

Thereafter, Skinner's reputation as an experiential historian largely paid the rent. Almost from the newspaper's founding in 1924, Skinner became a regular paid reviewer of books on frontier history for the Sunday *New York Herald Tribune* and, about the same time, began to write a steady stream of juvenile novels for Macmillan combining historical and fictionalized characters, which were also serialized in children's magazines. In January 1925, Skinner proudly 'banked my MacMillan cheque for 250.–,' received $15 from the *New York Herald Tribune* for a book review, and was going to 'do a serial this summer for Boy's Life, not to be paid for till Sept & then only by installments.'[156] The earliest of her juveniles borrowed both setting and characters from *Pioneers of the Old Southwest,* notably Daniel Boone and family: *Silent Scot* (1925), *Becky Landers* (1926), and *The White Leader* (1926). At the end of 1925, Skinner quipped that 'I'm literally drowning in a quicksand of "juveniles."'[157] Next came three wide-ranging tales, which like their predecessors were unusual for the time in having heroines just as resourceful as their heroes: *Roselle of the North* (1927), set among the Cree in the Canadian Northwest; *The Tiger Who Walks Alone* (1927), in South America; and *The Ranch of the Golden Flowers* (1928), in Spanish California. They were not as successful as their predecessors, so she returned to a more familiar frontier. *Andy Breaks Trail* (1928) used the very successful *Silent Scot* motif to follow the Lewis and Clark expedition, whereas her last two juveniles, *Debbie Barnes, Trader* (1932) and *Rob Roy, The Frontier Twins*, retreated to the earliest stories' setting. *Silent Scot* and *Becky Landers* each sold about 25,000 copies in Skinner's lifetime, the nine altogether about 125,000.[158]

If reviews and juveniles provided a living and a certain reputation, poetry and fiction still consumed Skinner. Even as she was reading the proofs for her final volume for Yale University Press in 1925, she was busy writing: 'This week I have to finish two stories and do a short article (all on contract).'[159] At about the same time Skinner wrote Stefansson with great delight that his English agent had asked her 'to send him everything to read, even my poems, chiefly in an enthusiasm roused in him by a story I sent him,' which he considered a '"true literary achievement"' and '"by far the best short story I have read by an English or an American writer in a good number of years."'[160] Skinner was always certain that the next nibble would be the making of her. As she wrote to Stefansson in early 1925: 'I have 4 stories out going the rounds & there have been several inquiries by movie co's about rights to two of my pubd stories, my agent reports recently, but nothing cinched yet. One movie sale of course would end my worries for a year & probably repay you in full too. I've got out a lot of work this winter – seems as if some of it *must* land somewhere before too long.'[161]

While the southeastern United States became perforce the frontier Skinner portrayed for financial gain, it was its British Columbia counterpart to which she turned when writing as she would. Skinner's long-awaited historical novel *Red Willows* appeared in 1929, and the poetry she considered her finest was brought together a year later as *Songs of the Coast Dwellers*, both published by Coward-McCann.[162] Neither made any money, but they did enjoy credible reviews. *Red Willows* offered a sweeping portrayal of the fur trade and early settlement in the Cariboo, building on characters from Skinner's childhood, while *Songs of the Coast Dwellers* embodied British Columbia Indian motifs. Both consolidated Skinner's literary reputation as an interpreter of the frontier experience.

Red Willows and *Songs of the Coast Dwellers* also helped to maintain Skinner's standing among historians. A 1928 article described her as 'Constance Lindsay Skinner, historian, recently elected Fellow of the American Geographical Society, whose first novel will appear soon,' this being *Red Willows*.[163] She was also named a Fellow of the Royal Geographical Society, the result being 'a two-fold distinction held by few women.'[164] An article appearing at the time of *Red Willows'* publication in 1929 identified her as a longtime 'authority on historical days in the west.'[165] The same year the head of the Wisconsin Historical Society wrote concerning

Turner's earlier autobiographical letter and asked as a matter of course whether he would have the opportunity to talk with her at the American Historical Association convention that December.[166] Just as revealing of Skinner's transitional status were the recent doctorates in history who asked her to read their theses to see how they could be 'highlighted' for publication. One self-described 'poor university professor' first flattered her by reference to her 'extraordinary ability as a stylist in historical writing' and then pronounced that he 'could not afford to put much more than $200 or $300 into the project.'[167] The lack of subsequent correspondence suggests that Skinner did not respond to the request.

Skinner was always conscious of the differences between her experiential approach and self-proclaimed professionals, whatever the discipline, and she was not afraid to be critical. Writing to an acquaintance in 1930, Skinner took aim at English professors: 'No doubt there are teachers of literature somewhere in USA who *feel* literature as art and beauty and really help students to a true appreciation of it. But it hasn't been my good fortune to meet them. What I have seen of literary teaching has scared & horrified me & I still thank God I never came under its influence myself – never having attended a school or college.'[168] Skinner extended the argument to professional historians in her introduction to the published Turner letter: 'He was a great scholar without being scholastic: scholarship, to him, was not an amulet to be worn round the necks of caste: all arrogance and ambition were foreign to him ... being sincere, he labored for knowledge and not for ambition.'[169] Over time she became even more acerbic, writing shortly before her death in 1939 about her longtime social acquaintance 'Mr Nevins (or "professor") ... Allan Nevins is just such a nice, modest, kind human being, though he knows as much as the most arrogant and myopic academics.'[170]

Skinner also continued to write history, notably a popular account of the fur trade, *Beaver, Kings and Cabins*, published in 1933 by Macmillan. The concept had been in her mind ever since writing *Adventurers of Oregon*, as she confided to a friend on the earlier volume's completion: 'This is very *subrosa*, but what I would love to do would be to write a much longer & detailed history of the Fur Trade, detailing fully with its political aspects & influences, & its influence on colonization – and making its grand old pioneers *live* again as vital forces in the work they did & in the building they left for generations to come. I say this is *subrosa* because I don't want someone else, better equipped than I am financially, to get hold of the same idea.[171] In many ways *Beaver, Kings and Cabins* was Skinner's most sophisticated work, linking fictionalized autobiography with general history. A contemporary sketch described its creation. 'To write it, she has drawn on her own memories, of course, and has talked to fur-traders all over the land, and she has read everything authentic on the subject of the fur-trade in America.'[172] Skinner described 'my own "Beaver, Kings and Cabins"':

> This is not only, nor chiefly, a resume of old trader-explorer records &, therefore, a history of the fur trade per se. It has a thesis, an idea -- i.e., the influence of the fur trade in re[ference] to exploration, inter-colonial wars, settlement. It presents a new idea not expressed before in Amer. Histories and, hence, sheds a new light on facts already well known. This is why scholars recommend it. Anyone, given time and integrity, can make a fine compilation. What is more needed, however, is ideas. History (polar or not) should bring something to the man & woman who will never experience the scene in actuality.

Skinner was absolutely convinced that 'what we don't need is another academic compilation.' She continued: 'I suppose my own view on writing biases all I say. Writing, to me, is not something one *does*, but is experience, a way of living; & its *first* aim is individual growth, enlargement of one's own faculties of heart and mind. *Surface* scholarship i.e. the gleanings of other people's thoughts & experiences, is all right as a starter. If one stops there one isn't (by *my* standards) a *writer* – only a bookkeeper.'[173] From Skinner's perspective, *Beaver, Kings and Cabins* was experiential history at its best.

Perhaps in part because of the profession's growing ability to dictate what constituted good history, reviews of *Beaver, Kings and Cabins* were lukewarm and sales slim.[174] It was neither the literary nor the financial success that Skinner would have had it be. While she retained the support of a clutch of male professional historians with whom she had interacted since her Yale University Press days, she fared less well with others. Whether or not the far more difficult path that women had to tread to enter the academy played a role, it was a female professor, Grace Lee Nute of Hamline University in St. Paul, Minnesota, who was particularly scathing about *Beaver, Kings and Cabins*. Skinner had likely been the original protagonist, having two years earlier 'set Miss Nute right' in a review in *Minnesota History*.[175] Now was pay-back time. Granting that 'her enthusiasm is boundless,' Skinner was, according to Nute, far too ambitious – and by inference presumptuous as a non-scholar – to attempt to crowd 'more than four centuries in her narrative.'[176] 'Needless to say, details go by the board in such a handling of data,' leading to 'mistakes, inaccuracies, and omissions.' While 'Miss Skinner's method of embroidering the background of a known historical event with all the colors and glamor that characterized the period has much to commend it ... the more prosaic historian, on the other hand, will be perplexed to know at times where fact ends and fiction begins.'[177]

The experiential historian was not about to be done in by a professional, and a female one at that. In a letter to the journal's editor, Skinner not only repudiated the specific errors asserted in the review, but went on the offensive, noting that *Beaver, Kings and Cabins* 'has drawn friendly, even enthusiastic, comment from historians and teachers of pioneer history: such as Dr. Joseph Schafer, Professor Henry Steele Commager, and Dr. Allan Nevins, scholars whose profound knowledge of American history makes mere school girls of both Miss Nute and myself.' What right had the reviewer, whose 'studies evidently have been along other lines,' to 'belittle' Skinner's scholarship? 'The value of my material and of the thesis built upon it can only be appraised by one familiar with the rise and development of the fur trade in the various sections of North America in the different periods of time: one who is also well informed on pioneer history in general and has more than a slight knowledge of the European backgrounds.'[178] Nute shot back, using as virtually her sole ammunition her academic credentials and professional status. Instead of responding to the substance of Skinner's letter, Nute referred pointedly to 'my doctoral dissertation ... many years of research in European manuscripts' and 'numerous monographs and articles.' Unlike the original review, Skinner's protagonist prominently identified herself as an 'Assistant Professor of History.'[179] She was inside the academy, and Skinner was not.

In the mid-1930s, Skinner became involved in a major new project that also drew on her reputation as an experiential historian, the *Rivers of America* series combining folklore, literature, and history to tell rivers' stories. In her obituary, Commager considered that Skinner's Yale 'books and the many articles and reviews which she wrote, were preparation for a more ambitious and more significant venture, an interpretation of the whole of American history in terms of its rivers and the folks who were drawn to them and followed them.'[180] Skinner had asked Turner, during their correspondence, to 'scan an outline I had made for a long historical work, or for a series of volumes' on rivers.[181] This link with Turner undoubtedly boosted the *Rivers of America* project, and Skinner made a point of mentioning it in her introduction to the *Wisconsin Magazine of History*'s publication of his autobiographical letter. Skinner recalled in its preface how 'he pointed out to me, after reading the outline, that I had set myself work and study which might occupy twenty years to a lifetime,' and so she had temporarily abandoned 'this ambitious, not to say monumental project (for the carrying out of which, by the way, I had no funds whatsoever!).' Over time she had shifted the project's emphasis to being, 'not a several-volume work for me to write, for any single author to write, but a series to be written by authors from the various river sections who "had it in their blood."'[182]

Farrar & Rinehart took on the series, and in the fall of 1937 Skinner travelled across the United States, speaking to librarians and others.[183] Her California cousin observed perceptively that she hoped 'this series will mean some money for you so you can look forward to security in your old age.'[184] The first volume was the story of Maine's Kennebec River by Robert P. Tristram Coffin, which by Skinner's death in 1939 had sold almost 12,000 copies.[185] Five other volumes were published before then and many others were planned, so that perhaps Skinner, if far too late to have the leisure to write as she would, finally acquired a steady source of income.

For Skinner the work of history had satisfactory outcomes. Perseverance had its rewards. Skinner maintained her standing at the edge of the emerging profession. In January 1939 she was the only woman, and one of very few non-academics, among a group of fifteen invited by Allan Nevins of Columbia to found a new Society of American Historians.[186] The public dimension of her life was flourishing at her death, whereas the private dimension that could not be revealed had dropped away. Skinner increasingly became the public person. To the extent that she had a private life, it revolved around literary friends and Nip the cat. In 1922, Skinner told Stefansson how 'I found Nip sitting on the little table the other pm in rapt contemplation of your portrait! Aren't you flattered? His interest was so concentrated – I wonder what was passing through his little cat mind.'[187] And a year later in a postscript: '(Nip is prancing over your letter & over my back as I write it. He sends his greetings to you, o great Imperialist).'[188] As Stefansson receded, so Nip became front and centre, and eventually part of her public image. A reporter interviewing Skinner in her apartment in 1933 found her 'literally barricaded by books with Nip, her black cat who thinks he is an otter, standing guard on top of the barricade.'[189] Over a cup of tea Skinner revealed how she had 'just

Nip the cat

done over the entire apartment myself. I used Nip for my color motif.'[190] Three years later a literary acquaintance told Skinner that 'My pussy-cats send their regards to your pussy-cat.'[191] Nip's death of old age in January 1938 brought a spate of sympathy notes from Skinner's public. Her own death followed just over a year later.

Skinner was always far more than a historian. Despite a certain acceptability at the fringes of the emerging profession, she did not become encased in the discipline but rather used the insights gained there to further her writing career. Recovering from a trio of personal dilemmas – unrequited love, a smothering mother, and ill health – Skinner built on her identification with the frontier to write in a style that was essentially international and interdisciplinary. She did not consider that, by virtue of being a Canadian, she could not also identify with the United States, for as she once put it, 'If indirectly, yet certainly, the writing of American history serves Canada and all Great & Greater Britain.'[192] From Skinner's perspective, she and Turner shared a common formative experience that knew no national boundaries. In her writing Skinner readily transferred the insights from her childhood to the American frontier and then back again to her native British Columbia.

As well as being international, Skinner was interdisciplinary. Her fiction sought the status of great literature, her poetry drew on ethnography, her *Rivers of America* series valued folklore, and her history writing incorporated all these disciplinary traditions and more. As well as plumbing the written record favoured by professional historians, Skinner understood the importance of individual accounts, or oral history. Through combining all of these sources, Skinner sought, whatever the genre, to retrieve the everyday experience of women and children as well as men, and of aboriginal peoples and other racial groups as well as mainstream society. If in writing history Skinner was behind the times in lacking the credentials of most of her male counterparts, she also presaged the future when, two generations later, the academy itself would turn in similar directions.[193]

Today, the historian Constance Lindsay Skinner survives as a handful of dusty volumes still on many library shelves, and as a reference or two in biographies of professional historians like Frederick Jackson Turner and Herbert Bolton[194] and of some of the better-known persons her life crossed, notably Jack London and Vilhjalmur Stefansson.[195] Skinner is generally portrayed as a handmaiden, assisting but not fundamentally altering the course of greater lives, as with Bolton.[196] To some extent Skinner was a willing handmaiden in the professionalization of history, just as she, at least for a time, sought subservience to Stefansson. But if the history profession used Constance Lindsay Skinner to further itself, she also used history. The boost that its writing gave Skinner was likely critical to her survival as a writer and then to her redefining herself, in the interests of finances, as a writer of historical juveniles and book reviews as well as poems, fiction, and more history.

Skinner's legitimacy as an experiential historian was grounded in her childhood but made feasible through her encounter with the emerging discipline. She did not aspire to become a professional historian, nor could she have, but was rather a transitional figure whose experience exemplifies the life choices faced by early twentieth-century women writing history and of career women more generally. Skinner's experience also demonstrates the great extent to which the boundaries that the profession was erecting around the work of history were a gendered social construction.

Acknowledgments
I am grateful to the Social Sciences and Humanities Research Council of Canada for funding the research on which this essay is based; to the New York Public Library's Rare Books and Manuscript Division for facilitating access to Constance Lindsay Skinner's papers; to Evelyn Stefansson Nef, widow of Vilhjalmur Stefansson, for generously permitting me to quote from his correspondence; to the Dartmouth College Library and National Archives for facilitating access to Stefansson's correspondence; to Carole Gerson of Simon Fraser University and Donald Smith of the University of Calgary for sharing locations of Skinner correspondence; and to Anita van Weerden and Chris Hanna for research assistance.

Notes

1 Quotation in title taken from Constance Lindsay Skinner (hereafter CLS) to Annie Lindsay Skinner (hereafter ALS), 20 April 1908, in box 4 of Skinner Papers in the Rare Books and Manuscripts Division of the New York Public Library (hereafter identified by box number).

2 Jacqueline Goggin, 'Challenging Sexual Discrimination in the Historical Profession: Women Historians and the American Historical Association, 1890-1940,' *American Historical Review* 97 (1992): 771.

3 CLS to Vilhjalmur Stefansson (hereafter VS), n.d. [November 1918], Stefansson Papers, Dartmouth College Library (hereafter DCL).

4 CLS to Snowdon Dunn Scott, 8 January 1920, Scott Papers, box 2, file 3, University of British Columbia Archives (hereafter UBCA).

5 CLS to VS, n.d. [November 1918], DCL.

6 For a checklist of writings, see Ann Heidbreder Eastman, ed., *Constance Lindsay Skinner, Author and Editor* (New York: Women's National Book Association 1980), 56-77. Skinner's career is discussed more fully in Jean Barman, 'Constance Lindsay Skinner and the Marketing of the Western Frontier,' in Donald H. Akenson, ed., *Canadian Papers in Rural History*, vol. 10 (Gananoque, ON: Langdale Press 1996), 82-116.

7 Henry Steele Commager, 'Constance Lindsay Skinner,' unidentified obituary [March 1939], DCL.

8 Such letters are perforce difficult to find. To date, Skinner correspondence has been located at Columbia University, Dartmouth College, Minnesota Historical Society, National Archives, Newbury Library, Rollins College, State Historical Society of Wisconsin, University of British Columbia, University of Chicago, and University of Virginia. I am grateful to the respective librarians and archivists for their kind assistance, and especially to George Brandak of UBC Special Collections for putting a request for assistance on an archival network.

9 *The New Historians: A Booklet About the Authors of the Chronicles of America* (New York: Yale University Press 1920), 4.

10 Allen Johnson (hereafter AJ) to Herbert Eugene Bolton (hereafter HEB), 22 November 1916, cited in John Francis Bannon, *Herbert Eugene Bolton: The Historian and the Man, 1870-1953* (Tucson: University of Arizona Press 1978), 120.

11 *New Historians*, 5.

12 *Yale Alumni Weekly* 31, 20 (14 April 1922), 1; Glasgow obituary, box 1.

13 CLS, *Pioneers of the Old Southwest: A Chronicle of the Dark and Bloody Ground* (New Haven: Yale University Press 1919); CLS, *Adventurers of Oregon: A Chronicle of the Fur Trade* (New Haven: Yale University Press 1920).

14 AJ to CLS, 3 June 1920, box 3.

15 *New Historians*, 13-48. The favoured locations for Ph.D. degrees were Harvard and Columbia. Most academic positions were in history or politics, but other individuals taught law, literature, and even chemistry.

16 Ibid., 27, 33.

17 Ibid., 26.

18 Ibid., 16, 20, 48.

19 Robert Glasgow to CLS, Toronto, 18 September 1900, box 1; Agnes C. Laut, *The 'Adventures of England' on Hudson Bay: A Chronicle of the Fur Trade in the North; Pioneers of the Pacific Coast: A Chronicle of Sea Rovers and Fur Hunters; The Cariboo Trail: A Chronicle of the Gold-fields of British Columbia* (Toronto: Glasgow, Brook 1914-16).

20 AJ to HEB, 23 June 1919, cited in Albert L. Hurtado, 'Parkmanizing the Spanish Borderlands: Bolton, Turner, and the Historians' World,' *Western Historical Quarterly* 26 (summer 1995): 160.

21 Bannon, *Bolton*, 117-21.

22 AJ to Robert Glasgow, in AJ to CLS, 26 December 1918, box 3.

23 AJ to CLS, 3 June 1920, box 3.

24 AJ to CLS, 13 June 1921, box 3.

25 CLS to VS, New York, 7 August 1920, DCL.

26 CLS to Eunice Tietjens, 31 May 1921, Tietjens Papers, Modern Manuscripts Collection, Newberry Library.

27 CLS, *Pioneers of the Old Southwest*, 107.

28 CLS to Snowdon Dunn Scott, 31 May 1920, Scott Papers, box 2, file 3, UBCA.

29 CLS, *Pioneers of the Old Southwest*, vii; also see bibliographical note, 287-92

30 CLS to Methuen [1925], in Annie Laurie Williams file, box 3.

31 Herbert E. Bolton, *The Spanish Borderlands: A Chronicle of Old Florida and the Southwest* (New Haven: Yale University Press 1921); *New Historians*, 31.

32 HEB to AJ, 16 October 1916; AJ to HEB [December 1916/January 1917], cited in Bannon, *Bolton*, 117, 120.

33 AJ to HEB, 20 January 1918, cited in Bannon, *Bolton*, 130.

34 HEB to Frederick E. Bolton, September 1918, cited in Bannon, *Bolton*, 111.

35 HEB to AJ, 28 March 1919, cited in Bannon, *Bolton*, 131.

36 Robert Glasgow to AJ, reprinted in AJ to HEB, 23 April 1919, cited in Bannon, *Bolton*, 132.

37 AJ to HEB, 23 April 1919, cited in Bannon, *Bolton*, 132.

38 HEB to AJ, n.d., cited in Bannon, *Bolton*, 133.

39 AJ to CLS, 25 September 1919, box 3.

40 AJ to CLS, 19 October 1919, box 3.

41 AJ to HEB, 7 March 1920, cited in Bannon, *Bolton*, 135.

42 CLS comments, enclosed in AJ to HEB, 7 March 1920, cited in Bannon, *Bolton*, 135.

43 HEB to AJ, 17 March and 3 April 1920, cited in Bannon, *Bolton*, 135, 136; Albert L. Hurtado, 'Introduction' to Herbert E. Bolton, *The Spanish Borderlands: A Chronicle of Old Florida and the Southwest* (Albuquerque: University of New Mexico Press 1996), xxxi.

44 HEB to AJ, 5 May 1920, cited in Bannon, *Bolton*, 136.

45 AJ to CLS, 3 June 1920, box 3.

46 Bannon, *Bolton*, 105-6.

47 Robert Glasgow to HEB, 21 January 1921, cited in Bannon, *Bolton*, 138.

48 Bolton, *Spanish Borderlands*, x.
49 Bannon, *Bolton*, 140.
50 Hurtado, 'Introduction,' xxxiii; Hurtado, 'Parkmanizing,' 165.
51 CLS to VS, 28 December 1921, in Stefansson Papers, National Archives, Washington D.C. (hereafter NA).
52 Clark Wissler, Constance Lindsay Skinner, and William Wood, *Adventures in the Wilderness* (New Haven: Yale University Press 1925).
53 *Republican* (Waterbury CN), 27 October 1929, enclosed in Arthur H. Brook to CLS, 3 December 1929, box 3; Augustus H. Shearer, review of five volumes of *Pageant of America* series, including vol. 1, *Mississippi Valley Historical Review* 13 (1926-7): 414.
54 Shearer, in *Mississippi Valley Historical Review*, 414.
55 Draft letter from CLS to Arthur H. Brook, Chronicles of America Agency, Yale University Press, 11 July 1925, box 3.
56 Draft letter from CLS to Ralph H. Gabriel, Yale University Press, 25 July 1925, box 3.
57 Robert Glasgow, United States Publishing Association, to CLS, New York, 21 May 1918, box 2.
58 CLS to VS, 3 September 1920, DCL.
59 CLS, 'History as Literature: And the Individual Definition,' *Bookman* 49 (August 1919): 750-1.
60 AJ to CLS, 3 January 1921, box 3.
61 CLS, 'Documents: Turner's Autobiographic Letter,' *Wisconsin Magazine of History* 19 (September 1935), 92.
62 Frederick Jackson Turner to CLS, 20 March 1923, box 2.
63 CLS, 'Documents,' 94; CLS, 'Turner the Frontiersman,' *New York Herald Tribune*, 19 March 1932.
64 Frederick Jackson Turner to CLS, 15 March 1922, box 2; CLS, 'Documents,' 101-2.
65 Joseph Schafer, review of *Pioneers of the Old Southwest*, in *American Historical Review* 36 (October 1920): 112-3.
66 Joseph Schafer, review of *Adventurers of Oregon*, in *American Historical Review* 36 (October 1920): 117-8.
67 AJ to CLS, 8 October 1920, box 3.
68 Edward T. James, ed., *Notable American Women 1607-1950: A Biographical Dictionary*, vol. 1 (Cambridge: Harvard University Press, 1971), xi, 716-7.
69 Bannon, *Bolton*, 91-2.
70 HEB Jr., cited in Bannon, *Bolton*, 94.
71 Henry Steele Commager to CLS, 4 November [n.d.], box 3.
72 Contract between Robert Glasgow and CLS, 21 June 1918, box 16.
73 Arthur H. Brook to CLS, 25 September 1922, box 3.
74 Robert James Skinner (hereafter RJS) to ALS, 30 October 1880, box 4.
75 A. Van Valkenburgh to CLS, 20 June 1932, box 2.
76 RJS to ALS, n.d. [December 1877], and subsequent letters, box 4.
77 RJS to ALS, 30 October 1880, box 4.
78 RJS to CLS, 6 October 1905, box 4.
79 RJS to CLS, 23 April 1902, box 4.
80 RJS to CLS, 10 December 1902, box 4.
81 RJS to CLS, 12 April 1902, box 4.
82 RJS to CLS, 7 August 1902, box 4.
83 RJS to CLS, 26 July 1903, box 4.
84 Box 14.
85 CLS to ALS, 20 April 1908, box 4.
86 CLS to ALS, n.d., box 4.
87 CLS to ALS, n.d. [1914?], box 4.
88 Mother and daughter were living together in New York City by October 1914; see 'B.C. Writer of Poems on Indian Lore,' *Vancouver Daily News-Advertiser*, 25 October 1914.
89 CLS to ALS, n.d. [1914?], box 4.
90 CLS to VS, 1921 memo, NA.
91 CLS, cited in Helen Hoke Watts, 'Recollections of a Friend,' in Eastman, ed., *Skinner*, 35.

92 CLS to VS, 28 December 1921, NA; VS to Mr. Winburne, 14 November 1925, box 2.
93 William R. Hunt, *Steff: A Biography of Vilhjalmur Stefansson, Canadian Arctic Explorer* (Vancouver: UBC Press 1986), 3-17.
94 CLS to VS, n.d. [November 1918], DCL.
95 CLS to VS, 1921 memo, NA.
96 Undated clippings and obituary of Annie Skinner, *Province*, 25 November 1925, box 4; she likely returned to Vancouver in 1916, as indicated by George H. Cowan to CLS, Vancouver, 22 January 1926, box 1.
97 CLS to VS, n.d. [November 1918], DCL. By this time Skinner had published poetry with Indian motifs in at least eight popular magazines of the day.
98 CLS to VS, 23 November 1918, DCL.
99 CLS to VS, 16 January [1919], DCL.
100 CLS to VS, 28 December 1921, NA.
101 CLS to VS, 1921 memo, NA.
102 VS to CLS, 6 March 1922, DCL.
103 CLS to VS, 15 March 1922, NA.
104 CLS to VS, 29 March 1922, NA.
105 CLS to VS, n.d. [November 1922], NA.
106 CLS to VS, 8 January 1923, NA.
107 CLS to VS, 2 February 1923, NA.
108 AJ to CLS, 13 June 1921, and 7 June 1922, quoting CLS's letter of 5 June 1922 to him, box 3.
109 CLS to VS, 2 February 1923, NA.
110 CLS to VS, 2 February 1923, NA.
111 CLS to Mrs. Rhodes, ca. 1896, box 2.
112 Jean West Maury, 'From a Fur-Trading Post to New York: Constance Lindsay Skinner's Progress from Her Earliest Days in British Columbia,' *Boston Evening Transcript*, 6 May 1933.
113 CLS to VS, 28 December 1921, NA.
114 CLS to VS, 4 July 1923, DCL.
115 CLS to VS, 4 July 1923, DCL.
116 CLS to VS, 11 August 1923, DCL.
117 VS to CLS, 23 August 1923, DCL.
118 VS to CLS, 24 August 1923, DCL.
119 VS to CLS, 11 September 1923, DCL and box 2.
120 CLS to VS, 18 January 1923 [*sic*; 1924], DCL.
121 CLS to VS, 2 February 1924, NA.
122 CLS to VS, n.d. [8 November 1924], NA.
123 CLS to VS, 18 January 1923 [*sic*; 1924], DCL.
124 CLS to VS, n.d. [18 March 1924], NA.
125 CLS to VS, n.d. [20 March 1924], NA.
126 CLS to VS, 10 June 1924, NA.
127 CLS to VS, n.d. [8 November 1924], NA.
128 CLS to VS, 5 October 1924, DCL.
129 CLS to VS, n.d. [8 November 1924], NA.
130 CLS to VS, 5 October 1924, DCL.
131 CLS to VS, 6 October 1925, NA.
132 Mollie Welsh to CLS, 21 February 1925, box 2.
133 CLS to VS, 22 July 1925, DCL.
134 CLS to VS, n.d. [June 1925?], DCL.
135 Copy letter of Muna Lee, Mrs. Luis Munoz Marin, to George W. Cowan, 1 December 1925, box 1.
136 CLS to VS, 2 July 1927, DCL.
137 CLS to VS [February 1925], NA.
138 CLS to VS, n.d. [June 1925?], DCL.
139 CLS to VS, 5 January 1926, DCL.
140 CLS to VS, 2 February 1927, DCL.

141 CLS to VS, n.d. [April 1927], DCL.
142 CLS to VS, 10 February [1928], DCL.
143 CLS to VS, 4 December 1934, DCL.
144 After Skinner's death in March 1939, Stefansson attempted to collect the remainder owed him from her estate, writing that: 'At various times, following 1919, I lent Miss Skinner smaller and larger sums of money, chiefly when she was ill. I kept no account; but she said she was doing so. We both said she would pay if and when she could. It is my approximate notation that I advanced her in all around $1500. During the latter half of the period since 1919 Miss Skinner was on the whole more prosperous and she repaid me in several small amounts, always, so far as I can remember, by check.' Stefansson then reproduced her 1934 letter with its reference to an account book. 'My impression is that she had repaid approximately half of the total sum lent her, but the said account book may give the right figures.' The account book was never located, and in the end Stefansson settled for Skinner's set of the publications of the Champlain Society, which a friend of Skinner's told him she had wanted him to have. VS to James Egan, Public Administrator, County of New York, 15 and 23 June 1939, 3 July 1939, 16 August 1939; H.M. Lydenberg, Director of New York Public Library, to VS, 26 June 1939; Mary Skinner to VS, 23 July 1939; VS to Mary Skinner, 28 July 1939; Egan to VS, 27 October 1939, all in DCL.
145 CLS to VS, 20 September [1929], Stefansson Papers, DCL; also VS to CLS, New York, 5 January 1937, box 2.
146 CLS to VS, n.d. [1933], in Stefansson Papers, DCL.
147 VS to Betty Smyth, 16 March 1931, in Stefansson Papers, DCL.
148 CLS to Methuen, n.d. [1925], in Annie Laurie Williams file, box 3.
149 CLS to M. Lincoln Schuster, 25 July 1925, DCL.
150 'Junior authors galley 442,' box 3.
151 Constance Lindsay Skinner, *'Good-Morning, Rosamond!'* (Garden City, NY: Doubleday, Page 1917).
152 Constance Lindsay Skinner, *The Search Relentless* (London: Methuen 1925; New York: Coward McCann 1926).
153 CLS to VS, n.d. [mid- or late 1925], DCL.
154 CLS to VS, 22 July 1925, DCL.
155 CLS to Lincoln Shuster, 25 July 1925, DCL.
156 CLS to VS, 5 January 1925, DCL.
157 CLS to VS, n.d. [mid- or late 1925], DCL.
158 Calculations based on sales and royalty statements, box 16.
159 CLS to Arthur H. Brook, 16 July 1925, box 3.
160 CLS to VS, n.d. [mid- or late 1925], DCL.
161 CLS to VS [February 1925], NA.
162 Skinner also published a fur trade novel set around Fort William, *Red Man's Luck*, with Coward-McCann in 1930.
163 'Historian Sees Decline of Male,' *Telegram* (Salt Lake City), 8 July 1928, box 12.
164 'Demand Preservation of Alva Belmont House,' *Equal Rights* 18 (April 1931): 83.
165 *Republican* (Waterbury, CT), 27 October 1929, enclosed in Arthur H. Brook to CLS, 3 December 1929, box 3.
166 Joseph Schafer to CLS, 18 October 1929, box 3.
167 Lawrence F. Hill, Ohio State University, to CLS, Columbus, 28 March 1931, box 1; also C.J. Brosnan, University of Idaho, to CLS, Moscow, 28 March 1930, box 1.
168 CLS to Owen Small, 3 December 1930, in Women's National Book Association Collection, Rare Book and Manuscript Library, Columbia University.
169 CLS, 'Documents,' 94.
170 CLS to VS, 15 February [1939], DCL.
171 CLS to Snowdon Dunn Scott, 31 May 1920, Scott Papers, box 2, file 3, UBCA.
172 Maury, 'From a Fur-Trading Post to New York.'
173 CLS to VS, 20 October 1934, DCL.
174 See, for instance, Ellsworth Huntington, 'The Power of the Beaver,' *Yale Review* 23 (December 1933): 430-2; Edna Kenton in *New Republic* 76 (11 October 1933): 252-3.
175 Arthur H. Brook to CLS, 25 March 1932, box 3.

176 Grace Lee Nute, review of *Beaver, Kings and Cabins* in *Mississippi Valley Historical Review* 20 (1933-4): 405.
177 Ibid.
178 CLS, 'A Communication,' *Mississippi Valley Historical Review* 21 (1934-5): 130-2.
179 'Miss Nute's Reply,' *Mississippi Valley Historical Review* 21 (1934-5): 132.
180 Henry Steele Commager, 'Constance Lindsay Skinner,' unidentified obituary [1939], Stefansson Papers, DCL.
181 Obituary in *Library Journal* 64 (1939): 313; CLS, 'Documents,' 92-3.
182 CLS, 'Documents,' 93.
183 Obituary in *Library Journal* 64 (1939): 313.
184 Bess Hallock to CLS, 21 August 1938, box 1.
185 Sales and royalty statements, box 16.
186 Allan Nevins to CLS, New York, 27 January 1939, and enclosures, box 2. The other fourteen were Julian P. Boyd, Henry Seidel Canby, Harry Carman, Henry Steele Commager, Carlton J.H. Hayes, Burton J. Hendrick, Marquis James, William L. Langer, Walter Millis, Frank Monaghan, Conyers Read, Holland Thompson, Carl Van Doren, and Nevins himself. Jaques Cattell, *Directory of American Scholars* (Lancaster: Science Press 1942), gives four of the group as teaching in 1939 at Columbia, two others at Yale, and one each at Harvard and Pennsylvania; one was New York State History Association librarian, and most of the remainder were, given their ages, likely retired.
187 CLS to VS, 14 June 1922, DCL.
188 CLS to VS, 11 September 1923, DCL.
189 Maury, 'From a Fur-Trading Post to New York.'
190 Ibid.
191 Clare Tulay Newberry (Mrs. David Newberry) to CLS, 3 December 1936 and 9 August 1937, box 2.
192 CLS to Snowdon Dunn Scott, 8 January 1920, Scott Papers, box 2, file 3, UBCA.
193 For example, Julie Cruikshank, *Life Lived Like a Story: Life Stories of Three Yukon Elders* (Vancouver: UBC Press 1990), which won the Canadian Historical Association's annual John A. Macdonald Prize for the best book in Canadian history.
194 Bannon, *Bolton*, 140.
195 Earle Labor, Robert C. Leitz III, and I. Milo Shepard, eds., *The Letters of Jack London*, 3 vols. (Stanford: Stanford University Press 1988), passim; Hunt, *Stef*, 58-60. It should be noted that Hunt did not apparently consult, at least not quote from, Stefansson's correspondence with Skinner in the Dartmouth College Library, but rather used only the National Archives letters.
196 See especially, Hurtado, 'Parkmanizing,' 149-67.

7
Isabel Skelton: Precursor to Canadian Cultural History

Terry Crowley

That women have contributed to the development of Canadian historiography is no longer a matter of contention, but the nature of their contribution remains to be ascertained. The work of Isabel Murphy Skelton is a case in point. Beginning in 1909 and ending in 1947, Isabel Skelton produced a series of literary studies, nonfiction articles, three histories, and three high-school history readers. As with all contributions to historiography, her work needs to be assessed in its own right and in its own time, while avoiding many of the criteria that have characterized Canadian historiographical studies focusing on men. On what basis can Skelton's work or that of any other women historians be analyzed? International developments in the area of cultural history can afford some answers.

Early in the twentieth century, Isabel Skelton envisioned a broader world of history beyond the confines of the subject as defined by male academics. While these historians concentrated on politics, constitutional affairs, economic matters, diplomacy, war, and French/English relations, Skelton's perspective as a woman interested in literature, theatre, music, and religion led her to pursue historical research in what is now called cultural history. In the United States, Mary Beard also headed in that direction when she advocated in the early 1930s that historians follow the lead forged by cultural anthropology.[1] 'The concept of culture,' American historian Caroline Ware wrote in furthering this orientation in 1940, 'implies that any given society is an integral – though not necessarily a completely integrated – whole, in which basic processes of living and characteristic social relationships constitute a pattern of social behaviour.'[2] Following the thought of anthropologists, Ware stressed the social rather than the intellectual component in cultural history, whereas Skelton's writings bridged the gap between the two in practical rather than theoretical expression.

Born when Canada was still a colony of Britain and Confederation was but ten years old, Skelton arrived at this position through the same incipient Canadian nationalism shown by some of her male counterparts, even though regional identities figured more prominently in her publications. Gender more than social class appeared in her work, but neither was an exclusive object of consideration. She wrote about women, Jesuit missionaries, literary nationalism, Canadian politics, and religious matters; geographically, her studies were limited to Quebec and Ontario, particularly the eastern part of the latter province where she spent most of her life. Although Skelton conceptualized her own work as social history and came to be influenced by British historian George Trevelyan, her historical contributions combined the social and intellectual in the way that cultural history has evolved.[3] Skelton became a precursor to the subdiscipline of cultural history that emerged later in the century.

Family Background and Education

Isabel Murphy Skelton was as much a product of her Scottish-Irish upbringing in the Ottawa Valley as she was influenced by the times in which she lived. Born on 9 July 1877 in Antrim, a hamlet in Fitzroy township in Carleton County thirty-five kilometres northwest of the national capital, Isabella Murphy was the eldest of three surviving children from the ten born to Mary Jane (Jeannie) Halliday and Alexander Murphy. Her mother was descended from the McNab clan who had left Scotland to settle in eastern Ontario early in the nineteenth century; her father came from an equally large family of Protestants originating in County Mayo on Ireland's western coast. Jeannie Halliday became an elementary school teacher in 1867, taught for seven years, and married in 1874. Relative prosperity eventually arrived through dint of hard effort, but Jeannie experienced such great personal tragedies that she demanded much of her eldest child Isabel, who was expected to set an example for brother Herbert, born four years later. Criticism of Isabel's behaviour was intended to induce conformity, but the young girl interpreted her mother's rigidity as a lack of confidence in her abilities.[4]

As with other young people in similar circumstances, Isabel Murphy sought escape from family constraints by seeking refuge with neighbours like the Sparrows, a family who lived across the road, and through friendships of her own. At school in Arnprior, twelve kilometres to the north of Antrim, she met a young woman named Jessie Muir who, although two years younger, remained her friend for life. Besides the intimacies that adolescents generally share, the imaginations of the two were fired by Indian lore, stories of early Scottish settlement in eastern Ontario, and tales of rafting timber on the Ottawa River.[5] Particularly significant were the experiences of Isabel's great grandfather, the illiterate settler Duncan McNab, who had fought the feudal pretensions of clan chieftain Archibald McNab after the government had granted him Fitzroy township in 1823.

Not for them the legend of the good-hearted but misguided clan chieftain that often appeared in print; Bella, as Isabel was called, interpreted Duncan McNab's court battles between 1837 and 1840 as a fight of the common people against a transplanted aristocracy.[6]

The two young women stayed together when they attended Almonte high school, an institution that enjoyed a superior academic reputation. Among its graduates in their era were Edward Peacock, who later became a financier knighted in Britain; Andrew Haydon, who entered law and then became an organizer for the Liberal party; and future Harvard government professor William B. Munro.[7]

As a girl, Isabel was drawn emotionally to her father and to a much younger sister, Edith Alexandra Murphy, born on 28 February 1891. The arrival of a baby brought new expenses and a lot more work to a family saving to advance financially, but Isabel was enchanted with her sister. The Murphy household was modest. Alexander Murphy had initially farmed on a small scale, but to augment his income he had parlayed an interest in carpentry into a business as a building contractor. As well, he became a justice of the peace, ran the local post office for three decades, and served as Fitzroy township clerk for two, operating this enterprise out of a tiny office cabin on the farm property so that locals could not snoop inside the house.

While some of Alex Murphy's brothers were hard-drinking rowdies and four of them moved off to Manitoba in search of better prospects in 1879, Alex chose to become a pillar of the community. He joined the Orange lodge in 1859, the Masons later in life, and served as a local school trustee. His intelligence was applied to practical matters, but Skelton's father admired clearly written prose and became a good storyteller able to recount vividly the vicissitudes of life in early nineteenth-century Ontario.[8] A substantial stone farmhouse was built, yet Alex Murphy never got around to replacing the small log barn behind it. Although he and Jeannie saved all they could to provide their children with a good education, there appears to have been some dispute whether Bella should advance to university. While she graduated from high school with honours in mathematics and English, she did not enter the arts course at Queen's University until 1897 when she was twenty years old, the same year that her friend Jessie Muir headed off for university.[9]

As women had first entered Queen's University in Kingston in 1878, Isabel Murphy formed part of the second generation to study there. Although they were numerically stronger by 1897, women at Queen's were still a very select group who comprised only 13 per cent of the student body by 1901; only .5 per cent of Canadians aged fifteen to twenty-four years of age attended university.[10] A strong bond existed between the generations because Isabel arrived on campus with a letter of introduction

Isabel Skelton (upper right) with women classmates at Queen's University, 1897-1901

to Elizabeth Shortt from Andrew Haydon, a young man from Pakenham who had graduated from the university; Haydon had found Alex Murphy a sound source of counsel when he was a teenager. One of the first female graduates of Queen's, Elizabeth Shortt was a physician, social activist, and wife of Adam Shortt, the John A. Macdonald professor of political and economic science. Elizabeth greeted Isabel cordially with her daughter Lorraine bedecked in a flowing blue dress in the manner of contemporary illustrations of ideal childhood. Although raising her own family, Elizabeth Shortt felt a special responsibility for women undergraduates because the university spent no money to provide them guidance. She took Isabel under her wing, and the two remained lifelong friends.

Adjustment to Queen's academic life was difficult initially. Because Isabel had been out of school for a couple of years, her grades tumbled during first year, partially as a result of the usual first-year social distractions. The Levana Society that had been established in 1889 provided a forum for Queen's women to meet and debate their future, but there was also a round of parties and outings where Isabel met a host of young people. One award-winning sophomore, Oscar Douglas Skelton, spotted her particular charm and ability during that first year and declared her to be 'great inspiration.'[11] Oscar's background was more obscure than Isabel's. His father scraped by as a poorly paid school teacher in Cornwall, Ontario, later running a grocery store and ending his career selling Hoover vacuum cleaners in Toronto. A brilliant young man who was one year her junior in age, Oscar was fully as earnest and intent as the young woman who enchanted him from first encounter, but he was so diffident as to be almost retiring. Isabel could be expressive, but Oscar was more likely to confide his thoughts to his diary – in Latin!

As their relationship deepened over the next two years, Isabel Murphy adjusted to university life and saw her grades improve as she came to major in English and history. Her interest in Levana also grew because the society attempted to emulate the collective spirit displayed by Queen's men; some undertook charity work by sending clothes to Africa while others began a ladies' column in the *Queen's Journal* to counter the condescension of male editors of this student newspaper.[12] Isabel became treasurer of Levana while Oscar continued to win academic prizes. When he graduated in 1899, he was awarded an M.A.: Queen's followed the practice of the Scottish universities in according the graduate degree to undergraduates in arts who achieved firsts in both their honours subjects. After saving enough money from summer employment, Oscar returned to Queen's for another year, attracted not only by a challenging new classics professor who breathed life into his subject, but also by the allure of Bella Murphy.

In 1900, he left for graduate study in classics at the University of Chicago, but finding the program as dry as dust, he took off for London, England. There he passed the Indian Civil Service examination, financing his trip by selling the latest popular technical marvel, stereopticon cards. Suffering from poor eyesight and an undescended testicle, he either did not take the required medical examination or failed it. Oscar moved to the United States and got a job as assistant editor of the *Booklover's* (later, *Appleton's*) *Magazine*. When Isabel graduated from Queen's with an M.A. and the medal for history in 1901, Oscar proposed marriage. She refused for reasons unknown, but later in life she considered the three following years until she accepted Oscar's second proposal in 1904 to have been wasted.

Isabel Skelton distinguished herself in history at university, but English literature was her first love. Wars, monarchs, politics, and ecclesiastical conflicts constituted the fabric of the past as taught at Queen's by George D. Ferguson, a Presbyterian minister teaching the subject since 1869. James Cappon, Queen's professor of English, possessed a superior intellect, and his tempered enthusiasm for nineteenth-century British writers fuelled Isabel's imagination and appealed to her Victorian idealism. Literature, Cappon maintained, was 'an interpretation of life.'[13] The young graduate blended this concept with the idealism of progressiveness in her initial publications. If literature edified life as she had been taught, Isabel thought that in the twentieth century it needed to mirror a greater range of people than it had in the past.

First, however, was marriage, then a move to the University of Chicago for Oscar to pursue a doctorate in political economy in 1905 and 1906, the birth of a son, and a return to Kingston in the latter year when Adam Shortt arranged for Oscar to be awarded a fellowship in political science. Although the couple were passionately in love, the early years of marriage were not without turmoil. They were poor, by the standards of a labourer's wage although not those earned by working women, and Oscar devoted most of his time to his classes, publishing, and preparing his doctoral dissertation. Isabel was relegated hesitantly to housekeeping and child rearing, although she tried desperately to pursue intellectual projects. Bonded not only by love but also similar convictions, both hoped to wrench the twentieth century from the contradictions and hypocrisies of its nineteenth-century predecessor by standing 'for a liberal progressivism, against corporation or imperialist or sectarian interests.'[14]

After four years, marriage nevertheless wore more heavily on Isabel than Oscar. When she found it difficult to juggle family, household, and intellectual pursuits, she despaired that her husband would totally outdistance her intellectually and that she would be unable to write. After Oscar returned to the University of Chicago during the summer of 1908 to complete his dissertation on socialism, Isabel lapsed into despondency over the unattractive prospect of a life unwillingly devoted to 'greasy domesticity.'[15] He attempted to avert her pessimism, claiming inexplicably that marriage was more constraining on the man than the woman, although he acknowledged that child rearing clearly demanded more of the wife. He promised to take greater care of their son Sandy (Alexander) when he returned and extended the hope that their personal finances would improve so that she could be relieved of those burdens that so impinged on her time.

Good fortune struck at precisely the right moment to fulfil Oscar's optimism. When Adam Shortt was appointed to the federal Civil Service Commission in 1908, Skelton succeeded him as Macdonald professor; at the age of thirty he was one of the youngest men appointed to that rank in Canada. The family moved into the Shortts' house, and the additional salary, although low in comparison to those at the University of Toronto, allowed the couple to hire a servant girl.[16] Isabel soon learned that being an employer entailed new commitments, but she was at last able to set aside a small part of each day in a determined effort to study and write. A second stroke of good luck arrived later in the year when Oscar's thesis won the first prize of $1,000 in a contest sponsored by American clothiers; at a time when a researcher could get room and board for a dollar a day, the award was large.[17] Among these blessings, Isabel's only regret was Elizabeth Shortt's departure for Ottawa, as the two had grown close. 'Kingston's greatest attraction,' she wrote to Shortt, 'was that it held you and that I could always appeal to you for big or little advice.'[18]

An Author

Although now thirty years of age, Isabel Skelton had not fully developed a sense of intellectual direction. Oscar published widely in magazines and academic journals about political economy, current affairs, and even literature, but Isabel had not found her voice.[19] Accepting the conventions of her generation, she had to organize the household around Oscar; she also lacked the benefit of Oscar's doctoral work or the support and promotion provided by male university networks. Adam Shortt advanced Oscar's career in a way that Elizabeth could not do for Isabel because her interests were medicine and social service while the younger woman's were literary. Isabel knew from her undergraduate days that she had no penchant for philosophy; she tried writing fiction and drama, but failing abysmally, she quickly put it aside just as her husband had.[20] Expecting a second son, who arrived in 1909 and was named Herbert, literary criticism was easier to pursue at home. History, as it was emerging in the hands of Adam Shortt, her husband, and other scholars, required long bouts of primary research in libraries and archives.

While she was pregnant, Isabel completed studies of six late-nineteenth-century British intellectuals that the Toronto *Globe* published, changing her title from 'Grand Old Men of English Letters' to one with a more properly Edwardian ring: 'Rearguard of the Victorian Age.' In the *Westminster* (Toronto) Isabel also published a provocative study of American and British novelists Edith Wharton and Mary [Mrs Humphry] Ward, while *The World Today* in Chicago accepted her portrait of British playwright and novelist John Galsworthy. For the *Canadian Magazine* she produced an analysis of the women's suffrage movement in Canada in 1913 and others on derivations of surnames and the dispute over what to call the new country created by Confederation in 1867.[21]

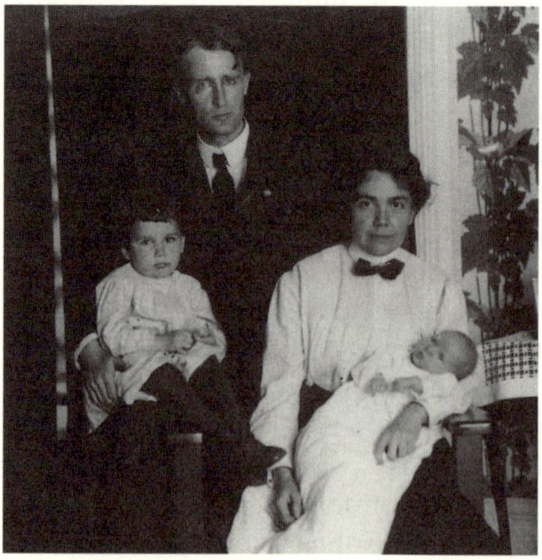

The young Isabel and Oscar with Sandy and Herbert, 1909

Besides providing money that made her less dependent on Oscar's income, these early publications allowed Isabel Skelton to hone her writing skills and improve the rigour of her thought. Her outlook was infused with the progressives' concern for broadening the focus of literature 'to include some of the sociological problems now demanding so much attention.'[22] This led her to the conclusion, new or at least innovative for its day, that what authors chose to exclude in writing was as important as what they wrote about. Narrative technique and the ability to establish a sense of place – important in her own historical writings later – also figured prominently in her criticism. Lastly, following British writer Arnold Bennett, Skelton emphasized the importance of convincing characterization in a novel.

Skelton's dissection of the women's suffrage movement in 1913 showed the strides she had made towards thoughtful and balanced analysis. The article asked an important question that continued to fascinate historians after her: Why had Canadian women made so little headway in securing suffrage before the First World War in contrast to the successes recorded in the United States, Australia, and New Zealand? The smaller proportion of Canadian women engaged in the paid workforce and the dispersion of a limited population within a vast geographical extent helped to explain the differences, Skelton thought, but perhaps more important was the absence of the American tradition of natural rights. Canadians, she noted in the article, prided themselves on being 'a sober unemotional people, practical we boast; living too much from hand to mouth in intellectual matters a critic might say.' She also took exception to the common argument that women's votes would right the wrongs that men had failed to address because she understood that such ideas created expectations impossible to fulfil. Women should vote, she maintained, 'to make mistakes and profit by them.' Not unaware of the antagonisms surrounding women's suffrage that had been aroused by critics who viewed suffragists as narrowly middle and upper class, she further argued for the vote to secure legislative 'justice in regard to property rights, marriage and divorce, and the guardianship of their children.' In all, her contribution was one of the more discerning and judicious pieces to appear during the course of a long polemic, even though her dispassionate work did not garner the attention of McGill professor Andrew Macphail's extended diatribe against the women's movement as a group of middle-class busy bodies when it was published in *University Magazine* shortly after her article appeared.[23] Still, Skelton had become a published author of note.

A Historian

Isabel Skelton's attention to British and American writers flowed from her undergraduate education in which Canadian subjects hardly figured. The history she had been taught was European; Canadian subject matter had been introduced by Adam Shortt at Queen's as early as 1890, but his courses were given in political economy. Adam Shortt would nevertheless be the formative influence in her transition to writing history in the same way that he was for Oscar. Shortt believed that academic work was often mere pedantry, spinning a surfeit of ideas around little concrete knowledge. 'Too much so-called scholarship is to me barren comment on what someone has said about reality,' Shortt wrote to Oscar Skelton in 1902, 'instead of a first-hand study of reality with such suggestive help from others as they may be able to give or one may be able to understand. Universities should not exist merely, or even largely, to thresh out old straw, but to get students into living contact with truth.'[24] Shortt hoped to expand the empirical base for scholarship by research into untapped primary sources. The documentation that had been collected by the Public (later, National) Archives of Canada from the federal government and from foreign repositories had been largely untouched. Shortt urged Oscar to venture into Canadian political history because it was 'almost virgin ground.'[25] These thoughts were not lost on Isabel. Although French Canadians had forged a distinctive historiography based primarily on their minority consciousness, English Canadians historiography was less well developed.

Canada's participation in the South African War of 1899 to 1902 moved Canada abruptly into the twentieth century. Attempts to tighten imperial ties prior to the First World War caused imperial sentiment to deepen in some quarters, while a stronger national outlook grew in others. Public controversies over the country's future direction increased people's interest in its past. The twenty-volume *Makers of Canada* series appeared between 1903 and 1908, the Champlain Society was founded in 1905 to publish primary sources, and the Public Archives also began new initiatives in the same area with the publication in 1907 of Shortt and Arthur Doughty's edition of documents relating to the constitutional history of Canada.

Isabel and Oscar Skelton hoisted their flag with the liberal nationalists, but there were greater opportunities for husband than wife. No women stood among either the authors or subjects of the *Makers of Canada* series, but selling the volumes convinced businessman Robert Glasgow that there was a market for well-written Canadian history books. Establishing a publishing company in conjunction with Arthur Brook, Glasgow secured George M. Wrong from the University of Toronto and H.H. Langton to edit the thirty-two-volume *Chronicles of Canada* series between 1914 and 1916. As this collection was intended for the public at large, the authorship was more varied: Agnes Laut and Ethel T. Raymond (from Brantford) were journalists who wrote about male subjects; Stephen Leacock, Charles

W. Colby, and William Bennett Munro were academics; and amateurs such as William Wood were also included.[26] Oscar Skelton contributed two of the volumes, one on politics during the Laurier era and the other on the development of railways.

The Chronicles series broke relatively little new intellectual ground, but Robert Glasgow projected a sixteen-volume supplement to fill in some of the holes apparent in the initial production. Before the outbreak of the First World War, he approached Oscar to see if Isabel, now with publications to her credit, would write a volume on Canadian heroines that would accompany a projected biography on Jean Mance, the first nurse in New France, and another by William Wood on the Ursulines. She accepted and signed a contract.

Isabel Skelton conceived her book more ambitiously than Glasgow's initial desire to satisfy popular interest in heroines. She wanted to write about the history of ordinary women in the settlement process and thereby unite experiences in New France with those in Upper Canada and the West. The emphasis on nameless women of no particular distinction marked a signal departure in Canadian historiography, but the subject of pioneering women flowed naturally from her family's background and her own intellectual development. The subject was also topical. After the 1911 census showed that a majority in Ontario lived in urban areas, anxiety about the eclipse of the rural past increased interest in the early years of settlement. However, the best means to give expression to such a vast topic presented Skelton with conceptual problems. From the beginning she excluded the Maritimes, even though there was much in common between their settlement experiences and those of women elsewhere in the country; eventually she was also forced to drop consideration of the Prairies because little information was readily available, and she had to make her project manageable. In this way she shaped her manuscript to be a regional study of central Canada.

The foremost difficulty Skelton encountered stemmed from attempting to reconcile Glasgow's initial interest in heroines with her own inclination to write a collective portrait of those who had remained largely faceless to history. Glasgow expressed his delight that Skelton was 'going to stress life in Upper Canada and the West rather than the stereotyped heroines of the French period,' yet there was too little known about the social history of New France to assume other than a biographical approach implicit in Glasgow's original conception.[27] Nevertheless, in writing about the French regime in Canada, Skelton presaged some important viewpoints not argued or examined by historians until much later in the twentieth century. She maintained that women in New France enjoyed a better position than had generally been portrayed by male authors; at the same time she expressed concerns about neglected elements in society, such as peasant farmers forced to sell their wheat to the government at low prices only to buy some of it back at higher cost.[28]

With two young boys – 'gorillas' Oscar called them – Isabel found it hard to secure the time to research and write her monograph even with paid help to assist with the housework.[29] Oscar was frequently away on archival research during the summer months, and Isabel had to rely on her mother and sister to care for their sons during the school vacation. She also had to draw regularly on her own self-discipline to get the book completed by 1917, when Glasgow paid $200 for the manuscript. An unexpected third child, Sheila, then arrived on 5 June 1918. Isabel's manuscript sat with Glasgow while he cooperated with Adam Shortt and Arthur Doughty to bring out the monumental *Canada and Its Provinces* series (1913-17), but during that period he purchased the larger *Chronicles of America* series and moved to the United States. When Robert Glasgow died unexpectedly in New York in 1922, Isabel and Oscar bought the manuscript back from publisher Arthur Brook for $250. By now Isabel had a provocative title, *The Backwoodswoman*, a wonderful fabrication that she derived from Confederation-era politician Thomas D'Arcy McGee, who signed three letters to John A. Macdonald as 'backwoodsman.'

Lorne Pierce at Ryerson Press in Toronto agreed to publish the manuscript in 1924 – over ten years after the book had been conceived. During the publication process, Isabel Skelton developed a straightforward working relationship with Pierce that avoided the sexual stereotyping he and other male publishers and critics brought to the work of such poets as Marjorie Pickthall and Audrey Alexander Brown.[30] By linking the French regime with the period of British rule, Skelton's themes appealed to the editor's desire to promote patriotism and morality in support of the bicultural nationalism he sought to further in the wake of the disunity aroused by the First World War. Her focus on ordinary women in familial settings also evoked the primitive frontier conditions that Pierce had experienced as a student teacher and Methodist minister in Saskatchewan from 1909 to 1914, after he graduated from Queen's and before he began work at Ryerson Press in 1920. Poetesses might be marketed as frail and emotive; history, as a reflection on lived experience, revealed women of courage and tenacity.

Skelton's *Backwoodswoman* was a significant contribution to Canadian historiography by virtue of its subject, methodology, and scholarly values. The book was not a journalistic effort in the manner of those by Agnes Machar, whom Skelton knew in Kingston; instead, it relied on what she called 'careful scientific research.'[31] Common at the time, the equation of historical with scientific research was an attempt to appropriate to history some of the prestige that science had attained, but the attempt fundamentally misconstrued the variety of cognitive processes and methodological approaches in both science and history.[32] To Skelton, however, the belief that good history rested on scientific research referred to the values a researcher brought to her inquiry and the manner in which she mapped her terrain. History conceived in dispassionate terms and based on a considered and unbiased examination of the relevant primary sources did not repeat the errors or prejudices passed on by less rigorous popularizers who only compounded the mistakes of their predecessors. If Canadian history were based on research and written elegantly, Skelton maintained, it would no longer be situated on 'the outskirts of history and literature,' but would deserve 'to rank as high in the world of cultural interests as the writing of history of an older country would do.'[33]

Skelton's *Backwoodswoman* signalled an important intellectual shift in the writing of Canadian women's history. The section on New France praised the exploits of exceptional individuals, while the larger part of the book assumed a newer approach that viewed ordinary women as active agents of historical change. The tradition of praising 'Women Worthies,' easily traced back to the writings of Christine de Pisan in the Middle Ages, found expression in Skelton's first three sections on Marie Hébert, Marie de l'Incarnation, and Madeleine de Verchères, which stemmed from Glasgow's desire for an account of heroines.[34] A chapter on United Empire Loyalist mothers provided Skelton with a bridge to a subject that was her own: the women of early Upper Canada whose lives she pieced together from a variety of primary sources. Here, where she was able to write about what she was most familiar, lay the strength of the book. To the written records Skelton was able to bring accounts passed on by her family about such things as women making potash, an important source of farm income in the early days of Upper Canada.

Skelton opened her preface with a criticism of the history generally pursued by men and indicated the presuppositions that she brought to the historical study of Canadian women. 'Few women are enroled among the Makers of Canada,' she wrote. 'Yet in all save the earliest years they have formed nearly half the population and have done almost half the work. But historians, absorbed in the annals of war and politics and business, tell us little of the part they played. The women's stage was not set in the limelight, but in the firelight.'[35]

Skelton therefore stressed women in their domestic and community settings, yet her own family background, marriage, and financial circumstances also attuned her to questions of social class. Although she wrapped all in a cultural nationalism that provided the intellectual backdrop for interpreting the meaning of these women's lives, she concluded that it was 'a reason for self-esteem among Canadians to-day that so many of their ancestors belonged to this class – the strong, the proud, the independent of the earth. Poverty could not degrade them.'[36] These views led

Skelton to steer away from an over-reliance on middle-class contemporary authors like Susanna Moodie or Catherine Parr Traill. 'The very artistic refinement and gentle training that made them so appreciative of the distant picture,' Skelton wrote of these literary precursors, 'robbed them of all sympathy with and understanding of it [Upper Canada] at closer range, and blinded them to the deep human pathos and tragedy – the toil, the poverty and the sickness that formed its details.'[37]

In returning to archival sources, Skelton was successful in moving beyond the conception of women as a general category in order to portray them in their cultural settings as part of social and ethnic groups, although aboriginal women figured only cursorily, and gender analysis was slight in her book. What was missing in her account was a provocative thesis or a consideration of the relationship between women and the larger structures of society. Skelton's account was primarily a self-affirmation of white women's roles in an effort to write them into history. Stemming from her study of the novel, she wanted to paint women into the picture rather than to adopt a gender analysis that would have questioned the underlying assumptions that governed people's lives. Marriage and children, for example, were accepted by her as the natural state for women; single women and those labouring outside the home received scant attention. Skelton surveyed women's terrain in home and fields with an anthropologist's delight in revealing detail, often about archaic processes or techniques. She conceived of the history of Canadian women as revolving primarily around home, work, family, and leisure; an examination of law or inheritance patterns, as undertaken by her American contemporary Mary Beard, would certainly have made Skelton's account less celebratory.[38] The illustrations for the volume prepared by noted graphic artist C.W. Jefferys reinforced this tendency, but Skelton herself criticized the improbability and class pretensions of his art work. Jefferys drew a soapmaking cauldron so big that the woman had to stand over it looking like a Trojan with a ladle high above her head; another engaged in weaving was overdressed, and a picture of a family arriving at a farm in the forest Skelton thought was too conventionally middle class.

Because Skelton's efforts appealed to a growing sense of cultural nationalism within the country, *The Backwoodswoman* was well received in the press, although it contested the values of male historians in subject and approach. In *Saturday Night* magazine, critic William Arthur Deacon reviewed the work favourably based on the premise that history was literary art. To Skelton he expressed personally 'the great pleasure I have taken in the reading of your book.'[39] Scholars were less favourable. Writing in the *Canadian Historical Review*, H.H. Langton accepted Deacon's basic presupposition that history was literature, then questioned most of Skelton's assumptions, including her criticisms of the commonly known writers whose portrayal of Upper Canadian society had prevailed for so long. He extolled the first section on the heroines of New France and derided Skelton's attempt to eschew elitism in recounting the experiences of ordinary women in the British period by concluding that the 'historian who wishes to introduce this generation to its great-grandmothers must give them names.'[40]

Elizabeth Shortt offered a woman's perspective, doubly impressed by Skelton's work because she knew how difficult it was for women to find time to engage in intellectual pursuits even when they had a servant. Shortt wrote to Skelton:

> I don't know how you manage to detach yourself. I've been able to do several things at once but not writing as one of them. Whenever I set to work to write even a report, I want a place & time [when] I can concentrate on it. That is where the men have the advantage – ie. when they are literary professionals – since they have no thousand humdrum details of sheets & towels & underwear & soup bones & salads to think of.[41]

Oscar, Isabel's most severe critic during manuscript revisions, was even more complimentary: 'it reads splendidly in type,' he wrote after seeing the book, 'good material, good style, good sense, good humour, and should bring you warm recognition from many quarters.' He suggested that Isabel write thanking Ryerson Press – 'it's as well to keep them in good humour' – and then closed his letter: 'Good night my dearest, mine, with my deepest love for my sweetheart & my pride in my author.'[42] Isabel returned the compliments in acknowledging his contribution. She confessed that she could never have done it alone, but owed it to him 'like the great majority of the good & happy things that come to me.'

The Backwoodswoman eventually sold its print run. Yet Skelton had not undertaken the project for the paltry royalty of twenty-five cents a copy that she received; rather, there was pride in accomplishment, and intellectual work constituted part of her being in the same way that it did her husband's. 'To attempt to do this kind of work has made all the difference,' she wrote, 'between a life of satisfaction (comparatively) and one that would have been – and had been – up to that restless and dissatisfied.'[43]

The significance of Skelton's achievement might best be evaluated by considering two other history books appearing in the same period. In 1923, W.J. Healy produced *Women of Red River*, a volume narrower in focus and heavily dependent on oral testimony.[44] Stemming from the desire of the Women's Canadian Club of Winnipeg to celebrate the past of women in their region in the era before the city's incorporation in 1873, Manitoba's provincial librarian was chosen to be the author. W.J.

Healy brought historical perspective, but at times his concern for the larger context distracted from his attention to women themselves. Relatively little work in historical sources was undertaken, and larger conceptions such as the role that social class played in the lives of women were excluded, although religion figured more prominently. His work was also demonstrably biased in that he chose educated, well-respected seniors to be interviewed because they were conceived as worthy precursors to those who belonged to the Women's Canadian Club. These women provided highly conventional accounts that generally avoided the less seemly side of life.

The narratives in *Women of Red River* were largely organized around particular localities, although concluding chapters tacked on accounts of travel, leisure, the Red River rebellion, and the onslaught of immigration from Ontario. Conflating oral interviews as a primary source with history as reflection on evidence provided by the past, *Women of Red River* sometimes lapsed inappropriately into intimate biographical details unsuited to its purpose. Moreover, Healy's book also ignored aboriginal women while covering some of the same ground as did Skelton's in relating production for domestic consumption, yet his attention to the latter was sporadic, and the book was not written in the direct, imaginative style of *The Backwoodswoman*. The line drawings created by artist Charles F. Comfort, however, were superior to the histrionics displayed in the illustrations of C.W. Jefferys.

Although Skelton's effort was arguably the best historical account of Canadian women produced up to that time, an international perspective reveals where it was wanting. In England in 1919, Alice Clark published a book entitled *Working Life of Women in the Seventeenth Century*. An adult student who enrolled at the London School of Economics in 1912, Clark enjoyed advantages over Skelton. Clark received intellectual support from a cluster of female scholars that included economic historian Lillian Knowles, medievalist Eileen Power, and historian M. Dorothy George, as well as a scholarship provided by Charlotte Shaw, wife of the playwright. Like Skelton, Clark turned to the archives and viewed women as belonging to social groups; however, differing intellectual environments accounted for the greater significance of what Clark produced when she combined feminist and socialist ideas current in London. The radical critique of capitalism undertaken by members of the Fabian Society led Clark to address women's relation to power, work, and property in a manner not suggested by Skelton's Canadian liberal outlook. In attempting to show that capitalism in seventeenth-century England had broken away from the family and that capitalistic organization had deprived women of sharing in the more profitable forms of economic production, Clark provided a stimulating thesis intended to provoke debate.[45]

Skelton's book was North American in outlook. Her approach was similar to that displayed in the *History of American Life* series, edited by Arthur Schlesinger Sr. and William Ryan Fox, and was thus subject to the same criticisms of old-fashioned positivism and aimless eclecticism that were levelled at the series.[46] Being an affirmation of progress in the course of human affairs, yet lacking in substantive argument other than confirming that women had played roles in history other than that of heroine, Skelton's *Backwoodswoman* represented an opening in Canadian historiography that lacked an immediate successor – if that had been possible considering almost total male domination of history departments at Canadian universities during the first quarter of the twentieth century. Her book retained historical interest for over seven decades until being relegated to historiography's bin by Jane Errington's account of women in Upper Canada.[47]

A Biographer

Isabel Skelton did not think that she was a women's historian; rather, she defined herself as a historian whose purpose was to reveal the past in a fuller amplitude than her male scholarly counterparts. Historiography dominated by Canadian men, she thought, was deficient in attention to the social, religious, literary, philosophical, and cultural arenas.[48] Even before her first book appeared in 1924, she had therefore begun work on another, a biography of Irishman Thomas D'Arcy McGee, an early proponent of a new nationality in British North America through Canadian Confederation. The origins of her interest in McGee were personal as well as intellectual. Skelton could remember being told as a child how her mother, then a young school teacher, had learned in 1868 that McGee had been fatally shot; her father had also related how impressive the man's oratorical abilities had been when he heard him speak. History had failed to do the man justice, Alex Murphy rightly maintained.[49] Because McGee was remembered in Canada primarily as a politician and martyr, he seemed an unlikely candidate for a historian other than one with the interests and outlook of Skelton. She saw the potential for a broader study of McGee's career as journalist, poet, polemicist, historian, and cabinet minister in Ireland and the United States as well as Canada. A fuller history, one that took intellectual life as seriously as politics and that considered literature as an essential feature of a nation's culture, was what Skelton strove to create in an effort to broaden her subject's appeal.

Skelton intended to write a full biography and therefore met fewer conceptional hurdles in the plan of this work, yet there were greater practical difficulties because the primary sources for McGee's life were dispersed across four countries on two continents. The Queen's library was woefully deficient in the areas of Irish and American history, and she had to purchase rare books from the Albert Britnell book shop in Toronto and other book sellers in Boston, Cleveland, New York City, and Troy (N.Y.). Research was undertaken in archives and libraries in Montreal, Toronto, Ottawa, Boston, New York, London, and Dublin. What Skelton lacked in financial support to pursue these investigations was compensated by her husband's efforts on her behalf. The couple subscribed to the *Irish Times* so that he could keep abreast of rapidly changing constitutional relations within the British Empire, and Oscar made a point of purchasing the most recent publications in Irish history. Access to the British Museum was facilitated in 1922 when the couple visited son Sandy, who was attending the experimental Bembridge private school on the Isle of Wight. In Rio de Janeiro later that year to represent Canada with her husband at an international meeting of historians marking the centennial of Brazil's independence, Skelton met Arthur Doughty, Dominion Archivist, and his assistant Gustave Lanctôt; both assured her that they would help her at the National Archives.

Oscar was also constantly proactive on her behalf. When he accepted a position as counsellor in the Department of External Affairs in 1924, he secured assistance from Sir Joseph Pope, a career civil servant with an unparalleled command of Canadian government records; and when he returned from Europe later that year, he stopped in Dublin to arrange for the hand copying of sources relating to McGee at the National Library. Always her best critic, her husband helped Skelton improve the manuscript. 'Oscar went at work on McGee today,' she recorded, '& knocks conceit out of me.'[50] Further, he arranged for Charles Murphy, Mackenzie King's postmaster general and avid McGee fan, to read some of Isabel's chapters, and when he heard that Murphy was ready to discuss them, decided to 'let affairs of state slide, as they had slidden [*sic*] for some days without anyone apparently coming to grief, and went over.'[51]

That Skelton's study of Thomas D'Arcy McGee was to be a public and intellectual biography was dictated as much by literary tastes as by the nature of the primary sources. McGee's private papers had been destroyed following the death of his son-in-law who had hoped, but failed, to write a biography; thus there could be no strong personal element in Skelton's work to garner the great attention earned, for example, by Lytton Strachey's biographical studies in England of Queen Victoria and other eminent Victorians.[52] Iconoclasm was also absent, as was the streak of cynicism characteristic of newer approaches to biography; although the British book market was large enough to find room for those looking askance at their ancestors, Canadian nationalists like the Skeltons were intent on celebrating forebears as precursors to the independence finalized in the Statute of Westminster in 1931.

Influenced by John Morley, author of a massive three-volume biography of British prime minister William Gladstone, Oscar had already produced big books on Alexander Tilloch Galt and Wilfrid Laurier in this older life and-times approach. Isabel created the same broad canvas for McGee by explaining fully the context of his career at each stage, focusing especially on his writings within their national and religious settings, and even devoting a chapter to establishing context for McGee's literary output in Ireland and Canada.[53] Unexpectedly, the majority of her manuscript dealt with Ireland and the United States, where McGee had been actively involved in a variety of Irish affairs before spending only eleven of his forty-two years in Canada. In the Canadian section, emphasis was laid not on politics, but on McGee's advocacy of a new nationality that would be neither British nor American. While naturally sympathetic to her subject, Skelton retained a critical distance that allowed her to take McGee to task when the occasion warranted.[54] Although she had been reared in Orange Ontario, she was as successful in avoiding any anti-Catholic bias as her father had been in shedding intolerance in the years prior to his death in 1916.

Research and writing entailed many days of slogging and those anxious moments that afflict all authors. Reading old newspapers was tedious. 'Work on *Globe*,' Skelton noted in 1924. 'Must push myself more at this kind of work.'[55] She also learned that the approaching centenary of McGee's death in 1925 had not gone unnoticed by others. At the University of Manitoba in 1923, historian D.C. Harvey published a long lecture on the Canadian aspects of McGee's career, and in 1924, the Macmillan publishing firm projected a biography by University of Toronto political economy professor Alexander Brady in its *Canadian Statesmen* series.[56] Neither study was as profound in conception or execution as to provide an intellectual challenge to Skelton's bolder pursuit of cultural history, but their appearance would detract from sales.

The decision that Isabel and Oscar Skelton made to allow Garden City Press to launch itself into publishing Canadian history with the McGee biography was, in retrospect, an error. A small publishing house owned by J.J. Harpell, whom the Skeltons had known since the time he served as business manager for *Queen's Quarterly*, Garden City Press produced trade journals and books on a site adjacent to the Macdonald campus of McGill University in Sainte-Anne-de-Bellevue. Harpell liked Skelton's manuscript and saw no need for the hand of an editor who would have required reductions, particularly where the text dealt excessively with well-known developments in Irish history and let the loquacious McGee speak too frequently. He did, however, accept suggestions from the author and her husband about everything from typeface to illustrations and paper quality. The result was an expensive publication that retailed at four times the cost of Professor Brady's slighter contribution that centred on politics. The copy editing was handled expertly by Marjorie Mackenzie, a talented woman with a master's degree who was serving as Oscar's secretary; she later published her own work and became a foreign service officer. Mackenzie took to her job with relish and a lively sense of humour, informing Skelton that her manuscript needed considerable editing "if the public is not to think that you have written parts of it in Turkish and other parts in cross-word puzzle."[57] Mackenzie and Isabel Skelton remained friends for the rest of their lives.

Skelton's *The Life of Thomas D'Arcy McGee* appeared in 1925 to generally favourable reviews, particularly in Ireland and the United States. Some Canadian newspaper reviewers found the sections dealing with those countries too long, and others wanting to read about a politician criticized the amount of literary detail. Journalist B.K. Sandwell, who knew the Skeltons at Queen's, best summarized the favourable comments when he wrote that what Skelton had produced stood among those 'reliable and realistic biographies' that 'recreate for the reader the living images of the men who acted, with all the personal attributes that contributed to the magnetism that enable them to accomplish their work, and endeared them to their contemporaries.'[58] The *Irish Statesman* was also favourably impressed, extolling the book as one that 'throws a flood of light on many obscure corners of Irish, American, and Canadian history.'[59] University of Toronto constitutional expert W.P.M. Kennedy acknowledged that the book would 'remain the standard biography of McGee' – as it has for three-quarters of a century.[60] Isabel's brother, however, cautioned her about the personal dangers attendant on publication: 'But after this superlative biography of McGee – the "Papist" – and your frequently kindly references to others of the same faith, how do you ever expect to go back to Orange Protestant Carleton county? Be sure that L.O.L. [Loyal Orange Lodge] no. 30 will find you out even in Ottawa.'[61]

Publishing a book to successful critical reviews is one process; securing its sale is another. Although J.J. Harpell had experience with niche publishing, he lacked Robert Glasgow's flair for marketing. A promotional flyer prepared by Oscar was printed, and Harpell sponsored a dinner for local dignitaries in Montreal to impress members of its Irish-Canadian community. However, these initiatives could not compensate for lack of familiarity with the book distribution systems in Canada, the United States, and Ireland, where more established publishers would have also pursued sales. Two thousand copies of *McGee* were printed and a thousand bound (some in Moroccan leather), but only 162 sold during its first year, the centenary of the man's birth. Harpell's desire for Garden City Press to enter new markets was shelved momentarily. 'I have come to the conclusion that the book-reading public of Canada is very limited,' he wrote, 'and the margin for a publisher is very difficult to attain.'[62] Author's royalties, negotiated at 10 per cent of gross sales for the first 1,000 copies, were again meagre. In following Adam Shortt's empiricism, Skelton had produced a definitive study intended 'to furnish a mine of reliable historical data and information' in the manner that the senior academic advocated.[63] The loss of sales entailed in such an approach was only partially compensated by scholarly appreciation of her work over the longer course.

Ottawa Interlude

The frenzy associated with publishing two major books in as many years coincided with a momentous upheaval in Isabel Skelton's life. Oscar's temporary posting to Ottawa in 1924 made him a commuter and increased Isabel's family responsibilities when she could least afford them. Early in 1925, the stress showed in such frequent headaches that she sought medical attention.[64] When Mackenzie King appointed her husband to replace Sir Joseph Pope as undersecretary of state for External Affairs later that year, strains in their relationship reached unprecedented heights as they prepared to leave Kingston after two decades. Oscar worked desperately hard during sixteen-hour days for a prime minister who seldom considered that his advisors had a personal life. The appointment was his moment of triumph, his chance to affect the course of the country's public life after writing it about for so many years. While Isabel knew that their sedate, intellectual lives had been changing immutably since 1922, when she had convinced Oscar that they both should begin keeping diaries, she had been unable to realize how the life of one she loved so much might detract from her own. She deeply resented that Oscar's career took unquestioned precedence, leaving her to juggle everything outside his work. The children needed more direction than she was able to provide alone, particularly Sandy, a student at Queen's who had become totally unmanageable to his mother and who would have to be left in Kingston. As talented at football, boxing, and basketball as he was at the study of political economy, Sandy was more unpredictable than his father and prone to rashness. He incurred an eye injury that sent him to hospital during initiation at Queen's; later he boxed for money in a Buffalo, New York, tavern.

The ostensible source of the couple's estrangement was the choice of their new home in Ottawa, but its roots lay deeper than either acknowledged. Oscar wanted a big house in Ottawa's prestigious Rockcliffe Park, while Isabel preferred a smaller dwelling situated in a less fashionable area that would require less attention and allow her more time for intellectual work. 'All such things he feels he wants bulk far more with Oscar than with me,' Isabel wrote, 'and he feels hurt and irritated with me if I oppose him.'[65] After Oscar charged her with displaying plebian taste, communication shut down and sexual alienation ensued. 'The confounded house

[is] between us and I feel it quite impossible to discuss the question. On the surface we are quite ordinary and friends – wore pink and mauve pyjamas – but –.'[66] Oscar did not speak fully about his upbringing until much later in life, and Isabel was unable to comprehend how much stock he placed on being able to display the success that had allowed him to overcome the poverty of his youth.

The quarrel ended when Oscar prevailed, but its result signalled a larger victory of his concerns over hers. The household was thereafter organized completely around her husband. Isabel accepted this fate with resignation partially because it reflected the dutiful role she had played in regard to her father and mother and partially because, at age forty-eight, the time for the protest seen in the early years of their marriage had passed. There were also significant benefits as compensation: Oscar was increasingly affectionate as they both advanced in years, although somewhat absent-minded; and she had her children and the hours she could squeeze in for writing. But the pivotal change in life that the move to Ottawa entailed, together with Sandy's failure to complete a degree at Oxford while on a Rhodes scholarship, led Isabel to reassess her priorities in order to provide greater attention to her seven-year-old daughter Sheila. Later in life she concluded: 'As I look back I see how Oscar and Isabel were far too interested in just work and not enough in life to have children. We did not bring to the boys attention and ourselves enough. I have given more to Sheila and she is a joy.'[67]

Isabel Skelton trained herself for the social role expected of the wives of top civil servants in interwar Ottawa, but she never relished the part. Family and literary pursuits provided more genuine satisfaction. Her friends were personal and intimate, women like her childhood friend Jessie Muir, who taught modern languages at the Ottawa Ladies College, Elizabeth Shortt, and later Frances Rogers, wife of Labour minister Norman Rogers. Attentive to diplomatic functions and active in a women's reading circle, Skelton foreswore organizational involvement in anything but the Girl Guides (Sheila was a member) and in St. George's Anglican Church, which she attended even though Oscar had remained an agnostic since youth. Occasionally she gave addresses just as she had at the Women's Canadian Club in Kingston where she had been president in 1915. For the Canadian history reader series of Ryerson Press, a collection intended for high-school students, she extended her purview by preparing three short studies, on McGee (1928) and on seventeenth-century Jesuits Jean de Brébeuf and Isaac Jogues (1930).[68] Lauding the heroism of the Jesuit missionaries at the expense of the aboriginal peoples they attempted to convert revealed Skelton's inability to extend the tolerance she had brought to her earlier work.

From her close association with Senator Andrew Haydon, Skelton developed a growing appreciation that cultural history needed not only to be broadly conceived, but also tied intimately to locale. Haydon had published a series of pioneer sketches of eastern Ontario in 1925 and introduced Skelton to James Macintosh Bell, who had retained his great grandfather's lengthy diary that recorded the beginnings of Scottish settlement around Perth in eastern Ontario early in the nineteenth century.[69] Parson William Bell's writings were a primary source rich in historical insight about immigrant adjustment in early Upper Canada, and Skelton decided to follow in Haydon's footsteps by providing an in-depth study of the region from which they had emanated and never really left. She intended to combine the intellectual concerns of William Bell with the religious and social events he recorded to provide a richer cultural understanding of ordinary people than had been seen previously, but her progress on the work was slowed by two events. When Charles Murphy died in 1935, she accepted his brother Edward's suggestion that they complete the edition of Thomas D'Arcy McGee's speeches and writings that Murphy had begun.[70] Second, Skelton produced a stunning short study in 1939 based on the work of Frederick Philip Grove.

Skelton's article on Grove marked an important departure in Canadian literary criticism and revealed its author at the height of her intellectual ability. Using the author's novels and semi-autobiographical books, Skelton showed how Grove's naturalism and emphasis on narrative technique resulted in a literary output that lacked human understanding or empathy, especially with women and youth. Just as Virginia Woolf had in 1924 criticized Edwardian novelists for their failure to see their characters from the inside, mistaking a fascination with manners and material fabric for life's psychological dramas, Skelton contended that Grove's work 'jealously excludes human intrusion' because academic wordsmithing failed to make contact with the personal experiences of its readers.[71] Naturalism had so overcome characterization in Grove's novels, she argued, that people were revealed as pale reflections of an overpowering Prairie landscape rather than as entities in their own right.

This attack was so massive and well-argued that a rattled Grove wrote to Skelton. At first he affirmed that her article was 'one of the very few attempts which have been made so far to get behind the letter press of my books' and that 'in certain analytic passages, you lay your finger on the exact truth.'[72] But when he raised the words 'venomous' and 'vindictiveness' in regard to her critique, Isabel decided to defend herself. Although she had been infuriated by Grove's pomposity when she met him on social occasions in Ottawa, detesting the pretence that was a partial cover for charlatanism – the author had falsified his background and hidden a conviction for fraud in Germany in 1903 – Isabel responded solely in terms of the critic's duty. Those seeking to interpret literary work, she thought, needed to digest an author's complete output 'objectively and with a free mind' and then 'to have the courage of one's convictions and be true to one's standards.' Reflecting the relativistic outlook gaining ground in intellectual circles, she also maintained that unless 'a critic is honest according to her lights, her work is of no value whatsoever, whether the comments are favourable or the reverse.'[73] In the end, Oscar's devilish wit prevailed when he left a business card under the tree at Christmas: 'To my severest critic, With coals of fire. 1939 F.P. Grove.'[74]

At sixty-two, Skelton proceeded with her researches into early Ontario history. Overwhelmed by the value of William Bell's seventeen-volume diary and wanting to breathe literary life into a time and place whose traces were few, she completed a full-scale biography of the pioneer parson in 1939. Organizing her manuscript around themes rather than chronology, the work evoked the cultural milieu in relation to religion, economic life, and society among the British immigrant families, disbanded soldiers, and half-pay officers who had settled around Perth in eastern Upper Canada beginning in 1816. While her approach remained broad, the decision to write a biography rather than to create a portrait of eastern Ontario society was an error. William Bell (1780-1857) was a prickly, unpopular preacher who had emigrated from Scotland in 1817. Although he helped to establish churches, temperance societies, Sunday schools, and Bible classes, much of the minister's life was spent embroiled in arcane internecine quarrels among Presbyterians about their ecclesiastical structures.

A better approach might have been to prepare a critical edition of the diary for the Champlain Society, yet Skelton did not contemplate this alternative. Her project was thereby flawed even though her work exemplified the same scholarly and intellectual attributes that she had brought to her previous books. The bulky manuscript was sent to Ryerson Press in the summer of 1939 with the hopes of big royalties, but it was rejected as being over-written; wartime shortages of paper delayed the project further.

Montreal Years

Within the four short years between 1937 and 1941, the principal personal supports sustaining Isabel Skelton's life were cast out from under her: her sister, best friend Jessie Muir, mother, and husband all died. During the same period, her son Sandy went through such a tumultuous divorce that Skelton found herself unable to speak to him and could only communicate in writing. Following Oscar's unexpected death on 28 January 1941, when he succumbed to a heart attack while driving in downtown Ottawa and smashed into a streetcar, she decided to turn her back on what she described as 'that old exacting social life' in the 'lap of luxury glow.'[75] She moved from Ottawa to an apartment in Montreal where she could be close to son Herbert and his wife Daisy, but her disillusionment with life, marked by bouts of overwhelming loneliness, characterized the completion of her transition to old age. 'Utterly alone,' she wrote in April 1941. 'All my dearest ones gone – except the children and I hardly understand them and they all but understand me – we live in different worlds.'[76]

It took several years for Skelton to adjust fully to new circumstances, a process that was assisted by her children, old friends from Queen's, intellectual work, social service with Montreal's university settlement house, church attendance, and involvement with other groups such as the University Women's Club. In 1942, she joined Canadian scholars and authors such as H.F. Angus, S.D. Clark, Watson Kirkconnell, J. Murray Gibbon, and Margaret McWilliams on the Committee on Co-operation in Canadian Citizenship. The purpose of the committee was to advise the ministry of national war services about joining ethnic minorities – estimated at a fifth of the population – to patriotic efforts in order to promote loyalty during wartime.[77] Skelton suggested history books that newer Canadians might read and wrote a number of short pieces; the ministry published one on John Graves Simcoe. In 1943 she resigned. 'I am no longer at the centre of things,' she concluded. However, on her seventieth birthday four years later, she thought: 'I still have high hopes of living and doing for others and to improve myself. My prayer: "Take not thy holy spirit from me." When my brain and memory are gone, let me die. My creed: the little more and how much it is!'[78]

Although dismayed at the increasing restrictions imposed by advancing years, Skelton still hoped to publish her volume on William Bell. She experienced a new sense of freedom, no matter how difficult to bear, that accompanied release from past commitments. 'I am no longer driven by love or duty,' she wrote in 1942, 'I am the master of my fate.'[79] She attempted to pare 20,000 words from a manuscript that counted 140,000 and scoured Montreal's libraries for books that would improve her work; she also began two new literary projects. Even though she had deepened her investigations into intellectual history, Skelton was keenly cognizant of her failings. 'Feel the whole [Bell] thing is too dull and ponderous anyway, but am going to go thru with it,' she recorded. 'If making a fresh start ten years ago – I c[oul]d do better – but as it is, it is as well done as I can get it.'[80] In 1944, she opened protracted negotiations with Lorne Pierce at Ryerson and J.J. Harpell at Garden City Press. A second major revision had to be undertaken and a personal financial subsidy provided to Ryerson Press. While neither the historical nor literary merits of the book were ever questioned, Pierce knew that it would not sell well.[81] Personally anxious, Skelton taxed the press with queries, but Pierce displayed his usual wellspring of patience in pacifying demanding authors. She was despondent while checking proofs for the book, thinking that her approach was outdated. 'Thirteen years of work and thinking – for what?' she asked herself.[82]

Pierce was right. Only a few Presbyterians and a handful interested in a serious study of early Upper Canadian religious and cultural life were willing to purchase a biography of William Bell. Interdenominational rivalries led the Anglican Church's national newspaper to charge erroneously that her book lacked objectivity. 'I have a just enough appreciation of my own work to be able to stand unworried [by] any review,' Skelton tried to convince herself.[83] Old friends like journalist Grant Dexter were naturally favourable in their notices, and so was political economy professor Alexander Brady. One historian at the University of Western Ontario who specialized in the social history of nineteenth-century Ontario expressed genuine appreciation. 'You were fair,' J.J. Talman informed Isabel, 'and yet did not squeeze all the colour out of his life in an effort to be exact. I ... shall count this one of the good books in my library.'[84]

Skelton never abandoned the activities that formed an essential core of her life's fulfilment – intellectual pursuits – but at the age of seventy, her productive years had passed. Occasionally she was visited by a diplomat like Herbert Norman, whom her son-in-law Arthur Menzies had worked with at External Affairs, or historian J.I. Cooper of McGill University and his student G.R.C. Keep, who were interested in Irish-Canadian history. Increasingly feisty as she aged, she found Cooper shabbily clad and with a 'very meagre equipment of historical lore. In fact I find myself questioning whether my visitor were somebody just impersonating a history professor to size me up or something.'[85]

Greater wrath was reserved for University of Toronto historian Donald Creighton. Pontificating in 1950 on the larger course of Canadian history during an address on the country's first prime minister, Creighton attacked what he called the Liberal interpretation of the country's history. 'Liberal folklore,' he said before proceeding to impugn her husband's historical output. Skelton retorted with 'shallow, pompous, imperialist.'[86] Although she began work for a book about Tiger Dunlop, the erratic and controversial agent for the Canada Land Company in southwestern Upper Canada, another able historical writer eventually filled the historical void she had identified.[87]

Skelton took great delight in her three grandchildren even though she was plagued by circulatory ailments. She cared for herself with the support of her family while living on her own to the end. At seventy-seven years of age in 1954, Skelton was introduced to a microfilm reader for the first time, amazed at how it speeded research at the expense of tired eyes. Yet when unable to recall recent details, she confessed: 'I am terrified of what the future holds – if I live.'[88] The following year fainting spells began; on one occasion she lay unconscious in her apartment for two days until she was discovered and taken to hospital by her son and daughter-in-law. Skelton returned to living independently, and died in Montreal on 22 August 1956.

Conclusion

Isabel Skelton's intellectual contributions highlight the importance of independent scholarship. In moving towards cultural history, she departed the principal confines that academic male historians attempted to define during the first half of the twentieth century while her work exemplified the scholarly standards that they had evolved. Because she chose to follow her own intellectual convictions rather than mirror contemporary scholarly fashion, some of her work today appears less remote than that of professional male colleagues like George Trevelyan, who was born a year before she. Marriage to a prominent academic and federal civil servant provided the emotional and material support essential to her output, but proved constricting in the demands made on her time. Motherhood also figures prominently in assessing Skelton as historian. With little money and the arrival of babies shortly after marriage, writing often played second fiddle to more immediate tasks even though it remained central to her self-esteem.

Conscious of the differing rhythms governing the lives of women and men, Skelton addressed gender differences when speaking to the graduates of the Ottawa Ladies College in 1926. Whereas Virginia Woolf had stressed the importance of space and an independent income as essential supports to female creativity, Skelton struck at another dimension. Urging her young listeners to be their own masters by establishing personal goals for self-development and social betterment, she also thought that their 'greatest need will be to realize the value of your time to decide what you can do in a day and what you will have to leave out of a day – the latter will probably be the greater task of the two.'[89] Juggling the completing demands of scholarship, family, and household sometimes caused great emotional turmoil in her own life, yet Skelton's last years showed the importance of the familial as well as the intellectual. Viewed in this light, women's contribution to historiography acquires an accent often different from that of men.

Although her study of women in settlement established a new standard in Canadian historiography in 1924, Skelton saw her vocation as bringing to light elements of the Canadian past neglected by male scholars as unimportant. The sum of her work combined social with intellectual history in an inchoate manner later recognized as cultural history. While both 'history' and 'culture' remain problematic concepts due to the absence of any agreed-upon definitions, Skelton's attempt to depict

Canada's development in larger terms than it had generally been conceived before itself constituted cultural reconstruction. In her writing career she encountered intellectual disagreements, but little of the sexual stereotyping that sometimes greeted other women authors in her era. By stressing adaptation to a new environment throughout her histories and by highlighting improvements in the course of human affairs, Skelton contributed to the growing cultural nationalism characteristic of Canadian historiography in her day, but the nature of the history she wrote dictated that she assume a regional focus to elucidate the larger whole. Gender differences, ethnicity, social class, religion, and literature figured prominently in her work. Through helping to forge a different and broader appreciation of history, Skelton struck new historiographical ground before male professionals were willing to venture beyond existing confines.

Notes

1 Mary Beard, *On Understanding Women* (New York: Longmans, Green 1931), and *America Through Women's Eyes* (New York: Macmillan 1933). See also Bonnie Smith, 'Seeing Mary Beard,' *Feminist Studies* 10 (1984): 399-416.

2 Caroline Ware, *The Cultural Approach to History* (New York: Columbia University Press 1940), 10-11.

3 See George Trevelyan, *English Social History: A Survey of Six Centuries, Chaucer to Queen Victoria* (Toronto: Longmans, Green 1947). Lynn Hunt, ed., *The New Cultural History* (Berkeley: University of California Press 1989) reveals some of the contemporary concerns of cultural history that is social history-oriented, whereas Michael Roth, ed., *Rediscovering History: Culture, Politics, and the Psyche* (Stanford: Stanford University Press 1994) stresses the relationship between cultural and intellectual history.

4 Isabel Skelton personal diaries (hereafter IS diaries), 28-9 March, 1 April 1940, in the possession of Dr. Kenneth Menzies, Guelph, Ontario.

5 Isabel Skelton, 'Jessie Muir Tribute Book,' Isabel Skelton Papers (hereafter ISP), box 7, Queen's University Archives.

6 See Alan Cameron and Julian Gwyn, 'Archibald McNab,' *Dictionary of Canadian Biography, 1851-1860*, vol. 8 (Toronto: University of Toronto Press 1985), 584-9.

7 Obituary of Peter MacGregor in 1937, IS diaries.

8 Alex Murphy to the editor, *Arnprior Chronicle* (29 February 1884); obituary, *Arnprior Chronicle* (14 July 1916).

9 The hiatus in Isabel Skelton's education cannot be explained, but later in life she revered her father's memory while being critical of her mother's want of confidence in her abilities.

10 Lynn Marks and Chad Gaffield, 'Women at Queen's University, 1895-1905: A "Little Sphere" All Their Own,' *Ontario History* 78 (1986): 331-50.

11 Oscar Skelton diary, 22 May 1898, Oscar Douglas Skelton Papers (hereafter OSP), box 11, National Archives of Canada, Ottawa.

12 Isabel Skelton, 'The Beginnings of Levana,' *Queen's Journal* (February 1924).

13 S.E.D. Shortt, *The Search for an Ideal: Six Canadian Intellectuals and Their Conviction in an Age of Transition, 1890-1930* (Toronto: University of Toronto Press 1976), 61.

14 Oscar to I. Skelton, [1908?], box 1, OSP.

15 Ibid.

16 One of the Shortt daughters, Muriel, lived with the Skeltons for a year and recounted some amusing episodes: Muriel Clarke, 'Some Early Memories of Kingston,' *Historic Kingston* 16 (1967): 80-7.

17 I. Skelton to Oscar Skelton, 19 January 1912, box 1, OSP.

18 I. Skelton to Elizabeth Shortt, 31 August 1908, box 9, Adam Shortt Papers, Queen's University Archives.

19 See Barry Ferguson, *Remaking Liberalism: The Intellectual Legacy of Adam Shortt, O.D. Skelton, W.C. Clark, and W.A. Mackintosh, 1890-1925* (Montreal and Kingston: McGill-Queen's University Press 1993).

20 IS diaries, 1 February 1941; I. Skelton, untitled story and play, box 1, ISP.

21 Isabella MacVane [pseudonym for Isabel Skelton], 'The Rearguard of the Victorian Age,' *Globe* (18 September 1909; 16 October 1909; 6 November 1909); Isabel Skelton, 'Two Women Novelists,' *Westminster* (Toronto) (November 1910): 325-31; 'Canadian Women and Suffrage,' *Canadian Magazine* 44 (1913-14): 162-5; 'What's In a Name,' *Canadian Magazine* 46 (1915-16): 350-6; 'The Name "Canada,"' *Canadian Magazine* 52 (1921-2): 312-14. The article on Galsworthy for *The World Today* is in box 1, ISP, as is correspondence with its editor, Shailer Matthews, whom Oscar Skelton had known at the University of Chicago.

22 Skelton, 'Two Women Novelists,' 327.

23 Andrew Macphail, 'On Certain Aspects of Feminism,' *University Magazine* 13 (1914): 83-91. When the Montreal Local Council of Women challenged the appearance of such biased writing in a purportedly academic journal, Macphail (who taught at McGill) closed ranks with James Mavor of the University of Toronto to deflect the women's criticism. Grace Ritchie-England and Anna Lyman to Andrew Macphail [1914], and James Mavor to Andrew Macphail, 29 March 1914, Andrew Macphail Papers, boxes 3 and 11, National Archives of Canada.

24 Adam Shortt to Oscar Skelton, 26 February 1902, box 1, OSP.

25 Ibid., 15 September 1902.

26 See Kenneth Windsor, 'Historical Writing in Canada to 1920,' in Carl Klinck, ed., *Literary History of Canada*, 2nd ed., vol. 1 (Toronto: University of Toronto Press 1976), 230; Carl Berger, *The Writing of Canadian History: Aspects of English-Canadian Historical Writing, 1900-1970* (Toronto: University of Toronto Press 1976).

27 Robert Glasgow to I. Skelton, 8 and 11 August 1916, box 1, ISP.

28 I. Skelton, "Women of New France," [n.d.], box 2, ISP. This subject has been studied recently by Louise Dechêne, *Le partage des subsistances au Canada sous le régime français* (Montreal: Boréal 1994). See also N.E.S. Griffiths, *Penelope's Web: Some Perceptions of Women in European and Canadian Society* (Toronto: Oxford University Press 1976), and Jan Noel, 'New France: Les femmes favorisées,' in Veronica Strong-Boag, ed., *Rethinking Canada: The Promise of Women's History* (Toronto: Copp Clark Pitman 1986), 23-44.

29 Oscar to I. Skelton, 19 December 1914, box 1, OSP.

30 See Sandra Campbell, 'Nationalism, Morality, and Gender: Lorne Pierce and the Canadian Literary Canon, 1920-1960,' *Papers of the Bibliographic Society of Canada* 32 (1994): 134-60.

31 I. Skelton to Andrew Haydon, 1935 [1932?], box 2, ISP.

32 The conceptualization of history as science can be followed generally in Ernst Breisach, *Historiography: Ancient, Medieval & Modern* (Chicago: University of Chicago Press 1983), but as this idea was also associated with ideas about objectivity, see also Peter Novich, *That Noble Dream: The 'Objectivity Question' and the American Historical Profession* (Cambridge: Cambridge University Press 1988).

33 I. Skelton, remarks on a letter of Andrew Haydon, 1935, box 1, ISP. It should be noted that Skelton's personal proclivities led her to appreciate most fully women whom she described as 'ever keen and liberal,' but this personal view did not enter into her historical work except in her lecture, 'Women of New France,' where she used the phrase.

34 See Natalie Zemon Davis in '"Women's History" in Transition: The European Case,' *Feminist Studies* 3, 3-4 (1975-6): 83-103, for the term 'women worthies,' and Bonnie G. Smith, 'The Contribution of Women to Modern Historiography in Great Britain, France and the United States, 1750-1940,' *American Historical Review* 89, 3 (June 1984): 709-32.

35 Isabel Skelton, *The Backwoodswoman, A Chronicle of Pioneer Home Life in Upper and Lower Canada* (Toronto: Ryerson 1924), 7.

36 Ibid., 133.

37 Ibid., 165. Carl Ballstadt, Elizabeth Hopkins, and Michael Peterman, eds., *Susanna Moodie, Letters of a Lifetime* (Toronto: University of Toronto Press 1985) presents a very different image of the woman and her life than the published writings that were intended for a middle-class readership in mid-nineteenth-century Britain.
38 See Nancy Cott, ed., *Woman Making History: Mary Ritter Beard Through Her Letters* (New Haven: Yale University Press 1991).
39 William Deacon to I. Skelton, March 1925; William Arthur Deacon, review of *The Backwoodswoman*, in *Saturday Night* (14 March 1925), box 1, ISP.
40 H.H. Langton, review of *The Backwoodswoman*, in *Canadian Historical Review* 6 (1925): 69.
41 Elizabeth Shortt to I. Skelton, 2 January 1925, box 1, ISP.
42 Oscar Skelton to I. Skelton, 10 December [1924], box 1, ISP.
43 I. to Oscar Skelton, 11 December 1924, box 1, ISP.
44 W.J. Healy, *Women of Red River: Being a Book Written from the Recollections of Women Surviving from the Red River Era* (Winnipeg: Russell, Lang 1923).
45 Alice Clark, *Working Life of Women in the Seventeenth Century* (London: Routledge and Sons 1919), preface, 298-9, 301. Compare Clark's argument with that expounded more generally by South African-born feminist Olive Schreiner in her popular *Women and Labor*, 6th ed. (New York: F.A. Stokes 1911), 46-7.
46 See Ernst Breisach, *American Progressive History, An Experiment in Modernization* (Chicago: University of Chicago Press 1993), 119-21.
47 Jane Errington, *Wives and Mothers, School Mistresses and Scullery Maids: Working Women in Upper Canada, 1790-1840* (Montreal and Kingston: McGill-Queen's University Press 1995).
48 I. Skelton, 'Canadian Biography,' (n.d.), box 4, ISP.
49 *Catholic Record* (5 May 1934). Two contemporary sketches appeared following McGee's death, and an edition of his poems was published posthumously.
50 IS diaries, 11 May 1924.
51 Oscar Skelton to I. Skelton, 29 December 1924, box 1, ISP.
52 G. Lytton Strachey, *Eminent Victorians* (New York: Modern Library 1918); Strachey, *Queen Victoria* (New York: Harcourt, Brace & World 1921).
53 See Isabel Skelton, *The Life of Thomas D'Arcy McGee* (Gardenvale: Garden City Press 1925), 281-306.
54 Ibid., 187-92.
55 IS diaries, 17 January 1924.
56 D.C. Harvey, *Thomas D'Arcy McGee: Prophet of Canadian Nationality* (Winnipeg: University of Manitoba 1923); Alexander Brady, *Thomas D'Arcy McGee* (Toronto: Macmillan 1925).
57 Marjorie Mackenzie to I. Skelton, 15 December 1924, box 1, ISP. See John Hilliker, *Canada's Department of External Affairs*, vol. 1: *The Early Years, 1909-1946* (Montreal and Kingston: McGill-Queen's University Press 1990). Mackenzie's own writings were published in *Queen's Quarterly*.
58 B.K. Sandwell, review of *The Life of Thomas D'Arcy McGee*, in *Saturday Night* (11 April 1925). Box 1 of the ISP contains a variety of other reviews.
59 *Irish Statesman* (10 October 1925).
60 W.P.M. Kennedy, review of *The Life of Thomas D'Arcy McGee*, in *Canadian Historical Review* 6 (1925): 168. Josephine Phelan, *Ardent Exile: The Life and Times of Thomas D'Arcy McGee* (Toronto: Macmillan 1951), 307, also acknowledged Skelton's work as 'the definitive biography' and did not attempt to go beyond its predecessor in most areas.
61 Bert Skelton to I. Skelton, 19 April 1925, box 1, ISP.
62 J.J. Harpell to O.D. Skelton, 27 November 1925, box 1, ISP. The McGee book had cost $3,355.22 to produce and had returned only $530.75 by this time.
63 Adam Shortt, review of O.D. Skelton, *Life and Letters of Wilfrid Laurier, Canadian Historical Review* 3 (1922): 77-87.
64 IS diaries, 6 April 1925.
65 Ibid., 19 August 1925.
66 Ibid., 20 August 1925.

67 Ibid., 5 June 1940. I. Skelton to Sheila Menzies, 24 July 1946, Isabel Skelton private papers (in the possession of Dr. Kenneth Menzies, Guelph, Ontario).

68 Isabel Skelton, *Thomas D'Arcy McGee, Jean de Brébeuf, Isaac Jogues* (Toronto: Ryerson 1928, 1930). Skelton's contributions were no less whiggish than the series as a whole.

69 Andrew Haydon, *Pioneer Sketches in the District of Bathurst* (Toronto: Ryerson 1925).

70 Skelton did not claim credit for her work. The collection was published as Charles Murphy, ed., *1825 - D'Arcy McGee – 1925: A Collection of Speeches and Addresses ...* (Toronto: Macmillan 1937).

71 Isabel Skelton, 'Frederick Philip Grove,' *Dalhousie Review* 19 (1939): 147-63. See Virginia Woolf, 'Mr. Bennett and Mrs. Brown' (1924), in *Collected Essays* (London: Hogarth Press 1966), 319-37.

72 Frederick Grove to I. Skelton, 9 August, and 5 September 1939, box 1, ISP.

73 I. Skelton to F. Grove, 15 August 1939, box 1, ISP. The advent of intellectual relativism was examined most searchingly by contemporary German scholar Karl Mannheim whose work (1929) was unavailable in English until much later: *Ideology and Utopia: An Introduction to the Sociology of Knowledge*, trans. by Louis Wirth and Edward Shils (New York: Harcourt, Brace & World 1964).

74 IS diaries, 25 December 1939, box 1, ISP.

75 IS diaries, 24 December 1941, and 12 April 1943.

76 IS diaries, 29 April 1941.

77 The larger setting is established in N.F. Dreisziger, 'The Rise of Bureaucracy for Multiculturalism: The Origins of the Nationalities Branch, 1939-1941,' and W.R. Young, 'Chauvinism and Canadianism: Canadian Ethnic Groups and the Failure of Wartime Information," in Norman Hillmer, ed., *On Guard for Thee: War, Ethnicity, and the Canadian State, 1939-1945* (Ottawa 1988), 1-52.

78 Note written on G.W. Simpson to I. Skelton, 22 October 1943, box 1, ISP, and IS diaries, 9 July 1947. The creed was James Cappon's favourite line from Robert Browning's poetry.

79 IS diaries, 26 April 1942.

80 Ibid., 19 May 1944.

81 Isabel Skelton, *A Man Austere: William Bell, Parson and Pioneer* (Toronto: Ryerson 1947). Lorne Pierce noted that a similar book, Wilhelmina Gordon's biography of her father, who had been principal of Queen's, *Daniel M Gordon: His Life* (1941) had sold only 235 copies. Lorne Pierce to I. Skelton, 10 November 1944, box 1, ISP; I. Skelton to Lorne Pierce, 23 April 1946, Lorne Pierce Papers, Queen's University Archives.

82 IS diaries, 21 November 1946.

83 Ibid., 19 September 1947, 29 October 1948. *Canadian Churchman* (21 August 1947).

84 Alexander Brady, review of books in social science, *University of Toronto Quarterly* 27 (1947-8): 287; J.J. Talman to I. Skelton, 21 May 1948, box 1, ISP.

85 IS diaries, 27 October 1949. G.R.C. Keep to I. Skelton, 8 August 1951, box 1, ISP; Isabel Skelton, 'D'Arcy McGee and Montreal,' *Culture* 12 (1951): 16-28.

86 IS diaries, 29 November 1950. See Donald Creighton, 'Sir John A. Macdonald and Canadian Historians' (1948), in Carl Berger, ed., *Approaches to Canadian History* (Toronto: University of Toronto Press 1967), 50-62.

87 See W.H. Graham, *Tiger Dunlop* (London: Hutchison 1962).

88 IS diaries, 26 October 1954.

89 I. Skelton, speech to the graduates of the Ottawa Ladies College, 15 June 1926, box 1, ISP.

Part 3:
The Academy

8
Laying Siege to the History Professoriate

Alison Prentice

In October 1934, the British Columbia-born medievalist Sylvia Thrupp was enjoying a period of study in the United States after completing her doctorate at the University of London. A letter to her mentor, University of British Columbia history department head Walter Sage, sketched a delightful picture of her attempts to find a focus for her work and a job in her chosen field, British medieval history.[1] 'Dear Dr. Sage,' she wrote, 'I understand from my father that you were kind enough to offer me some sort of job, he wasn't very clear what, and that he told you that I was busy until the spring.' Thrupp thanked him for the offer, which she hoped could be renewed at a later date. She also apologized for her delay in contacting Sage. 'I meant to write before this, but have been rather occupied moving from place to place and from plan to plan.' Thrupp then described visits to Columbia and Harvard, the historians she had met there, and what she thought of them. She went on to outline her current research interests and plans for the winter.

Thrupp did not hide from Sage the fact that she was also on the lookout for a university position in other parts of Canada. But, so far, the job hunt had been unproductive. Reporting that she was 'slightly discouraged by the extent of anti-feminist feeling in the eastern universities,' Thrupp explained why. 'At McGill they once had a woman in history whom they didn't like and have never taken the risk again and never will while the present staff lives.' The head of history at Toronto, Chester Martin, 'also made it clear that he would appoint only men.' At the University of Western Ontario Thrupp found a more liberal spirit – and a better history library than at Toronto – but no greater prospect of a job. In the end, it was at her own home University of British Columbia, where she had done her first two degrees, that Thrupp found work as a sessional instructor, a position she held for nearly a decade.

Sylvia Thrupp's experience was not unique. Although some were more welcoming than others, history departments throughout English Canada cheerfully admitted women to undergraduate programs and also to master's programs, when these developed. Some talented women were even encouraged to go on to doctorates in history, typically in the United States or Britain and, eventually, in Canada itself. Where faculty men in most Anglophone history departments prior to the 1950s drew the line was at admitting women to their own ranks. Although few articulated their intentions as clearly as the McGill and University of Toronto professors apparently did to Thrupp in 1934, it is evident that the majority of those in a position to hire historians saw university departments of history as enclaves that should be inhabited, almost exclusively, by men like themselves.[2] The records of universities and history departments prior to the 1950s nevertheless reveal some exceptions to the rule and the existence of more than a few women who were well qualified to join the history professoriate had they been given the chance. We must first, of course, wonder if they wanted to.

Assessing motivation is among the historian's trickiest tasks, and motives for pursuing university degrees are no exception. Yet the research of Jo LaPierre and Nicole Neatby has persuasively demonstrated the professional orientation of many – perhaps most – women who attended universities like McGill, Queen's, and Toronto in the early years. Working with information about subsequent careers and, in Neatby's case, with oral histories, their studies show that during the first few decades after their admission to universities and, perhaps even more in the 1920s, women undergraduates had distinct occupational goals.[3] Arguably, women who pursued graduate degrees were even more likely to have been professionally oriented, with those in doctoral programs at least considering the possibility of university employment.[4]

The majority of women who received advanced university training in English Canada prior to the 1950s, however, understood that there were few opportunities for permanent employment in university teaching.[5] The women who specialized in history typically abandoned formal study after the bachelor's or master's degree and found work in archives, libraries, university presses, and, especially, secondary schools, where they used their talents to develop manuscript and book collections or to build careers as editors or teachers.[6] It was extremely hard for this generation of women to break into the professoriate.

But the fact remains that some women did achieve careers as academic historians. These pioneers, who paved the way for later generations of English-Canadian women to claim a place in the ranks of the history professoriate, deserve our attention. Their story is not so much a tale of triumph as one of steady, ongoing persistence. Like all stories, it is also one in which context is important. By examining the experience of women in selected English-Canadian history departments prior to 1950,

I hope to uncover that context and the factors that helped or hindered the gradual, somewhat grudging admission of women to the professoriate in history.

My aims in selecting history departments to study were two: first, to seek regional representation; second, to look for departments where women were most likely to be found. Choosing departments from western Canadian universities was easy. The Canadian Historical Association's first women presidents, Hilda Neatby and Margaret Ormsby,[7] received not only their initial training, but also permanent positions as history professors at the Universities of Saskatchewan and British Columbia (UBC), respectively. Selecting central and eastern universities to examine was more difficult. Despite what Sylvia Thrupp said about them, Toronto and McGill had to be part of the story. At these key, research-oriented universities where graduate programs in history developed relatively early, women ought to have found encouragement – and possibly even employment – especially as undergraduate numbers and faculty workloads increased during the interwar years and the 1940s. Finally, I chose Queen's and Dalhousie to represent smaller central and eastern institutions, speculating that they might have exhibited similarities to the smaller universities in the West. A gradually accumulating roster of women historians also suggested that Toronto, McGill, Queen's, and Dalhousie, along with Saskatchewan and UBC, had educated (and occasionally employed for brief periods) several very interesting women historians, some of whom made careers for themselves in their respective regions or elsewhere.

My goal, in the end, has been to throw some light on the way in which the historical profession and, thus, historical knowledge were socially constructed in the period under study. There are many facets to this question but, here, the spotlight is on gender.

Women Students and Departmental Cultures

That women studied history at Dalhousie, McGill, Queen's, Toronto, Saskatchewan, and UBC prior to 1950 is singularly apparent. It is impossible to count all female history undergraduates for each university during the whole period; indeed, university records vary considerably in the amount of information of this sort that can be gleaned. Nevertheless, an examination of calendars and presidents' reports does reveal that early twentieth-century women undergraduates quickly became involved in history and history programs. The *Principal's Reports* at Queen's, for the three years between 1912 and 1915, for example, note roughly equal numbers of men and women taking the various history courses offered. Women also enrolled in preliminary honours history, but fell away sharply when it came to senior honours.[8] The number of Queen's women graduating in honours history or history and English (counted for most years between 1910 and 1950) indicate women's continuing interest in the subject, although they also show a decline in the 1940s. Between 1910 and 1916, women took nine or about 25 per cent of the thirty-five bachelor's degrees in history or history and English; between 1923 and 1939, when both degrees seem to have been especially popular, nearly half (166 out of 342, or 48.5 per cent) of all honours graduates in history or history and English were women. But after this, there was a falling off, as Queen's women dropped to less than one-third of the students graduating in these programs.[9]

University of Toronto women undergraduates were similarly attracted to history courses and programs. Prior to the 1920s, the presidents' reports made some effort to track women's enrolment in the various courses in the Faculty of Arts. The 1910-11 report recorded, for example, that of the ninety-eight first-year University College women students registered, a total of fifteen were taking English and history. The numbers for the three subsequent years were twenty out of eighty-four, fourteen out of seventy, and eleven out of fifty-eight. Modern history by itself, in contrast, attracted fewer students, both male and female. In 1917-18, the last report recording female enrolments separately, English and history again saw high enrolments for women – and women were now beginning to catch up to men in modern history. For that year, among University College students, women comprised slightly more than half of all students enrolled in the former; they were now exactly one-third of those taking modern history alone.[10] Subsequent numbers and proportions at Toronto, unfortunately, are not so easily documented.

Only at UBC has it been possible to count undergraduate numbers for a substantial period. There, in the 1920's, women comprised precisely one-half of the twenty-eight students in history and history and English; total numbers of students enrolled in these programs rose somewhat after 1929, but the proportion of women fell to approximately one-third of all students in history or history and English at UBC between 1930 and 1950.[11]

Tracking graduate students in history is slightly easier than tracking undergraduates, as many universities made an effort to record the names of all students who were awarded graduate degrees, sometimes even recording their specialties or the titles of their theses. All six of the universities examined encouraged substantial numbers of women to pursue master's degrees in history, once such degrees were actually in place. Far fewer women were encouraged to enter the few small doctoral programs in history. Those wishing to continue their historical training after the master's – especially in the early years – were usually advised to seek advanced degrees outside of Canada. This was the advice given to both Margaret Ormsby and Hilda Neatby at least, and the experience of other women suggests that they were not alone.[12]

Despite inconsistencies in universities' reporting practices, it is possible to see shifts over time and make some comparisons. McGill calendars, for example, reveal a total of forty-seven master's degrees in history granted prior to the 1950s, with fourteen (nearly 30 per cent) of them awarded to women. If we look at master's degrees by decade, however, it is clear that after a slow start, women's acquisition of M.A.s in history shot up in the 1930s, from 25 per cent to nearly 50 per cent of those granted – then dropped quite dramatically in the 1940s to 20 per cent or only one in five. Yet between 1939 and 1950, four women successfully completed doctorates in history at McGill.[13]

For graduate students, Toronto and Queen's calendars provide enrolment rather than graduation figures, and it is not possible to compare women and men. Still, the Queen's records suggest quite large numbers of women enrolled in master's programs in history, although, as at McGill, there was a sharp decline in the 1940s. The Toronto figures are distinctive for the sheer numbers enrolled in history M.A.s altogether, frequently equalling or topping in a single year those enrolled over an entire decade at Queen's. Even before 1920, Toronto often had over ten master's students registered in any given year; numbers dropped slightly during the following decade, but jumped up again subsequently – rising to twenty-one men and women in 1945-6 and thirty-six in 1950-1.[14] In terms of student numbers, Toronto evidently deserved its reputation as the preeminent department for graduate study prior to the 1950s. In an interesting examination of Toronto's history department prior to 1940, Duncan Meikle found that 45 out of 122 (well over one-third) of the master's theses he tracked down were written by women. Women were proportionally most active in the 1920s, when they were the authors of exactly twelve of the twenty-four theses listed in the university's card catalogues. Before 1920, they had contributed slightly less than one-third; in the 1930s, the proportion settled at 40 per cent. Women were less active in Toronto's doctoral program, completing (in the 1940s) only two of the fifteen history Ph.D.s awarded by Toronto between 1925 and 1951.[15]

Like Dalhousie and Queen's, British Columbia and Saskatchewan offered no doctorates in history prior to the 1950s, but they did have vigorous master's programs. Saskatchewan numbers are not easy to determine, but at UBC women earned three of the eight history M.A.s granted in the 1920s, nine out of twenty-nine in the 1930s, and seven of the eighteen awarded in the 1940s.[16] Even more telling figures are the eight interwar UBC women graduates in history who eventually went on to complete doctorates, in history or related fields, at other universities.[17]

A key to their later success was the many scholarships and prizes that women historians could win at UBC. The university calendars recorded their achievements meticulously. Examined for the 1920s, 1930s, and

1940s, the calendars show the women doing better than the men in the first decade, with eighteen women history students winning scholarships or prizes compared to fifteen men. That they were less successful in the 1930s and 1940s presumably reflects their lower enrolment in undergraduate honours history (and honours history and English) during those two decades. Between 1930 and 1950, women students won about one-third of the prizes and scholarships awarded to historians. They were more successful when it came to the few IODE or Carnegie scholarships for graduate study in the United States or Great Britain, winning three of the six given out to history students at UBC between 1931 and 1947.[18] Women at UBC and elsewhere, of course, were not eligible for the prestigious Rhodes scholarships, which went exclusively to men and were occasionally won by historians.[19]

Comparisons of success rates in prize winning are not easily made, as most university records examined for this study either had fewer awards for history students or did not follow UBC in providing details about these competitions. Queen's, for example, did not have as many history prizes; nor did the calendars report them consistently. It is possible nevertheless to get some idea of women's success in winning two awards at Queen's: the Andrew Haydon Scholarship in Colonial History for the best marks in the 'pass' class in that subject and the annual History Medal for the highest marks in honours history courses. Women did extremely well in the first case, winning 43 per cent (thirteen out of thirty) of the scholarships in the years that could be examined between 1910 and 1940, when the scholarship seems to have been discontinued for a period. Although less successful in winning the honours history medal, women carried off six of twenty-nine (about 20 per cent) of these prizes in the years examined between 1910 and 1950. This proportion held at the graduate level, with women winning four of the nineteen Sir James Aikens Fellowships in Canadian History granted between 1926 and 1949, and four, or more than 25 per cent, of the fifteen Western Ontario Graduate Fellowships in History between 1931 and 1949.[20] Women entering the graduate history program at Toronto did even better, but only at first. Prior to 1930, seven of the sixteen graduate fellowships in history (about 40 per cent) went to women. During the next two decades, however, women were much less successful, earning only three of the nineteen fellowships granted in the 1930s and three of the twenty awarded in the 1940s.[21]

Numbers of women enrolled in undergraduate and graduate degrees and winning prizes cannot tell the whole story of women in academic history, but they are certainly suggestive. The figures show that women were encouraged to do history as undergraduates and at the master's level in these English-Canadian universities; they also demonstrate that women found more encouragement in this respect during the 1920s than they were to find by the 1940s, and in some places, in both the 1930s and 1940s. Some women were encouraged to go on to doctorates in history. But few women made it through the Ph.D. programs that McGill and Toronto established prior to 1950. The numbers (and proportions) of women students dropped dramatically when it came to the doctorate at the two universities offering that degree.

What kind of learning environments did women encounter in the history departments they entered during the first half of the twentieth century? It is fascinating to glimpse in the records departments that varied considerably from university to university and to see how departmental cultures changed over time.[22] In an era of all-powerful department heads and university presidents, when most history departments had only three or four faculty members, the character and interests of their teachers could make a profound difference to women. Also significant were the growth patterns of departments (for those that grew) and the impact of events such as war and depression on the history departments of our six English-Canadian universities.

Both world wars fostered enormous changes. Studies of Acadia University during the First World War have shown that women students there revelled in the opportunities provided them by the relative absence of men on campus. We also know that the First World War opened the door to university teaching for women in a variety of disciplines.[23] While the 1920s continued to be a positive period for women in many if not all faculties, the 1930s were more ambiguous. Still courted as students, perhaps for the fees that they could bring in, women may have been somewhat less welcome as competitors for the rewards of scholarship: fellowships and teaching posts in universities. Indeed, in many families, women may not have been able to afford undergraduate education, or graduate study, in the first place. Both factors could have produced the drop in the proportion of history graduates and graduate students who were women at several universities during this decade.[24] Nor did the expansionist 1940s bring immediate relief, as women historians continued to be viewed by the men as unlikely or, at best, awkward colleagues.

It is apparent that most male historians of the early twentieth century found it almost impossible to contemplate women as members of a profession that resembled a gentlemen's club. What is remarkable is the fact that it was evidently not much easier for their mid-century successors to see women participating in the new professionalism either, as historians competed for place as experts and creators of knowledge. Thus, the Second World War and its aftermath – with their shortages of teaching personnel, large classes, and the focus on military concerns during the war and on veterans' interests afterwards – also had a less than positive impact on women, even though a few women did get university history jobs because of the war.[25] As some departments grew and specialized, their leaders appeared to worry that too much female involvement might undermine the professional status that academic historians increasingly sought for themselves and their more serious students during this period.[26]

Interestingly, however, there were regional differences in how departments responded to the pressures of the times. As Sylvia Thrupp's comment on the prejudice she encountered at several 'eastern universities' suggests, Thrupp certainly saw a difference between central Canada and the West when it came to women. Her early experience at UBC, at least, had been in a relatively forward-looking department. In her undergraduate days, the head of history had been Mack Eastman, a dedicated internationalist who, a year after Thrupp graduated in 1924, left university teaching to work at the International Labour Office in Geneva.[27] Eastman's papers contain fascinating clues to his reputation as a rabble rouser. A letter from O.D. Skelton inviting his membership on a committee of the Canadian Political Science Association in 1914 pointed out that there was room on the committee 'for both the most desperate and the most conservative characters,' making it quite clear that Eastman was not viewed as one of the conservatives.[28] Indeed, by 1921 Eastman was defending himself from newspaper charges that he was a socialist. To avoid further trouble, he asked the UBC 'Socialist Society,' of which he was honorary president, to change its name to the 'Social Study Club.'[29]

An undated text for a lecture on the teaching of history reveals not only Eastman's interest in economic and social history, but some interest in the political and social history of women. Under the heading 'Feminism,' he noted the possibility of studying 'woman suffrage,' its origins in the period of the French Revolution, and its more recent past. A handwritten addendum wondered what subject could be more fitting for 'some woman candidate for a Master's degree at the University of British Columbia.' Not a topic a man should take up, perhaps, but to suggest it as a legitimate topic for a woman was radical enough for the time.

However, the two earliest women master's students at UBC, Sylvia Thrupp and Margaret Ormsby, did not choose this route, selecting instead other topics and focusing on the history of their province. They did this no doubt partly because the documents were to hand. But the interwar years were also witness to the development of a growing movement in local and regional history in which Ormsby, especially, was destined to play an important role. At UBC work in local history may have been encouraged by the temporary presence of P.E.I. Rhodes scholar Daniel C. Harvey, who took over the leadership of the department three years after Eastman's departure. It was clearly further encouraged by Walter Sage, who succeeded Harvey when the latter found his permanent niche at the Public Archives of Nova Scotia (PANS) in 1931.

At the University of Saskatchewan, a similar interest in regional history was fostered during the same period by the history department's interwar head, Arthur S. Morton. Morton's papers also reveal a major reason why Canadianists at some universities may have been particularly welcoming to women undergraduates and graduate students in their field. In a period when most professors of history at Canadian universities focused on political or constitutional history and the study of international diplomacy, Morton devoted much of his energy to the founding of a regional history museum and archives, welcoming the contributions that students and former students could make to this work. Long after they had left the university, Morton kept in touch with women who were teaching school or raising families, encouraging them to seek out artefacts and papers documenting the histories of their respective localities for the university's collections. It was thus in a history department that considered women's contributions useful that the Canadian Historical Association's first woman president, Hilda Neatby, received her early training, studying not only with Morton but also with Frank Underhill, who taught there before he moved to Toronto in the late 1920s.[30]

No other individual, perhaps, was as keen on the exploration of local and regional history as Daniel C. Harvey. As department head at UBC and provincial archivist of Nova Scotia, he too encouraged the work of women who shared his interests. Before he joined the graduate history faculty at Dalhousie, history at the university appears to have been dominated by men oriented to the study of international politics. During the interwar years, history was more or less the preserve of A.S. Walker and department head George E. Wilson. The latter, who held an M.A. from Queen's and a doctorate from Harvard, was also for some time dean of men students and eventually dean of arts and science. Until Harvey's appointment to the graduate faculty in 1940, the heavy responsibilities carried by these men must have made the training of graduate students of either sex difficult.[31]

Yet Dalhousie was by no means an impossible environment for would-be women historians during the interwar years. Wilson encouraged at least two women who pursued master's degrees in history. Sister Francis d'Assisi was awarded an M.A. by Dalhousie in 1926, a prelude to her career teaching history at Mount Saint Vincent College, the Halifax Roman Catholic women's college she eventually directed for many years. Four years later, Margaret Ells received her master's from Dalhousie. Ells, who would go on to doctoral study at the University of London, was employed by Harvey at the Public Archives of Nova Scotia from 1932 until she left to teach at the Halifax Ladies' College in 1945. Like Phyllis Blakeley, who replaced her at PANS, Ells modelled herself on Harvey, the archivist-historian, and was a writer as well as a collector and cataloguer of Nova Scotia history. Her teaching career – and perhaps her ability to continue as a historian – was cut short by her marriage and move to the United States, where a surprised family eventually discovered a draft of the London doctoral thesis among her effects at her death.[32]

That Harvey encouraged more than one woman historian there can be no doubt. His chief female protegées were Margaret Ells and Phyllis Blakeley.[33] But his papers include letters from Sister Maura of Mount Saint Vincent, who published a history of her college in 1956,[34] and from several of his former women history students in British Columbia. There is also a letter from Relief Williams, whose innovative master's thesis on Nova Scotian social history for McGill must have received some input from Harvey when she was conducting her research at the Nova Scotia archives.[35] Certainly, when I interviewed her in 1992, Relief Williams Mackay recalled having received little assistance from her McGill supervisor, an Englishman who knew almost nothing about Nova Scotia.[36]

Relief Williams's experience of thesis supervision may have been an exception;[37] of the fourteen women who earned master's degrees at McGill in history prior to 1950, seven wrote theses on Canadian topics, and the majority dealt with the history of Quebec. Indeed, as graduate research grew in the 1930s, the McGill history department deliberately focused it on the 'reconstruction of the history of the French regime in Canada, with additional research on the economic side of that period,' and on '19th century Canadian history, reinterpreting the conclusions of Canadian historians a generation ago.'[38] Of the four women who won doctoral degrees in history from McGill between the late 1930s and the early 1950s (Dorothy Ross, Alice J.E. Lunn, Marion Elizabeth Arthur, and Allana G. Reid), all but Ross wrote on the history of New France or Quebec. Women graduates of McGill who wished to continue their studies beyond the master's degree in non-Canadian topics were encouraged to pursue their doctorates elsewhere. At least two of these women completed their Ph.D.s.[39]

The history departments at both Queen's and Toronto were profoundly oriented towards the production of men well versed in history as a preparation for their future work in government. Under the leadership of George M. Wrong, the Toronto department prior to the late 1920s modelled itself on Oxford, appointed instructors from Balliol, and focused on undergraduate teaching. Only towards the latter part of Wrong's regime did the emphasis begin to shift very gradually towards research and graduate study. But the idea of the professional gentleman lingered, and Ottawa continued to beckon history graduates for many years to come.[40] An artefact of this program was Toronto's exclusive Historical Club, an institution founded by Wrong in 1904-5 and designed to introduce bright young men to the political and economic elites of the city as well as encourage their study of the day's issues, presumably from a historical perspective. The club was limited, at various times, to between twenty-five and thirty male students, from the third and fourth years. Meeting fortnightly in the homes of their professors or of prominent Torontonians, its members prepared papers on topics of the day – and occasionally on the subject of history. Perhaps in order to justify the name of the club in the face of criticism, an account of its activities in the late 1920s noted, with unintended humour, that papers were given 'not only on historical but even political and educational subjects having historical backgrounds.'[41]

The elitist character of the club produced resentment on campus, and women were the first to react. A parallel society, which can be traced back to 1911, was the Women's Discussion Club of University College, organized by Toronto history graduate student and tutor Winnifred Harvey. The club soon expanded to include three sections and women from Victoria College. At least two other budding historians, Helen McMurchie and Helen Cowan, belonged to this association.[42] In 1912-13, Harvey and McMurchie founded the more radical, co-educational Interrogative Club. Hosted by a faculty wife, this club explicitly aimed to include equal numbers of women and men and to debate provocative topics in an open atmosphere. At least two other future historians joined McMurchie and Harvey in promoting 'uncensored thinking' in the Interrogative Club: Fred Soward, who would later teach at UBC, and Isabel Jones, who would be associated with the University of Saskatchewan.[43]

These two clubs must have died out, for there is no trace of either after the First World War. In contrast, the Historical Club thrived, although there were further attempts to steal its thunder. In 1913-14, an International Polity Club boasted University of Toronto president Robert Falconer as honorary president and two women on a seven-person executive, including the ubiquitous Helen McMurchie. Ambitious in its aims, the club claimed to be the 'product, not of a clique, nor of any single college, but of this remarkable age' and to have a membership that was entirely open.[44] In 1923, a newly constituted Polity Club, founded by history instructor Marjorie Reid, was for women only. The club was explicit in modelling itself on the all-male Historical Club; membership was by invitation and meetings followed the format of the men's society. However, this club does not appear to have survived past 1930.[45]

While there is evidence that students tried once again to form a co-educational history club in the late 1920s,[46] the Modern History Club did not make its appearance until the late 1930s. *Torontonensis*, the University of Toronto yearbook, noted its founding in 1939, reporting that Gerald Craig and Maurice Careless were president and vice-president, respectively, of a society that included four women on its executive. This club owed its comparative longevity, perhaps, to its focus on guest speakers and social events rather than on student papers or debates.[47]

Only two women, Dorothy Toye Long and Anna M. Wright, completed doctorates at Toronto in these years. Long, who was married to a United Church clergyman, took over ten years to finish her thesis, but did complete the Ph.D. Wright was a 1931 graduate who, after a fairly long stint teaching secondary school in Orangeville and completing an M.A. at Queen's, earned a Toronto doctorate in 1943.[48] At least three other women candidates for doctorates appear to have dropped out. One, a Mrs. Shirley Gordon, appears briefly in departmental records in the winter of 1936-7, when her fields were established and a supervisory committee put in place, only to disappear in the years following.[49] A second, Elizabeth Sims, completed both her B.A. and M.A. at Toronto in 1931 and 1934, respectively, and was beginning her doctorate by the fall of 1935. Her marriage to a German economic historian does not seem to have interfered with these plans, as they worked together on medieval history, but the Second World War brought her Toronto studies to a halt.[50] A third woman doctoral candidate, Angela Hannen, reported that she had suffered 'a very severe nervous collapse ... due to overwork' during her second year of doctoral studies in 1945 as well suffering 'a serious disappointment' concerning her 'original thesis-problem' the previous year.[51] Hannen also disappears from the records after the mid-1940s.[52]

During the mid-1930s, a history club exclusively for graduate students welcomed such women and it appears to have continued into the 1940s.[53] But, like the undergraduate Modern History Club, it seems to have led a shadowy existence compared to the more flamboyant Historical Club. The exclusion of women from the latter clearly did not prevent them from entering graduate study in history, but the chequered history of the clubs that were founded in reaction to it and the late founding of departmentally sponsored co-educational clubs may have taken their toll. The persistence of the exclusively male Historical Club was always a reminder that there were worlds that no women could enter.

McGill, the other research-oriented university able to offer doctorates to women, had a club very similar to Toronto's all-male history society. The McGill Historical Club has been traced only to 1927-8, the last year it was reported in the university's calendars. Lists of its executives suggest that, like Toronto's, it did not welcome women.

Fortunately for women, the smaller universities did not replicate this exclusion. If Dalhousie had a historical club for men, its existence was never mentioned in the university calendars; a Sociology Club, founded in the late 1920s, admitted women both to membership and executive positions.[54] Queen's does not appear to have had a history club either although, again, there may have been similar associations attached to other disciplines. In contrast, Saskatchewan and British Columbia did have history clubs. And both avoided the exclusive Historical Club model, creating very early in their histories successful, relatively long-lived co-educational clubs in which women participated fully.

The Historical Association of the University of Saskatchewan, which was founded in 1917-18, described itself as a 'live' organization, open to all students who had taken 'at least one class in history in the university.' With a branch 'devoted to ethnological, archaeological, as well as historical research in this province [and a] committee ... collecting everything which will illustrate the life of the races which have helped to build up the Canadian nation,[55] the historical association clearly had an agenda to promote regional social history. But it also fostered the development of students' interests in national and international history and, significantly, promoted the work of the women students who joined. From at least 1921, women were on the executive of the society and, in 1923-4, Hilda Neatby was a member of an executive that included altogether five women and four men. In 1927-8, Neatby, as a master's student, was again on an executive of six women and four men. That year, the club sponsored lectures on 'the Chinese situation,' Nova Scotia history, and Gandhi. Students presented papers on 'Danger Spots in Europe' and on the Ukrainian and Icelandic settlers of Saskatchewan. A final meeting in the spring of 1928 debated whether 'Canada should pursue a policy of separation from the Empire.'[56]

As these topics suggest, most of the Historical Association lectures and discussions dealt with themes in local Saskatchewan or Canadian history or with international questions. Only in 1929, the year Canadian women became 'persons' and the year that Hilda Neatby's sister Kate was president, were women's issues addressed. One meeting in 1929 debated the resolution that 'the admission of women to the franchise has materially weakened democratic institutions.' The affirmative was described as having been 'valiantly upheld by the men, depicting their ideal of the home-keeping woman, while the young ladies declared that an enlightened age demanded enlightened women who would best serve the interests of the home by taking an active interest in the world about them.'[57] At the closing meeting that year, Bernard Shaw's *The Intelligent Woman's Guide to Socialism* was the subject chosen for debate, but Saskatchewan's yearbook said nothing about who argued what.[58] The Historical Association carried on throughout most of the 1930s, but its momentum dwindled somewhat after what had obviously been a lively decade. It seems to have been disbanded in 1939 with Morton's retirement.

The University of British Columbia has preserved some records of its Historical Society, which was established in 1919 with three classes of members: honorary (presumably faculty), life or associate (members who had graduated), and ordinary (undergraduate) members. Once again, women were included, although initially the club was limited to fourteen third- or fourth-year students, and later on to twenty. The society's purpose, as stated in the constitution, was 'the study of historical problems' and, as the limitation on numbers suggests, the club was more exclusive than Saskatchewan's, prospective members having to apply for membership in writing. Judging by the programs, the club may also have had slightly more scholarly goals, discussing such topics as 'the New Social Science and History.' Membership lists and programs from the 1920s reveal that there were usually more or less equal numbers of men and women in the club, that women were sometimes elected president and gave papers almost as often as men did. Membership lists disappear in the 1930s, although not programs or announcements of the executive. Although some women continued to be active, giving papers at club meetings, there appears to have been no woman president in the 1930s, and I found no records for the 1940s.[59]

However, by 1934, UBC had a new 'Graduate Historical Society' designed to encourage among graduates 'an interest in the discussion of historical subjects.' Unlike the undergraduate society, which usually met in people's homes, this society sometimes met in a library seminar room. Membership in the club was more open, with former members of the undergraduate society, graduates who had majored in history, master's students in history, summer school and extra-sessional students in the field, and people who were especially recommended to the executive all welcomed. Once again, women clearly participated in the society. In 1942, Dr. Sylvia Thrupp of the class of 1924 entertained the membership with a talk entitled 'A Historian at the Gate of Heaven,' in which she contemplated what might befall various famous characters who had written history as they sought to pass through the pearly gates. Although she 'did not presume to define the fate of each,' her paper resulted in 'lively discussion about the role of the historian,' including the question of whether 'intellectually honest' work had to be dull.[60]

Women on Faculty

Sylvia Thrupp was present on this occasion not only because she was a University of British Columbia graduate, but because she was also a member of the UBC faculty between 1935 and 1945. The fact that women were able to join and be equal members of the UBC and University of Saskatchewan undergraduate history clubs from their earliest days seems particularly significant, in light of the fact that these two universities produced, and also employed, the few women historians who found relatively secure jobs in Canadian history departments prior to 1950. Women were not as successful in landing, or keeping, history jobs at other universities in Canada.

George Wrong's department at Toronto might have been an exception had things continued as they were in the late teens and early 1920s. Beginning with the 1914-15 calendar and ending only with that of 1925-6, for every year but 1922-3 one or two women held the rank of 'instructor in history' at Toronto. Three women were involved altogether: Helen McMurchie; Margaret Wrong, one of Wrong's daughters; and Marjorie Reid. At the time, the department employed from six to ten men, although as many as four were on service leave during the First World War. And yet it was not solely the war that allowed women to be instructors at Toronto; Polly Armstrong, Wrong's younger daughter, remembered her father as adamant that he 'had to have a woman' on the teaching staff. In Wrong's day, the history department took on some of the characteristics of a family, the entire staff coming regularly for Sunday lunch; the women instructors, and at least one woman fellow, Winnifred Harvey, must have been among those dining, as Wrong's daughter remembered meeting them.[61]

That wartime exigencies were not the only reason for putting women into teaching roles in history is made clear in correspondence between George Wrong and Toronto's president Robert Falconer that dates from two years before the war. In October 1912, Wrong reported that women were trying to raise money for Helen McMurchie's salary, but had not yet completed their campaign. Since this was the case, he was 'now trying to secure the amount required' for McMurchie (and also for Winnifred Harvey) himself. Wrong had not initiated this campaign to get women on the staff: 'I may say that the movement was begun by the women undergraduates of the recent fourth year. I had nothing to do with it but the object is so good and the results are certain to be so useful that I am ready to see it carried through.' The campaign evidently worked for Helen McMurchie, as she was made a fellow, obviously with teaching responsibilities. The following year, it appears the university was willing to foot the bill, or at least a substantial portion of it. In June 1913, Falconer wrote to Wrong that he had 'succeeded in securing from the Governors $750 for Miss McMurchy [*sic*], who is made instructor.' Wrong may not have been as successful in getting what he wanted for Harvey. Correspondence between Falconer and Wrong in 1915, at least, suggests that the university was unable to pay the entire cost.[62] Yet it is clear, from Polly Armstrong's memories, that Winnifred Harvey, like Helen McMurchie, played an important teaching role in the department for a number of years.[63]

In 1922, Wrong was beginning to be concerned that women fellows and instructors were not going on to suitable employment after their apprenticeships at the university. Toronto, apparently, could not keep them; perhaps he wondered if it would be better not to encourage them in the first place. This may have been the subtext of letters between Wrong and the president regarding the candidacy of a Miss Macfarlane, who was a Saskatchewan graduate and strongly supported by Saskatchewan's president Walter Murray, evidently in competition with a man from British Columbia. Wrong noted that Macfarlane was 'a pass student,' while the 'B.C. man, Herd, submitted an essay that showed a touch of genius.' The clinching argument, however, was that there were almost no prospects for women historians. As Wrong continued, 'it is not easy to get work for women ... while men are in some demand. Four or five women who have been with me are still seeking work. I deplore the lack of openings for them but I cannot help it.'

In spite of such misgivings, in the end Wrong apparently supported Macfarlane's appointment to a fellowship and, five days later, Falconer confirmed it, recalling that Murray 'looked upon her as one of the best students in History they had ever had.'[64]

Wrong continued to worry, however. In 1925, it was probably Wrong who wrote to Mary McGeachy advising her to apply for a fellowship at Radcliffe rather than at Toronto. 'If you did well at Radcliffe ... they would back you for an appointment.' This would give her a start; maybe later she could return to Canada. The problem was 'that in Canada there are very few colleges for women, and in co-educational institutions it is very hard to secure the appointment of a woman to the staff. I know this very well, for over and over again I have backed women for appointments in Canada and hitherto the authorities, especially in the West, have preferred to appoint a man.' An interesting perception, given Thrupp's experience later on and, indeed, the situation at Wrong's own university as his leadership in history drew to a close.[65]

Marjorie Reid was the instructor who managed to hang on the longest at Toronto, but ultimately, her career too was blocked. In 1922, during a period of study at Somerville College at Oxford, Reid attempted, unsuccessfully, to move to UBC. By 1925, aware that she could not go on at Toronto, she evidently contemplated leaving and asked her mentors to make inquiries about possible appointments for her elsewhere. W.P.M. Kennedy wrote three letters on her behalf. In all three he admitted that there were no prospects for a woman in history at Toronto. As he put it to the dean of arts at the University of Wisconsin, 'our policy is not (whether rightly or wrongly does not matter) to give higher appointments to women.' Kennedy was concerned about his former student and expressed the hope that Reid would 'be given a chance to develop her academic ability' at some other institution.[66] Evidently Wrong too was concerned; indeed, it may have been the Reid case that caused the frustration he expressed to Mary McGeachy. Whatever the source, Reid was no doubt even more frustrated.[67]

Reid's departure marked the end of an era at Toronto. By this time, Winnifred Harvey was long gone; Margaret Wrong had left to take up her life's work with the International Student Christian Movement; and Helen McMurchie was pursuing new interests in child psychology that developed when she married Professor Alexander Bott. Although at least two women applied for positions in history at Toronto during the 1930s,[68] after 1925 no woman was employed above the rank of tutor until Hilda Neatby was made a 'special lecturer' in the department for two years beginning in 1944, with a Miss Macdonald following her in 1947, and Anna Wright (for one term) in 1949.[69] Margaret Albright also began a lectureship in 1948-9, but it too proved to be a temporary post.[70] Clearly, Sylvia Thrupp's impression of the climate Chester Martin and his colleagues had created was all too accurate.

Thrupp's impression of McGill was equally on the mark, although the history department that encouraged Relief Williams did employ women assistants at a time when Martin's Toronto department was reluctant to do so. Charles W. Colby ran a small department that, until the early 1920s, often had only one other man on the faculty, assistant professor Charles Edmund Fryer. But Colby did have the help of Ethel Hurlbatt, warden and 'resident tutor' in history at the Royal Victoria College for women. Hurlbatt had read honours history at Oxford's Somerville College and had a master's degree from Trinity College, Dublin.[71] Her title suggests the possibility that male and female students were segregated in

Miss Hurlbatt and male colleagues in the McGill convocation procession, 1922

some early history classes, a fact that may also have motivated Wrong's wish to have at least one woman teacher on his staff at Toronto.[72] That there was some ambiguity about her role is suggested by the fact that, after 1916, Hurlbatt ceased to be listed as a member of the history department in the McGill calendars.

Whatever the logistics of teaching history to women and men at McGill, in the early years of the First World War Colby did manage to expand the department briefly by hiring the radical British social scientist, Harold Laski. Possibly in a vain hope to retain his services, Laski was promoted after only one year from lecturer to assistant professor, but he left soon afterwards. In 1916, therefore, Colby was able to create a sessional lectureship for Vera Lee Brown, a New Brunswicker who had completed a B.A. and an M.A. at McGill, in 1912 and 1913 respectively. By this time, Brown was working on a doctorate in European history for Bryn Mawr and continued with this project during her four-year tenure at McGill. These years may have been especially difficult ones; at some point between her acceptance of the job in 1916 and her departure in 1920, Brown lost her entire thesis in a fire and had to begin her research once more from scratch. Although she persevered and earned her Ph.D. in 1922, she did not stay at McGill. A brief account of the department, written in the early 1980s, suggests that Brown was 'eased out as her teaching had been criticized in the faculty.'[73] She spent the next several years doing research in England and teaching in two different schools in the United States before taking up her appointment as an assistant professor at Smith College in 1924. Smith's gain was McGill's loss, as Vera Brown's work in Spanish-American history and her two-volume text on the history of the Americas was to earn her considerable respect in years to come.[74]

It was probably Charles Fryer who, temporarily put in charge of the department when Colby retired but denied the title of head for many years, was so set against having any women on the history faculty. Finally promoted to the headship in 1932,[75] it certainly must have been Fryer who told Thrupp in 1934 that the experiment of employing a woman had been a failure and would not be repeated. He may have been referring to Ethel Hurlbatt when he remarked that McGill had once employed a woman that 'they did not like,' but it is more likely that Vera Brown was the woman in question. Brown may have had problems with her teaching, but she was also a strong and feisty woman. Among the early activists of the Berkshire Conference of Women Historians, Brown also pioneered the idea of commuter marriage, when she became the wife of John Holmes of Fredericton and, later, Halifax. There is no doubt that, in her latter years at Smith College, Vera Brown Holmes was regarded as 'formidable' by both younger colleagues and students.[76]

An undated portrait of Vera Brown Holmes

In the meantime, Hurlbatt continued to teach history off and on at Royal Victoria College (RVC) until close to her retirement as warden in 1929, even though she was increasingly plagued by poor health.[77] She was replaced at RVC by Joan M. Foster, whose title was 'assistant in history' for three years; after this a history post particularly connected with RVC seems to have been discontinued. However, another history job for a woman had been created with the advent of a lectureship in history and geography at McGill's domestic science school, Macdonald College. Held first by John Grant Thompson, then briefly by Mabel Price, it was eventually taken up by Dorothy Sievwright, who taught these subjects at Macdonald until the late 1940s.

For all their reluctance to have women on the history faculty, as the McGill history department grew so did the burden of the work. In the mid-1920s, readers and assistants began to be hired, first one, then two or three. And finally, in 1928-9, Beatrice Lyman was engaged as the first woman assistant. She was joined soon afterwards by Joan Foster (the RVC appointment), and in the mid-1930s by Dorothy Ross, Isabel Craig, Alice Lunn, and Relief Williams. By the end of the 1930s, assistantships for women graduate students in history were firmly established at McGill and, in the 1940s when research fellowships began to be offered, these were also sometimes held by women. Yet, although the department grew by one or two each decade to a complement of six professors by 1950, none of these women, several of whom earned doctorates from McGill, landed permanent jobs there.

Queen's and Dalhousie began with similarly small departments in the early decades of the twentieth century. At Dalhousie, Wilson, Walker, and, later, Harvey constituted the entire history department until the mid-1940s, despite considerable growth in the university as a whole prior to the late 1930s. Only after the Second World War did history finally expand, with the engagement of two lecturers, both men.[78]

Queen's was a different story. The history department grew at about the same pace as McGill's, numbering four men by the end of the 1920s; it rarely fell below that number during the following decade. Like McGill also, Queen's hired tutors and fellows. As early as 1911-12, the calendar lists a woman in a teaching role, although this interlude was brief: no tutors of either sex are in evidence between 1914 and 1924. After that, the department, now led by Duncan A. McArthur, enjoyed the assistance of both male and female fellows and tutors, with Amy Williams, who had an M.A. from Cornell, and Jean Malcolm, a Queen's B.A., the first women to fill these roles. From then on Queen's was rarely without female assistants, although there was a three-year hiatus in the mid-1930s and again in the early 1940s. In the calendar for 1939-40, one of three tutors and two of the four fellows listed were women.[79] The following year, the single tutor was the Toronto graduate, Anna M. Wright, while Anne Sedgewick held one of the three fellowships in history. Wright, who, as we have seen, did her master's at Queen's before returning to complete her doctorate at Toronto in 1943, held the rank of instructor at Queen's from 1943 until 1946. Her reasons for resigning in 1946 are unknown. But the fact that she appeared as a special lecturer at Toronto in 1949 suggests that she was still interested in university teaching at that point and, thus, that it was probably the authorities at Queen's, rather than Wright, who precipitated the decision.[80] At the time of her resignation, history at Queen's was growing again, but not because there were more women on the scene. Operating with a faculty of four or five men between 1946 and 1950, the department continued to depend on large numbers of tutors and fellows, but now most of them were men.

Thus, it was left to the Universities of Saskatchewan and British Columbia to pioneer in the matter of making women permanent members of faculty in history. How and why did they do this? History department heads like Walter Sage and Arthur Morton may have been able to perceive women as potential fellow workers in a way that their counterparts in central and eastern Canada could not, perhaps in large part because of their interest in promoting local and regional history. But this was by no means the whole story. The Saskatchewan case, especially, alerts us to the need to probe more deeply. During the interwar years, at least three women historians – Jean Murray, Hilda Neatby, and Vera Reynolds Kilduff – were encouraged to continue their studies to the doctoral level; two of them, Murray and Neatby, ended up teaching in the history department at Saskatchewan. A fourth, Isabel Jones, was encouraged to do advanced research and evidently did some work for the department.

The University of Saskatchewan Historical Association, 1933-4. Jean Murray, in the front row centre, was honorary president

Of the four, only Jean Murray appears to have had a strong and lasting interest in Saskatchewan history.

About Isabel Jones and Vera Reynolds Kilduff we know little. Jones appears, as we have seen, in the Toronto records as a member of the Interrogative Club in 1917, and there is correspondence between Jones and Morton from the early 1920s, indicating that she was then pursuing a graduate degree in the east. Later, notes about the authorship of an innovative article on the women of Three Rivers, New France, published posthumously in the June 1940 issue of the *Canadian Historical Review*, reveal that the deceased author was Isabel Jones Foulché-Delbosc and that she had taught history at Saskatchewan. But there the trail ends.[81] The history of Vera Reynolds Kilduff is even more obscure. Kilduff did her B.A. and M.A. at Saskatchewan in 1934 and 1935, completing a Ph.D. at Bryn Mawr in 1938. Her subsequent path is unknown.[82]

Fortunately, the career of Jean Murray is more easily documented. The first woman to receive a real job in the history department at Saskatchewan, her special circumstances may have opened Morton's eyes to women's talents as well as to some of the more unpredictable aspects of university politics. Murray was one of the three daughters of the university's much-admired but autocratic president, Walter Murray. All three daughters chose careers other than marriage, and Murray's choice was to be a historian. Her path was undoubtedly smoothed by her father's influence and by family friends such as Robert Falconer, who was president of the University of Toronto when Murray applied for a fellowship to do an M.A. there. But Murray did not win her position by her father's influence alone. According to Arthur Morton, Murray was also a very fine instructor.[83] A stint teaching school in rural Saskatchewan preceded her pursuit of a master's degree at Toronto and, as soon as her doctoral course work was completed at Chicago in 1928, Murray was offered a job at the University of Alberta.[84] By the time her doctorate was awarded in 1936, however, Murray was a member of the history faculty at Saskatchewan with a salary reputedly paid out of the pocket of her father.[85] Here she remained in active service, teaching Canadian history and writing about Saskatchewan's past and the history of the university, gathering and preserving her father's and other university papers, and generally making herself useful to her colleagues and her students.[86]

In the mid-1940s, Murray was joined by the second woman to secure permanent employment in Saskatchewan's history department, Hilda Neatby. Unlike Murray's, Neatby's journey to a tenured appointment on Saskatchewan's main campus in Saskatoon was long and circuitous.[87] She began her teaching career with temporary jobs at Saskatchewan, first replacing Margaret Cameron in French and then Frank Underhill in history. Having completed a master's degree in 1928, Neatby moved on to doctoral studies and a teaching assistantship at Minnesota under A.L. Burt. While she would have preferred to study with Underhill (by then at Toronto), Neatby reluctantly accepted the generally held view that, since there were few jobs for women Ph.D.s in Canada and Americans would never hire a person with a University of Toronto degree, the only choice for a woman was to take her doctorate at some university outside of Canada. But even with her Minnesota degree, Neatby was unable to get either a job or a post-doctoral fellowship in the early 1930s. As she wrote to her sister, 'a Ph.D. in Canadian history is practically an unsalable article and when it is saddled with the wrong sex things are even worse.' Finally, Neatby landed a teaching position, cobbled together for her when the University of Saskatchewan took over Regina College in 1934. As Michael Hayden describes this job, Neatby was hired to teach modern European history at three different institutions: 'Regina College, Luther College, and in Moose Jaw for a total of nine hours a week.' In addition, she taught five hours of grade-twelve French and handled the correspondence work in both courses.

This regime only came to an end when Neatby was given a temporary post at the University of Toronto in 1944-5. Hayden suggests that she yearned to teach in a history department almost anywhere except at home in Saskatchewan but, if she hoped for a permanent job in Toronto, these hopes were dashed. The fall of 1946 saw her return to Saskatoon where she took up a position in her old undergraduate department.[88] From this base, Neatby eventually made a name for herself as one of Canada's most distinguished historians of French Canada, as a key member of the Massey Commission on the Arts, Letters and Sciences, and, more controversially, as an outspoken critic of Canadian education.[89] She was elected the first woman president of the Canadian Historical Association in 1962.

Margaret Ormsby, of the University of British Columbia, would be the second woman to be so honoured. And this brings us to a consideration of the hiring policies and practices of the history department at UBC, where women were considered for positions as early as 1922. Departmental papers for that year contain letters from, or promoting the candidacies of, four women who were interested in a position that had evidently been advertised. Toronto's Marjorie G. Reid wrote on her own behalf from Somerville College at Oxford. Vincent Massey of Toronto recommended Dorothea Bidwell; A.B. Balcom wrote recommending Esther I. Clark of Acadia University; a final recommendation came from A.L. Burt, who was promoting Aileen Dunham, a 1919 Alberta graduate with a 1921 M.A. from Toronto.

Burt left no doubt about Aileen Dunham's qualifications for a faculty position: 'She is by far the most brilliant student that I have ever had and I expect that it will be many years before I encounter her like again.'[90] Clearly Burt, who directed the studies of a number of distinguished Canadians after he left the University of Alberta to teach at Minnesota, should be counted among the Canadian historians who were less troubled than others by the prospect of women instructors joining the ranks of professional historians.[91] Despite his praise, however, the job did not go to Dunham; Fred Soward, who had debated with Helen McMurchie, Winnifred Harvey, and Isabel Jones in Toronto's Interrogative Club, and who also had a degree from Oxford, was hired instead.[92] The next appointment in history at British Columbia went to Hugh Keenleyside, a UBC graduate who obtained his doctorate from Clark University and was first listed in the calendar as a member of the faculty in 1926-7. Keenleyside taught history at UBC for two years only, but the courses listed under his name in the calendars suggest that he shared some of the progressive ideas of his undergraduate mentor, Mack Eastman. He introduced a new course entitled 'An Outline of the Social History of the Western World'; during the first year it was offered, the three essay topics assigned for the fall term included one on the position of women in ancient Babylon and Egypt.[93]

By 1928-9, the UBC history department had been transformed. Eastman had been replaced by D.C. Harvey, of Dalhousie and Oxford, as head of the department; Keenleyside was gone and three new men were listed as special lecturers or assistants. The next year, Sylvia Thrupp was among those listed in the new category of 'assistant.' Other women would follow her: Gwen Musgrave, Margaret Ross, Margaret Ormsby, who was an assistant in 1935-6, and Patricia Johnson, who played this role in 1937-8.[94] By then Harvey was gone, Walter Sage was department head, and Thrupp, who now had a University of London doctorate, had rejoined the department with the rank of 'instructor.'

Thrupp continued the department's interest in social history, offering a course entitled 'Social and Economic History of Medieval Europe' and other courses that emphasized social and cultural themes. She also worked very hard in a department that appears to have been somewhat understaffed, teaching three or four courses every year. Sage was among those who clearly felt overloaded, especially when the war depleted the department's resources in the early 1940s. His correspondence from that period reveals that he was increasingly turning over departmental tasks to Thrupp, including the provision of criticism and commentary to students on their theses.[95] Despite these contributions, the university did not promote her. Moreover, a letter from UBC's president, L.S. Klinck, to Sage regarding history appointments in 1944 suggests that even after nine years of service, Thrupp's appointment had to be renewed annually. She was also discriminated against when it came to salaries. By 1944, her annual pay was $2,000. In contrast, the pay of A.C. Cooke, an Oxford graduate whose scholarship was minimal compared to Thrupp's, but who had been appointed directly into the professorial ranks in 1929-30 and promoted to associate in 1940-1, was increased in 1944 from $3,400 to $3,600.[96]

The wonder is that Thrupp stayed at UBC as long as she did. Undoubtedly she was, at least in part, motivated by a measure of gratitude; given the state of the job market and the prejudice against women when she first began to seek employment in the 1930s, she probably felt lucky to have any job at all. Her letters to Sage during that decade are fascinating not only for their revelations of prejudice against women seeking faculty positions at McGill and Toronto, but also for what they say about efforts that were made to help women scholars find jobs during this period and the negative feelings that might be found among those at the bottom of developing professional hierarchies. In 1933, she wrote that a committee of the Canadian Federation of University Women was 'canvassing all the Canadian universities on behalf of me and three other women in the same boat, but the story all round is the old one of the economy. [Harold] Laski talks about the "intellectual proletariat," naming the research assistants who have to spend all their energy doing the dirty work for professors who take all the credit.' Although by this stage she may have begun to worry about her own job prospects, Thrupp felt fortunate that, so far, she had been able to avoid joining 'the proletarian ranks.'[97]

But by the mid-1940s, Thrupp must have sensed the unfairness of her situation. In the academic year (1944-5) that followed Klinck's letter,

Thrupp was still listed in the calendar as a member of the department, but one who was on leave of absence; she never returned to a regular post at UBC after this leave. Perhaps the fact that she was invited by Harold Innis to spend the year in Toronto's political economy department was responsible for her last-minute promotion to assistant professor. This belated recognition did not persuade her to return to UBC, however. The Toronto post launched a career in the United States and, from 1945 on, Thrupp was employed by American universities, which were either more willing or more able to reward her considerable talents appropriately.[98]

The year before Sylvia Thrupp left British Columbia permanently, Margaret Ormsby joined the history department as a special lecturer. After the completion of her Bryn Mawr Ph.D. in 1937, Ormsby had first taught at a girls' school in California before landing a wartime position in the short-staffed history department at McMaster University in Hamilton, Ontario.[99] At UBC, she was initially viewed as a temporary replacement for Fred Soward, who had been seconded to the Department of External Affairs during the war.[100] Like Thrupp, Ormsby had a heavy teaching load, taking on the duties usually assigned to an assistant as well as the lecturing for her courses. Perhaps learning from the Thrupp experience, however, the University of British Columbia did see to it that Ormsby was promoted and, within three years, she had become an assistant professor. According to Professor Ormsby, this and other promotions were not solicited, and P.B. Waite suggests that they came directly from the university's new president, Larry Mackenzie, 'who liked to reward talent.'[101]

Given the powerful role of the central administration at UBC, it is hard to know how much to blame Sage for the university's failure to promote Thrupp on the one hand, or credit him for its success in engaging the permanent services of Ormsby on the other. At the very least, he deserves credit for his support of UBC's women history graduates in the early stages of their careers. Sage wrote to Thrupp in 1934 telling her not to despair of getting a post in Canada; he also backed her for a Rockefeller fellowship and presumably got her the UBC job, by means of which she kept body and soul together for nine years. Sage also wrote to Ormsby when she was at Bryn Mawr, suggesting in great detail what research she might do for her proposed doctorate in British Columbia history and, later on, about his efforts to help her get a scholarship.[102] Eventually, as in the case of Thrupp, he did give Ormsby a job.[103] In the latter's case, however, it was evidently the university president who provided the most important support: appropriate job security and promotions. Only Jean Murray and Hilda Neatby, in Ormsby's era, joined her in this important achievement.

A Foot in the Door

It may not be altogether appropriate to refer to women historians as 'laying siege' to Canadian university history departments during the first half of the twentieth century. As I have suggested, most women receiving professional training in history during those years would have been acutely aware of the hurdles they faced in seeking employment at the top of the professional ladder. Especially during the 1930s, they knew that men supporting wives and children were perceived to have the larger claim to jobs in university history departments, despite the very single status of some male historians when they were first hired – or even later – and the undoubted fact that single women often also had dependants to support.[104]

To some women, goals other than university teaching must often have seemed more practical or more interesting. Relief Williams Mckay, who recalled that she was encouraged to do a doctorate at McGill, confessed that she was both pushed and pulled away from this course of action by contradictory feelings and concerns. For one thing, she was put off the academic route by another woman doctoral candidate at McGill whom she found 'unfeminine.' For another, her interests were broad, and she tended to go to the theatre on evenings when she should have been studying for exams. Most important perhaps, she very much wanted to bring education to poor children in rural Nova Scotia, citing the example of a university friend who had chosen to do similar work in Newfoundland. Her M.A. in history completed, Williams's future course was set when she sought teacher training in her home province and gave up further formal study.[105] Relief Williams Mackay did not altogether abandon her historical interests however. Rural school teaching, marriage, and the raising of four children, followed by a second career teaching English in a secondary school that opened near her home, were capped by a return to research and writing. In the mid-1980s she published an engaging and valuable history of her own Nova Scotia forebears.[106] Perhaps the Nova Scotia women historians, Relief Williams Mackay, Margaret Ells, and Phyllis Blakeley, are as good examples as any of the fact that women had other fish to fry besides laying siege to university history departments.

The substantial number of Canadian women who did seek doctoral degrees, however, and the struggles of many of them to find satisfactory university employment in Canada, nevertheless confirm a story of embattlement, as department after department found it difficult or impossible to hire the extremely well-qualified women historians in their midst. Some women who applied for university jobs, like Juliana Cotton who wrote to D.C. Harvey when he was head of history at UBC, were advised that they might be better off seeking work, at least initially, in secondary teaching. The argument in this case was that, as Cotton was an Englishwoman, taking such a job would be a good way to familiarize herself with

'Canadian conditions.' But it is also true that, in this period, high-school teaching was regarded as the most suitable destination for women with graduate degrees.[107] Vera Brown and Margaret Ormsby both taught in American girls' schools briefly. Becoming an expatriate was another path to employment. Brown and Sylvia Thrupp were among a substantial number who found jobs in American colleges or universities. Before the 1950s, only Jean Murray, Hilda Neatby, and Ormsby appear to have been able to create what would amount to lifetime careers teaching in university history departments in English Canada.

There are at least two points to be made about their success. The first is that the careers of these three women and of their female colleagues who headed for the United States did not occur in a vacuum. Theirs were not solo roles, performed without a supporting cast of other women graduate students and would-be women scholars. Indeed, their careers probably would not have been possible had it not been for the existence of many other women knocking at the doors of university history departments, however tentatively.[108] Second, and happily for those that followed, the careers of Murray, Ormsby, and Neatby proved that women could not only teach at the university level but, especially in the cases of Neatby and Ormsby, could also excel as scholars. And, although they may have grumbled, male students did not faint at the sight or sound of a woman professor at the front of the lecture hall. Indeed, at least one future historian of the male variety rather appreciated the smart hats and fine legs of the elegant woman professor he encountered at UBC when he was a student there after the Second World War. Moreover, P.B. Waite also appreciated the 'revolutionary' character of Ormsby's course which, he recalls, covered new ground in the economic and social history of Canada.[109] Finally, in the 1960s, both Ormsby and Saskatchewan's Neatby were elected to the presidency of the Canadian Historical Association, an important badge of their full acceptance as 'professional' historians.

University doors were hardly wide open to women historians during the post-Second World War years or even the years that followed. Indeed, the struggles were by no means over. At the University of Toronto in 1950 – and as late as 1967 – it was still possible for women entering doctoral programs in history to be queried about their intentions in pursuing this degree. Men with the power to admit or reject them expressed reservations about the advisability of such a course, either stating or implying that there would be no jobs for women Ph.D.s when they graduated.[110] At the same time, despite these continuing prejudices, the women who pursued academic careers in history prior to 1950 achieved a good deal. If the doors were not wide open, neither were they entirely closed. This was a considerable improvement on the conditions that Sylvia Thrupp encountered in 1934.

Acknowledgments

The research for this study has been supported by the Social Sciences and Humanities Research Council of Canada. I am also grateful for the expert assistance, at an early stage of the research, of Cathy James and, more recently, of Alyson King who did much of the investigation of sources on the Toronto, Queen's, and McGill history departments for this paper. Thanks are due as well, for important technical help, to Elizabeth Fear, Beulah Worrell, and Chris Olsen. Finally, my special thanks to Margaret Banks, Jean Burnet, Terry Crowley, Michiel Horn, Alyson King, Duncan Meikle, Margaret Ormsby, Jim Prentice, Patricia Roy, and P.B. Waite for their extremely helpful comments on earlier versions of this paper.

Notes

1 Sylvia Thrupp to Sage, 8 October 1934, Walter Sage Papers (hereafter WSP), University of British Columbia Archives (hereafter UBCA). Thrupp had already completed a two-year postdoctoral fellowship at the London School of Economics (1931-3); from 1933 to 1935 she was on a second fellowship.

2 William Duncan Meikle has explored what might best be characterized as the class aspects of this tendency in his account of the Oxford-oriented history department of the University of Toronto under George M. Wrong. See Meikle, 'And Gladly Teach: G.M. Wrong and the Department of History at the University of Toronto' (Ph.D. diss., Michigan State University 1977).

3 Jo LaPierre, 'The Academic Life of Canadian Coeds, 1880-1900,' and Nicole Neatby, 'Preparing for the Working World: Women at Queen's During the 1920s,' in Ruby Heap and Alison Prentice, eds., *Gender and Education in Ontario* (Toronto: Canadian Scholars Press 1991).

4 Most studies of early Canadian women academics see women looking for meaningful work and to support themselves. Judith Fingard, 'Gender and Inequality at Dalhousie: Women Faculty before 1950,' *Dalhousie Review* 59, 4 (winter 1984-5): 687-703; Alison Prentice, 'Bluestockings, Feminists or Women Workers? A Preliminary Look at Women's Early Employment at the University of Toronto,' *Journal of Canadian Historical Association*, 2 (1991): 231-61; Mary Kinnear, 'Disappointed in Discourse: Women Professors at the University of Manitoba before 1970,' *Historical Studies in Education/Revue d'histoire de l'éducation* 4, 2 (fall 1992): 269-87, reprinted, in a revised form, as chapter 2 of Mary Kinnear, *In Subordination: Women and the Professions, 1870-1970* (Montreal and Kingston: McGill-Queen's University Press 1995). Biographical studies of early women professors include Margaret Gillett, 'The Lonely Heart: Maude E. Abbott, 1869-1940,' in Geraldine Jonçich Clifford, ed., *Lone Voyagers: Academic Women in Coeducational Institutions, 1870-1937* (New York: The Feminist Press 1989); Alison Prentice, 'Scholarly Passion: Two Women Who Caught It,' in Alison Prentice and Marjorie R. Theobald, eds., *Women Who Taught: Perspectives on the History of Women and Teaching* (Toronto: University of Toronto Press 1990); Prentice, 'Elizabeth Allin: Physicist,' in Elspeth Cameron and Janice Dickin, eds., *Great Dames* (Toronto: University of Toronto Press 1997). See also the studies of women scientists in Marianne Gosztonyi Ainley, ed., *Despite the Odds: Essays on Canadian Women and Science* (Montreal: Véhicule Press 1990).

5 Certainly, this was the opinion of Mossie May Waddington Kirkwood, English professor and dean of women at the University of Toronto, when speaking of women graduate students generally. Most women with scholarly aspirations and career goals, she noted in a 1973 interview, expected, or were expected, to seek employment in secondary school teaching. Mossie May Kirkwood interview, B74-020, University of Toronto Archives (hereafter UTA).

6 Such women include historian/archivists like Margaret Ells and Phyllis Blakeley of the Public Archives of Nova Scotia and teacher historians like Katherine Lamont, whose career unfolded in Ontario and Quebec, or Relief Williams Mackay of Nova Scotia. These and many other women historians who could be added to the list will, I hope, be the subjects of a future study.

7 Hilda Neatby was president of the CHA in 1962-3; Margaret Ormsby followed her in 1965-6.

8 Queen's University, *Principal's Report for 1914-15*, 9; 'Report of the Dean of Women, Hilda C. Laird,' Queen's University, *Principal's Report for 1925-26*, 64.

9 Queen's University, *Calendars*. The calendars, printed in April of each year, listed students who had graduated the previous year. Counted in these numbers were those honours students who listed either 'History' or 'History and English' as their courses of study. My thanks to Alyson King, who conducted the research on student numbers at Queen's, McGill, and Toronto.

10 University of Toronto, *President's Report* (1910-11): 35, and (1917-18): 42-3. At the other universities studied (except for UBC, which is described below), printed materials do not clearly indicate courses of study pursued by male and female undergraduates, although graduating students could undoubtedly be tracked using students' yearbooks such as the Dalhousie University *Pharos* or lists of individual students and their courses.

11 University of British Columbia, *Calendars*. As with the Queen's records, we counted only those who listed either 'History' or 'History and English' as a course of study.

12 Much of the information about Hilda Neatby's career included in this essay is derived from Michael Hayden, *So Much to Do, So Little Time: The Writings of Hilda Neatby* (Vancouver: UBC Press 1983), especially chapter 1; also, Margaret A. Ormsby, interview with author, June 1990. For an account of Professor Ormsby's career, see John Norris, 'Margaret Ormsby,' in John Norris and Margaret Prang, eds., 'Personality and History in British Columbia: Essays in Honour of Margaret Ormsby,' *BC Studies* 32 (winter 1976-7): 11-27.

13 McGill University, *Calendars*. Although it did not list many non-Canadian items, the *Canadian Historical Review* lists of completed M.A. and Ph.D. theses were also examined for evidence of women's graduate degrees in history.

14 Queen's University, *Calendars*; University of Toronto, *Calendars*. Looking at five-year intervals at Toronto, the figures were fourteen enrolled in 1930-1 and again in 1935-6, followed by a drop to only seven in 1940-1, before the very large numbers of the following decade.

15 Meikle, 'And Gladly Teach,' appendixes H and I, 304-17. Unfortunately, Meikle's M.A. list does not include the 1940s.

16 *Calendars* of the Universities of Toronto, Saskatchewan, and British Columbia.

17 From the class of 1924, Lillian Gates (Ph.D. Radcliffe 1956) and Winnifred B. Ramsell (Ph.D. Wisconsin 193l); from the class of 1925, Sylvia Thrupp (Ph.D. London 1931); from the class of 1926, Marion M. Spector (Ph.D. Columbia 1940) and M. Marion Mitchell (Ph.D. Columbia 1938); from the class of 1929, Margaret A. Ormsby (Ph.D. Bryn Mawr 1938); from the class of 1931, Idele L. Wilson (Ph.D. Toronto 1944); and from the class of 1932, Norah Louise Hughes (Ph.D. Chicago 1945).

18 *Calendars*, UBC. The numbers are as follows: In the 1920s, 14 out of 28 honours history students at UBC were women, who won 18 of the 33 prizes; in the 1920s, 18 out of 60 students were women, who won 10 of the 32 prizes; in the 1940s, women students in honours history numbered 12 out of a total of 37, winning 10 of the 35 prizes awarded. The awards for undergraduates included the Vancouver Women's Canadian Club Scholarship, the History Society Prize (1920-9), the Graduate History Society Prize (1936-44), the History Society Silver Medal (1921-3), the History Society Gold Medal (1920-32), the United Empire Loyalist Silver Medal (1935-47), and the John and Annie Southcott Memorial Scholarship in early B.C. History (1937-47). Graduate awards for which both women and men were eligible included the Imperial Order of the Daughters of Empire War Memorial Post Graduate Scholarship (first granted to history student Phyllis M. Freeman in 1931) and the Carnegie Corporation Scholarships for Graduate Study (first awarded to history students Arthur J. Johnson and Margaret A. Ormsby in 1935).

19 The importance of the Rhodes scholarship to continuing the Oxford influence on the development of history in Canada emerges in Lewis H. Thomas, *The Renaissance of Canadian History: A Biography of A.L. Burt* (Toronto: University of Toronto Press 1975), x and chapter 1.

20 Queen's University, *Calendars* and *President's Reports*. Most years between 1910 and 1950 were examined. Aikens Fellowship winners were Alice Oswald, Bessye Sheffield (whose

prize reverted to W.D.R. McHoull), Gladys Hentz, and Kathryn E. Dawson. The winners of the Western Ontario award were Jessie C. Ward, Verna Walton Burgess, M. Phyllis Nunn, and Jacqueline Coté.

21 University of Toronto, *President's Reports*.

22 History department records have been explored at the Universities of British Columbia, Saskatchewan, and Toronto. For Queen's, McGill, and Dalhousie, I relied largely although not exclusively on university-printed materials, such as calendars and presidents' reports, or other historians' university or biographical studies. The Toronto history department is also the subject of two studies: Meikle, 'And Gladly Teach,' and Robert Bothwell, *Laying the Foundation: A Century of History at University of Toronto* (University of Toronto: Department of History 1991). For Ontario universities considered collectively, see A.B. McKillop, *Matters of Mind: The University in Ontario, 1791-1951* (Toronto: University of Toronto Press 1994), which has excellent sections on gender relations in the universities and women's experience of higher education in Ontario during the period explored. On the topic of history as a scholarly endeavour in twentieth-century English Canada, see Carl Berger, *The Writing of Canadian History: Aspects of English-Canadian Historical Writing, 1900-1970* (Toronto: University of Toronto Press 1976).

23 See Prentice, 'Bluestockings' and 'Scholarly Passion' for examples of women being hired at the University of Toronto. On Acadia, see Barry Moody, 'Acadia and the Great War,' in Paul Axelrod and John G. Reid, eds., *Youth, University and Canadian Society: Essays in the Social History of Higher Education* (Montreal and Kingston: McGill-Queen's University Press 1989); also see Moody's essay in this collection.

24 Lack of funds for graduate study determined the life course of Katharine Lamont, who travelled to Europe and also studied at Oxford after her graduation from Regina College in 1926, but could not afford to continue during the Depression. Falling into a private girls' school job in Toronto instead, she made her career teaching history at the secondary level and, later, as headmistress of a girls' school in Montreal. Katharine Lamont, interview with author, April 1996.

25 Both the Saskatchewan and UBC history departments sent men to Ottawa during the war; the calendars of both universities reveal a heavy emphasis on the sciences throughout the period studied, but especially in the 1940s. For a discussion of one university's recruitment of women students into war work and the negative effects on their studies, see Nancy Kiefer and Ruth Roach Pierson, 'The War Effort and Women Students at the University of Toronto, 1939-1945,' in Axelrod and Reid, *Youth, University and Canadian Society*.

26 See Meikle, 'And Gladly Teach,' for a discussion of the shifting emphasis at the University of Toronto, as George Wrong's devotion to teaching and general education began to be replaced in the 1930s by increasing specialization and a focus on research and professional graduate training.

27 Eastman remained with the ILO until forced to leave Europe in the late 1930s. When he returned to teaching, he found a position in the history department of the University of Saskatchewan.

28 O.D. Skelton to Mack Eastman, 21 August 1914, S. Mack Eastman Papers, UBCA.

29 Eastman to the editor of *Empire Weekly*, 4 October 1921, Eastman Papers. Eastman was also attacked for being insufficiently attached to the British Empire, a fact that was demonstrated by his allowing an American text, which gave short shrift to the empire's role in the First World War, to be used in the modern history course. Communication from Pat Roy, April 1996.

30 A.S. Morton Papers, subject file 33, University of Saskatchewan History Department, 1914-41, University of Saskatchewan Archives (hereafter USA). In the light of the Saskatchewan department's interest in local history during the interwar years, it's fascinating to discover Neatby's later disparagement of the movement, reported in the essay by Ambrose in this collection.

31 Dalhousie, *Calendars*. See also Wilson's reports as Dean of Arts and Science, Dalhousie University, *Reports of the President* (1945-50): 45-7, and (1950-4): 59-61.

32 Evidence of George Wilson's support for Ells may be found in a brief account of her life, which notes that Wilson had wanted to grant high honours to Margaret Ells but

had been prevented from doing so by a colleague. Public Archives of Nova Scotia (hereafter PANS), Margaret Ells Collection, MG1 vol. 2,676, A and B. For a brief review of Ells's doctoral thesis, which was either never examined or never pronounced satisfactory, see *Nova Scotia Historical Review* 7, 1 (1987). Four of Margaret Ells's publications may be found in the Phyllis Blakeley Papers, vol. 3,113, file 14, PANS.

33 Phyllis Blakeley was a prolific writer of Nova Scotia history. For a list of her many publications, see Wendy Duff, 'Bibliography of the Writings of Phyllis Ruth Blakeley,' *Nova Scotia Historical Review* 7, 2 (1987): 88-100.

34 Sister Maura, *The Sisters of Charity, Halifax* (Toronto: Ryerson Press 1956).

35 Sister Maura to Harvey, 11 March 1950; Isabel Bescoby to Harvey, 29 November 1935; Helen R. Boutilier to Harvey, 30 November 1935; Relief Williams to Harvey, 16 January 1936. Located in Daniel Cobb Harvey Papers, MG1 vols. 1200-01, PANS. Three of the four letters expressed their authors' appreciation of radio broadcasts on Canadian history that Harvey made in the mid-1930s.

36 Relief Williams Mackay, interview with author, June 1992.

37 A brief examination of the McGill history department by Michael Perceval-Maxwell does suggest that it was badly understaffed in the early 1930s when Relief Williams was doing her masters. McGill University Archives (hereafter MUA), 'The History of History at McGill,' typescript (April 1981), 21-2.

38 McGill University, *Annual Report* (1937-8): 8.

39 McGill University, *Calendars* (1909-10 to 1949-50). These women were Vera L. Brown, whose Bryn Mawr doctorate is dated 1923, and Cicely M. Greer, who earned a Ph.D. from Radcliffe in the late 1940s.

40 These themes are explored in Meikle, 'And Gladly Teach,' and are further taken up in Bothwell, *Laying the Foundation*. For an analysis of the development of the professions and gentlemanly professional codes prior to the twentieth century, see R.D. Gidney and W.J.P. Millar, *Professional Gentlemen: The Professions in Nineteenth-Century Ontario* (Toronto: University of Toronto Press 1994).

41 *Varsity* (18 October 1928), A73-0051/249 (40), UTA.

42 The Women's Discussion Club is described in *Torontonensis*, vol. 14 (1912): 221, and vol. 16 (1914): 226. It's not clear what Harvey's status was at the time of the club's founding. McMurchie was probably a graduate student at this point, as was Cowan in 1913-14.

43 *Torontonensis*, vol. 19 (1917): 200. Although this account suggests that the club was limited to ten men and ten women, the list of members included thirteen women and twelve men, in addition to the seven members listed as 'on active service.'

44 *Torontonensis*, vol. 16 (1914): 250.

45 *Torontonensis*, vol. 27 (1925): 305; vol. 30 (1928): 259; vol. 31 (1929): 255; vol. 32 (1930): 385. In 1928, Gwendolyn Carter, later a renowned specialist in African government at Smith College, was president of the club.

46 *World* (19 November 1929), A73-0051/249 (40), UTA. The new historical club 'for both men and women' got as far as electing a president, a secretary, and a 'councillor,' but no further evidence of its existence has been found. It may have evolved into the Letters Club, a society for English and history students that lasted from 1930 to 1938 and accented English more than history, and quite explicitly, social more than intellectual activities. 'There seemed to be a general feeling that the intellectual gymnastics of the lectures were sufficient.' *Varsity* (26 November 1930), A73-0051/249 (51), UTA.

47 *Torontonensis*, vol. 41 (1939): 236; vol. 42 (1940): 243; vol. 48 (1946): 253; vol. 49 (1947): 329.

48 Dorothy Elizabeth Toye Long Papers, B90-0049, UTA; clippings files, Anna Margaret Wright, A73-0026/527 (25), UTA. See also the G.W Brown Papers, B72-0023/23 (01), UTA, for a letter from Wright to her thesis supervisor in August 1943, and December n.d.; Department of History Papers, A70-0025/8 (67) and (68), UTA, for letters placing Wright at the top of a list of history candidates recommended for fellowships in 1941 and 1942.

49 Department of History minutes, 5 December 1936, and 5 February 1937, A90-0023/027 (01), UTA.

50 Cody Papers, January 1934, A68-0006/12, UTA; Chester Martin to President Cody, 15 November 1935, A68-0006/23; *Telegram* (26 October 1939), A73-0026/419 (88). Elizabeth Sims Hoemberg, who eventually published a book about her wartime experiences in Germany, lectured on the British Commonwealth after the war at the University of Munster; 'Raised 3 Children, Farmed Acre on German Battlefield,' *Telegram* (4 May 1950), A73-0026/419 (88).
51 Angela Hannen to President Smith, 27 June 1946, A68-0007/02 (01), Sidney Earle Smith Papers, UTA.
52 Two other doctoral candidates from the 1940s are referred to in the records: Mrs. W.F. Mitchell, noted in a 1945 communication between Chester Martin and Sidney Smith, and Phyllis Walden, who is listed as a Ph.D. student in a 1946-7 list of members of the Graduate History Club. Martin to Smith, 25 October 1945, A68-0007/02 (01), UTA; Graduate History Club mailing lists, A90-0023/27, UTA. No trace has been found of doctoral theses by these two or the other three women Ph.D. students at the University of Toronto.
53 There are few records of this club, but it appears to have been founded in 1936. It is mentioned in the papers of Dorothy Toye Long, B90-0049/11, UTA, and there is a file in the Department of History Papers, B90-0023/27, UTA, entitled Graduate History Club. Anna Wright was secretary of the club in 1940-1.
54 Dalhousie University, *Calendars*. Judith Fingard's study of women students at Dalhousie suggests that the large numbers of brothers and sisters who attended, along with the small numbers overall, may have worked against the development of some forms of gender exclusivity. See Fingard, 'College, Career, and Community: Dalhousie Coeds, 1881-1921,' in Axelrod and Reid, *Youth, University and Canadian Society*.
55 *The Spectrum* (University of Saskatchewan Yearbook) 1921: 39, USA.
56 *The Greystone* (University of Saskatchewan Yearbook) 1928: 70, USA.
57 *The Greystone* 1929: 85.
58 Ibid.
59 Papers of the Historical Society of the University of British Columbia, UBCA.
60 Records of the Graduate Historical Society of the University of British Columbia, UBCA.
61 Conversation with Polly Armstrong, 8 January 1995.
62 Falconer to Wrong, 10 March 1915, A67-0007/036, UTA. In an unpublished summary of the Toronto careers of Winnifred Harvey, Helen McMurchie, Margaret Wrong, and Marjorie Reid, entitled 'Four Teachers' and kindly sent to me by Duncan Meikle, Meikle indicates that Harvey's initial salary, like McMurchie's, had also been raised in the first instance by the women students.
63 Meikle, in 'Four Teachers,' confirms this perception.
64 Wrong to Falconer, 24 June 1922; Falconer to Wrong, 29 June 1922, A67-007/80, UTA.
65 Unsigned letter to McGeachy, 9 March 1925, A70-0025/3, UTA. History department records at McGill reveal that among Wrong's earlier efforts was an attempt to get a job at McGill for his daughter Margaret. In his reply to Wrong, the principal noted that there 'ought to be some readjustment in the history staff here, but I doubt if any additional appointment will be made in the way of a woman teacher.' W. Peterson to Wrong, 25 January 1915, Department of History, MUA, file 991. My thanks to Colin Coates and Megan Davies, who called this letter to my attention.
66 W.P.M.K. to (Mack) Eastman to 'King,' and to Dean Sellery, 9 May 1925, A70-0025/5 (150), UTA.
67 By 1926, Marjorie Reid had left Toronto and had become Marjorie Reid Jackson. I have not yet been able to trace her subsequent career.
68 Juliana M.S. Cotton, of the University of Wisconsin, applied in 1932; Audrey Baker, with an honours degree from Oxford and a doctorate in medieval history from the University of London, applied in 1938. Chester Martin to Falconer, 29 January 1932, A67-0007/132a, UTA; Helen Millichamp to Cody, 4 January 1938, A68-0006/040 (01).
69 See departmental minutes, 1944-5, A90-0023/027 (01), UTA; Chester Martin to President Sidney Smith, 23 October 1947, A68-0007/33 (7); Chester Martin to Dean Beatty, 28 January 1949, A68-0007/048/13.
70 Martin to Smith, 3 September 1948, A68-0007/48 (13). Margaret Albright was still in her lectureship in May 1951 however, and Martin may have even been trying to

promote her, although the evidence is ambiguous as he was complaining that none of the eight lecturers in history had been promoted. The dean had pointed out that all had received substantial salary increases, if not promotions, including Albright. She married and eventually made her career at Atkinson College, York University, as Margaret A. Knittl.

71 McGill University, *Calendars* (1909-10 to 1930-1), and *Annual Report* (1933-4): 18. See also Susan E. Vaughan, 'Ethel Hurlbatt, LL.D.: Warden of the Royal Victoria College, 1907-1929,' *McGill News* 15, 3 (June 1934): 19-23, and Muriel V. Roscoe, 'The Royal Victoria College, 1899-1962, A Report to the Principal' (1964), MUA. Hurlbatt (1866-1934) had attended Oxford from 1888 to 1892 and was warden of Aberdare Hall, University of Wales, and Bedford College for Women, University of London, before taking up the post at McGill, which she held from 1907 to 1929.

72 Margaret Ormsby mentioned that history was often taught separately to men and women. Margaret Ormsby, interview with author, June 1990.

73 Perceval-Maxwell, 'The History of History at McGill,' 14.

74 McGill University, *Calendars* (1915-16 to 1919-20); *Annual Reports* (1914-15, 1915-16, and 1920-1); Vera Lee Brown Holmes Papers, Smith College Archives (hereafter SCA).

75 That Basil Williams, with an M.A. from Oxford, was brought in over Fryer's head to be Kingsford Professor of History and head of the department several years after Colby left must have been somewhat galling. Fryer was promoted to full professor in the same year, but had to see one more person promoted ahead of him when William Templeton Waugh, with a master's from Manchester, was made head of history in the late 1920s. Fryer finally won his promotion to the chair, after serving McGill since 1906, when Waugh died in 1932. See McGill University, *Annual Report* (1920-1): 21, and (1932-3): 19. Perceval-Maxwell speculates that Waugh's sudden death may have been 'the result of overwork,' 'The History of History,' 21.

76 For a brief reference to Vera Brown Holmes's role in the Berkshire Conference of Women Historians, see Jacqueline Goggin, 'Challenging Sexual Discrimination in the Historical Profession: Women Historians and the American Historical Association, 1890-1940,' *American Historical Review* 47, 3 (June 1992) n. 69, 794. As a student of Holmes in 1954-5, I certainly found her formidable and was interested to have my view corroborated: a discussion conducted by Professor Nellie Hoyt on earlier years in the history department at Smith, Oral History Collection, SCA; and Nellie Hoyt, professor emerita, conversation with author, May 1995.

77 Hurlbatt was given an honorary doctorate by McGill in 1930 and was much eulogized when she died several years later for 'her brilliant scholarship and charm of personality.' McGill University, *Annual Report* (1933-4): 18.

78 The appointments of J.P. Heisler and D. Mitton as lecturer and special lecturer in history are reported for the year 1948-9; see Dalhousie University, 'New Appointments, 1948-9,' *Report of the President* (1945-50): 72. On the fluctuations in student numbers, see 'Report of the Dean of the Faculty of Arts and Science,' *Report of the President* (1945-50): 45.

79 The tutors were G.P. Grant, Dorothy Harlow, and M.B. Parnell; the fellows were J.B. Conacher, Gladys Heintz, Donald C. MacDonald, and M. Phyllis Nunn. Queen's University, *Calendar* (1939-40).

80 Queen's University, *Calendars* (1944-5 to 1950-1). It is interesting to note that Anna Wright was listed as a member of the history department in the calendars but not as a member of the Queen's faculty, although her appointment was never identified as sessional. *Queen's Review* of March 1950 reported that Anna Wright, now Mrs. Percy M. Robinson, had delivered a lecture on 'Education in Canada' to the Royal Society of Arts in London. According to Joy Parr, people at Queen's believed that after her marriage she moved to California. Undated communication.

81 Isabel Jones to Morton, 19 June 1923, and 24 June 1923, Arthur Morton Papers, USA. Jones was writing from Paris, requesting letters of recommendation and describing her thesis on the history of New France. Her posthumously published article was entitled 'Women of New France (Three Rivers: 1651-63),' *Canadian Historical Review* 21, 2 (June 1940): 132-49. *CHR* describes Jones as a graduate of the University of Toronto, who was

'for a time a member of the staff in history at the University of Saskatchewan' and 'later associated with her husband in historical work on France.' In 1931, she published, with Julio Puyol, *Bibliographia de R. Foulché-Delbosc (1864-1929)* in Madrid, but I have not been able to find any further traces of her career. For a brief discussion of her article, see the Introduction to this collection.

82 Vera Reynolds's degrees were unearthed in *Canadian Historical Review* lists, researched by Cathy James.

83 Handwritten draft letter recommending Jean Murray to the University of Chicago for a fellowship, n.d., Arthur Morton Papers, USA.

84 R.F. Blackblock to Jean Murray, 10 October 1921; Robert Falconer to Jean Murray, 4 June 1923; G.M. Wrong to Jean Murray, 25 June 1925; registration for the degree of Doctor of Philosophy, University of Chicago, 1 December 1924; letters from personnel at the University of Chicago, regarding award of a fellowship, 1 April 1 1927; regarding field for the final exam, 8 February 1928; letters from the University of Alberta regarding her appointment, 18 April 1928, 11 May 1928, and 1 June 1928. Personal correspondence, general, Jean E. Murray Collection, USA.

85 David R. and Robert A. Murray, *The Prairie Builder: Walter Murray of Saskatchewan* (Edmonton: NeWest Press 1984), 237. The authors' discussion of Walter Murray's relations with his three daughters and concerns for their welfare is intriguing and suggests that not everyone at Saskatchewan admired all aspects of Murray's administration or family life, despite his overall popularity.

86 Conversations with Michael Hayden of the University of Saskatchewan history department and with Stan Hanson of the University of Saskatchewan Archives, spring 1994. See also James S. to Jean Murray, 4 May 1949, Jean E. Murray Collection, USA, in which she is asked to run the history department during one session in the absence of both the head, G.W. Simpson, and the acting head, Hilda Neatby. See also appreciative letters from students in Jean Murray's personal papers.

87 As indicated above, for this account of Neatby's career, I rely largely on Hayden, *So Much to Do, So Little Time*, especially chapter 1.

88 Ibid., 24.

89 Hilda Neatby's famous study of Canadian education, *So Little for the Mind*, was published by Clarke, Irwin in 1953, shortly after her stint with the Massey Commission.

90 A.L. Burt to Mack Eastman, 28 November 1922, WSP, UBCA. Also Marjorie G. Reid application, 27 March 1922; Vincent Massey to Dean Coleman, 27 June 1922; A.B. Balcom to President Klinck, n.d. Reid, as we have seen, taught at Toronto until 1926; Clark is the subject of Barry Moody's essay in this collection. I have not, so far, been able to trace Dorothea Bidwell. According to Lewis Thomas, Dunham went on to a distinguished career as a historian in the United States. Thomas, *The Renaissance*, 14.

91 That it was probably Burt who was in charge when Jean Murray was offered the job at Alberta is further evidence of this. He was also mentor not only to Aileen Dunham (see note 90) but to another Alberta student, Lillian Cobb, who also became a professor of history in the United States. See Thomas, *The Renaissance*, 14-5. He may also have encouraged Georgina Talbot Droitcour, who completed a doctorate in British history at Minnesota in 1922 and was employed at Minnesota when she wrote to Walter Sage applying for a job at UBC in 1923. Droitcour to Sage, 19 February 1923, WSP, UBCA.

92 This is not clear in the UBC calendars, but W.P.M. Kennedy's letter to Mack Eastman (cited in note 66) reminded Eastman that Reid had applied at the time 'you appointed Soward.' See also H.T.J. Coleman to Evan L. Donaldson, 20 July 1922, WSP.

93 UBC, *Calendars*, especially 1926-7.

94 While the interwar assistants, with the exception of Stanley Moodie and Margaret Ormsby, were probably all master's students, after the war the junior teachers were appointed at the instructor level and already had their M.A.s. See UBC *Calendars* for 1929-30 to 1931-2, 1935-6, 1937-8, and 1946-7.

95 See, for example, Sage to Eleanor Piggott, 2 October 1942; Sage to D. Brown, 21 January 1943; Sage to Kathleen Reynolds, 21 January 1943, WSP, UBCA. In all three cases, it is clear that Thrupp read the theses of these students and made comments, which Sage then passed on with a brief covering letter explaining her role to the students.

Thrupp was also the author of a guide for history M.A. students working in the department at UBC. See Sage to Mollie Cottingham, 8 February 1943.

96 L.S. Klinck to Sage, 30 May 1944, WSP, UBCA. Cooke evidently was not only no scholar, he was also a 'disorganized' teacher. Private communication, spring 1996.

97 Thrupp to Sage, 29 January 1933; see also Thrupp to Sage, 8 October 1933, and 17 October 1933, WSP.

98 It was Margaret Ormsby who offered the opinion that the year in Toronto launched Thrupp's American career; Ormsby to the author, 4 April 1996. For the information about her promotion to assistant professor, I am indebted to Michiel Horn who mentions it in 'The Exclusive University,' draft chapter of his forthcoming *Academic Freedom in Canada: A History*. Thrupp's career took her to several American universities, but she was chiefly employed at the Universities of Chicago and Michigan. She returned to teach summer school at UBC on at least one occasion. Letters to Sage regarding this employment suggest that her father's residence in Vancouver was a drawing card; this may also have been another reason she was willing to endure the temporary position at UBC for so long. Thrupp to Sage, 7 January 1950, 22 January 1950, and 23 August 1951, WSP.

99 Margaret Ormsby, interview with author, June 1990; Norris, 'Margaret Ormsby,' 22; 'A Western Woman Looks at Her Work,' unpublished typescript of Professor Ormsby's address to the Canadian Historical Association, McMaster University, 7 June 1987. According to the latter, Chester New was the department head at McMaster who hired Margaret Ormsby in 1940.

100 Sage to Patricia Johnson, 16 June 1943, and Sage to Dr. C.K. Smith, 24 July 1943, WSP, UBCA. It is in the latter letter that Sage noted that 'Professor Soward's place has been temporarily filled by the appointment of Dr. Margaret Ormsby.' There is some evidence that Sage tried to hire J.B. Brebner the following year, but that Brebner could not afford to move his family from New York, where he was in the history department at Columbia. Brebner suggested that Sage think about Donald Creighton. 'Do you suppose that you could get Creighton? He seems to be the pick of the crop on many counts, and it would be much easier to move within Canada.' Brebner to Sage, 23 October 1944.

101 Larry Mackenzie evidently exacted some payment, often asking Ormsby 'to help' at presidential social events during the frequent absences of his wife. The latter, interestingly, seems to have been able to avoid the role of 'president's wife' to an unusual extent. P.B. Waite, *Lord of Point Grey: Larry Mackenzie of U.B.C.* (Vancouver: University of British Columbia Press 1987), 142, 170.

102 Thrupp to Sage, 29 January 1933; Sage to Thrupp, 17 October 1934; Sage to Ormsby, 21 December 1931; Sage to Ormsby, 15 February 1933, WSP, UBCA.

103 For Sage's support of other, lesser-known women historians, see Sage to the University of Toronto Dean of Graduate Studies (regarding Helen Boutilier) 15 March 1933; Sage to Boutilier, 9 March 1933, 23 August 1934, and 15 September 1934; Sage to 'Whom It May Concern' (regarding Margaret Little), 8 April 1935; Sage to Hubert E. Bolton (regarding Anne Eleanor Carroll, UBC exchange student to the University of California), 21 January 1943; Sage to Dr. J.E. Robbins (regarding Anne Carroll), 13 May 1943, WSP.

104 Ormsby mentioned that both she and Hilda Neatby had obligations to elderly mothers during important stages of their careers; Margaret Ormsby, interview with author, June 1990. Dalhousie's George Wilson was among the male professors who never married; Lester Pearson was one of many who were single when they were first employed at Toronto. A study published in the American Association of University Professors *Bulletin* in 1949 exploded the myth that single women scholars had only themselves to support, demonstrating that more than half of a group of 158 Northeastern women faculty supported one or more dependents. Cited in Margaret W. Rossiter, *Women Scientists in America: Before Affirmative Action, 1940-1972* (Baltimore: Johns Hopkins University Press 1995), 38.

105 Relief Williams Mackay, interview with author, June 1992.

106 Relief Williams Mackay, *Simple Annals: The Story of the McQueen's of Sutherland's River* (Pictou NS: Advocate Printing and Publishing 1986); Relief Williams Mackay, interview with author, June 1992. The McQueen family correspondence is now to be found in the Public Archives of Nova Scotia.

107 Cotton to chairman, 29 March 1929, and Harvey to Cotton, 6 April 1929, WSP, UBCA. Cotton had a doctorate in progress, a master's degree from Wisconsin, and one on the way from Oxford. In 1932, Cotton tried again to get a Canadian position, this time at the University of Toronto. See note 68. That high-school teaching was the normal expectation for women with advanced degrees emerges in an oral history of Mossie May Kirkwood of the University of Toronto. See Prentice, 'Scholarly Passion,' 272.

108 Maxine Berg makes a similar argument in 'Eileen Power and Women's History,' *Gender & History* 6, 2 (August 1994).

109 Conversation with P.B. Waite, April 1995; Waite to author, 16 March 1996.

110 Margaret Banks was the student in question in 1950. Bothwell, *Laying the Foundation*, 130, errs in dating this event 1949, which was the year Banks began her M.A. Banks to author, 9 March 1996. Professor Banks persevered with her doctorate nevertheless, but found the warning – at least initially – proved to be all too true. Although a full-time history job would undoubtedly have given her more time for her scholarly work, Banks ultimately found her niche in the law library at the University of Western Ontario. From this position, she was able to make important contributions to the development of Canadian legal history, eventually joining the graduate history department at UWO in 1969. My own experience in 1967 was more subtle. Who, the then graduate secretary wanted to know, would look after my children? And what did I expect to do with the degree once I got it? Tolerant bemusement bordering on scepticism was this gentleman's response to my application.

9

A View from the Front Steps: Esther Clark Wright and the Making of a Maritime Historian

Barry M. Moody

When, at age ninety, Maritime historian Esther Clark Wright collected her memoirs for publication, she began with a description of one of her earliest and most important childhood memories: sitting on the front steps of her family home in Fredericton, New Brunswick, watching the world go by. From that vantage point, she was able to observe and interact with two elements that would mould her approach to life and to the writing of history for the rest of her long life. Greeting the neighbours, talking with passersby, and watching the flow of life around her helped to forge an abiding interest in people, their activities, and their individual life stories. Across the road from those front steps flowed the broad St. John River, which defined so much of the character of that part of New Brunswick and of the people who occupied it.[1] The young Esther Clark responded early to the strong influence of nature and of her surrounding environment, marking the child and the mature woman in significant ways as she evolved as a person and as a historian. It would be the people of New Brunswick – people firmly rooted in place – about which she would write in later years. However, it would be a long journey from the front steps of the home in Fredericton to the writing of the dozens of books and articles that would mark her later career. If the view from the front steps of the family home in Fredericton helped determine *what* subjects the future historian would be interested in, her upbringing, her education, and especially her marriage would shape *how* and even *if* she would write about those subjects.

While the influences and events of her early life can be seen as providing the crucial factors in shaping the future historian, it was not until well into middle age before Wright would possess the confidence, education, encouragement, and leisure to begin producing the many books that would characterize the last half of her very long life. Her first tentative venture into the field came only at age forty-five, with the publication of a short study of one of her Loyalist ancestors.[2] For nearly half a

Watercolour of Esther Clark Wright by her friend Helen Beals

century following this, there would be a steady stream of books and articles, most of them focused on the people and geography of her native province. Her most significant work, *The Loyalists of New Brunswick*, which challenged so many of the assumptions of the nature of loyalism, and therefore of the American Revolution,[3] did not appear until she was sixty. It was only in the mid-1970s that she turned her attention to the New England settlers of the Maritime provinces and to shipbuilding in the Bay of Fundy region.[4] Her last book appeared at age ninety, only a short time before her death in 1990. In many respects, the first half of her long life can be seen as a prologue, the fashioning of the woman who would become the successful historian of later life. It is that early process that is the focus of this essay.

The birth of Esther Isabelle on 4 May 1895 was an event of considerable moment in the Clark household, marking the appearance of the first child and, as it turned out, the only daughter of an upwardly mobile young Fredericton couple. The home life created by William G. and Harriett (Richardson) Clark proved a decisive influence in the shaping of their young daughter, providing her with the intellectual stimulus, strong religious convictions, educational opportunities, and financial security that would prove so crucial in Esther Clark's later life.

The Clarks were committed adherents of the Baptist Church, and their involvement extended far beyond the obligatory Sunday church attendance. Esther was thus raised in a home in which regular family devotions and discussions of things spiritual were part of daily activity.[5] Both parents were active in the local church and in the wider Baptist community. William Clark was a long-serving deacon and Sunday School superintendent and teacher.[6] The Baptist Church in the Maritimes provided significant, if not equal, scope of action for women as well as for men, and Harriett Clark was at least as well known as her husband in the greater Baptist community. Aside from her activities in the local church, she was deeply involved in the women's missionary movement, serving for many years on the executive of the United Baptist Women's Missionary Union and eventually as its president.[7] Such a home atmosphere not only shaped Esther's religious convictions, but also determined the university that she would attend, a crucial factor in moulding her future life. The Baptist connection also provided her with an extensive network of contacts and friends, especially female ones, which extended far beyond the Maritimes. In later years, Clark would on occasion question some of the religious teachings of her youth and would alter some of her beliefs, but her commitment to the Baptist Church remained one of the cornerstones of her life.[8]

Intricately connected with the religious climate of the Clark home were the attitudes concerning and respect for education. Although her father had had only six years of education in a rural school, her mother had completed school and attended the provincial Normal School in Fredericton. Both parents were active in the promotion of education in the Maritimes, with Harriett serving as a member of the local school board and William as a long-time member of the board of governors of Acadia University, the Maritime Baptist institution of higher learning.[9] Acadia would recognize their contributions to education and to the denomination with honorary degrees; Harriett received an honorary M.A. in 1926 and William an honorary D.C.L. in 1940.[10] All three Clark children were eventually sent to Acadia, and throughout her prolonged excursion into higher education, Esther always had her parents' firm encouragement and substantial financial support.

By the time of Esther's birth, William G. Clark was in the process of building a very successful business in Fredericton, which would later be extended to other parts of the province. In the second decade of the twentieth century, Clark sensed the coming importance of the automobile and opened a series of car dealerships, which are still operated by members of his family.[11] For her entire life, Esther was provided with the financial backing that allowed her freedom to pursue interests and a lifestyle unhampered by the need to earn a living. The family also became increasingly important socially and politically. Her father served first as mayor of Fredericton, and then as member of Parliament and eventually lieutenant-governor of New Brunswick.[12] This secure financial and social position, however, never adversely affected the developing young Esther. Although it may well have contributed to her strong sense of confidence and independence that she exhibited throughout much of her life, there was nothing of the social snob about her.[13] As Esther wrote to her mother to announce her engagement: 'You trained me to be a professor's wife, didn't you? to like plain living and high thinking, not to put material values too high.'[14] Certainly 'plain living and high thinking' would appear to have characterized her life.

After a sound education in the schools of Fredericton, Clark was sent to the neighbouring province of Nova Scotia for university training, to Acadia University in Wolfville.[15] Few decisions made by or for her during her lifetime proved as decisive in shaping her future. The University of New Brunswick was only a few blocks away from the family home in Fredericton and might well have been considered the appropriate place of education for a seventeen-year-old woman, but the ties of denomination were stronger for the Clark family than the advantages of proximity. Her arrival on campus in the fall of 1912 began a nearly eighty-year love affair and established for the young Clark patterns of thinking, and circles of friends, that remained constants for the rest of her life. A dozen years later, in attempting to explain herself to her fiancé, she listed her love of Acadia as one of the three key ingredients of her makeup:

> Three things, though perhaps in reality they are only two, even you shall not change in me. Deep in my heart I shall always be a Canadian and a Baptist and a loyal daughter of Acadia. Acadia is so much an expression of my country and my church that it is a part of the other two. I shall be perfectly contented to live in another country if that is where our work takes us, and completely satisfied to worship with another denomination, and I may learn to love other halls of learning, but never as I love Acadia.[16]

At Acadia, Clark was moulded by the powerful sentiments of the Social Gospel, which reinforced the teachings of church and home and gave them a sharper intellectual focus. There too she blossomed academically and socially, as her newsy, weekly letters home revealed. Acadia clearly provided her not only with intellectual stimulus, but also engendered considerable confidence in the young scholar.[17] Acadia had admitted women to its classrooms for more than a generation (it was the second university in the British Empire to do so),[18] and Clark found the atmosphere both accepting and challenging. The position of women at the university was greatly enhanced by the departure of most of the male students after the outbreak of war in 1914, leaving the women to dominate the classes, carry off the prizes, run the student newspaper, and organize the social life of the institution.[19] The women graduates of the war years would be considerably marked by the absence of their male counterparts and the resulting attention and encouragement they received from their professors.[20] The confidence produced by this experience would be reflected in the later careers and accomplishments of many of these women.[21] They would pursue careers in medicine, foreign missions, university teaching, social work, biological research, and economics, among others. The years spent at Acadia were clearly crucial in such developments.

The Acadia experience provided Clark not merely with a solid education and considerable confidence, but, perhaps as important for her emotional equilibrium, an extensive network of friends – especially female friends – that would form a firm foundation upon which her life would be built. Lacking any sisters or close female cousins, Clark was immediately drawn to the lively set of young women she found at Acadia. The close ties thus formed were exaggerated, but certainly not created, by the

'The Girls' in residence, Acadia University, ca. 1915. Esther Clark is the one underneath the pennant

increasing scarcity of male classmates by early 1915, as more and more of the young men enlisted as soon as they came of age.

In many respects, Clark and her fellow female students exemplified what Carroll Smith-Rosenberg has described as 'the female world of love and ritual,' but with a number of important differences.[22] The establishment of such strong female friendships was clearly not only a nineteenth-century phenomenon, nor did it flourish only as long as women inhabited a world 'bounded by home, church, and the institution of visiting.'[23] It was perhaps precisely because they were thrust into a traditionally male and foreign environment that the preservation of such strong friendships and networks was so important. For Clark and her friends at Acadia, female relationships would form a solid base upon which they would construct much of the rest of their lives, extending those important friendships into the late twentieth century.[24] Her letters over the next seventy years reveal just how important those female relationships were.[25]

Clark emerged from her four years at Acadia with a firm grounding in her chosen field (economics), a well-trained mind, a heightened sense of Christian duty, a wide circle of friends, both male and female, and a deep and abiding love for the university. Although she would travel extensively throughout her life, she would never be able to pull up the roots that were thrust deep into the Wolfville soil during her Acadia sojourn. She lived for extended periods in other communities and even other countries, but she never again felt completely at home living anywhere else. Thus, Clark graduated in 1916 with important components of her future already in place; what she still lacked was any firm direction for her life. The only thing that was clear was that for her and her contemporaries, many of the traditional career paths for women held few attractions.

In her views and attitudes, Clark at age twenty-one seemed to exemplify many of the characteristics of the 'new woman' who was so admired and so feared in North America in the early twentieth century.[26] Confident, independent, athletic, well-educated, and highly motivated, she was quite prepared to challenge what she saw as the stifling atmosphere of the Victorian era, to question traditional attitudes, and to seek a career for herself quite different from that of her mother. For Clark, an honours degree in economics from Acadia was only a beginning.

After a year spent teaching school in New Brunswick and visiting with 'the girls,'[27] a clearly restless Clark began graduate studies at the University of Toronto, another important step in the shaping of the future historian. The exposure to intellectual stimulus as well as the variety and challenges of the university and the city greatly excited her and opened new aspects of her thinking. She revelled in the music, the public speakers, the theatre, the range of peoples and minds, and the new friendships she was developing.[28] Here again the female friends from Acadia and her mother's extensive network proved invaluable in giving Clark a sense of belonging and providing entrées into a number of important circles.[29]

If the social and intellectual life of the city stimulated Clark, her experience at the University of Toronto was to prove more of a mixed blessing. There she came under the powerful influence of Prof. Robert M. MacIver, a sociologist from Scotland and member of the political science department whose chief interest was in the study of community. Although he would later preside over a department of increasing specialization, he saw himself primarily as a social scientist, 'not as a sociologist or a political scientist or an economist. I had come to the conclusion that the demarcation of the social sciences into separate departmental boxes was artificial, mainly a device for the convenience of administration.'[30] At the time Clark studied under him, he was still working on *The Elements of Social Science*, published in 1921, in which he would outline 'the relationships between society and its physical, economic, and social environments.'[31] His approach to the study of society struck responsive cords in the young woman from New Brunswick, with her interest in and concern for individual people and her love of the natural environment. Her short exposure to MacIver would leave a lasting impression.[32]

Clark must have found Frederick Tracey, her professor of ethics, much tougher sledding. His views on the different natures and consequently separate spheres of men and women stood in sharp contrast to her own ideas and experience. In his important textbook *The Psychology of Adolescence* (1920), Tracey argued that woman

> is much less disposed than [man] to make new discoveries, to find fresh ways of doing things, or to call in question established customs, traditions or beliefs. Her attitude toward all that has been sanctified by tradition, custom and convention is more docile and less critical than his. By nature she is neither a radical nor a non-conformist; nor does she find so much difficulty as he in believing that what is is right, and that the existing order had better not be disturbed.[33]

However, Clark always found even contrary views stimulating, and although she doubtless heard much to disagree with in his classes, her letters home made no complaint about the course.

Not surprisingly, Clark found the University of Toronto overwhelmingly male in its outlook and makeup. While she chafed against this, she did not find it overly intimidating and got along well with both her professors and her fellow students. She loved using the Knox library but couldn't go there often as 'it is sacred to men especially Presbyterian theologues!'[34] She more frequently encountered not hostility, but too much deference in the class room: 'I don't like to talk too much [in political philosophy class] as I'm the only girl & the overwhelmingly respectful silence with which the men listen is discouraging.'[35]

The Toronto experience, brief as it was, was important in expanding Clark's understanding of sociology and in exposing her in a major way to primary research. Partly through her contacts with MacIver, she increasingly saw the study of society as an academic exercise worth pursuing for its own sake, divorced from social reform and social work.[36] She was also greatly encouraged to explore the social history of her home province through the study of statistics, doing primary research in Ottawa on the 'Social and Vital Statistics of New Brunswick.'[37] Both of these developments would help shape her approach to history.

A year spent at Oxford University[38] did not seem to make as much of an impression on Clark, perhaps because the condescending attitudes towards 'colonials' so annoyed her.[39] After the rather free and easy male-female relationships of Acadia, Clark had found the constraints of Toronto bad enough; yet they were much worse in England, and she obviously missed the give-and-take that had characterized her time at Acadia.[40] A year after returning to Canada, she wrote that 'Co-education in this country, however, does much to make easier a sense of comradeship and cooperation between men and women which seems rather difficult of attainment in England.'[41] She obtained her Diploma in Education in 1921,[42] but the rest of her intended three-year stay in England was cut short by family matters.[43] Clark's younger brother Thurston became seriously ill, probably the result of his wartime service, and died 17 October 1921.[44] It was on board the *Minnedosa* in mid-Atlantic on her way back to Canada that Clark became acquainted with an aloof but interesting Englishman, Conrad Payling Wright.

While the time at Toronto and Oxford provided Clark with much food for thought, her studies did not appear to provide a firm direction in the choice of a career. Until the early 1920s, a life of social service still powerfully attracted the young Clark. At Acadia she was strongly influenced by the missionary movement and gave serious consideration to the foreign mission field, especially after her best friend, Bessie Lockhart, dedicated her life to Baptist work in India.[45] In the winter of 1919-20, 'A chance came ... to go to Burma with a friend of the family who was in charge of the school there, but Mother said, "No," and I consented to let the matter rest'; this, when Clark was nearly twenty-five.[46] In 1922, she again sought work in the foreign mission field, receiving an offer to teach at Ginling College, Nanking, China, [47] which she was still considering when the proposal of marriage came from Wright.[48] Even the attractive field of home missions seemed closed to her. In 1919, Clark was licensed to preach by the Baptist Church (the first woman in New Brunswick to serve the Regular Baptist Church is this fashion) [49] and spent the summer pastoring a small rural church, an experience that she (and the congregation) clearly found satisfying and fulfilling.[50] However, once again the long arm of Fredericton intervened: 'I would love to have continued in the work, but Mother was far from well and I felt I was needed at home.'[51] 'Home' was well on the way to stifling the young Esther Clark.

Given this early interest in and commitment to social service, her initial inclinations would probably have led her down the path marked 'maternal feminism.' Ironically, it was the pressures of home and the opportunity for marriage that steered her in other directions, shaped her future career into quite a different form, and freed her from what some have seen as 'the forces of conservative women's social service.'[52] For the rest of her life she would remain greatly interested in social issues, especially those concerning women and children, and give strong support to a number of social causes, but a career in this field never evolved, and she was freed to pursue other interests.

The death of her younger brother and her mother's subsequent emotional collapse seemed to tie Clark to the Fredericton home more securely than ever. After the exhilarating and formative days at Acadia, Toronto, and Oxford, a hiatus had been reached in her development, and she seemed unable to progress further. The depressing situation at home and the uncongenial task of teaching school in Fredericton combined to cast Clark into a 'slough of despond,' as she phrased it. 'School had been so wearing that my nerves were strained to the breaking point and only sheer determination not to be beaten had kept me from giving up ... Your [Conrad Wright's] letter by giving me something else besides troublesome pupils to think of, really saved me from a nervous collapse I think.'[53] Her loneliness, sense of isolation and alienation, and frustration created what she termed 'that awful time of despair and despondency.'[54] All of her habitual confidence and vivacity seem to have fled. 'Have you read "Main Street" by Sinclair Lewis?' she wrote Wright. 'It is a tale of the ingloriousness of life in a small town and in my cynical moments I say that Fredericton is another Main Street.'[55] From this trap a dispirited Clark could see little chance of escape.

A Husband's Influence

Conrad Wright, her acquaintance from the *Minnedosa*, proved to be the force that liberated Clark from the stifling constraints of her home, community, and job. However much in later years she would chafe at his vagaries, indecisiveness, and procrastination, it was his confidence in her, his advanced thinking concerning marriage, and his desire to accept her as an equal that restored her equilibrium and provided the necessary context for the development of the successful writer and historian that she became. Both his remarkable strengths and his obvious weaknesses were essential components of this process.

Esther Clark and Conrad Wright on their wedding day

Wright was in 1922 a well-educated Englishman (Oxford, B.A. Hons. 1921) about a year younger than Clark, with eclectic and diverse interests.[56] Trained in physics, he had recently turned to economics and developed strong interests in politics and history. As he rather laughingly described himself to his future wife: 'Put me down as a social engineer, who will attempt to furnish a constitution or a kitchen with equal readiness.'[57] It was not a bad description. Clark was obviously attracted to this man who was crossing the Atlantic to take up a research position in California, attracted enough to overcome her usual shyness where strange men were concerned. From the beginning, Wright brought out the nonconformist side of Clark, encouraging her to do and think things that shocked her more conservative side.

On 24 October 1922, Wright sent a letter to Clark that was the start of a remarkable courtship by mail, culminating in their marriage on 31 July 1924. The letters of these two, plus those written by both to her mother, provide a wonderful insight into the views held by this modern couple on politics, religion, love and marriage, women, society, literature, and much more. They also reveal how Clark was liberated by the courtship experience, deriving strength from Wright's confidence in her, which encouraged her to break the confining bonds of her Victorian upbringing.

Having known Clark for a very limited time – a few hours at Oxford, a few days on the *Minnedosa,* and a weekend in Fredericton – Wright wrote in October 1922 to propose marriage: 'I am offering, not seeking, surrender.'[58] Although he realized that she could not give an immediate reply, as they needed to know more about each other, he was clearly attracted by her mind; in Clark's case, that was the most direct route to her heart. 'I know that I take a keen and intense delight in you yourself, your character and personality, your words, your actions,' he wrote. 'I do not think that I possess any friend to whom I could open my mind so freely in so many different ways as I could to you.' He told her of his family history, wartime service, economic prospects, and future plans. In many ways, this was a fairly conventional Victorian proposal. However, he soon indicated just how different many of his views were. Although he hoped to enter the British House of Commons as a Labour M.P., the choice of a career was not his alone. 'It is because I esteem you so highly that I desire to marry you. Feeling such esteem I cannot offer you a marriage which will give you less than perfect equality. We must choose our path together.' Wright was prepared to cast other conventions overboard as well, declaring that he would write to inform her mother of what he had proposed, but he would not ask her parents' permission. 'I say this simply because I feel that I should be showing disrespect for you if I treated you as even your parents' property. Yet in the best sense of the word, you must always remain their most cherished possession and, unfortunately, I must always appear to them as a thief and a robber.'

The letter from Wright, coming almost out of the blue, evoked an immediate and very positive response from Clark. It was not 'love' that either wrote about, but regard, respect, admiration, and congeniality. Coming at a time when her own self-confidence was at its lowest ebb, Wright's letter revitalized Clark, opening new vistas and stimulating new ideas. 'From the first you inspired me with confidence,' she wrote in response to his proposal, although she agreed that they needed to know each other better before marriage. At this stage of her development, with her views of marriage still shaped by her Victorian upbringing, she saw herself essentially in the role of wife and helpmate. 'On one point, I have no doubts, – I could be very happy doing my own housework, doing it economically, quickly and quietly, and allowing time and strength for giving help and inspiration in the home and outside it.'[59] Courtship by and marriage to Conrad Wright would help change those views.

In the subsequent letters, one detects a transformation of Esther Clark, a shedding of the veneer that her mother and the conventions of the time had tried to impose. As she herself noted: 'A very prudent and cautious I wrote that letter, a person who seems to be vanishing.' Her '*proper* self' still wrestled with the new ideas and desires that arose, but was increasingly losing the battle. Although she did not fall in with all of Wright's ideas, the talk of equality in marriage stimulated her. He even went so far as to suggest that she should also propose to him, to place them on an equal footing. 'I assume there of course that you desire that kind of equality, but for all I know, you may prefer to reject it, feeling that you may be freer, safer & stronger if you place your reliance on well-established conventions.'[60] On the issue of proposal, at least, the conventional conquered, as she replied: 'I don't want to miss a bit of the thrill of having you do the seeking and I the responding.'[61]

Clark fairly bubbled under the tutelage of Wright, developing and expressing ideas that she had long kept tightly under wraps. Any and every topic now seemed open for discussion. She wrote excitedly:

> I was interested in the references to your religious beliefs. What heaps of things we shall have to talk over and find out each other's ideas upon. On that point, I fancy we shall more or less agree, on fundamentals, anyway. I have so often found people shocked by my views on religion (even the girls at Oxford) that I seldom express them. My poor father would never recover, he is the most orthodox of mortals and only recently heard of evolution.[62]

He told her about his debates with the fundamentalists in California, while she educated him about the political scene in Canada. Economics, social theory, recently read books, education, Canada's British ties, and much more formed grist for the mill of their relationship. It was an exhilarating time for Clark; as she herself expressed it: 'I've changed so much since I first began to know myself that I'm not sure yet what I may turn out to be.'[63]

Clark was particularly struck by Wright's thinking concerning women, a topic to which he had clearly given much thought. He wrote:

> I see myself giving such high respect to the individuality of women in a world which tends to immure them in marriage. I have seen two or three of my friends and acquaintances before & after marriage & in each case I have felt that in some way the wife had surrendered some of the liberty that in her heart she desired to keep. It seemed as if in some way her personality had been withdrawn from the world & that she now made contact with the world only by and through and for her husband.[64]

Clark was not yet concerned about her identity apart from her future husband and was able to reply briefly: 'It is very kind of you to be concerned about the question of women keeping their individuality in marriage for I shall therefore not have to worry about it.'[65] His varied interests clearly were part of his attraction for Clark, however, as she wrote: 'I do like your being interested in all sorts of things that most men would not take the trouble to interest themselves in. That quality in you is one of the things that helps to make my dreams of the future such very, very happy ones.'[66] Although she still saw her own future research work as an extension of his, she was gradually beginning to envision at least a parallel if not a separate road for herself. 'I am not at all worried at the prospect of losing my independence by becoming absorbed in *your* work. [He had raised the issue.] If I am working on it too, it will be *our* work. And I shan't always sit back & let you take the initiative, but shall branch out on my own lines of research sometimes.'[67]

As Clark became more and more absorbed in her relationship with Wright, she moved perceptibly further away from the conventions of her Fredericton upbringing, exercising more of her own judgement, and plotting her own course. This was clearly revealed in the clash over her proposal to go to California to visit Wright before she had absolutely made up her mind whether to marry him. As she confided to Conrad, 'Mother seemed somewhat shocked at mention of the idea. It is, of course, a most un-Victorian proceeding and looks dreadfully like chasing a man!' Even Esther herself was getting cold feet at the thought of such a daring idea.[68] But visit him she would, although it caused a major disruption in the Clark household. 'What my family will say I don't know! But I feel dreadfully reckless.'[69] As Clark finally wrote sharply to her mother: 'I'm sorry you disapprove but I am going down to California ... If you are afraid people will talk, you needn't tell them anything about California.'[70]

The trip to California brought the desired conclusion to the courtship by mail, and Clark returned to Canada exhilarated and fulfilled. In spite of the much-talked-about sexual freedom of the postwar period,[71] and despite the unchaperoned trip to California, this was a remarkably chaste courtship. As Clark reported to her mother: 'We were very shy and dreadfully sensible until the last two or three days when he developed a most unexpected and surprising tendency to hold my hand at all sorts of odd moments, the which he was not allowed to do.'[72] Although in many respects Clark and Wright represented a 'new couple' with thinking considerably in advance of the standard wisdom of the Victorian-Edwardian period, they had not necessarily thrown all conventions overboard. Those that remained, however, were *their* conventions, adopted because they believed in them, not because either their parents or their contemporaries did.

The marriage of Esther Clark and Conrad Wright took place on 31 July 1924, not at the Fredericton Baptist Church, where her family wished it, but at the family farm just outside the city. The newspaper might enthuse about the 'sylvan surroundings,'[73] but for Clark it was one last opportunity to thumb her nose at the community from which she felt increasingly alienated. As she wrote her future mother-in-law about her plans to be married at the farm, 'Fredericton, since it is a small town and therefore very conventional, will be very much shocked. My chief delight is shocking Fredericton.'[74] The choice of location for the wedding reveals not only Clark's desire to be unconventional, but also her deeply rooted love of the countryside and close association with nature.

The wedding was to be Esther's last fling at rebellion. She quickly settled into a fairly conventional life as housewife in California, looking after their tiny home, preparing Conrad's meals, making social visits, and waiting for the arrival of the much-desired babies.[75] The failure of the latter to put in an appearance was to prove one of the decisive factors in the development of Esther Clark Wright as productive historian and writer. Given her great love of children, she would have undoubtedly poured great energy and much time into the role of mother, but several miscarriages and unsuccessful consultations with specialists finally forced the couple to accept the fact that there would be no children as a focus for their lives.[76]

It was to keep 'from brooding too much over things that have not happened' that Esther turned to research, something for which she had always exhibited a passion.[77] While Conrad worked at the Food Research Institute at Stanford University, Esther began doing research for him in one of his fields of interest, the history of engineering in Great Britain, finding the work stimulating and interesting.[78] But it was not Conrad's work alone in which she was interested. Her love of New Brunswick history surfaced early, as she presented a paper on the Loyalists to the History Club at Stanford. The time that sometimes weighed heavily on her hands provided the opportunity for her to write for the *Canadian Forum* on another of her favourite themes, 'On Being Canadian.'[79] Free of the usual financial concerns of newlyweds, thanks to her family money, encouraged by the intellectual stimulus of her husband, and sadly unencumbered by the pressures of a young family, Esther turned more and more of her attention to further academic pursuits, both for Conrad and for herself.

In spite of Conrad's encouragement, and still hoping for the fulfilling role of mother, Esther continued to see her career as decidedly secondary to that of her husband. However, life with the brilliant but erratic man whom she had married had turned out to be more difficult than she had envisioned. It was she who planned and worked for his admission to the Harvard Ph.D. program after she discovered that Conrad was more talk than action. 'He will not plan out his time & consider how he is coming out. It's evidently one of the duties that will have to fall to me & I hate to have to prod the poor old thing too much,' Esther grumbled to her mother.[80] But prod him she must, and did. It was still his career, his academic pursuits that came first. As she confided to her mother: 'I felt tempted to register for a Ph.D. myself but decided I ought not to take the time this year for myself but do what I could to help him. I want him to get through his general examination this year if it is at all possible & I'll have to see that he doesn't leave too much reading till the last minute.'[81]

Certainly getting Conrad through the Ph.D. process would prove to be a demanding job for them both. Instead of the expected year, he would spend five at Harvard, pursuing obscure readings and topics, and often forgetting the main thread, to his wife's growing impatience. Esther herself began classes at Radcliffe, worked as a marker in the Harvard School of Business, undertook research in England, and nudged an infuriatingly slow Conrad. By the spring of 1931, Esther had caught up with her husband. She was prepared to submit her Ph.D. thesis in economic history and take the required special exam, in spite of having suffered her first miscarriage only two months before, a devastating experience for both of them. A surprised, disappointed, triumphant, and confused Esther reported to her family back in Fredericton: 'The most absurd thing has happened. I passed the special exam & Conrad failed! Harvard says that I am qualified to teach economic history and Conrad isn't! Conrad has been an instructor here for four years; I have kept house & done economics on the side & they pass me & fail him. It is too preposterous for anything.'[82] It was Esther who now possessed the coveted Ph.D. in economics while Conrad did not.

The events of the spring precipitated a crisis in the relationship that was to have profound consequences. To this point, Esther had been the supportive if prodding wife, placing her husband's education and career before her own. As was often the case in times of turmoil, Esther looked to the Wolfville area and her female friends from Acadia days for solace and direction. While visiting there in the summer following her exams, Esther learned of a temporary vacancy in the history department at Acadia and, through her contacts, was able to secure the offer of the appointment for Conrad (she seems to have given no thought to seeking it for herself). His temporizing over the offer finally let loose a torrent of frustration that had been building for years, signalling a virtual declaration of independence by a woman who had clearly grown a great deal since the days of her courtship and marriage. Writing to Conrad, who had remained in Cambridge, Esther exploded:

> Well now, I'm going to be frank, brutally frank. You've been 10 years in the United States & you haven't yet got your Ph.D. I think you're jolly lucky to get any kind of a job at all, & I think that if you didn't live in

> a world of illusions & self-delusions, you'd be thanking your lucky stars that you've got a wife who was at the right spot & had sufficient influence to get you something when Harvard had dropped you ... You needn't try any martyr complex on me ...
>
> You've had things your own way for seven years & look what a mess we've been landed in. Suppose you let me manage things for a bit & you take orders ... For the sake of peace & quietness, to avoid scenes, I've let you have your own way these years even when I've known you were making wrong decisions. Nobody knows what I've suffered these last two years at Harvard ... For the sake of having children I let things go, but there were times when I felt that children could be too dearly bought. I still believe that you have brains, but I can no longer trust you on decisions as to a course of action ... I'm fed up with standing by & seeing you wreck our career, especially when I could see a wiser course of action ...
>
> I shall go further. If you persist in overriding my judgment on this matter [accepting the Acadia offer], I shall not hand out one cent to support you & me while you write or to enable you to travel. I'm not going to be flaunted & scorned & then hand out as I've done in the past. If your judgments turned out to be correct it would be different.[83]

The letter charted a new course for their relationship and for Esther's own career. Completely confident in her own judgment, secure in her own financial position, Esther was now prepared to determine her own future – and Conrad's too, if necessary. Esther reported to her mother: 'He [Conrad] hasn't said definitely that he's taken the Acadia post but I gather that he has. He sounds sulky but he'll get over it.'[84]

The airing of her frustrations, renewed contact with her beloved Acadia, her own secure financial position, and her second miscarriage in 1932 freed Esther from some of the constraints of conventional marriage. She was determined not to leave Acadia for extended periods of time again, nor did she, no matter where Conrad might be settled. Her interests and research increasingly diverged from those of her husband; they spent more and more time apart, often in the years ahead operating completely separate residences, she in Wolfville and he frequently in Ottawa. In many respects, she had moved beyond him and was impatient and sometimes angry with his vagaries and procrastination. In 1932, Esther wrote revealingly to her mother that she, impatient with how long it took Conrad to shave on Sunday morning, had started out for church without him; she was at the church door before he caught up.[85] In later years, she was often seated for five or ten minutes before Conrad came puffing in, to the great amusement of the congregation. This scene seems to have characterized their entire relationship. In spite of such difficulties, their marriage nevertheless lasted for over sixty-five years.[86]

Although she would undoubtedly have chosen to live her life otherwise, the absence of children and the distant relationship (literally and figuratively) with Conrad provided Esther with the freedom to pursue her interests in history and economics as well as the time for the extensive writing career that might not otherwise have been hers. However, it is difficult to read the early letters between Conrad and Esther without realizing the key role that his advanced thinking and sympathetic understanding played in liberating her from the constraints of her situation in Fredericton and in building her self-confidence. Without Conrad Payling Wright, there might well have been no Esther Clark Wright, historian.

A Historian Emerges

With the years of academic study behind her, her marital relationship on a new footing, and all hope of children now gone, Wright was about to embark on a new phase of life: that of published historian. Although she had written for publication many times before, beginning in high school in Fredericton, most of this work had been short pieces for newspapers and religious magazines. In the mid-1930s, she began writing and submitting articles for more substantial publications, focusing first on nature and then on history. In the fifteen books and numerous substantial articles that she produced between the mid-1930s and 1985, the impact of these early years is evident.

Her interest in and love of her native province of New Brunswick provided Wright with the geographic focus of much of her work. Although she might rail against the cloying atmosphere of Fredericton, Wright was nevertheless greatly attached to the region, and most of her works of history focused on the province. In doing this, she clearly, if at first unconsciously, rejected the idea of 'national' history. Long before there was any discussion of 'regional history' and 'limited identities,' Wright was exploring and writing about what interested her, which was the history of her own province or at least certain parts of it.[87]

Her abiding interest in people was also to be well reflected in her work – not the 'great' people, even in the New Brunswick context, but the ordinary people. Her passion for the everyday lives of ordinary people led her inevitably down the path to genealogy and convinced her that no understanding of even great events was possible without examining individual lives. Her most important work, *The Loyalists of New Brunswick* (1955), was thus the result of the meticulous piecing together of the lives of thousands of individual Loyalists. People counted, and were counted, in her work, building her image of the past from the ground up. The great and the near-great held no interest for her; it would be the people she could observe from her front steps about whom she would write.

Her rejection of the constraints and standards of the Victorian era, incipient during her university days, had been brought to full flower with the encouragement of Conrad Wright. Her interest in the eighteenth, rather than the nineteenth, century would result, providing an important focus for much of her work. In her important studies of the Loyalists and the New England Planters, it was to the eighteenth century that she looked. In reviewing Thomas Raddall's *His Majesty's Yankees*, Wright revealed much about herself when she wrote:

> The later nineteenth century, basking delightedly in the warm appreciation of its own greatness, was inclined to dismiss the eighteenth century as a rude and barbarous age which had had the misfortune to exist before real progress began. It was an unsatisfactory era, the Victorians thought, when an artificial veneer had to take the place of the refinements of the later period; a regrettable era, with all sorts of plainness, and vulgarity, and smouldering discontents underneath, and occasional explosions, rather unpleasant ones. The twentieth century, jolted out of complacency by a succession of catastrophic events, is not so sure that the Victorians were right, either about themselves or about the eighteenth century. The twentieth century is curious about the eighteenth, about its simplicity, about its interest in nature, about its refusals to be satisfied with what the ruling classes did and with what they told it to think, about its ferment of ideas and its violence.[88]

Here she was talking as much about her own interests and work as she was about Raddall's.

By the 1930s, all the necessary ingredients were thus in place to produce the accomplished historian who would emerge over the next several decades. Wright possessed a geographic and class focus as well as a preference for the eighteenth century, which had sprung from her early Fredericton days. Her years at Acadia, Toronto, Oxford, and Radcliffe had provided her with the academic training and exposure to primary research necessary for a successful historian in the twentieth century. From the family businesses she derived the financial independence that would provide the money and leisure to engage in extended periods of research and writing. Her husband's strengths gave her confidence in herself as a woman and as a person, and encouraged her to expand her mind at a crucial stage in her development; his weaknesses, and the lack of children, freed her from some of the constraints of ordinary marriage. The blending of all these factors and forces, combined with her own superior intellect and strong personality, would produce the successful writer and historian, Esther Clark Wright.

Notes

1 Esther Clark Wright, *Back a Long Way* (n.p.: 1986), 1-3.

2 Esther Clark Wright, *Alexander Clark, Loyalist: A Contribution to the History of New Brunswick* (Kentville NS: Kentville Publishing 1940).

3 Esther Clark Wright, *The Loyalists of New Brunswick* (Fredericton 1955).

4 Esther Clark Wright, *Planters and Pioneers* (Wolfville NS: self-published 1978); Wright, *The Ships of St. Martins: Shipbuilding and a List of Vessels Built at St. Martins, New Brunswick, 1800-1899* (Saint John: New Brunswick Museum 1974).

5 Esther Clark Wright, 'Without Intervention of Prophet, Priest or King,' in Barry M. Moody, ed., *Repent and Believe: The Baptist Experience in Maritime Canada* (Hantsport NS: Lancelot Press 1980), 66.

6 Ibid., 72; Wright, *Back a Long Way*, 9.

7 *The Acadia Record, 1836-1953*, revised and enlarged by Watson Kirkconnell (Wolfville NS: Acadia University 1953), 493.

8 See, for examples, Esther Clark to Conrad Wright, 6 February 1923; E. Clark to C. Wright, 27 April 1924; E. Clark to C. Wright, 27 May 1924. Unless otherwise stated, all correspondence to and from Esther Clark Wright cited here is in the Esther Clark Wright Archives (hereafter ECWA), Acadia University, Wolfville, NS.

9 Wright, *Back a Long Way*, 7, 9, 34; minutes of the Board of Governors, Acadia University.

10 *Acadia Record*, 493, 498.

11 R.P. Allen, 'Hon. William G. Clark, D.C.L., LL.D., Lieut.-Governor of New Brunswick,' *Maritime Advocate and Busy East* (June 1943): 5.

12 Wright, *Back a Long Way*, 9; Wright, 'Without Intervention of Prophet,' 66; E. Clark to C. Wright, 25 November 1922; 'Governor of Acadia University Passes Away,' *Acadia Bulletin* (February 1948): 19-20.

13 This is particularly obvious in the relationships developed during her four pivotal years at Acadia. Clark wrote more than 280 letters to her family while at Acadia between 1912 and 1916 (in the possession of this author); the letters reveal a remarkable picture of life at a Canadian university through the eyes of a young woman.

14 E. Clark to Mother, 12 September 1923.

15 See R.S. Longley, *Acadia University, 1838-1938* (Wolfville NS: Acadia University 1938) for a history of the institution.

16 E. Clark to C. Wright, 17 May 1924. However, she also admitted that she had said she would never live in England and, most emphatically, would never marry an Englishman. E. Clark to C. Wright, 25 November 1922.

17 Clark's years at Acadia are discussed in Barry Moody, 'Acadia and the Great War,' in Paul Axelrod and John G. Reid, eds., *Youth, University and Canadian Society: Essays in the Social History of Higher Education* (Montreal and Kingston: McGill-Queen's Press 1989), 143-60; Barry Moody, 'Esther Clark Goes to College,' in *Atlantis: A Women's Studies Journal* 20, 1 (fall-winter 1995): 39-48.

18 Acadia's first female graduate was Clara Marshall, 1884. See Barry Moody, 'Breadth of Vision, Breadth of Mind: The Baptists and Acadia College,' in G.A. Rawlyk, ed., *Canadian Baptists and Christian Higher Education* (Montreal and Kingston: McGill-Queen's Press 1988), 21-4. In 1875, Mount Allison College (Sackville, NB) became the first institution in the British Empire to grant a degree to a woman. John G. Reid, 'The Education of Women at Mount Allison, 1854-1914,' *Acadiensis* 12, 2 (spring 1983): 18-19.

19 Moody, 'Acadia and the Great War,' 153-6.

20 Tammy Pettigrew, 'Womanly in Their Strength: The Women Graduates of Acadia University in 1916,' (unpublished B.A. hons. thesis, Acadia University 1994).

21 Pettigrew, 'Womanly in Their Strength,' *Acadia Record*, 124-31.

22 Carroll Smith-Rosenberg, 'The Female World of Love and Ritual: Relations Between Women in Nineteenth-Century America,' in Nancy F. Cott and Elizabeth H. Peck, eds., *A History of Her Own* (New York: Simon & Schuster 1979).

23 Smith-Rosenberg, 'Female World of Love and Ritual,' 316-18.

24 At the end of her life, and more than seventy years after their graduation, Clark would write a sad farewell to her female classmates, ending 'Miss Chase, Miss Chute, Miss Clark: of the trio and the larger group there remains only Miss Clark – forlorn, for there

is no one with whom to exchange reminiscences of those varied and valued friends and of the good years at Acadia.' Esther Clark Wright, 'Miss Chase, Miss Chute, Miss Clark,' Acadia University Alumni *Bulletin*, 72, 1 (winter 1987-8): 13.

25 Smith-Rosenberg would appear to assign too early a date for the demise of such relationships. For Clark and her friends at least, there seemed to be no 'cultural taboos' restricting such relationships. Smith-Rosenberg, 'The Female World of Love and Ritual,' 330-1.

26 See Lois W. Banner, *American Beauty* (New York: Alfred A. Knopf 1983), 187; Wayne Roberts, '"Rocking the Cradle for the World:" The New Woman and Maternal Feminism, Toronto 1877-1914,' in Linda Kealey, ed., *A Not Unreasonable Claim: Women and Social Reform in Canada, 1880s-1920s* (Toronto: Women's Press 1979), 15-18; Rosalind Rosenberg, *Beyond Separate Spheres: Intellectual Roots of Modern Feminism* (New Haven: Yale University Press 1982), 54, 77.

27 See E. Clark to mother, 21 May 1917, and 6 August 1917; E. Clark to father, 11 May 1917.

28 See, for examples, E. Clark to mother, 8 January 1918; 11 January 1918; 25 January 1918; 29 January 1918; 7 February 1918; 6 March 1918; 18 March 1918; E. Clark to father, 2 March 1918.

29 E. Clark to mother, 7 February 1918; E. Clark to father, 2 March 1918; see Veronica Strong-Boag, 'Growing Up Female,' in R. Douglas Francis and Donald B. Smith, eds., *Readings in Canadian History: Post-Confederation* (Toronto: Holt, Rinehart & Winston 1990), 292.

30 Quoted in A.B. McKillop, *Matters of Mind: The University in Ontario 1791-1951* (Toronto: University of Toronto Press 1994), 503.

31 McKillop, *Matters of Mind*, 504.

32 For more on MacIver's years at Toronto, see *As a Tale That Is Told: The Autobiography of R.M. MacIver* (Chicago: University of Chicago Press 1968).

33 Quoted in Beth Light and Ruth Roach Pierson, eds., *No Easy Road: Women in Canada 1920s to 1960s* (Toronto: New Hogtown Press 1990), 23-4.

34 E. Clark to mother, 29 January 1918.

35 E. Clark to mother, 25 January 1918.

36 McKillop, *Matters of Mind*, 486-98, discusses the competing American and British models; he also notes the growing influence of Acadia graduate (1912) Carl Dawson, professor at McGill, 496-7.

37 E. Clark to mother, 25 March 1918; 3 April 1918; 29 April 1918.

38 *Acadia Bulletin*, 8 & 9 (September-October 1920): 5.

39 E. Clark to C. Wright, 2 July 1922, and 4 February 1924.

40 See Carol Dyhouse, *No Distinction of Sex? Women in British Universities, 1870-1939* (London: UCL Press 1995) for a discussion of the position of women in British universities at this time.

41 E. Clark to C. Wright, 2 July 1922.

42 E. Clark to mother, 11 July 1921.

43 E. Clark to Mrs. Mary E. Wright, 2 December 1923.

44 *Acadia Bulletin* 11, 8 & 9 (September-October 1921): 6.

45 *The Acadia Record*, 125.

46 E. Clark to C. Wright, 25 November 1922.

47 Ann Reid to E. Clark, 23 August 1922; Elizabeth R. Bender to E. Clark, 29 August 1922. Gingling College, for Chinese women, was operated by the Foreign Mission Society of the American Baptists.

48 For an excellent discussion of the mission-oriented milieu in which Clark was raised, see P. Lorraine Coops, 'Not a Romantic Notion: Single Women Missionaries from the Maritime Baptist Convention who Served in the Telugu Fields in India 1880-1912' (unpublished M.A. thesis, Queen's University 1992).

49 'License to preach,' 24 June 1919, Esther Clark and Conrad Payling Wright papers; *Maritime Baptist* (28 May 1919): 4.

50 Minutes of the Grangeville NB United Baptist Church, 7 May 1919, Baptist Collection; *Acadia Bulletin* 8, 6 (July 1919): 3; *Maritime Baptist* (28 May 1919): 4.

51 E. Clark to C. Wright, 25 November 1922.
52 Roberts, '"Rocking the Cradle for the World,"' 24.
53 E. Clark to C. Wright, 25 November 1922.
54 E. Clark to C. Wright, 20 December 1922.
55 E. Clark to C. Wright, 14 December 1921.
56 Obituary for Conrad Payling Wright, Halifax *Chronicle-Herald* (16 October 1991).
57 C. Wright to E. Clark, 3 January 1924.
58 C. Wright to E. Clark, 24 October 1922.
59 E. Clark to C. Wright, 25 November 1922.
60 C. Wright to E. Clark, 9 December 1922.
61 E. Clark to C. Wright, 20 December 1922.
62 E. Clark to C. Wright, 6 February 1923.
63 E. Clark to C. Wright, 31 May 1923.
64 C. Wright to E. Clark, 19 May 1924.
65 E. Clark to C. Wright, 27 May 1924.
66 E. Clark to C. Wright, 21 March 1924.
67 E. Clark to C. Wright, 16 June 1924.
68 E. Clark to C. Wright, 14 May 1923.
69 E. Clark to C. Wright, 25 July 1923.
70 E. Clark to mother, 15 August 1923.
71 Paula S. Fass. *The Damned and the Beautiful: American Youth in the 1920s* (New York: Oxford University Press 1977), 21.
72 E. Clark to mother, 12 September 1923.
73 Fredericton *Gleaner* (31 July 1924).
74 E. Clark to Mrs. Mary Esther Wright, 19 January 1924.
75 See the letters to her mother, fall, winter, and spring of 1924-5.
76 See E. Wright to mother, 11 February 1931; E. Wright to mother, 7 May 1931; E. Wright to mother, 15 January 1931 [1932]; C. Wright to Mrs. Clark, n.d. [February 1932].
77 E. Wright to mother, 18 March 1928.
78 E. Wright to mother, 22 October 1924; E. Wright to mother, 2 August 1926.
79 E. Wright to mother, 12 December 1924; E. Wright to mother, 23 May 1926.
80 E. Wright to mother, 12 August 1926.
81 E. Wright to mother, 22 September 1926.
82 E. Wright to mother, 9 June 1931.
83 E. Wright to C. Wright, 4-5 July 1931.
84 E. Wright to mother, 26 July 1931.
85 E. Wright to mother, 21 March 1932.
86 Conrad Wright survived his wife by a little over a year, dying 14 October 1991 at the age of ninety-five; obituary, Halifax *Chronicle Herald*, 16 October 1991. Esther Clark Wright died 17 June 1990, aged ninety-five; obituary, Halifax *Chronicle Herald*, 20 June 1990.
87 See John G. Reid, 'Writing about Regions,' in John Schultz ed., *Writing about Canada: A Handbook for Modern Canadian History* (Scarborough: Prentice-Hall Canada 1990), 71-96.
88 Esther Clark Wright, 'A Conflict of Loyalties,' in *Dalhousie Review* 23, 1 (April 1943): 83.

10
Kathleen Wood-Legh: A Canadian in Cambridge

Megan J. Davies and Colin M. Coates

On 10 June 1967, Dr. Kathleen Louise Wood-Legh strode to centre stage at Senate House, Cambridge, to receive an earned Litt.D. degree in recognition of the quality of her life's work.[1] In a rare gesture of appreciation, the audience burst into applause to acclaim Wood-Legh's achievement.[2] From friends' reminiscences of the event, it is clear that much more than academic excellence was being honoured on that day: the ovation for Wood-Legh celebrated a woman who had lived her life courageously, shaping an intellectual haven for herself and providing crucial inspiration and support for a new college for Cambridge women.

Kathleen Wood-Legh was born in 1901 in Mount Forest, Ontario, the only child of Charles Wood-Legh and Katie Stevenson.[3] Working for the Canadian Pacific Railway, Charles Wood-Legh moved his family to Portland, Maine, where Wood-Legh was educated by private tutors and at Deering High School.[4] She was an accomplished musician who performed publicly on a number of occasions.[5]

Kathleen Wood-Legh typing in her back garden

In 1919, Wood-Legh began her history studies at Montreal's McGill University. The period following the First World War was a relatively open time for Canadian women going to university; the proportion of women in higher education in that period would not be reached again until the 1970s.[6] Compared to the experience of pioneering women, the presence of female undergraduates in universities was increasingly accepted by the war years.[7] Women were active at the postgraduate level as well. Taking medieval history as an example, in the United States in the early 1920s, approximately 40 per cent of all postgraduate theses were prepared by women.[8] A small number had even forged successful academic careers. Nellie Neilson and Bertha Putnam, both in the United States, were well-established historians of medieval England.[9]

Similar trends were apparent for McGill's Department of History. Ethel Hurlbatt, warden of Royal Victoria College, tutored in the department from 1907 to 1916.[10] Vera Brown, who went on to pursue a successful career at Smith College, lectured in the department from 1916 to 1920.[11] Eleven McGill women completed their M.A.s in history in the 1920s, a ten-year figure that was not surpassed until the 1960s.[12] While postgraduate studies did not necessarily lead to full-time university-level careers in Canada, some international precedents existed for aspiring women historians.

As a postgraduate at McGill, Wood-Legh worked under the direction of William Waugh. Her focus on medieval history reflected not only Wood-Legh's own intellectual interests, but also the nature of history teaching at Canadian universities during this period, dominated as they were by British-trained staff.[13] At McGill, for example, Canadian history was not part of the undergraduate curriculum until the final year of study.[14] The teaching of British history at McGill was reputed to be strong, according to an alumnus: 'It became not only possible, but easy, for a keen student to obtain a first rate undergraduate training, fitting him [*sic*] to rank with the best history schools in England.'[15]

Wood-Legh performed brilliantly in McGill's history department, receiving a first class honours B.A. in 1923 and an M.A. the following year. Along with Sir Robert Baden-Powell, who received an honorary degree in 1923, Wood-Legh was singled out in the *Montreal Gazette*'s coverage of that year's convocation. 'Certain things stand out in recollecting the event,' wrote the reporter, 'one, an incident which occurred when the women graduates in the Faculty of Arts were being presented for their degrees. All received a measure of applause, but there was ovation when a tall, slightly hesitant candidate, with a quiet radiance in her face, was led gently across the stage by a class-mate – blind.'[16] This nameless woman (all the men mentioned in the article are named) was Wood-Legh, and she later returned to the stage to collect a prize in history.

Although this clipping was included in Wood-Legh's papers, it is doubtful that she would have cared to be singled out in this fashion. An unspoken rule among family, colleagues, and friends was that her blindness was never commented upon and never catered to.[17] She received a blind pension later in life, but Wood-Legh never made use of a cane or a seeing-eye dog nor did she associate with other blind people, professionally or personally. One close friend of Wood-Legh's, the philosopher Dorothy Emmet, recalled the 1920s at Oxford and the birth of a lifelong companionship between the two women scholars:

> our friendship began when I took her for a walk on Port Meadow, and we got bogged down in a quagmire of mud, and the only way out was to climb along the bottom slats of a fence – which she did with great agility; and I realised that what she really liked was to be treated, as far as possible, as a sighted person, to do tough things with a spice of adventure, and what she did not want was to be fussed over as a 'poor blind woman.'[18]

Wood-Legh was able to negotiate the streets of Cambridge by herself. She frequently travelled in the United Kingdom and on the continent, relying on friends to meet her but travelling solo. In middle age she boldly tried horse-back riding and skating.[19] The acknowledgments in Wood-Legh's articles and books do not explicitly refer to her absolute reliance on people who read the research material to her, although she carefully thanked those who had assisted her.

Wood-Legh faced the fact of her blindness with fortitude. One student of hers wrote: 'I never did believe that she really was blind – and in the most important sense she wasn't. Anything but.'[20] Although Wood-Legh was first and foremost an intellectual, she was also well rooted, and comprehensively trained by her mother, in the practical tasks of daily life.[21] Yet Wood-Legh's physical handicap, coupled with the fact that she was a woman, undoubtedly would obstruct the path to the academic career to which she aspired in 1923.[22]

One can imagine the discussions that took place between Kathleen and her parents in 1923 concerning her future. Prof. Basil Williams of McGill's history department encouraged her to pursue her studies and suggested a thesis topic.[23] Katie and Charles Wood-Legh, no intellectuals themselves, seem to have appreciated the fact that their daughter was first and foremost a scholar. Charles Wood-Legh read and took notes for his daughter and guided her about.[24] Their support for their only child's academic career is even more extraordinary in the context of contemporary views about the kind of work blind people were fit for: basket-making and massage therapy.[25] It is possible that Wood-Legh's blindness in fact released her and her parents from traditional expectations that she would marry and have children, choices that narrowed the academic possibilities of other women of her generation. Katie Wood-Legh once told her daughter, 'If you marry, that will be good; if you do not marry, that will be equally good.'[26]

Oxbridge Life

The selection of England rather than the United States as the locale for Wood-Legh's graduate studies may have been due to both McGill's connections with British academia and her father's roots in that country. Whatever the rationale, by the mid-1920s the entire Wood-Legh household had relocated to Oxford.[27] Wood-Legh studied at St. Hilda's, one of Oxford's women's colleges. In 1926, the family moved to Cambridge in order that Kathleen Wood-Legh might work with G.G. Coulton, the eminent medievalist. Coulton was a specialist in church history and a staunch Protestant with whom, in a friend's phrase, Wood-Legh 'saw eye to eye.'[28] Wood-Legh completed her B.Litt. at Oxford in 1929 and her Ph.D. at Cambridge in 1932. Eileen Power, Helen Cam, Dorothy George, and Wood-Legh's near-contemporary, Dorothy Whitelock, were among the women historians engaged in fruitful careers at the time Wood-Legh crossed the Atlantic. Cambridge tolerated two women's colleges at this time, Girton and Newnham, the latter from which Wood-Legh obtained her degree.

The Oxbridge world was certainly a bastion of male privilege. A historian of women at Cambridge reports that, in the 1920s, 'some lecturers made great play of seating the women separately and addressing themselves solely to the "gentlemen."'[29] Indeed, Cambridge University's regulations denied official membership to women as late as 1947. This meant that women could not of their own right borrow books from the university library and were not permitted to attend Senate, where the highest academic policies were determined. Furthermore, statutes limited women to no more than 10 per cent of the undergraduate student body.[30] Nevertheless, women did teach at the university, both as tutors and staff members from 1926.[31]

Wood-Legh published three journal articles from her research on the English parliament, the subject of her McGill M.A. and her Oxford B.Litt. theses.[32] In these pieces, her meticulous approach to medieval institutions is apparent: providing detailed lists of the men who attended parliament and of their periods in attendance. These were not path-breaking, but rather solid, contributions to the field, taking a scientific approach in their inclusiveness.

Like other women, Wood-Legh was drawn to the developing field of economic and social history. As historian Maxine Berg argues, women were able to carve a niche for themselves in this expanding field, often choosing different topics and emphases than their male colleagues.[33] Some male historians at Cambridge were supportive of academic women, and Wood-Legh allied herself with these men as she had at McGill. G.M. Trevelyan, Regius Professor of Modern History at Cambridge, and the author of the preface to one of Wood-Legh's books, took the scholarship of women historians seriously. In his renowned *English Social History*, published in 1942, he relied on and cited many women's contributions to social history, including Wood-Legh's.[34] Wood-Legh, in turn, greatly admired Trevelyan and indeed shared his essential conservatism and love of the English countryside and all things English.[35] G.G. Coulton, Wood-Legh's supervisor, taught many of the female students at Girton and Newnham, including Eileen Power and Helen Cam. More positive concerning women's roles in the university than many of his colleagues, he believed in providing a place for women to enter academic discussion by lecturing to them separately from male students. This practice did not succeed in the more egalitarian atmosphere of the University of Toronto, where Coulton spent the years of the Second World War.[36]

Wood-Legh completed her Ph.D. dissertation in 1932 and published it in 1935 in a series edited by Coulton.[37] Her survey of English church life in the fourteenth century included a chapter on chantries, endowments for the chanting of masses for the benefactor's soul. Chantries sometimes fulfilled practical educational purposes; influenced by German colleagues' sense of the importance of this institution, Wood-Legh would dedicate the rest of her life to exploring the nature of chantries in Britain.[38]

In the early 1930s, everything suggests that Wood-Legh was set on an academic career, and indeed, she applied unsuccessfully for positions at University College, Southampton, and King's College, London, in 1934.[39] From May to July 1931, she was the history mistress at The King's High School for Girls in Warwick, but returned to Cambridge subsequently. Despite positive recommendations from her mentors, Coulton and Trevelyan, she was not able to obtain a teaching fellowship or lectureship.[40] Instead, Wood-Legh worked as a casual tutor, filling the important role of one-to-one tuition that is the hallmark of Oxbridge teaching. The Oxbridge system served to make a marginal female scholar like Wood-Legh dependent on male allies; it was mostly male colleagues who sent her male tutorial students. Later, C. Cheney, eminent medievalist at Cambridge and a close friend of Wood-Legh, shepherded her last book through its final editorial stages and publication after her death.[41] Wood-Legh's experience illustrates the strong roots of male power within the Oxbridge system and perhaps the failure of the older colleges for women to promote adequately the interests of female academics.

Notwithstanding the limitations imposed by the patriarchal structure that she encountered at Cambridge, Wood-Legh felt that this was where she wanted to make her home. Until her death in 1981, she lived in a small house in the Newnham Croft neighbourhood of Cambridge, the location of which seems to sum up the key elements in her life. St. Edward's, the local parish church where she was a committed member of the congregation, stands just around the corner. A short stroll to the east brings one to the University Library where Wood-Legh conducted much of her research; to the west one enters the countryside where she loved to walk, often covering twenty miles in one day. Themes of faith, intellect, and community are evident in the manner in which Wood-Legh managed to retain her independence and continue her work.

At Cambridge, Wood-Legh nurtured a wide circle of friends whose members called themselves Owlstonians after the name of the street where Wood-Legh lived.[42] Wood-Legh's social world opened through the 'Owlstone door' to admit men and women gathered from all stages and facets of her life.[43] Common interests were intellectual discussion, often about religion, and an appreciation of classical music, the English countryside, and good food. One member of Wood-Legh's social circle, Canon David Isitt, described his friend in 1981: 'You can't have high seriousness without profound good humour; and, like her great hero Erasmus of Rotterdam, she is one of those who have contributed to the life of Cambridge a rare combination of piety, wit and common-sense. Playing the flute, and enjoying good food, both have something to do with it. Can any of us think of anybody who enjoys life more than she does?'[44] Her friends characterized Wood-Legh in friendship as fun. 'Yes, the standard she asked of you was high, but still you could say it was *fun*.'[45]

Although a permanent post at Cambridge eluded Wood-Legh, she continued to work in the university community. On an informal basis and increasingly on a formal basis for Trinity and Caius Colleges, she tutored in medieval Latin and medieval history. Lady Kathleen Balfour (Oldfield), Christopher Milne, Lord (Asa) Briggs, John Silkin, later Labour minister of agriculture, and David Sheppard, later bishop of Liverpool, were among her many students. While Briggs requested a different tutor soon after their sessions began,[46] other students were greatly influenced by Wood-Legh's scholarly passion and personal courage. Robert Lacey wrote: 'I can see what a lot she taught me. At first she frightened me. But then I came to see that the principles upon which she insisted were the only viable ones ... It seems only a few months ago that I was finding my way to her little house down by the river to sit reading out my latest essay while she peered at me quizzically.[47]

A number of these intellectual relationships that began as tutorials evolved into long-term connections. Wood-Legh became a keen cricket fan, listening to radio broadcasts of test matches, in order to follow the sporting career of David Sheppard. Lady Kathleen Balfour and she remained life-long friends, hiking in England and Germany and working together in the Modern Churchmen's Union.

The monetary rewards of tutoring were also important to Wood-Legh. Both she and her father received small pensions, but Charles Wood-Legh apparently brought little further income into the household once they left Canada. It seems likely that Kathleen Wood-Legh supported her parents and possibly Miss Stevenson, the aunt who came to live at 49 Owlstone Road after her mother's death, on the limited pay that she received as a tutor.[48] Finances were clearly difficult. A sense of genteel poverty pervades descriptions of Wood-Legh's daily routine. One woman who came from Germany to live with Wood-Legh in the 1950s recalls receiving one pound per week and a bicycle without brakes to make her way around Cambridge. It was not until Wood-Legh inherited a sum of money from her uncle in the mid-1960s that her financial situation stabilized.[49]

Despite financial hardships, Wood-Legh found ways of pursuing her academic work and published a variety of studies. While her earliest work relied on published patent rolls and other such documentation, she increasingly integrated unpublished archival material as well. Given her blindness, she required help with both published materials and primary documents. Friends, neighbours, and a succession of personal 'secretaries' read to her, and she taught many of the latter the intricacies of medieval palaeography. Wood-Legh's work is striking more for its meticulousness than for its theoretical brilliance. She clearly fit into a generation of historians who felt the importance of institutional studies as contributions to scientific perspectives on the past, freed from partisanship and prejudice.[50]

In addition to her analyses of published and unpublished sources, Wood-Legh also performed many of the tasks of other historians of the medieval period. She translated, edited, and annotated a German study of medieval English electoral law.[51] She edited two collections of primary sources. In 1956, she published the Latin account book of a small household, with a short preface by Trevelyan. In her lengthy introduction, Wood-Legh argued that the account book provided glimpses into 'middle class' life that few other contemporary documents allowed.[52] She also published the records of the official visitations to religious establishments in Kent in the early sixteenth century.[53] She was working on this latter collection in her last decade of life, and in the certain knowledge that she was dying, she reduced the pain-killing drugs in her final days so that she could dictate the introduction to this work, which was published posthumously.

On two occasions, Wood-Legh was asked to prepare prestigious, funded lecture series. In 1955, she delivered the Birkbeck Lectures at Trinity

College, Cambridge, on the subject of medieval chantries, which she later published as *Perpetual Chantries*, probably her most lasting contribution to medieval historiography.[54] This volume remains the standard work on the topic. In 1972, she was asked to provide the Hulsean lectures, a series of theological talks based in the Faculty of Divinity at Cambridge. Wood-Legh was the first woman to give this series of lectures, speaking on the practice of 'good works.'[55] In her seventies, Wood-Legh taught extramural courses for Cambridge on various topics, including 'Medieval Trade in Western Europe' and 'Parish Life in Medieval England.'[56]

Faith and Heritage

Like any scholar's work, Wood-Legh's writings are in a certain way autobiographical. Her attraction to church history dovetailed with her staunch Protestantism. She attended church faithfully, and critically, often commenting on the sermon. On at least one occasion, she delivered the sermon herself. Active in the Student Christian Movement at McGill,[57] Wood-Legh later participated in the Modern Churchmen's Union (MCU) of the Church of England, which provided a liberal, intellectual critique of Anglican thought.[58] Wood-Legh brought Lady Kathleen Balfour into the group, and the two friends attended MCU conferences and worked together to promote their shared religious and political views within the group.[59]

Wood-Legh's strong religious faith, a shift from early agnosticism, was evident in all facets of her life.[60] Several of the young German women who came to live with Wood-Legh after the Second World War left with a new sense of Christian belief that they attributed to her influence.[61] Friends' memories of Wood-Legh's last days are redolent of religious faith and joy, as they watched her grapple with terrible pain and the knowledge of her imminent death.[62]

Wood-Legh's Christian beliefs found a place in her historiographical contributions. She believed that there was something particularly English about the Church even before the Reformation. Specifically, she was interested in the relationship between the state and the church, and the impact that relationship had on the people. Her interest in chantries reflected her liberal religiosity. Not merely concerned with eschatology, chantries also had practical purposes: 'in no other [form of piety],' Wood-Legh wrote in 1944, 'could the men of that age find such a combination of spiritual and temporal advantages.'[63]

Her love of medieval history was deep and tactile. Wood-Legh could ascertain the age of an ancient font by touch.[64] At a Sealed Knot re-enactment of a Civil War scene in Wells, Somerset, she 'revelled' to the sound of the marching feet of the Roundheads. Running her fingers over the recumbent effigies on a medieval tomb in a Dorset church, she exclaimed in delighted tones, 'Oh, I know him!'[65] Undoubtedly Wood-Legh would have agreed with Trevelyan's argument that the medieval period was the cornerstone for the British tradition: 'unless we become a Totalitarian State and forget all our Englishry, there will always be something medieval in our ways of thinking, especially in our idea that people and corporations have rights and liberties which the State ought in some degree to respect, in spite of the legal omnicompetence of Parliament.'[66]

Also in kinship with Trevelyan, Wood-Legh's love for time past sometimes bordered on the nostalgic. On a fifty-mile 'pilgrimage' from the Shrine of St. Martha to Canterbury in 1932 with her friend Lady Kathleen Balfour, she delighted in the unchanging character of the English countryside and in the form of ancient buildings. Modelling a story of the journey on Chaucer's *Canterbury Tales*, Lady Balfour cast Wood-Legh as the scholar. In her role as the 'Clerk of Oxenford' to Balfour's 'Squire,' Wood-Legh lamented the changes that were transforming the country: 'Up there on the Downs and among those neat Kent gardens, the people really belong to their own English soil. But here on the highways, I feel there is something alien that has affected the dwellers.'[67]

Wood-Legh adopted other quintessential elements of 'respectable' middle-class English life. Afternoon tea, for example, was a longstanding tradition at 49 Owlstone Road.[68] Wood-Legh's fondness for country walking, which was a passion for her and an activity she often pursued during her holidays, is another hallmark of an English manner of living. Such sentiments are striking, at least in retrospect, coming from a Canadian who had immigrated to the United Kingdom, but they also reflect Wood-Legh's cultural conservatism. Although urban British society was increasingly multiracial by the 1960s, Wood-Legh's own view of her adopted country does not appear to have incorporated such changes.

Moreover, there are few hints of Wood-Legh's Canadian origins in her writing. A short, rather sentimental poem about Canada, probably written when she visited her uncle in Saskatchewan in 1918, survives.[69] She wrote regularly to this same uncle until his death in the mid-1960s, but apparently did not maintain any other Canadian connections. A woman who lived at Owlstone Road at the end of Wood-Legh's life felt that Canada 'represented a small, closed, early chapter of her life, of less interest to her than her lifelong love, a university career.'[70] According to another colleague, 'her whole personality and style seemed so much that of a single English academic female that one would never normally have thought she had an upbringing elsewhere.'[71]

Wood-Legh's time in Montreal did not impress upon her the qualities of French culture. Rather, she was attracted to Anglo-Saxon traditions. She developed a strong bond with Germany and often travelled there during the 1930s, attending academic conferences and hiking between rural youth hostels.[72] She remained close to many German friends; indeed, Professor Stengel of the University of Marburg inspired her life's research into chantries.[73] She was a member of a local refugee committee during the 1930s and through this organization befriended German refugees during the Second World War.[74]

Following her father's death in 1945, Wood-Legh had a long series of German 'secretaries' until her own death in 1981. These women, young university students, would help Wood-Legh by reading books and documents aloud and by performing various household tasks. In exchange, the women received room and board, practise with their English, tuition in medieval Latin, and a memorable introduction to a British way of life.[75] In many cases, the friendships that developed between the older historian and the young students were of profound emotional importance to both parties. For Wood-Legh, the presence of these young companions helped fill the emotional void left by the death of her father.[76] And for many of the German women, Wood-Legh became a life-long source of personal inspiration.[77] During Wood-Legh's last illness, four of these women made special trips to England to visit their former mentor.[78]

A New Women's College

Undoubtedly her work on chantries influenced one of her most lasting endeavours, the founding of Lucy Cavendish College. After Wood-Legh's father died, her friends, particularly zoologist Dr. Anna Bidder and philosopher Dr. Margaret Braithwaite, were concerned that she would become reclusive and depressed. In 1950, they established a women's Dining Group to provide her company. Each Tuesday night, a group of women academics would gather for a meal and intellectual discussion. At one of the early meetings, Braithwaite exclaimed that they were establishing a potential 'high table': 'We are the kind of people who could be used to make the nucleus of a new College in Cambridge.'[79] This Dining Group was a place for marginalized women in Cambridge, set aside because of personal demands on their time, often due to their familial duties.[80] The group was open to any woman member of the Regent House, the governing body of the university, who did not have an official connection with an existing college.

Although many of the women agreed with the goal of establishing a new women's college, there was much debate and delay in setting up the institution. Some wished for a college to admit undergraduate women, while others, like Wood-Legh, Bidder, and Braithwaite, wanted a college to enhance the position of women who had completed their studies, to provide a 'high table' for intellectual exchange in which they could flourish. In 1954, there was a split, as Dame Myra Curtis of Newnham took the lead away from the Dining Group and contributed to the founding of New Hall. This college aimed at increasing the number of female undergraduates, but did not intend to address the status of female tutors unattached to particular colleges.[81]

Despite the establishment of New College along very different principles, the Dining Group persisted in its aim. As Margaret Braithwaite stated, 'The thing we all really know about is the academic woman who has home responsibilities and wants to get back or to keep going her academic work.'[82] Wood-Legh played an important role, serving as chair of the Dining Group for nearly eight years, drafting memoranda and writing the constitution for the college. Her blindness only hindered her when she was barred from serving as a trustee.[83] In 1965, Lucy Cavendish College was founded, dedicated to providing a place for women academics as well as a residence for returning women students. Wood-Legh became a fellow of the college and the pro-president (deputy president).

Among the women of the Dining Group, Wood-Legh had been the most assiduous, often taking on the task of telephoning members to encourage them to attend.[84] This group was of vital importance to her. The Dining Group, and eventually Lucy Cavendish College itself, seem to have given Wood-Legh a real home as an intellectual at Cambridge. It is possible that the death of her most important male anchor, her father, ushered in a more female-centred phase of her life, a phase in which she helped establish Lucy Cavendish College and enjoyed a succession of friendships with the young German women who came to live with her.

Was Wood-Legh a feminist? Both Anna Bidder and Lady Kathleen Balfour deny that Wood-Legh would have defined herself as a feminist, even during the days when she fought hard to establish a new college for Cambridge women.[85] She told one of her German 'secretaries' that she wished she had been a man, preferably one born in Victorian times![86] Wood-Legh did, however, adopt 'feminist' positions, as in her support of the ordination of women in the Church of England.[87] And her achievements during the last twenty years of her life were often framed by others in feminist terms. For example, the newspaper report of her Hulsean lecture series was titled 'Breaking a Barrier.'[88] Some female friends, too, apparently viewed Wood-Legh's actions during the latter years of her life within the context of contemporary feminism. Kay Baxter's tribute for her old friend's eightieth birthday refers to Wood-Legh's 'unequivocal statements concerning women's rights and duties.' One of the values that L. Zinn of Germany acquired during her stay with Wood-Legh was 'to struggle for women's rights.'[89]

It is not too much of an exaggeration to see Lucy Cavendish College as being analogous to the chantries to which Wood-Legh had dedicated her career. While chantries were established to pray for the souls of the departed, they often had very practical aims, in particular educational ones. Indeed, some of the colleges at Oxford and Cambridge can trace their origins back to medieval chantries. Because of her knowledge of the history of chantries, Wood-Legh was of particular help in developing the constitution of the new college, given her deep understanding of their historic role.[90] Yet this Cambridge chantry was for women rather than men – and Kathleen Wood-Legh, specialist of medieval chantries, played a key role in founding it.

Conclusion

For Wood-Legh, the notion of community and an elevated sense of the importance of intellectual thought and spiritual commitment became the organizing principles not just for her research, but for the way in which she lived her life. To exist as she did as a woman without independent means in early twentieth-century Canada would have been next to impossible.[91] Instead, Wood-Legh made her home in Cambridge, England, creating a life for herself as a scholar, a teacher, and a lover of all that was traditionally English.

On one level, the story of Wood-Legh's life fits easily into broader trends of opportunity and constraint that faced all female Canadian historians of her time. Opportunity is evident in the fact that she received her B.A. and M.A. at McGill, a B.Litt. at Oxford, and a Ph.D. at Cambridge during the 1920s and early 1930s. She published well-respected works, primarily on the church history of medieval England.

Kathleen Wood-Legh

While she was relatively well-connected within her field of historical study, the limitations of possibility are also evident. Early efforts to obtain employment at English universities and girls' schools proved unsuccessful, and her subsequent teaching career was spent as a casual tutor for various Cambridge colleges. Like many other academic women of her period, Wood-Legh would not have called herself a feminist. Yet her efforts to establish Lucy Cavendish College at Cambridge demonstrate an appreciation for the particular difficulties women face in pursuing academic careers. Certainly, Wood-Legh provides an example of a courageous life, but her story also illuminates other elements that may sustain women who venture into the male world of academe: personal faith, a devotion to the quest of intellect, and a community of fellow scholars who are also friends.

Acknowledgments

Many people helped in the preparation of this article. Many of Kathleen Wood-Legh's colleagues and friends generously gave their time to share their memories of Wood-Legh. The letters and tapes that we collected during the course of this project will be placed in the archives of Lucy Cavendish College, Cambridge. Prof. Ged Martin and Dr. Adam Fox of the University of Edinburgh explained aspects of Cambridge culture. Joan Bullock-Anderson, archivist of Lucy Cavendish College, was also very helpful.

Notes

1 Unlike an honorary doctorate, scholars may apply for a Litt.D. degree, the determination being made by a group of scholars at the university.

2 Dorothy Emmet, tribute, box 1, file 13, Cambridge University Library, Add MS 8384, Papers of Dr. K.L. Wood-Legh (hereafter KLW-L).

3 Information concerning Wood-Legh's family background was particularly difficult to locate. A handwritten copy of a newspaper account of her parents' wedding states that Miss Katie Stevenson married Mr. Charles F. Wood-Legh on 13 November 1900, box 23, file 8, KLW-L. The article notes that the groom was a member of a prominent English family, 'being a son of the late Baron.' We could find no evidence of an aristocratic family connection.

4 Prof. Dorothy Emmet reported that Charles Wood-Legh had some sort of clerical job with the railway but retired early. Emmet, telephone interview with Megan Davies, 19 May 1995.

5 In 1912, Wood-Legh performed several pieces in a public recital in Portland, Maine, box 3, file 8, KLW-L.

6 Margaret Gillett, *We Walked Very Warily: A History of Women at McGill* (Montreal: Eden Press 1981), 435.

7 Judith Fingard, 'College, Career, and Community: Dalhousie Coeds, 1881-1921,' in Paul Axelrod and John G. Reid, eds., *Youth, University and Canadian Society: Essays in the Social History of Higher Education* (Montreal and Kingston: McGill-Queen's University Press 1989), 26-50; Gillett, *We Walked Very Warily*; Helen MacGill Hughes, 'Wasp/Woman/Sociologist,' *Society* 14, 5 (July/August 1977): 69-80.

8 James R. Willard, comp., *Progress of Medieval Studies in the United States of America*, bulletin no. 1 (1923): 16-19.

9 Margaret Hastings and Elisabeth G. Kimball, 'Two Distinguished Medievalists – Nellie Neilson and Bertha Putnam,' *Journal of British Studies* 18, 2 (spring 1979): 142-59.

10 Muriel V. Roscoe, 'The Royal Victoria College, 1899-1962. A Report to the Principal' (1964), 91-4, McGill University Archives.

11 Stanley Brice Frost, *McGill University: For the Advancement of Learning, Vol. II: 1895-1971* (Kingston and Montreal, McGill-Queen's University Press 1984), 182.
12 Statistics compiled from graduate calendars, McGill University Archives.
13 Maxine Berg, *A Woman in History: Eileen Power, 1889-1940* (Cambridge: Cambridge University Press 1996), 6.
14 Nevertheless, Wood-Legh's M.A. supervisor, William Waugh, also had research interests related to Canada.
15 Frost, *McGill University, Vol. II*, 146-7; Rushton Coulborne cited, 183.
16 Clipping from *Montreal Gazette* (3 May 1923): 4, box 3, file 8, KLW-L.
17 This attitude towards Wood-Legh's blindness seems to have emanated from her mother, who insisted that her daughter take care of her own personal needs. Althea Tyndale, letter to authors, 20 August 1995, and also funeral address by D. Emmet, box 1, file 13, KLW-L.
18 Funeral address by Emmet.
19 Barbara Schmeidler, letter to authors, 18 May 1995.
20 'Birthday Book of Tributes,' contribution by Robert Lacey, 30 September 1981, box 1, file 13, KLW-L.
21 Althea I. Tyndale, letter to authors, 25 June 1995; Ingeborg Amanzi, letter to authors, 6 June 1995; funeral address by Emmet.
22 It is worth noting that a fellow blind Canadian, Charles Malcolm MacInnes, taught for decades at Bristol University, published important works on the British maritime empire, and served as dean of the Faculty of Arts for many years. Alan F. Williams, 'Bristol and C.M. MacInnes: The Canadian Dean of the Gateway of Empire,' *British Journal of Canadian Studies* 1, 2 (December 1986): 303-17.
23 Williams to Wood-Legh, 7 June 1923, box 3, file 7, KLW-L. Williams was undoubtedly an important intellectual mentor for Wood-Legh.
24 Wood-Legh's friends note the assistance that her father gave her; Tony Chase, letter to authors, 5 June 1995; memorial address, Gert Rathenau, n.d., box 1, file 13, KLW-L.
25 For a few examples, see 'A Profession for the Blind,' *Public Health* 44, 5 (February 1931): 133; E.K. Macdonald, 'The Responsibility of the Local Authority for the Blind,' *Public Health* 47, 4 (January 1934): 123-9.
26 Althea Tyndale, letter to authors, 20 August 1995.
27 It seems likely that the move took place in 1924. Wood-Legh's papers include a handwritten list of moving expenses dated May 1924, box 1, file 3, KLW-L.
28 Dorothy Emmet, telephone interview with Megan Davies, 19 May 1995.
29 Rita McWilliams-Tullberg, *Women at Cambridge: A Men's University – Though of a Mixed Type* (London: Victor Gollancz 1975), 207.
30 Vera Brittain, *Lady into Woman: A History of Women from Victoria to Elizabeth II* (London: Andrew Dakers 1953), 87.
31 T.E.B. Howarth, *Cambridge between Two Wars* (London: Collins 1978), 42.
32 Kathleen Wood-Legh, 'The Franklin,' *Review of English Studies* (April 1928); 'Sheriffs, Lawyers, and Belted Knights in the Parliaments of Edward III,' *English Historical Review* (July 1931): 372-88; 'The Knights' Attendance in the Parliaments of Edward III,' *English Historical Review* (July 1932): 398-413.
33 Berg, *A Woman in History*, 12.
34 G.M. Trevelyan, *English Social History: A Survey of Six Centuries, Chaucer to Queen Victoria* (London: Longmans, Green 1942), 24, footnote. He dedicated the book to the memory of Eileen Power. On that dedication, see Berg, *A Woman in History*, 247-9.
35 Tony Chase, letter to authors, 5 June 1995. David Cannadine, *G.M. Trevelyan: A Life in History* (London: Fontana 1992), chapter iv.
36 G.G. Coulton, *Fourscore Years: An Autobiography* (Cambridge; Cambridge University Press 1942), 313; Sarah Campion, *Father: A Portrait of G.G. Coulton at Home* (London: Michael Joseph 1948), 176.
37 Kathleen Wood-Legh, *Studies in Church Life in England under Edward III* (Cambridge: Cambridge University Press 1934). She published an earlier article related to church history: 'The Appropriation of Parish Churches during the Reign of Edward III,' *Cambridge Historical Journal* 3, 1 (1929): 15-22.

38 Articles on chantries include 'Some Aspects of the History of Chantries during the Reign of Edward III,' *Cambridge Historical Journal* 4, 1 (1932): 26-50; 'Some Aspects of the History of Chantries in the Later Middle Ages,' *Transactions of the Royal Historical Society*, 4th series, vol. 28 (1946): 47-60; 'Chantries and Corporations sole,' *Law Quarterly Review* 74 (1958): 272-84.

39 Wood-Legh to Registrar, University College, Southampton, 26 May 1934, and Wood-Legh to Registrar, King's College, London, 30 May 1934, box 3, file 12, KLW-L.

40 Ibid. Trevelyan wrote in his testimonial: 'I think her moral and intellectual power very remarkable and well suited to teaching,' 1 March 1933.

41 Kathleen Wood-Legh, ed., *Kentish Visitations of Archbishop William Warham and his Deputies, 1511-1512* (Maidstone, Kent: Kent Archaeological Society 1984). Cheney also helped with editing and references dealing with earlier projects; Cheney to Wood-Legh, 7 August 1964, box 3, file 4, KLW-L.

42 The phase 'Owlstonian' is taken from F. Gordon Addenbrooke's contribution to the 'Birthday Book of Tributes,' n.d., KLW-L.

43 Ibid. Kay Baxter makes reference to the 'Owlstone door' in her birthday book tribute, 9 August 1981. This group included Canon David Isitt; Mala and F. Gordon Addenbrooke (the latter of Trinity College, Oxford), who had initially made contact with Wood-Legh at her uncle's home in Saskatchewan; Dr. James and Dorothy Parkes (the former an authority on the Jewish people, a much-published commentator on Israel and Palestine, and the author of two books of popular theology under the pseudonym of 'James Hadham'); Dr. Anna Bidder, a zoologist; Dr. Margaret Braithwaite, a philosopher; Kay Baxter; Lady Kathleen Oldfield (Wood-Legh, Baxter, and Oldfield were sometimes referred to as 'the three Kays'); and Barbara Reynolds (translator of two Cambridge Italian-English dictionaries, a close friend and subsequent biographer of Dorothy Sayers).

44 'Birthday Book of Tributes,' contribution by Canon David Isitt, 1981.

45 Dr. Anna Bidder, 'Tributes to Dr. K.L. Wood-Legh,' 31 October 1981, reference no. 238, Lucy Cavendish College Archives.

46 Lord Briggs, letter to authors, 29 August 1995.

47 'Birthday Book of Tributes,' contribution by Robert Lacey, 30 September 1981; Kathleen Oldfield recalled that Wood-Legh made 'medieval latin come alive.' Copy of Wood-Legh's obituary, *Modern Churchman*, n.d., box 1, file 13, KLW-L.

48 It seems likely that her father did not work again after the Wood-Legh household relocated to England. Tony Chase notes that 'Her father was devoted to her but was never very successful at earning his living;' Tony Chase, letter to authors, 5 June 1995. The aunt either died during the 1950s or went to live in a nursing home. Christa Kümpel, letter to authors, 22 August 1995.

49 William Ernest Stephenson died in Victoria in November, 1965. Obituary, *Victoria Daily Colonist*, 9 November 1965. This must have been the same 'Uncle Ernie' whom Wood-Legh visited at the Rectory in Balcarres, Saskatchewan, in 1918. Dr. Anna Bidder noted that Wood-Legh received an unexpected and much appreciated inheritance; Bidder, taped interview with Megan Davies, Cambridge, 6 June 1995.

50 Peter Novick, *That Noble Dream: The 'Objectivity Question' and the American Historical Profession* (Cambridge: Cambridge University Press 1988).

51 Ludwig Riess, *The History of English Electoral Law in the Middle Ages*, trans. Kathleen Wood-Legh (Cambridge: Cambridge University Press 1940).

52 Kathleen Wood-Legh, ed., *A Small Household of the Fifteenth Century* (Manchester: Manchester University Press 1956).

53 Wood-Legh, *Kentish Visitations.*

54 Kathleen Wood-Legh, *Perpetual Chantries in Britain* (Cambridge: Cambridge University Press 1965). A scholar of a later period in the history of chantries acknowledged his 'immense' debt to Wood-Legh's work: Alan Kreider, *English Chantries: The Road to Dissolution* (Cambridge, MA: Harvard University Press 1979), 219.

55 Kathleen Wood-Legh, 'Breaking a barrier,' *Daily Telegraph* (3 November 1972).

56 Cambridge University Board of Extra-mural Studies, course syllabi, 1976, n.d., box 1, file 11, KLW-L.

57 *Old McGill* (1923), 127.

58 On the philosophy of the Modern Churchman's Union, see Alan M.G. Stephenson, *The Rise and Decline of English Modernism: The Hulsean Lectures 1979-1980* (London: SPCK 1984).
59 Lady Oldfield, taped interview with Megan Davies, 19 June 1995.
60 Wood-Legh's obituary, *Modern Churchman.*
61 Leni Challenger, who stayed with Wood-Legh for one year in 1956 and was in fact married from Wood-Legh's house, reported that her own faith was 'shaky' and Wood-Legh helped strengthen her Christian belief. Challenger, telephone interview with Megan Davies, 18 May 1995.
62 Dr. Anna Bidder, 'Tributes to Dr. K.L. Wood-Legh;' E.H.W., 'Kathleen Louise Wood-Legh, 1901-1981,' *Newnham College Roll Letter* (1982): 63.
63 Wood-Legh, 'Some Aspects of the History of Chantries in the Later Middle Ages,' 48.
64 Wood-Legh's obituary, *Modern Churchman.*
65 Both these incidents are recounted in a letter from Tony Chase to authors, 11 May 1995.
66 Trevelyan, *English Social History*, 96.
67 Lady Kathleen Balfour, 'A Canterbury Tale,' *Blackwood's Magazine,* 232 (July 1932): 119.
68 Lady Oldfield, taped interview with Megan Davies, 19 June 1995.
69 This poem, titled 'What the West Is To Me' was apparently published. Wood-Legh gave a copy to Barbara Schmeidler; Schmeidler, letter to authors, 18 May 1995. Again, the way in which Wood-Legh's blindness is obscured is striking: 'Though here we find no mountains grand,/ And here no sparkling sea,/ There's something in this Western land / That has a charm for me.'
70 Althea I. Tyndale, letter to authors, 20 August 1995. Lady Oldfield corroborated this view in her taped interview with Megan Davies, 19 June 1995.
71 Felicity Heal, letter to authors, 17 August 1995.
72 Wood-Legh's first visit to Germany likely took place in 1929 when she made important contacts with German historians, including the young Dr. Matthes; Wood-Legh to father, 27 July 1929, box 1, file 2, KLW-L. In the summer of 1934, Kathleen Oldfield and Wood-Legh walked up the Rhine from Bonn to Mainz; Wood-Legh's obituary, *Modern Churchman.*
73 Wood-Legh contributed a chapter to Professor Stengel's festschrift: 'The chantries in some medieval English towns' in E. Kunz, ed., *Festschrift Edmund E. Stengel zum 70 geburtstag* (Münster: Böhlan 1952), 428-42.
74 Tony Chase, letter to authors, 5 June 1995.
75 'I will never forget the evenings we spent in the library listening to the music of the London Promenade Concerts. With that she opened for me the door to music in a wonderful way,' Birgit Sicels, letter to authors, 23 May 1995.
76 Dr. Anna Bidder, taped interview with Megan Davies, 6 June 1995.
77 Barbara Schmeidler, for example, recalls that the time, 'spent with her [Wood-Legh] belongs to the most fascinating periods in my life. I was ca. 22 years then and open to any new ideas,' Schmeidler, letter to authors, 18 May 1995. More poignantly, Brigitte Frank, who arrived at Owlstone Road in the first decade following the war, wrote, 'One of the deepest impressions I have to thank you for is an understanding of the value of tradition ... when you remember the inner situation of a young German girl in those days, whose really shattering experience had been the destruction of all values and a deep sense of insecurity;' 'Birthday Book of Tributes,' contribution by Brigitte Frank.
78 'Scholar who never let blindness hinder her,' *Cambridge Evening News* (27 October 1981).
79 C. Kate Bertram, *Lucy Cavendish College Cambridge: A History of the Early Years* (Cambridge 1989), 1. A 'High Table', at which senior members took their meals separate from undergraduates, formed the centre of social and intellectual stimulus for the college.
80 Bidder, 'Tributes to Dr. K.L. Wood-Legh'; she notes that many of the women in the Dining Group had young children and ties to the home.
81 Wood-Legh to President of St. John's, 16 June 1954, KLW-L. See also Rosemary Murray, *New Hall, 1954-1972: The Making of a College* (Cambridge 1980).
82 A.M. Bidder, 'Prehistory of the College,' 4, Lucy Cavendish College Archives.
83 Bertram, *Lucy Cavendish College*, 18, 23, 29.
84 Bidder, 'Tributes to Dr. K.L. Wood-Legh'; she described Wood-Legh as 'the king-pin of

the first three, who gathered together that group of women known as the Women's Dining Group.'

85 Dr. Anna Bidder, taped interview with Megan Davies, 6 June 1995; Lady Oldfield, taped interview with Megan Davies, 19 June 1995.

86 Barbara Schmeidler, letter to authors, 18 May 1995.

87 'Scholar who never let blindness hinder her,' *Cambridge Evening News*.

88 *The Daily Telegraph*, 3 November 1972.

89 L. Zinn, letter to authors, 20 May 1995.

90 Bidder, 'Tributes to Dr. K.L. Wood-Legh.'

91 Wood-Legh's career reflects the experience of other Canadian women historians of the period. Vera Brown of McGill and Sylvia Thrupp of the University of British Columbia are two scholars who left Canada to pursue career opportunities in the United States.

Part 4:
New Departures

11
Making History: Women's History in Canadian Universities in the 1970s

Deborah Gorham

In September 1971, during my third year as an assistant professor at Carleton University, I offered a course in women's history for the first time. It was the same year that Natalie Zemon Davis and Jill Ker Conway first offered their women's history course at the University of Toronto. By the 1974-5 academic year, at least eight such courses were being taught at Canadian universities.[1] Moreover, in the early 1970s, research, publication, and teaching on women's history began to develop in Canada, both inside and outside of universities. Within the academic historical profession, the annual conferences of the Canadian Historical Association reflect a growth in women's history beginning in 1969, when the program included two papers on women. In 1975, with the founding of the Canadian Committee on Women's History, women's history gained an institutional base within the Canadian Historical Association.

The course offerings, scholarly activities, and institution-building of the early 1970s are evidence of the emergence of women's history as a distinct field in Canadian universities. Academic women's history in Canada has continued to grow, as it has internationally. In the 1990s, most universities and colleges across the country offer courses in the history of women at the undergraduate and graduate levels; not only has the teaching of women's history expanded since the early 1970s, so also has scholarly research and publication.[2] Moreover, in the 1990s, Canada now has a younger group of academic historians of women, some of whom define themselves as constituting a second, successor generation to their predecessors of the 1970s and early 1980s.[3]

The establishment of women's history as an academic field in Canada is a major achievement whose history deserves to be recorded and understood not only for its own sake but also because it is part of the history of higher education in Canada, of women's experience as university scholars and teachers, and of the history of feminism and the women's movement in Canada. This essay is offered as an attempt to encourage such a history. I will sketch the early years of women's history, focusing on the 1970s. Based as it is on preliminary research and on the recollections of a small number of individuals, one of whom is myself, and another of whom, Alison Prentice, is an editor of this collection, this essay is offered as a partial and, in part, a personal narrative and preliminary analysis; in no way is it a definitive or comprehensive study.[4]

Teaching Women's History at Canadian Universities

The best known and most influential course on women's history taught before 1975 was the University of Toronto's 'Topics in the History of Women' co-taught by Natalie Zemon Davis and Jill Ker Conway.[5] The course was offered for the first time in 1971-2 with an enrolment of over 200 students. More than simply a new course, History 348 was both a new departure for Toronto's Department of History and a significant event within Toronto's blossoming feminist community. According to Conway, it soon became known as 'the most intellectually exciting course on campus,' and the numerous auditors included faculty members and students.[6]

When they introduced the course, Jill Ker Conway and Natalie Zemon Davis were among a handful of women professors at the University of Toronto. Neither was Canadian by birth or upbringing and neither was a Canadianist, Davis's field being early modern Europe and Conway's the nineteenth-century United States. (Conway, it should be mentioned, was a rare example of a scholar who had written a dissertation on women in the 1960s.) Davis and Conway would go on to achieve distinguished professional reputations and become major figures in North American academic life, in both cases in the United States. In 1971-2, both Davis and Conway had been at the University of Toronto for some years, and both had the talent and academic qualifications necessary to assure the soundness of their scholarship. As well, they each possessed personal qualities of strength and self-assurance that allowed them to be confident pioneers.

In *True North*, the second volume of her autobiography, Jill Conway describes how she and Davis planned carefully for the course. 'The main themes were to be developed from the concepts historians used to explain the contours of society in any period: class, urbanization, professionalization, demography, the institution of the family, sexuality. Over happily argumentative lunches we mapped out a year-long course, and discussed the documents and texts students should read.'[7] Davis would deal with the early modern period, and Conway with the nineteenth and twentieth centuries.

Why did these two people undertake this experiment? Both Davis and Conway were primarily scholars, with a deep love of scholarship and a commitment to teaching and scholarship as a vocation whose all-consuming nature left little time for political activism separated from scholarship.[8] But sympathy with the newly reborn feminist movement did play a role in their decision to launch their women's history course.

Born in Detroit, Michigan, Natalie Zemon became active in Left politics and scholarship when she was an undergraduate at Smith College in Northhampton, Massachusetts, in the late 1940s.[9] But her sense of the importance of social activism went back even further: she was the daughter of well-to-do Jewish parents and was raised in a household sympathetic to radical politics. When she attended a private high school for girls, both her sympathies with radical politics and her Jewishness helped to reinforce a salutary sense of her outsider status: 'I was very eager to be a good student and to be popular and do all the other things you were supposed to do, but I was Jewish. Although I wasn't poor, I was certainly an outsider ... I see that as a very creative experience.'[10]

When Davis arrived in Toronto in 1962, 'there were no university nursery schools, there was no housing for married students, and scheduling and residence requirements [for graduate degrees] were inflexible. This made it very difficult for married women.'[11] In 1969, when feminist groups at the University of Toronto had become active and visible, a coalition of women organized a protest designed to pressure the university administration to provide day-care facilities for employees and students. The protests culminated with the occupation of the university's administration building by day-care activists.[12] When Natalie Davis, who taught some of the women involved in the protest, talked to and encouraged the organizers of the sit-in, some of her senior colleagues in Toronto's history department were so angry that they threatened to bring forward a vote of censure against her at a departmental meeting. The censure vote was averted through the efforts of Jill Conway.[13]

Conway herself was involved in working for the rights of women faculty at the University of Toronto and in the wider world of Canadian academic life. In *True North*, she describes her anger and frustration when, in 1970, after six years at the university, she was not promoted to associate professor, although all the other members of her cohort of junior faculty (all men) were. She had read about such discrimination but had not herself been subjected to it: 'Now that it was happening to me, my rage was so powerful, it startled me.'[14] Conway fought for her promotion, successfully. She tells us that the confrontation caused her to begin 'thinking about the situation of other women faculty.'[15]

In contrast to Davis and Conway, both by then scholars with considerable standing at a powerful institution, when I offered 'Women and Society in Western Europe and North America, 1700-1970' at the St. Patrick's College campus of Carleton University, Ottawa, for the first time in 1971-2, I was a junior, untenured faculty member with a still unfinished Ph.D.[16] My energy for introducing and then teaching the course sprang primarily from my growing commitment to and involvement with the revival of feminism.

I had since childhood been familiar with feminism as an integral part of radicalism and had considered myself to be a feminist since early adulthood. My mother was always employed and valued her right to work in the labour force, and both my parents had been active in Left politics in the 1930s. My parents assumed not only that I would attend university, but also that I would prepare for serious professional work. I attended excellent girls' schools in New York City (my birthplace) where, although little was said overtly about feminism, all the pupils were encouraged to take themselves seriously and to achieve academic success. My first year of university at Barnard College reinforced these values, although even a woman's college like Barnard had lost some of its edge in the antifeminist 1950s. I dropped out of college for a year, returning not to Barnard, but to McGill University, Montreal. McGill was my first encounter with co-education since primary school. Although I received a fine education there, McGill unquestionably did not take its women students as seriously as it took its men. However, I knew I wanted to go to graduate school, and did so, even though I received little encouragement or advice from my professors at McGill.

The year 1970 was a turning point for me: I began reading seriously the new feminist literature. The book with the most profound personal impact was Kate Millett's *Sexual Politics*, which I read when it was published that year.[17] Millett's analysis forced me to recognize the unfinished revolution in my own life. Betty Friedan's *The Feminine Mystique* had certainly moved me in 1963, yet without the same effect; although I had been married for several years and in 1963 had given birth to my only child, I was, after all, also enrolled in a doctoral program at the University of Wisconsin. I did not see 'the feminine mystique' as my problem. In 1965, I left my Ph.D. studies at Wisconsin prematurely, following my husband to Ottawa where he was offered a job with the Canadian federal public service. I was lucky enough to be offered a tenure-track position at Carleton in 1969, but my primary identity in the late 1960s was that of wife and mother. In the early 1970s, I had few links to a wider scholarly community, and during the first few years of my appointment at Carleton, I was much more interested in teaching than I was in research. Reading *Sexual Politics* and becoming involved in Ottawa's emerging feminist community caused me to realize just how much I needed genuine personal autonomy and the opportunity to pursue serious professional work of my own.

I first learned about new developments for feminist scholarship and feminist teaching from Greta Hofmann-Nemiroff, a pioneer in women's studies in Canada.[18] It was after discussions with Hofmann-Nemiroff that

I initiated a proposal for a course in women's history in 1970-1. I saw the course proposal as a way to link my newly awakened and transformed feminist commitment with my work as a teacher. Not only was 'Women and Society' the first women's history course to be offered at Carleton, it was the first course of any kind explicitly on women offered at the university. (At Carleton, Women's Studies courses, in which I was also involved, followed the first discipline-based courses.)[19]

I attribute the relative ease with which I introduced 'Women and Society' in large measure to the fact that I was at that time appointed to St. Patrick's College rather than the university's 'main' campus Department of History. St. Patrick's College, a Roman Catholic institution run by the Oblate order, had fallen on hard times, and Carleton University purchased it in the late 1960s. For a few wonderful years, St. Pat's was invited to be experimental. The courses on women introduced through St. Pat's in the early 1970s were accepted because of the college's mandate to be innovative. In addition, the college's marginality and the fact that its status was not as high as that of the university's main campus had several consequences helpful to the development of feminist teaching. First, although men still greatly outnumbered women as faculty members, proportionally more women were hired at St. Pat's than at the main campus during the expansionist late 1960s.[20] Second, because the college program was not taken seriously by many on the main campus, the larger institution felt comfortable in relegating innovation to the margins. Nevertheless, that first women's history course did need the approval of the chairman of the main Department of History. Fortunately, in 1970-1 the chairman was H. Blair Neatby, a man of liberal principles who knew and respected women scholars; he supported 'Women and Society' largely out of a sense of fair-mindedness.

I was fortunate that my interest in feminist scholarship meshed with my historical area of expertise. Trained initially at the University of Wisconsin as a British social historian specializing in the Victorian period, the course I devised for 1971-2 was largely based on this background. The readings included selections from the excellent work on women produced by historians influenced by the early twentieth-century women's movement (Alice Clark, Ivy Pinchbeck, Eileen Power, and Mildred Campbell are notable examples), but we also read Simone de Beauvoir and Kate Millett.[21] I remember the class and the students fondly. Thirty-four students registered in the class, including one African student, whose passionate interest in African liberation issues as well as in feminism encouraged both the other students and myself to be aware on many levels of the dimensions of race as well as class in shaping women's experience. Nine men registered for the course, several of whom defined themselves as student radicals with a commitment to women's liberation. In

1971-2, I was teaching the only explicitly feminist course at Carleton, and I therefore allowed the students to write papers on a wide range of topics, some of which could not be considered properly historical, but were nevertheless exciting and original. In short, for the young instructor (myself) and for the varied group of students, the classroom overflowed with energy, passionate commitment, and creativity. On the other hand, I know that the course I offered that first year did lack a well-formulated framework, and we did have a tendency to stray from the assigned readings to discuss anything and everything related to feminism. Teaching the course that first year involved educating myself as well as the students, finding out about courses and reading lists being developed elsewhere, and building up a library collection.

A third course in women's history was introduced in 1973-4 at the University of Manitoba by historian Mary Kinnear.[22] Kinnear, an Oxford graduate, came to Manitoba in 1965 when her husband, also a historian, was offered a position. She was hired in 1966 as a lecturer by St. John's College, a founding and affiliated college on the campus of the university; its academic departments (other than theology) became fully integrated with the University of Manitoba in 1968. By 1973 when Kinnear completed her dissertation for the University of Oregon, she was the mother of three young children with a fourth born later that year.

As a teacher and a scholar of women's history, Kinnear has done important work since the early 1970s, contributing to the development of teaching in the field through her excellent textbook, *Daughters of Time* (1982).[23] Her interest in women's history was sparked in 1971-2 when Shirley Smith was dean of women at the University of Manitoba. Smith, a feminist, sponsored a lecture series on women in which Kinnear, then the only woman member of the Department of History, was asked to lecture on women and history. In 1972, when she was approached by a colleague in the Department of Religion to teach a team-taught interdisciplinary course on Women's Studies, Kinnear responded that she thought women's history deserved a course of its own. Shortly afterward, she was asked by the dean of arts to teach just such a course: 'Somewhat astonished, both at the university and myself, I agreed.' She comments on her initial involvement in the history of women as follows: 'I responded, willingly, to others' initiatives in developing a new course in history ... I quickly became determined to make this my future teaching and research interest.'

Kinnear remembers her students in this early course as 'a wonderful mix, marvellously motivated.' Kinnear knew about the University of Toronto course, and she recalls that she was 'tremendously helped by the generosity of N.Z. Davis and Jill Conway at the U. of T. ... J. Conway gave advice and shared reading lists and I was very grateful for this help.'

Kinnear prepared for the course during a sabbatical leave spent in Oxford, and in choosing readings for the class, she was inspired by the 'huge packet' Jill Conway sent along. She also found 'inspiration' from 'a new book, Sheila Rowbotham's *Hidden from History*.' Back at Manitoba, she says, 'Frankly, I had to scramble' to make assigned readings available to students and to build up the library collection. From the very first year Kinnear taught her course, she encouraged students to do work in regional history. This developed her own research interests in Canadian and specifically in Manitoba history.

Summing up her involvement with women's history over more than two decades, Kinnear says:

> In retrospect, I am grateful I was employed in the right place (a university) at the right time, on the cusp of a newly developing intellectual area. I had enough general political support to establish my own history course, and then to help establish a Women's Studies minor ... [After some early years of isolation], my relationship with other scholars grew slowly and tentatively, and in the eighties my own publishing career ... became more established. Yes, things in the 1970s could have been easier. Then and now, I wish there were more women on staff. But I can't complain that it was an excessively rocky road with huge obstacles placed in the way. Barriers there were, but these were as much related to the general situation of any working mother as arising out of the nature of academic culture.[24]

In 1973-4, Alison Prentice, then in the second year of her appointment to York University's Atkinson College, also taught a course on women's history, 'Women, the Family and Education in Canada.'[25] To the best of my knowledge, this was the first course taught at a Canadian university that focused on women in Canada. Prentice, who had been firmly committed to feminism for several years, initiated this course. She experienced little difficulty in doing so, partly because, like myself, she was teaching at a marginal institution. Atkinson 'was an unusually radical small college, devoted to the education of mature students.'[26] The department was small and when Prentice was hired, two women already held posts, one of which was chair. Only one of her Atkinson colleagues objected when she introduced the course proposal, but his objections were easily overruled.

Prentice recalls that

> about half the course was on the history of women and the family (having family history ... helped a lot, given the paucity of resources) and the other half was on the history of education ... My most memorable class

> had two men and about thirty women. The men were a bit sceptical, but the women were uniformly supportive ... They ... really got into their research papers – often on their own family backgrounds, or using the census. One Jewish woman had served in the Canadian armed forces during the Second World War and said [the experience] had changed her life. She also had a lot to say about women and education in her tradition and her Rabbi ancestors ... Another brought in her grandmother's incredible diary – which Marta Danylewycz, Beth Light and I eventually quoted in 'The Evolution of the Sexual Division of Labour in Teaching.' What delighted them, I think, was the idea that they and their families were part of history and that the things they were interested in ... were also part of history.[27]

During her career as a teacher and scholar, Prentice has made major contributions to women's history. She was one of the editors of the pathbreaking collection *The Neglected Majority* and is the first author of *Canadian Women: A History*, the book generally recognized as the field's major synthesizing work.[28] However, Prentice did not begin her adult life with ambitions to become a university professor. She was from a successful business family and received a privileged education, which included the Bishop Strachan School in Toronto, a private school for girls, followed by Smith College. In responding to my queries for this paper, Prentice characterized her education at Smith as 'both positive and negative.' Smith, she acknowledges, offered a 'wonderful new and exciting intellectual world.' However, in the 1950s (in contrast to the 1940s, when Natalie Zemon Davis attended Smith), the college's attitude towards women's achievement was ambivalent. On the one hand, Smith had a proud tradition of educating women. But in that decade of heightened gender constraints, even Smith projected mixed messages: 'the women professors seemed to me, at the time, old, rather irritable and not very expansive personalities ... in some peculiar way, we were not encouraged as women ... I think our professors thought we weren't serious – and would marry and be boring. Sylvia Plath [Prentice's contemporary at Smith] said it all in *The Bell Jar*.'[29] With hindsight and a knowledge of history, Prentice says, 'clearly women professors in the 1950s had a lot to be tired and bitter about; I'm reminded of how terrible the prejudice against them was – even at the women's colleges.'[30]

After Smith, Prentice's intention was to become a school teacher. Her introduction to history at the graduate level came about by accident. It was only because the Ontario College of Education would not accept her B.A. from Smith as the equivalent of an Ontario Honours B.A. that she enrolled in the M.A. program in history at the University of Toronto before studying to be a teacher. She left her second teaching job after 'two marvellous years' because she was by then married (to University of Toronto physicist James Prentice) and pregnant with her first child, and 'Toronto Board of Education rules required that pregnant teachers get out of the classroom four months before the due date!'

During the early 1960s, Prentice raised two children and taught 'the odd tutorial' for the University of Toronto's Department of History.

> At a certain point, when I was in my early thirties, the phone rang on the last day of June, and once again I was asked to take a bunch of tutorials for the history department the following year. I happened to be scrubbing the kitchen floor at the time. That was the moment when the light bulb went on, I think. I liked the work – in fact I loved teaching. But I did not like being asked to take the left-over courses at the last minute ... So I decided to get the union ticket – which is exactly how I thought of it. Teaching was my interest: I never really connected teaching history at university to being a historian and writing history.

Prentice enrolled in Toronto's Ph.D. program in 1967, working with Michael Katz and J.M.S. Careless. She received her doctorate in 1974 during her second year at Atkinson, a time in which she discovered her passion and talent for scholarship as well as for teaching.[31] But her commitment to women's history grew out of her feminism. By the early 1970s, Prentice had close links to Toronto's New Feminists, although she never became a member and did not have time to attend meetings regularly. Ironically, her husband Jim was a participating member of the New Feminists men's group.[32]

A 'key moment' for Prentice, as it was for me, was reading Kate Millett's *Sexual Politics*: 'That had an enormous influence, and I identified myself as a feminist from then on.' It was that feminist commitment that led her to propose and teach her course at Atkinson and to go on, when she moved from Atkinson to the Ontario Institute for Studies in Education (OISE) in 1975, to make women's history a central focus of her research and teaching.

Prentice says that one reason she landed her job at OISE is that she was prepared to teach a course that was already on the books: 'History of the Education of Women in Canadian Society.'[33] The course was instituted in 1974-5 and was one of at least three additional courses in women's history taught for the first time at a Canadian university during that year.

At Acadia University in Wolfville, Nova Scotia, feminist scholarship first made its impact on teaching through interdisciplinary course offerings.[34] In 1973-4, the university introduced an interdisciplinary course with the title 'Women in the Modern World,' which was crosslisted by sociology and home economics. Historian Lois Vallely-Fischer coordinated it during its first year, a responsibility for which she received no teaching credit. She recalls that 'it was very difficult to get the course approved because not only was it about women, but it was an interdisciplinary course.'[35] There were over a hundred students enrolled and a number of instructors involved, none of whom received any teaching credit. The history course taught at Acadia in 1974-5[36] was introduced because colleagues in the history department were annoyed that the department itself received no recognition for the students enrolled in the interdisciplinary course. Vallely-Fischer recalls, 'Marg Conrad [historian Margaret Conrad] and I responded that for that we needed a second course, on history of women, and so I proposed the course which we offered the following year'; the students who enrolled were mainly from the arts faculty. She remembers that she used two important collections of readings, both of which came out in 1973: Julia O'Faolain and Lauro Martines, *Not in God's Image,* and Susan Bell, *Women, from the Greeks to the French Revolution.*[37]

Also in 1974-5, Victorianist Ann Robson, a member of Toronto's Department of History, introduced a third-year seminar on Victorian women.[38] For the course, Robson assembled an admirable set of readings including such important new contributions as S. Barbara Kanner's pioneering bibliography from Martha Vicinus's *Suffer and Be Still: Women in the Victorian Age,* articles by Carl Degler and Ann Douglas Wood, and such contemporary sources as an 1859 article from the *Edinburgh Review* on 'Female Industry.'[39] Robson, who has contributed to the field yet does not define herself as a historian of women (indeed, she is wary about women's history's links to feminism), did not wish this course to be identified narrowly as a women's history course. In later years, when she realized that men students were reluctant to take the course because it had 'women' in the title, she changed it to 'Victorian Beliefs and Attitudes.' When I talked to her, Robson remarked that she was pleased but surprised to be identified as a pioneer teacher of women's history in Canada.[40]

Ruth Roach Pierson has made major contributions to women's history in Canada and internationally and is best known for her work on Canadian women and the Second World War.[41] Pierson introduced a course on women's history in the spring of 1975 at Memorial University in St. John's, Newfoundland. Pierson's motivation for introducing the course arose from her activist involvement in the feminist movement in St. John's in the early 1970s, where she was one of the founding members of the Newfoundland Council on the Status of Women and the St. John's Women's Centre; her interest in feminist history was sparked when she attended the second Berkshire Conference on the History of Women in 1974.[42] In an article written ten years later, she described how important that conference had been to her:

> It is hard to describe what a galvanizing experience that was ... I heard Natalie Zemon Davis deliver her groundbreaking paper 'Women's History in Transition: The European Case,' and Linda Gordon, her equally trail-blazing paper on women's campaign for voluntary motherhood ... The effect was exhilarating. Dare I say liberating? I went from knowing little or nothing about the history of women and the history of feminism to knowing that that's what I wanted to study and that gaining such knowledge was a legitimate enterprise.[43]

Recalling her experiences in the mid-1970s, Pierson explains that after the Berkshire conference she 'returned to Memorial all fired up to teach a course in women's history. I asked to be able to do this, and was granted permission to offer a course on the history of feminism under the elastic rubric ... "Contemporary Problems in Historical Perspective." I began the course by saying that I thought feminism was not a contemporary problem but rather a solution to a set of contemporary problems.'[44]

Pierson was born and grew up in Seattle, Washington. She had an outstanding career as a student, first at the University of Washington and then at Yale University where she began studies for her Ph.D. in 1964. Pierson's major field at Yale was German history; she did her thesis, on German-Jewish identity in the Weimar Republic, under the supervision of a major historian of twentieth-century Germany who respected her intelligence and encouraged her work. However, she was 'never exposed to any women's history' at Yale. 'I'm certain I would have written a very different Ph.D. thesis had I been aware of gender as a critical category of social historical analysis.' Pierson went to St. John's in 1970 because her husband was hired by Memorial University's Department of History. Memorial had the sense to hire Ruth Roach Pierson as well, but only to a 'junior division' category it then had, a position with considerably less status and security than a regular, tenure-track appointment.

Like others, Pierson read Kate Millett's *Sexual Politics* soon after it was published. 'I bought Kate Millett's *Sexual Politics* at the Yale Co-op,' she recalls, while waiting to collect the bound copies of her dissertation. Reading Millett brought to the surface her unrecognized anger that after her hard work and excellence as a student, everyone involved in the situation – including her thesis adviser, her husband, and, worst of all, herself – assumed that she would simply follow her husband when he was offered a job. Pierson had not encountered feminism as a child or young woman. Her mother, aunts, and family friends in the Seattle of her childhood were all 'stay-at-home moms' and 'feminism was not a word in my vocabulary.' Describing her feminist commitment now, she says that, looking back, she was 'a woman who was waiting for feminism to come along and articulate many of the inchoate thoughts and feelings I had been struggling with for years. I first consciously identified myself as a feminist once the word resurfaced within my milieu – sometime towards the end of the 1960s.'

For that first course at Memorial in the spring of 1975, Pierson assigned her students such works as Mary Wollstonecraft's *A Vindication of the Rights of Woman*, Friedrich Engels's *The Origins of the Family, Private Property and the State*, and Betty Friedan's *The Feminine Mystique*. Pierson recollects that she read Ivy Pinchbeck's *Women Workers and the Industrial Revolution* in preparation for the course. She emphasizes that she not only taught her 'keenly interested' and responsive students, she learned from them. Pierson recalls the particular influence of one mature student who had been a WREN during the war (a member of the Women's Royal Naval Service in Great Britain); in 1975, the woman was active in the women's movement in St. John's and incorporated her wartime experiences into a paper she did for Pierson's class. Pierson says, 'Her paper is what prompted me to go off that summer and begin researching the history of women's labour in the Second World War.'

Canadian Academics and the Research and Writing of Women's History in Canada

From the late 1960s to 1975, Canadian historians began to engage in scholarly research on women and introduce courses on women's history. During these years, papers on women's history presented at the Canadian Historical Association (CHA) provide one significant bellwether of the development in Canadian universities of historical scholarship on women. The annual meetings of the CHA were then, as they remain today, the most widely recognized forum for the presentation of historical papers in Canada.

From 1969 to 1973, presentation of papers on the history of women at the CHA amounted to a few isolated examples.[45] The presenter of one such early paper was historian Kathleen McCrone. In 1971, McCrone, then a recently hired junior faculty member at the University of Windsor,[46] had just completed her dissertation 'The Advancement of Women During the Age of Reform, 1832-1870'; hers was one of a handful of dissertations on women's history written in the 1960s. In October 1971, she sent in a proposal to the CHA program committee, offering to give a paper at the 1972 meetings on 'The Advancement of English Women during the Age of Reform.' The proposal was accepted, and the paper was presented at the 1972 meeting. Subsequently it received the significant recognition of acceptance by *Historical Papers*.[47]

When McCrone and I discussed this early paper in 1995, she remarked that she had not realized at the time how unusual it was for her to be proposing a paper on a women's history topic. McCrone has enjoyed a successful career as both researcher and university administrator; in recollecting the past, she spoke movingly about her own experiences as a young scholar. She graduated from the University of Saskatchewan in 1963. As an undergraduate, McCrone had been introduced to Victorian history by Hilda Neatby and Peter Marsh. She selected New York University for her graduate work partly for personal reasons: her older brother, a geologist, taught there. McCrone enjoyed New York City and New York University's Department of History, and she received 'generous assistance from a number of professors, including ... Leo Gershoy, the distinguished French historian.'[48] However, it was not anyone at New York University who suggested that she do a thesis on women, but rather her old mentor from Saskatchewan, Hilda Neatby, whom she continued to consult when she went home to Saskatchewan on vacation. McCrone still retains, as a valued memento, the piece of paper on which Neatby wrote out suggestions for thesis topics on women. McCrone emphasizes that she was 'pretty naive' about the nature of academia as a professional milieu; her 'first exposure to the profession' was at the CHA meetings in Canada's centennial year, 1967. McCrone was encouraged then, and at subsequent CHA meetings, by the fact that some of the few women historians teaching in Canadian universities did attend the CHA: people like Margaret Ormsby, Margaret Prang, and Hilda Neatby herself.

In 1973, the CHA mounted a full session on women's history for the first time. Participants included D. Suzanne Cross, Veronica Strong-Boag, and Jennifer Stoddart.[49] The 1973 session represented a landmark for academic women's history in Canada: not only was it the first session dedicated specifically to women's history sponsored by the CHA, the participants were part of a cohort that differed in significant ways from the scholars who taught women's history before 1975 or did research before 1970. For example, while Conway and McCrone did their dissertations on women in the 1960s, they were exceptions. In contrast, Cross, Stoddart, and Strong-Boag were all graduate students working on dissertations in women's history in the 1970s; moreover, they were Canadianists. Thus, as graduate students they enjoyed the advantages of being part of a small but growing community of historians of women, and of historians creating the new social history of Canada.[50] Strong-Boag, for example, was a teaching assistant for Davis's and Conway's course 'Topics in the History of Women.'[51] Wendy Mitchinson, another member of this cohort, recollects that she had considerable support from historian Ramsay Cook when she first decided to do work on women during her M.A. year at York University in 1970-1. Later she was encouraged by both Cook and Paul Stevens (her thesis advisor) when she decided to make women the focus of her Ph.D. research.[52]

In 1975, the Canadian Historical Association program included another session on women's history, this time with three papers.[53] It was after that panel that some seventeen people met for the founding meeting of the Canadian Committee on Women's History.[54] As one of the presenters at the women's history session, I attended the meeting, which was organized by the group of young Canadianist scholars mentioned above. Veronica Strong-Boag, newly appointed as an assistant professor at Trent University, was a chief convenor; she and Ann Leger Anderson would become coordinators of the new organization. On that pleasant June afternoon, the small group met in a comfortable lounge equipped with sofas and easy chairs. As a group, we presented some visual contrast to the usual CHA gathering: not only were all but two of us women, but we were also not wearing the women's version of academic tweed. In the summer of 1975, long skirts with flowered prints were in fashion. I recollect that I was wearing an ankle-length Indian print skirt, a black tee-shirt, and several strands of Indian beads. Several others were wearing similar clothing.

The costumes enhanced the air of informality and the sense that this was a bold venture, as indeed it was in many ways. However, the organization that was founded and that quickly grew emphatically did not align itself with the political or social counter-cultures of the 1960s and 1970s. Certain individuals present that day as well as others who later had contacts with the CCWH did indeed have links to the Women's Liberation Movement, peace activism, and Left politics.[55] However, the group that scheduled the meeting and led the CCWH designed an organization that, although infused with the excitement of the new women's history, would first and foremost promote scholarship on women within universities and existing professional organizations, most notably the Canadian Historical Association. True, the initial statement of goals did include the following acknowledgment of women's history's connection to a wider community: 'The committee wants to reach historians and others with an interest in this area, and it wants to contact not only academics but also people who are not formally affiliated with universities and colleges.' But the CCWH did not and never has made the forging of links to groups outside the academy a primary goal, nor has it ever seen itself as an advocacy group designed to promote the interests of women in the historical profession. Its primary purpose, during its more than twenty-year life span, has been 'to promote teaching of, and research on, women's history,' to encourage 'presentation of scholarly papers on women's history at appropriate conferences,' and to promote the preservation of archival materials.[56]

CCWH correspondence reveals that in its first decade the organization did a formidable job of building a network of faculty members and graduate students at Canadian universities. The committee circulated questionnaires and coordinated information about the research and teaching interests of its members; it facilitated sessions at the CHA on women's history; and it worked to increase the influence of the CCWH and its members within the CHA. While archivists were active in the 1970s, and some individuals who taught at community colleges were involved, the CCWH's membership came primarily from the universities. By 1977, the mailing list had grown to fifty-six people, the majority of whom were Canadianists.

Within its well-defined limits, the Canadian Committee on Women's History has been remarkably successful. Since 1975, it has provided women's history in Canada with visibility, and historians working on women's history, especially those whose research interests are Canadianist, with a scholarly community. Two decades after its founding, CCWH membership has expanded to close to 200 members.[57]

Although the presentation of papers at academic conferences and the creation of institutions were crucial to the growth of women's history in Canada, publications are the real fruits of academic research. The mid-1970s represent a key moment in the development of publications in Canadianist women's history; as well, it was in these years that feminist periodical publications were initiated. The *Canadian Newsletter of Research on Women* began publication in 1972, and the first issue of *Atlantis: A Women's Studies Journal* appeared in 1975. During its early years, *Atlantis* was published from Acadia University; two feminist historians who taught at Acadia, Margaret Conrad and Lois Vallely-Fischer, were on its editorial board. Historical articles figured prominently in the early volumes of *Atlantis*.[58] Between 1974 and 1979, three important collections of articles on Canadian women's history appeared. The first book-length publication of major significance came from a collective of women who positioned themselves as activists in the women's movement rather than as academics, although several of the contributors did have links to the academy: *Women at Work: Ontario, 1850-1930* was published by the Canadian Women's Educational Press in 1974.

The press was founded in 1972 with the publication of *Women Unite! An Anthology of the Canadian Women's Movement*.[59] The founders of the press described themselves as 'a group of women working together because of our concern for the appalling absence of available material written by or about Canadian women.'[60] The Canadian Women's Educational Press was a non-profit collective drawn from activists in women's liberation groups in Toronto. *Women at Work* was one of the Women's Press's most important early contributions. Its significance was acknowledged not only by women's movement activists, but also by university-based scholars and by the wider Canadian literary and cultural community. It was used as an assigned text in university courses in the 1970s and 1980s; some of its articles continue to be cited in scholarly works more than twenty years after the book's publication.

The anthology came out of the socialist labour history tradition, and its bibliography cites some major works influenced both by socialism and the early twentieth-century women's movement, including Alice Clark's *Working Life of Women in the Seventeenth Century* (1919). The contributors to *Women at Work* also explicitly recognized their connection to the 'new social history' of the 1970s: 'Recently ... women's rekindled interest in their own history has linked up with an academic interest in a "new history," a social history which seeks both to extend the boundaries of the historical discipline and to redefine the way we look at history.'[61] Some of the contributors – notably, Linda Kealey, who wrote the introduction – would go on to play major roles as feminist academics. However, the collective as a whole distanced itself from academic history, including the new women's history. 'The Women's Movement of the past ten years encouraged women to rediscover their history,'[62] Kealey states in her introduction; the volume's concluding chapter, the 'Research Guide' by Patricia Schulz, asserts that history can and must be written by ordinary people and that women's history must be written by ordinary women:

> One purpose of this book is to encourage the writing of women's history ... The way women's history is written and disseminated into the community will be determined in part by who writes it. Traditionally, history has been written by male, middle-class academics ... [but] ... economic and social history should ... take history out of the textbooks and make it personal and relevant. It should be the history of your family, your town, the local industry ... your union.[63]

In contrast, *The Neglected Majority: Essays in Canadian Women's History* (1977), edited by Susan Mann Trofimenkoff and Alison Prentice, positioned itself as a volume of scholarship by professional academic historians, although the editors certainly acknowledged that there were connections between the women's movement, feminist scholarship, and women's history: 'Partly as a result of a women's movement which has inspired women's studies courses and programmes across the western world, and partly because of new directions in historical writing itself, an intriguing new field has emerged, a field which is at once a challenge and a response to a contemporary scholarship increasingly aware of its own past biases.'[64] The volume was published by McClelland and Stewart in the prestigious Canadian Social History series; the contributors for the most part were young Canadianist scholars with new academic appointments; and several of the papers had been presented either at the Canadian Historical Association or at other academic conferences.

In 1979, four years after the publication of *Women at Work*, the Women's Press brought out *A Not Unreasonable Claim: Women and Reform in Canada*

(1979), edited by Linda Kealey. Although there was considerable overlap between *Women at Work* and *A Not Unreasonable Claim* (Linda Kealey contributed to both volumes, as did historian Wayne Roberts), there were sharp differences between the two collections in terms of presentation. In order to honour the collective responsible for the book, the editors are not named on the cover or title page of *Women at Work*.[65] In contrast, Linda Kealey is named as editor of *A Not Unreasonable Claim*, and the contributors, with their academic affiliations, are described on a 'Contributors' page. Moreover, the book's preface includes a clear statement about the Women's Press's view of the difference between the two collections: 'Unlike *Women at Work: Ontario, 1850-1930*, which was largely written by women within the Press itself, this book is the product of academic historians, employed for the most part at Canadian colleges and universities.'[66]

In the late 1990s, the similarities shared by these three volumes seem more important than the ways in which they differ.[67] At the time, however, in terms of overt political message, direct statement, and mode of presentation, *Women at Work* on the one hand, and *The Neglected Majority* and *A Not Unreasonable Claim* on the other, represented contrasting approaches. *Women at Work* takes the position that ordinary women must not only claim their own history, they must also claim the writing of it. The style and presentation of the two later volumes is designed to support the assumption that the writing of history is a professional occupation, appropriately situated within the academy. Yet it is significant to note that all three volumes had an impact on university-based feminist scholarship. To establish the impact that any of these volumes had on the women's movement or on women readers goes well beyond the scope of this essay, although it would be fascinating to explore whether these volumes and their successors have indeed inspired women, if not to write their own history, at least to take that history seriously.

Conclusion

This brief overview of teaching and research on women's history in Canadian universities in the 1970s is merely a beginning. However, it does point to questions that future researchers might explore.

What, for example, have been the interconnections between Canadian women's history and women's history in the United States, in Britain, and in other parts of the world? Women's history emerged earlier in the United States than it did in Canada, and from its very beginning those involved were preoccupied with the overarching questions posed by a feminist perspective on history. Historians such as Gerda Lerner, Joan Kelly, Natalie Zemon Davis, and Linda Gordon developed theoretical concepts that questioned the very foundations of traditional history from a feminist perspective.[68] How influential were those developments on individuals in Canada? Ruth Roach Pierson has written of the enormous influence the second Berkshire Conference on the History of Women had on her. In their communications with me, other individuals recollected the influence of the early 'Berks conferences' and other contacts with American scholars.[69] The influence of American, British, and other national scholarship on Canadians, and the influence of Canadian scholarship internationally, could fruitfully be explored.

So also could the effect of a trend that began in 1975 and has continued to the present: the increasing Canadianization of women's history in Canada. The majority of the eight women's history courses taught before 1975 and discussed in this essay were taught by non-Canadianists; research in Canadian women's history really got under way only in the mid-1970s, but since then has rapidly expanded. It is of course quite appropriate that, since 1975, women's history in Canada should be dominated by Canadian women's history, whether through the voice of the Canadian Committee on Women's History, through courses taught at Canadian universities, or through Canada's publication networks. However, there are negative features to this Canadianist hegemony. It marginalizes those of us (like myself) whose primary research interests lie in other national histories. Moreover, the fact that academic women's history in Canada has, perhaps inevitably, shaped itself to fit dominant academic models has meant that, like university-based scholarship generally, it has tended to marginalize minority voices. In her history of the Canadian Committee on Women's History, Veronica Strong-Boag acknowledges that the women who founded the CCWH in 1975 were, as a group, 'relatively young, white, and heterosexual.'[70] In the 1990s, the dominance of a white Canadian perspective continues in the historical profession. Certainly the contributors to the important collection of articles on African-Canadian women's history, *'We're Rooted Here and They Can't Pull Us Up': Essays in African Canadian Women's History*, believe this to be the case. In their introduction, they comment: 'The growth of women's history in Canada over the last twenty years has not reflected the lives of Black women ... From early works ... to more recent publications ... barely a mention is made of the existence of Black women on the historical landscape.'[71]

The material gathered for this essay also raises questions concerning the relationship between historical scholarship on women and gender on the one hand and feminism and the women's movement on the other. In *Challenging Times: The Women's Movement in Canada and the United States* (1993), sociologist Margrit Eichler, who did pathbreaking research in the 1980s on Canadian women's studies scholars, writes in her essay 'Not Always an Easy Alliance': 'It is part of our conventional wisdom that women's studies have emerged "out of the women's movement," not just in Canada, but in other countries as well.'[72] Eichler derived the title of her essay from a comment made by one of her respondents who, in answer to the question, 'How would you describe the general relationship between feminist studies and the women's movement?' said, 'Hmmm. Well. Not always an easy alliance, I guess.' The respondent, a professor, could well have been a historian. The sample of people I interviewed for this essay or encountered in published or manuscript sources is not large. However, it is clear even from this small group of people that there was a diversity of opinion concerning the relationship between scholarship and activism. When dealing with historians, we need to take to heart Eichler's comments: we cannot assume a simple relationship between activism in the women's movement and a commitment to women's and/or gender history in the 1970s or later, nor can we assume that this relationship is an easy one.

The small sample gathered here reveals a variety of perspectives. On the one hand, there are Ruth Roach Pierson, Alison Prentice, and myself, all of whom experienced our initial involvement with the women's movement in the early 1970s as intense and personal and see our scholarship as arising out of our commitment to feminism. This does not mean that we view scholarship and activism as identical, or view the relationship between the two as unproblematic. I have found the views of American historian Linda Gordon, who has struggled with and commented on the connection between activism and scholarship, to be especially illuminating. In 1981, Gordon said: 'I once believed that there could be a perfect harmony between activists and scholars: scholars could see the needs of activists for more understanding and fill them. Now I see, and it's saddening, that, to some extent, there is an inevitable tension between activists and scholars.'[73]

At the other end of the spectrum from Pierson, Prentice, and myself is Ann Robson who, although deeply interested in women's history, continues to see an engaged feminism as a threat to good scholarship.[74] Robson's discomfort with any connection between the feminist movement and scholarship is more pronounced than that of many historians working on women in Canada, but it could well be that the majority of university-based women's history scholars of the 1970s, even if they did and do identify themselves as feminist, did not come to women's history through feminism.

Some of the comments that Wendy Mitchinson made while responding to my questions are relevant here. It will be recalled that Mitchinson, as a graduate student at York University, received encouragement in her choice of women's organizations as a thesis topic from Ramsay Cook and Paul Stevens. She also described for me how she became interested in women's institution-building as a topic. Her initial interest during 1970-1, her M.A. year, did indeed come from learning about 'a number of feminist protests at Toronto City Hall.' She was led to 'do something on women (women's organizations) because I knew absolutely nothing about the history of women.' She remembers 'being labelled in the department (in a good-natured way), that is, people kept asking me how the movement was – since I wasn't a card-carrying feminist at the time I found this all rather interesting. Indeed I've always said that my research made me a feminist rather than my research initially being a result of any conscious feminist orientation.'[75]

A cautious approach to feminism is also reflected in comments Kathleen McCrone made in 1971 concerning her research on Victorian middle-class women reformers: 'An examination of the subject reveals that although literature on the many aspects of the woman question abounds, there is little specifically on the early and mid-Victorian period, and what does exist is all too often characterized by either condescension or fervour. Much of this material demonstrates the danger of looking at the nineteenth century through feminist eyes alone, of ignoring the disabilities suffered by men as well as women, of regarding feminism as the most important social question of its time, and one whose solution was wholly due to female efforts.'[76]

Again, a similar sort of caution is reflected in comments historian Sylvia Van Kirk made to Veronica Strong-Boag in 1975, when Van Kirk was preparing to teach a course on women's history at the University of Toronto in 1976. Van Kirk's letter to Strong-Boag, asking for suggestions and advice, expresses her concern that the proposed course should avoid too much emphasis on 'famous women' and also that it should avoid being excessively influenced by the Women's Liberation Movement.[77]

This cautious, arm's-length approach on the part of many Canadian historians of women is, as we have seen, also reflected in the professionalizing strategies of the Canadian Committee on Women's History.[78] Not only was this a prudent strategy in the 1970s, the emphasis that Canadian historians of women placed on maintaining the traditional canons of historical scholarship has led to the production, over the past twenty-five years, of an admirable body of historical writing on women.

But eschewing activism and political commitment also left Canadian historians of women vulnerable. In the 1990s, the Canadian university system as a whole is in crisis; not only are universities experiencing funding problems, the very nature and purpose of higher education and scholarship is being called into question by governments, by the media, and by some segments of the Canadian public itself. For women's history, this has meant many losses, the most important of which is that in the present situation, very few younger colleagues among historians of women are able to find academic employment, much less the time and resources to continue their research after completing graduate training. In the 1990s, I would suggest, Canadian historians of women need to become politically active in defence not only of women's history, but of feminist scholarship and of women historians.

Dedication

This paper is dedicated to my dear friend and colleague, Professor Elinor Burwell, Department of Psychology, Carleton University. Elinor Burwell and I taught 'Introduction to Women's Studies' together for several years in the 1970s and were both active in initiating Carleton's Interfaculty Committee on Women's Studies. The committee functioned from 1975 until 1987, when it was replaced by Carleton's Institute of Women's Studies (now the Pauline Jewett Institute of Women's Studies).

Notes

1 The eight history courses discussed in this essay were taught by the following people at the following institutions, beginning in the years indicated:
1971-2: Deborah Gorham (then Keith), St. Patrick's College, Carleton University.
1971-2: Natalie Zemon Davis and Jill Ker Conway, University of Toronto.
1973-4: Mary Kinnear, University of Manitoba.
1973-4: Alison Prentice, Atkinson College, York University.
1974-5: Trevor Wigney, Ontario Institute for Studies in Education.
1974-5: Lois Vallely-Fischer, Acadia University.
1974-5: Ann Robson, University of Toronto.
1974-5: Ruth Roach Pierson, Memorial University.

Most of the information about courses taught before 1975 was gathered from research done in Canadian university calendars during the summer of 1995 by Jayne Elliott, then a graduate student in the Department of History, Carleton University. She used the collection of calendars housed in the National Library of Canada. My thanks to Ms. Elliott for her careful, thorough research and for her keen interest in this project.

Checking the calendars, while it represents an important first step, offers only an incomplete survey: some calendars are missing from the National Library's collection, and there may well have been additional courses taught, for example, as Ruth Roach Pierson's was, as a 'Special Topics' course, which we overlooked.

It should be noted that the preliminary research done in 1995 also resulted in a SSHRC Research Grant Application, 'Making History: Canadian Historians and Women's History since 1965,' submitted in the 1995-6 competition by myself and five co-investigators. Although the grant application received four assessments from peer assessors, all of them very positive, the SSHRC adjudication committee rejected the grant. I hope that it will be possible, in future, for a group of historians to attempt the sort of project we had in mind.

2 The fall 1995 issue of the Canadian Committee on Women's History *Newsletter* lists over 160 'Recent Publications in Canadian Women's History.' The list was compiled by Diana Pedersen. See also Diana Pedersen, *Changing Women, Changing History: A Bibliography of the History of Women in Canada*, 2nd ed. (Ottawa: Carleton University Press 1996).

3 See, for example, the introduction to Franca Iacovetta and Mariana Valverde, eds., *Gender Conflicts: New Essays in Women's History* (Toronto: University of Toronto Press 1992).

4 A number of people generously wrote or talked to me about their experiences as historians of women in the 1970s: Kathleen McCrone, Mary Kinnear, Ruth Roach Pierson, Ann Robson, Lois Vallely-Fischer, Wendy Mitchinson, and Alison Prentice. Without their contributions, it would not have been possible for me to write this paper. I thank them all. I also thank my colleague Marilyn Barber for helping me formulate some of the questions I asked my respondents.

5 The course description appears in the University of Toronto *Calendar* (1971-2): 93. It was taught on the St. George Campus: 'His. 348 Topics in the History of Women: This

course will cover the period from the Fifteenth to the Twentieth Century, and will examine the following subjects in the context of both European and North American society: family structure and demographic patterns, female participation in the labour force and in religious and political movements, changes in sex roles, in attitudes towards women and in female consciousness. J.K. Conway, N.Z. Davis.'

1996-7 marked the twenty-fifth anniversary of the introduction of 'Topics in the History of Women' and of the first Women's Studies course offered at the University of Toronto. On the significance of these anniversaries and on the reunion held to celebrate the history course anniversary, see Val Ross, 'The Not So Quiet Revolution,' *University of Toronto Magazine* (spring 1997): 18-20. Thanks to Fran Klodawsky for calling this article to my attention.

6 Jill Ker Conway, *True North: A Memoir* (Toronto: Knopf 1994), 200. *True North* is the second volume of Conway's autobiography.

7 Conway, *True North*, 196.

8 'I would like to introduce a word I should have mentioned before. I think of myself as having a vocation. I hope I'm an intellectual and not just a professional.' From a 1981 interview with Davis, conducted by Rob Harding and Judy Coffin, in Henry Abelove et al., eds., *Visions of History* (New York: Pantheon Books 1984), 107-8.

9 Smith College is one of the original American 'Seven Sisters' women's colleges.

10 Abelove et al., *Visions*, 100.

11 Ibid., 108.

12 For this protest, see Nancy Adamson, Linda Briskin, and Margaret McPhail, *Feminist Organizing for Change: The Contemporary Women's Movement in Canada* (Toronto: Oxford University Press 1989), 47. Alison Prentice was present at this demonstration. She mentioned this in her communications with me in August 1996.

13 See Conway, *True North*, 190-4.

14 Ibid., 164.

15 Ibid., 184.

16 From the Carleton University Undergraduate *Calendar* (1971-2): 79. 'History 03.354 Women and Society in Western Europe and North America, 1700-1970. An examination of the changes that have taken place in the position of women since the eighteenth century and the relationship of those changes to other social, economic and intellectual developments. Deborah Keith [Gorham].'

17 Kate Millett, *Sexual Politics* (New York: Doubleday 1970).

18 Greta Hofmann-Nemiroff, along with Christine Garside (now Sister Prudence Allen), developed the first women's studies course taught in Canada at Sir George Williams University in Montreal. The course, 'Images of Women,' was developed in 1968, proposed in 1969, and taught for the first time in 1970. Some 100 students registered and almost as many attended as auditors. I thank Professor Hofmann-Nemiroff for providing me with this information.

19 Prof. Elinor Burwell, to whom this paper is dedicated, taught her 'Psychology of Women' course at Carleton's main campus Department of Psychology in 1973-4. At the St. Patrick's College campus, a 300-level seminar on women, history, and literature ('Women: Selected Topics in Literature and History') was taught in 1973-4 by Joan Jonkel and myself. 04.288: 'Introduction to Women's Studies' was first taught in 1974-5 at St. Pat's by Elinor Burwell, Florence Kellner, and myself.

20 At least two such women had come to Ottawa with husbands who had been hired by Carleton. The women, whose credentials were as good or better than those of their husbands, were offered jobs at St. Pat's, in what the departments perceived as a second-best option, good enough for a wife. Other women who were newly hired (I was one of them) were already living in Ottawa and, because of family ties, could not easily move in search of employment.

21 Alice Clark, *The Working Life of Women in the Seventeenth Century* (1919; reprint, London: Routledge 1992); Ivy Pinchbeck, *Women Workers and the Industrial Revolution, 1750-1850* (1930; reprint, London: Frank Cass 1969); Eileen Power, *Medieval English Nunneries* (Cambridge: Cambridge University Press 1922); Mildred Campbell, *The English Yeoman under Elizabeth to the Early Stuarts* (1942; reprint, New York: Kelley 1968).

22 See the University of Manitoba *Calendar* (1974-5): 115: '11.271 Women in History: A study of the personal, social, economic, religious, and political situation of women in Western society from the middle of the eighteenth century to the present, with particular interest in the situation of women in Manitoba.' Although the course is listed only in the 1974-5 *Calendar*, Kinnear taught it for the first time in 1973-4. Written communication, Mary Kinnear to author, 29 January 1996.

23 Mary Kinnear, *Daughters of Time: Women in the Western Tradition* (Ann Arbor: University of Michigan Press 1982).

24 All quotations are from Mary Kinnear, letter to author, 29 January 1996.

25 See Atkinson College course listings in the York University *Calendar* (1973-4): 89. 'AK/HS338: Women, the Family and Education in Canada: An exploration of the historical roles of women the family and educational institutions in Canadian society and literature.' Thanks to Alison Prentice for supplying me with the appropriate pages of the Atkinson section of York's *Calendar*.

26 From Alison Prentice's answers to my questionnaire, which she answered at length in August 1996.

27 Alison Prentice, 'The Evolution of the Sexual Division of Labour in Teaching,' *Social History/histoire sociale* 31 (May 1983).

28 Alison Prentice et al., *Canadian Women: A History* (Toronto: Harcourt Brace 1988). A second edition was published in 1996.

29 Sylvia Plath, *The Bell Jar* (London: Heineman 1963).

30 See, for example, Margaret W. Rossiter, *Women Scientists in America: Struggles and Strategies to 1940* (Baltimore: Johns Hopkins 1982) and Margaret W. Rossiter, *Women Scientists in America before Affirmative Action, 1940-1972* (Baltimore: Johns Hopkins 1995).

31 Alison Prentice, *The School Promoters: Education and Social Class in Mid-Nineteenth Century Upper Canada* (Toronto: McClelland and Stewart 1977).

32 On the New Feminists' position in the early 1970s, see for example Bonnie Kreps, 'Radical Feminism' in *Women Unite! An Anthology of the Canadian Women's Movement* (Toronto: Canadian Women's Educational Press 1972). Kreps was a founder of New Feminists and is identified in the anthology as 'a founder of Radical Feminism in Canada,' 71.

33 OISE, early in the 1970s, was active in feminist scholarship; a course on the Sociology of Women was first offered in 1972. The 'History of Education of Women' course was the second feminist course offered at OISE. See M. Anne Oakley, 'Women Creating Spaces: Feminist Practice in an Institution' (Ph.D. diss., Ontario Institute for Studies in Education 1993), 64. Thanks to Alison Prentice for calling this dissertation to my attention. The course was proposed and offered by historian Trevor Wigney, then a member of OISE's Department of History and Philosophy of Education: '1426X History of the Education of Women in Canadian Society: A consideration of the history of the education of women in Canada, with special reference to Ontario. The course will include studies of the relationship between education and the role of women's organizations and their educational aims and activities, and similar themes.' I obtained the course description from *OISE Bulletin* (1974-5): 111. Thanks to Alison Prentice for providing me with this page of the *Bulletin*. To the best of my knowledge, Trevor Wigney was the only man to teach a course on women's history in Canada before 1975. Professor Wigney left OISE later in the 1970s to return to Australia, his native country. Sadly, he died several years after his return home.

34 This was also the case at the University of Calgary, where historian Elaine Leslau Silverman taught Interdisciplinary Studies 305: 'Women and Contemporary Society' in 1971-2.

35 Lois Vallely-Fischer, e-mail to author, 19 December 1995.

36 'History 220: History of Women: A Survey of the history of women in Europe and North America.' Acadia *Calendar* (1974-5): 110.

37 Julia O'Faolain and Lauro Martines, *Not in God's Image* (London: Temple Smith 1973), and Susan Bell, *Women, From the Greeks to the French Revolution* (Stanford: Stanford University Press 1973).

38 'History 332: Victorian Women: The course will begin with an examination of the status of women in the major areas of 19th century life (e.g., law, politics, education, employment, literature) and the contemporary justification for the existing attitudes

and practices. The second half of the course will study some of the movements which attempted to alter the status of women. The aim of the course will be a greater understanding of Victorian society and of the men and women who created and shaped that society.' University of Toronto *Calendar* (1974-5).

39 I thank Prof. Ann Robson for kindly sending me a copy of the readings she used for 'History 332, Victorian Women' in 1974-5.

40 Prof. Ann Robson, telephone interview with author, 4 March 1996.

41 Ruth Roach Pierson, *'They're Still Women After All': The Second World War and Canadian Womanhood* (Toronto: McClelland and Stewart 1986).

42 On the Berkshire Conference, see Judith P. Zinsser, *History and Feminism: A Glass Half Full* (New York: Twayne Publishers 1993), 93-103, passim. Zinsser's useful study of women's history in the United States includes an account of the emergence of the Berkshire Conference on the History of Women out of the Berkshire Conference of Women Historians, an organization founded in 1930 by the first generation of women history scholars. The first Berkshire Conference on the History of Women took place in 1973.

43 Ruth Roach Pierson, '"Women Have Nothing To Gain From a Harvard of The North": The False Equation of Elitism with Excellence in Education,' in Frieda Forman et al., eds., *Feminism and Education: A Canadian Perspective*, vol. 1 (Toronto: OISE 1990), 278.

44 All quotes are Ruth Roach Pierson, e-mail to author, 6 August 1996.

45 The first papers explicitly on women's history were given as part of a session on 'Social History' at the 1969 CHA meetings; see 1969 CHA program, York University, June 1969. American suffrage historian William O'Neill chaired the session. There were two papers on women: Robert H. McNeal's 'Women in the Russian Revolutionary Movement,' and Jill Conway's 'American Feminist Radicals: 1870-1930.' Historian Robert McNeal was one of a small but active minority of academic men who contributed to Canadianist and non-Canadianist women's history in a Canadian setting during the past twenty-five years. Any extended history of women's history in Canada should consider their contributions and their points of view.

46 Professor McCrone, now a dean at Windsor, was hired in 1968; Kathleen McCrone, telephone interview with author, 12 December 1995.

47 The paper was published as 'The Assertion of Women's Rights in Mid-Victorian England' in *Historical Papers*, 1972.

48 Kathleen McCrone, e-mail to author, 5 November 1996.

49 This was a two-paper session. D. Suzanne Cross delivered her paper 'The Neglected Majority: The Changing Role of Women in 19th Century Montreal,' and Jennifer Stoddart and Veronica Strong-Boag delivered their joint paper 'The Female Domestic in the Urban Milieu: Montreal and Toronto 1890-1914.'

50 That there is no clear demarcation line between the two groups is demonstrated by Alison Prentice's experience. In the 1970s, Prentice was part of what I am calling the pioneer cohort active before 1975 *and* part of the cohort of Canadianists.

51 In her commemorative history of the Canadian Committee on Women's History, Strong-Boag mentions that she was a teaching assistant for Conway and Davis and that her 1975 thesis was the first doctoral thesis in Canadian women's history from the University of Toronto. Veronica Strong-Boag, *Work to Be Done: The Canadian Committee on Women's History* (Vancouver: Centre for Research in Women's Studies and Gender Relations, UBC 1995) unpaginated.

52 Wendy Mitchinson, e-mail to author, 20 December 1995.

53 The three presenters were Jane Lewis, Eliane Silverman, and myself. Ann Leger Anderson was the commentator; Veronica Strong-Boag served as chair.

54 Strong-Boag gives the number as seventeen, and the minutes indicate seventeen, but the mailing list 'compiled at organizational meeting, Edmonton, Alta., June 6, 1975' includes twenty. CCWH papers, MG 28 I 57, National Archives of Canada (hereafter NAC), Ottawa.

55 'The gender and youth of the majority and the fact most of us thought of ourselves as left-leaning, and in a few cases marxist, singled us out from most others in our profession ... Perhaps still more important was the fact that most people in the room ... identified publicly as feminists.' Strong-Boag, *Work to Be Done*.

56 Ibid., and *Bulletins to Membership*, 1975-8, first bulletin, vol. 1, file 2, CCWH papers, NAC.

57 See *Directory*, Canadian Committee on Women's History, 1994-5.

58 Judith Zinsser points out that historians made major contributions to the interdisciplinary journals founded in the United States in the early and mid-1970s. The first issue of *Signs* had three historical articles, including Carroll Smith-Rosenberg's famous 'The Female World of Love and Ritual,' which was the lead article. See Zinsser, *History and Feminism*, 92. Historians also figured prominently in early issues of *Feminist Studies*, which began publication in 1972.

59 *Women Unite!*

60 The quotation appears on the inside cover of *Women Unite!* Chris Gabriel and Katherine Scott contributed an article on the Women's Press entitled 'Women's Press at Twenty: The Politics of Feminist Publishing,' in Linda Carty, ed., *And Still We Rise: Feminist Political Mobilizing in Contemporary Canada* (Toronto: Women's Press 1993). The article discusses only *Women Unite!* and *Still Ain't Satisfied*, an anthology published in 1982; this focus suits the purpose of the article, which is not to write a history of the press, but rather to address the issue of racism and to tell one side of the story of the 1988 split in the press. A genuine history of the Women's Press would have to mention the historical works published by the press over its twenty-year history. In the 1970s, these books included Janice Acton et al., eds., *Women at Work: Ontario 1850-1930* (1974); Rasmussen et al., *A Harvest Yet to Reap: A History of Prairie Women* (1976), a wonderful contribution to Prairie history that grew out of Anne Wheeler and Lorna Rasmussen's documentary film *Great Grand Mother*; and Linda Kealey, ed., *A Not Unreasonable Claim: Women and Reform in Canada* (1979).

61 Acton et al., *Women at Work*, 1

62 Ibid., 1.

63 Ibid., 363.

64 Susan Mann Trofimenkoff and Alison Prentice, *The Neglected Majority: Essays in Canadian Women's History* (Toronto: McClelland and Stewart 1977), 7.

65 Janice Acton, Penny Goldsmith, and Bonnie Shepard are named only on the copyright page.

66 Kealey, *A Not Unreasonable Claim*, preface.

67 Note, for example, that the authors of the introduction to *Gender Conflicts: New Essays in Women's History* make no distinction between the circumstances of production and the intent of the three volumes.

68 Zinsser, *History and Feminism*, provides a good summary of this American scholarship.

69 Prentice mentions that she attended the second Berkshire Conference in 1974. In the mid-1970s, both Mary Kinnear and myself were influenced by active feminist historians' groups in London.

70 Strong-Boag, *Work to Be Done*.

71 Peggy Bristow et al., *'We're Rooted Here and They Can't Pull Us Up': Essays in African Canadian Women's History* (Toronto: University of Toronto 1994), 7.

72 Margrit Eichler, 'Not Always an Easy Alliance: The Relationship between Women's Studies and the Women's Movement in Canada,' in Constance Backhouse and David H. Flaherty, eds. *Challenging Times: The Women's Movement in Canada and the United States* (Montreal and Kingston: McGill-Queen's Press 1993), 120.

73 From Carol Lasser's 1981 interview with Linda Gordon in *Visions of History*, 85-6.

74 In answer to my interview questions about feminism and women's history, Robson said that she thought any direct relationship between the two could be 'harmful' to scholarship.

75 Wendy Mitchinson, e-mail to author, 20 December 1995.

76 McCrone to S.F. Wise (chair of the CHA program committee), 31 October 1971. I thank Kathleen McCrone for generously making this correspondence available to me.

77 Sylvia Van Kirk to Veronica Strong-Boag, 6 August 1975, CCWH correspondence files, CCWH papers, NAC.

78 There are parallels elsewhere. As a group, historians of women in the United States, according to American feminist scholar Bernice Carroll, have been insufficiently involved in activist engagement in feminist struggles within the academy. See Bernice A. Carroll, 'Scholarship and Action: CCWHP and the Movement(s),' *Journal of Women's History* 6, 3 (1994): 79-96.

Contributors

Linda M. Ambrose is an assistant professor at Laurentian University in Sudbury, Ontario, where she teaches Canadian history, women's history, and Ontario history. She recently published a book on rural women's history entitled *For Home and Country: The Centennial History of the Women's Institutes in Ontario*, and she is currently involved in a comparative study of the history of rural women's organizations throughout Canada.

Jean Barman teaches in the Department of Educational Studies at the University of British Columbia. She is the author of *The West beyond the West: A History of British Columbia* (rev. 1996) and co-editor of *First Nations Education in Canada: The Circle Unfolds* (1995) and *Children, Teachers and Schools in the History of British Columbia* (1995).

Beverly Boutilier is currently an advisor to the Women's Studies Program of CUSO in Indonesia. Her historical publications range widely and include research on the development of museum programs, the history of women's organizations, and the comparative history of women and colonization.

Colin M. Coates is Lecturer in Canadian Studies at the University of Edinburgh. He is the editor of *Imperial Canada, 1867-1917*.

Terry Crowley is a member of the History Department at the University of Guelph. His chapter in this volume forms part of a larger study on the intellectual contributions of Oscar and Isabel Skelton to Canadian history.

Megan J. Davies is a postdoctoral fellow at the Wellcome Institute for the History of Medicine at the University of Glasgow. Her research interests include women's history, the social history of medicine, and the history of old age. She is currently working on a comparative study of women in public health and social welfare bureaucracies in Scotland and Canada.

Deborah Gorham is a professor of history at Carleton University. She has published numerous articles and books on British and Canadian women's history, including *Vera Brittain: A Feminist Life, Caring and Curing: Historical Perspectives on Women and Healing in Canada* (co-edited with Dianne Dodd), and *Up and Doing: Canadian Women and Peace* (co-edited with Janice Williamson).

Dianne M. Hallman is an assistant professor of educational foundations in the College of Education, University of Saskatchewan. She is currently studying the history of teaching and has previously published in the areas of women's history and educational biography.

Barry M. Moody is the head of Acadia University's Department of History. He has lectured and written extensively on the history of the Maritime provinces and is chair of the Planter Studies Centre at Acadia. He is currently writing a history of Acadia and plans to publish a collection of letters written by Esther Clark while she was a student there from 1912 to 1916.

Alison Prentice is one of the authors of the pathbreaking *Canadian Women: A History* and has worked on numerous books on the history of women in Canada. She teaches at the Ontario Institute for Studies in Education of the University of Toronto.

Elizabeth Smyth is an associate professor with the Ontario Institute for Studies in Education of the University of Toronto. Her research interests include the history of women religious as teachers, gender and curriculum, technologically enhanced learning, and educational change.

Index